D0459027

Information Storage and Management

Storing, Managing, and Protecting Digital Information

Edited by
G. Somasundaram
Alok Shrivastava
EMC Education Services

Wiley Publishing, Inc.

Information Storage and Management

Published by
Wiley Publishing, Inc.
10475 Crosspoint Boulevard
Indianapolis, IN 46256
www.wiley.com

Copyright © 2009 by EMC Corporation

Published by Wiley Publishing, Inc., Indianapolis, Indiana

Published simultaneously in Canada

ISBN: 978-0-470-29421-5

Manufactured in the United States of America

10 9 8 7 6 5

No part of this publication may be reproduced, stored in a retrieval system or transmitted in any form or by any means, electronic, mechanical, photocopying, recording, scanning or otherwise, except as permitted under Sections 107 or 108 of the 1976 United States Copyright Act, without either the prior written permission of the Publisher, or authorization through payment of the appropriate per-copy fee to the Copyright Clearance Center, 222 Rosewood Drive, Danvers, MA 01923, (978) 750-8400, fax (978) 646-8600. Requests to the Publisher for permission should be addressed to the Legal Department, Wiley Publishing, Inc., 10475 Crosspoint Blvd., Indianapolis, IN 46256, (317) 572-3447, fax (317) 572-4355, or online at www.wiley.com/go/permissions.

Limit of Liability/Disclaimer of Warranty: The publisher and the author make no representations or warranties with respect to the accuracy or completeness of the contents of this work and specifically disclaim all warranties, including without limitation warranties of fitness for a particular purpose. No warranty may be created or extended by sales or promotional materials. The advice and strategies contained herein may not be suitable for every situation. This work is sold with the understanding that the publisher is not engaged in rendering legal, accounting, or other professional services. If professional assistance is required, the services of a competent professional person should be sought. Neither the publisher nor the author shall be liable for damages arising herefrom. The fact that an organization or Web site is referred to in this work as a citation and/or a potential source of further information does not mean that the author or the publisher endorses the information the organization or Web site may provide or recommendations it may make. Further, readers should be aware that Internet Web sites listed in this work may have changed or disappeared between when this work was written and when it is read.

For general information on our other products and services please contact our Customer Care Department within the United States at (800) 762-2974, outside the United States at (317) 572-3993 or fax (317) 572-4002.

Library of Congress Cataloging-in-Publication Data is available from the publisher.

Trademarks: Wiley and the Wiley logo are trademarks or registered trademarks of John Wiley & Sons, Inc. and/or its affiliates, in the United States and other countries, and may not be used without written permission. All other trademarks are the property of their respective owners. Wiley Publishing, Inc. is not associated with any product or vendor mentioned in this book.

Wiley also publishes its books in a variety of electronic formats. Some content that appears in print may not be available in electronic books.

EMC^2, EMC, EMC Centera, EMC ControlCenter, AdvantEdge, AlphaStor, ApplicationXtender, Avamar, Captiva, Catalog Solution, Celerra, Centera, CentraStar, ClaimPack, ClaimsEditor, ClaimsEditor Professional, CLARalert, CLARiiON, ClientPak, CodeLink, Connectrix, Co-StandbyServer, Dantz, Direct Matrix Architecture, DiskXtender, DiskXtender 2000, Document Sciences, Documentum, EmailXaminer, EmailXtender, EmailXtract, eRoom, Event Explorer, FLARE, FormWare, HighRoad, InputAccel, Invista, ISIS, Max Retriever, Navisphere, NetWorker, nLayers, OpenScale, PixTools, Powerlink, PowerPath, Rainfinity, RepliStor, ResourcePak, Retrospect, Smarts, SnapShotServer, SnapView/IP, SRDF, Symmetrix, TimeFinder, VisualSAN, Voyence, VSAM-Assist, WebXtender, where information lives, xPression, xPresso, Xtender, and Xtender Solutions are registered trademarks and EMC LifeLine, EMC OnCourse, EMC Proven, EMC Snap, EMC Storage Administrator, Acartus, Access Logix, ArchiveXtender, Atmos, Authentic Problems, Automated Resource Manager, AutoStart, AutoSwap, AVALONidm, C-Clip, Celerra Replicator, CenterStage, CLARevent, Codebook Correlation Technology, Common Information Model, CopyCross, CopyPoint, DatabaseXtender, Digital Mailroom, Direct Matrix, EDM, E-Lab, eInput, Enginuity, FarPoint, FirstPass, Fortress, Global File Virtualization, Graphic Visualization, InfiniFlex, InfoMover, Infoscape, InputAccel Express, MediaStor, MirrorView, Mozy, MozyEnterprise, MozyHome, MozyPro, OnAlert, PowerSnap, QuickScan, RepliCare, SafeLine, SAN Advisor, SAN Copy, SAN Manager, SDMS, SnapImage, SnapSure, SnapView, StorageScope, SupportMate, SymmAPI, SymmEnabler, Symmetrix DMX, UltraFlex, UltraPoint, UltraScale, Viewlets, Virtual Provisioning, and VisualSRM are trademarks of EMC Corporation. All other trademarks used herein are the property of their respective owners. © Copyright 2009 EMC Corporation. All rights reserved. Published in the USA. 01/09

About the Editors

G Somasundaram (Somu) is a graduate from the Indian Institute of Technology in Mumbai, India, and has over 22 years of experience in the IT industry, the last 10 with EMC Corporation. Currently he is director, EMC Global Services, leading worldwide industry readiness initiatives. Somu is the architect of EMC's open storage curriculum, aimed at addressing the storage knowledge "gap" that exists in the IT industry. Under his leadership and direction, industry readiness initiatives, such as the EMC Learning Partner and Academic Alliance programs, continue to experience significant growth and educate thousands of students worldwide on information storage and management technologies. Key areas of Somu's responsibility include guiding a global team of professionals, identifying and partnering with global IT education providers, and setting the overall direction for EMC's industry readiness initiatives. Prior to his current role, Somu held various managerial and leadership roles with EMC as well as other leading IT vendors.

Alok Shrivastava is senior director, EMC Global Services and has focused on education since 2003. Alok is the architect of several of EMC's successful education initiatives including the industry leading EMC Proven Professional program, industry readiness programs such as EMC's Academic Alliance, and most recently this unique and valuable book on information storage technology. Alok provides vision and leadership to a team of highly talented experts and professionals that develops world-class technical education for EMC's employees, partners, customers, and other industry professionals. Prior to his success in education, Alok built and led a highly successful team of EMC presales engineers in Asia-Pacific and Japan. Earlier in his career, Alok was a systems manager, storage manager, and a backup/restore/disaster recovery consultant working with some of the world's largest data centers and IT installations. He holds dual Masters degrees from the Indian Institute of Technology in Mumbai, India, and the University of Sagar in India. Alok has worked in information storage technology and has held a unique passion for this field for most of his 25-plus year career in IT.

Credits

Executive Editor
Carol Long

Senior Development Editor
Tom Dinse

Production Editor
Dassi Zeidel

Copy Editor
Luann Rouff

Editorial Manager
Mary Beth Wakefield

Production Manager
Tim Tate

**Vice President and Executive
Group Publisher**
Richard Swadley

**Vice President and Executive
Publisher**
Barry Pruett

Project Coordinator, Cover
Lynsey Stanford

Compositor
Jeffrey Lytle, Happenstance
Type-O-Rama

Proofreader
Nancy Bell

Indexer
Robert Swanson

Cover Image
© 2008 Ron Chapple/Ron Chapple
Stock/Photos To Go

Cover Designer
EMC Creative Development

Acknowledgments

When we embarked upon the project to develop this book, the very first challenge was to identify a team of subject matter experts covering the vast range of technologies that form the modern information storage infrastructure.

A key factor working in our favor is that at EMC, we have the technologies, the know-how, and many of the best talents in the industry. When we reached out to individual experts, they were as excited as we were about the prospect of publishing a comprehensive book on information storage technology. This was an opportunity to share their expertise with professionals and students worldwide.

This book is the result of efforts and contributions from a number of key EMC organizations led by EMC Education Services and supported by the office of CTO, Global Marketing, and EMC Engineering.

In addition to his own research and expertise, **Ganesh Rajaratnam,** from EMC Education Services, led the efforts with other subject matter experts to develop the first draft of the book. **Dr. David Black,** from the EMC CTO office, devoted many valuable hours to combing through the content and providing cogent advice on the key topics covered in this book.

We are very grateful to the following experts from EMC Education Services for developing the content for various sections and chapters of this book:

Rodrigo Alves	**Anbuselvi Jeyakumar**
Charlie Brooks	**Sagar Kotekar Patil**
Debasish Chakrabarty	**Andre Rossouw**
Diana Davis	**Tony Santamaria**
Amit Deshmukh	**Saravanaraj Sridharan**
Michael Dulavitz	**Ganesh Sundaresan**
Ashish Garg	**Jim Tracy**
Dr. Vanchi Gurumoorthy	**Anand Varkar**
Simon Hawkshaw	**Dr. Viswanth VS**

The following experts thoroughly reviewed the book at various stages and provided valuable feedback and guidance:

Ronen Artzi

Eric Baize

Greg Baltazar

Edward Bell

Christopher Chaulk

Roger Dupuis

Deborah Filer

Bala Ganeshan

Jason Gervickas

Nancy Gessler

Jody Goncalves

Jack Harwood

Arthur Johnson

Michelle Lavoie

Tom McGowan

Jeffery Moore

Toby Morral

Peter Popieniuck

Kevin Sheridan

Ed VanSickle

We also thank NIIT Limited for their help with the initial draft, **Muthaiah Thiagarajan** of EMC and DreaMarT Interactive Pvt. Ltd. for their support in creating all illustrations, and the publisher, John Wiley & Sons, for their timely support in bringing this book to the industry.

— **G. Somasundaram**
Director, Education Services, EMC Corporation

— **Alok Shrivastava**
Senior Director, Education Services, EMC Corporation

March 2009

Contents

Icons used in this book

 Host

 Host with Internal Storage

 Host with 1 HBA

 Host with 2 HBA

 Control Station

 NAS Head

 Client

 Tape Library

 Storage Array with ports

 CAS

 Integrated NAS

 Generic Array

 RAID Array

 JBOD

 IP connectivity

FC connectivity

 WAN

 LAN

 FC SAN

 Storage Network

 IP

 File System

 Standard disk

 LUN

 Striped disk

 Logical Volume

 Virtualization Appliance

 Firewall

 FC Hub

 FC Switch

 iSCSI Bridge

 FCIP Gateway

 FC Director

 IP Switch

FC Router

IP Router

Foreword

Ralph Waldo Emerson, the great American essayist, philosopher, and poet, once said that the invariable mark of wisdom is seeing the miraculous in the common. Today, common miracles surround us, and it is virtually impossible *not* to see them. Most of us have modern gadgetry such as digital cameras, video camcorders, cell phones, fast computers that can access millions of websites, instant messaging, social networking sites, search engines, music downloads … the list goes on. All of these examples have one thing in common: they generate huge volumes of data. Not only are we in an information age, we're in an age where information is exploding into a digital universe that requires enhanced technology and a new generation of professionals who are able to manage, leverage, and optimize *storage and information management* solutions.

Just to give you an idea of the challenges we face today, in one year the amount of digital information created, captured, and replicated is millions of times the amount of information in all the books ever written. Information is the most important asset of a business. To realize the inherent power of information, it must be intelligently and efficiently stored, protected, and managed—so that it can be made accessible, searchable, shareable, and, ultimately, actionable.

We are currently in the perfect storm. Everything is increasing: the information, the costs, and the skilled professionals needed to store and manage it—professionals who are not available in sufficient numbers to meet the growing need. The IT manager's number one concern is how to manage this storage growth. Enterprises simply cannot purchase bigger and better "boxes" to store their data. IT managers must not only worry about budgets for storage technology, but also be concerned with energy-efficient, footprint-reducing technology that is easy to install, manage, and use. Although many IT managers intend to hire more trained staff, they are facing a shortage of skilled, storage-educated professionals who can take control of managing and optimizing the data.

I was unable to find a comprehensive book in the marketplace that provided insight into the various technologies deployed to store and manage information. As an industry leader, we have the subject-matter expertise and practical experience to help fill this gap; and now this book can give you a behind-the-scenes view of the technologies used in information storage and management. You will learn where data goes, how it is managed, and how you can contribute to your company's profitability.

If you've chosen storage and information infrastructure management as your career, you are a pioneer in a profession that is undergoing constant change, but one in which the challenges lead to great rewards.

Regardless of your current role in IT, this book should be a key part of your IT library and professional development.

Thomas P. Clancy
Vice President, Education Services, EMC Corporation
March 2009

Introduction

Information storage is a central pillar of information technology. A large quantity of digital information is being created every moment by individual and corporate consumers of IT. This information needs to be stored, protected, optimized, and managed.

Not long ago, information storage was seen as only a bunch of disks or tapes attached to the back of the computer to store data. Even today, only those in the storage industry understand the critical role that information storage technology plays in the availability, performance, integration, and optimization of the entire IT infrastructure. Over the last two decades, information storage has developed into a highly sophisticated technology, providing a variety of solutions for storing, managing, connecting, protecting, securing, sharing, and optimizing digital information.

With the exponential growth of information and the development of sophisticated products and solutions, there is also a growing need for information storage professionals. IT managers are challenged by the ongoing task of employing and developing highly skilled information storage professionals.

Many leading universities and colleges have started to include storage technology courses in their regular computer technology or information technology curriculum, yet many of today's IT professionals, even those with years of experience, have not benefited from this formal education, therefore many seasoned professionals—including application, systems, database, and network administrators—do not share a common foundation about how storage technology affects their areas of expertise.

This book is designed and developed to enable professionals and students to achieve a comprehensive understanding of all segments of storage technology. While the product examples used in the book are from EMC Corporation, an understanding of the technology concepts and principles prepare the reader to easily understand products from various technology vendors.

This book has 16 chapters, organized in four sections. Advanced topics build upon the topics learned in previous chapters.

Part 1, "Information Storage and Management for Today's World": These four chapters cover information growth and challenges, define a storage system and its environment, review the evolution of storage technology, and introduce intelligent storage systems.

Part 2, "Storage Options and Protocols": These six chapters cover the SCSI and Fibre channel architecture, direct-attached storage (DAS), storage area networks (SANs), network-attached storage (NAS), Internet Protocol SAN (IP-SAN), content-addressed storage (CAS), and storage virtualization.

Part 3, "Business Continuity and Replication": These four chapters introduce business continuity, backup and recovery, local data replication, and remote data replication.

Part 4, "Security and Administration": These two chapters cover storage security and storage infrastructure monitoring and management.

This book has a supplementary website that provides additional up-to-date learning aids and reading material. Visit `http://education.EMC.com/ismbook` for details.

EMC Academic Alliance

Universities and colleges interested in offering an *information storage and management* curriculum are invited to join the Academic Alliance program. This program provides comprehensive support to institutes, including teaching aids, faculty guides, student projects, and more. Please visit `http://education.EMC .com/academicalliance`.

EMC Proven Professional Certification

This book prepares students and professionals to take the EMC Proven Professional Information Storage and Management exam E20-001. EMC Proven Professional is the premier certification program that validates your knowledge and helps establish your credibility in the information technology industry. For more information on certification as well as to access practice exams, visit `http://education.EMC.com`.

Storage System

In This Section

Chapter 1
Introduction to Information
Storage and Management

Information is increasingly important in our daily lives. We have become information dependents of the twenty-first century, living in an on-command, on-demand world that means we need information when and where it is required. We access the Internet every day to perform searches, participate in social networking, send and receive e-mails, share pictures and videos, and scores of other applications. Equipped with a growing number of content-generating devices, more information is being created by individuals than by businesses. Information created by individuals gains value when shared with others. When created, information resides locally on devices such as cell phones, cameras, and laptops. To share this information, it needs to be uploaded via networks to data centers. It is interesting to note that while the majority of information is created by individuals, it is stored and managed by a relatively small number of organizations. Figure 1-1 depicts this virtuous cycle of information.

KEY CONCEPTS

Data and Information

Structured and Unstructured Data

Storage Technology Architectures

Core Elements of a Data Center

Information Management

Information Lifecycle Management

The importance, dependency, and volume of information for the business world also continue to grow at astounding rates. Businesses depend on fast and reliable access to information critical to their success. Some of the business applications that process information include airline reservations, telephone billing systems, e-commerce, ATMs, product designs, inventory management, e-mail archives, Web portals, patient records, credit cards, life sciences, and global capital markets.

The increasing criticality of information to the businesses has amplified the challenges in protecting and managing the data. The volume of data that business must manage has driven strategies to classify data according to its value and create rules for the treatment of this data over its lifecycle. These strategies not only provide financial and regulatory benefits at the business level, but also manageability benefits at operational levels to the organization.

Data centers now view information storage as one of their core elements, along with applications, databases, operating systems, and networks. Storage technology continues to evolve with technical advancements offering increasingly higher levels of availability, security, scalability, performance, integrity, capacity, and manageability.

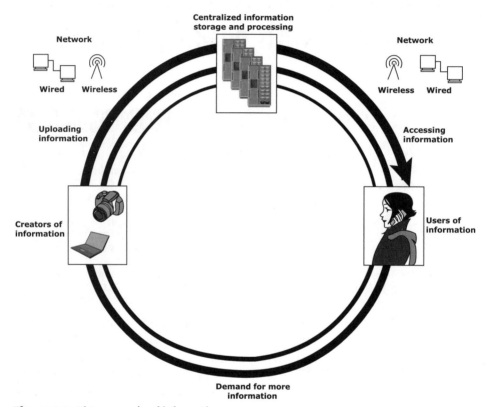

Figure 1-1: Virtuous cycle of information

This chapter describes the evolution of information storage architecture from simple direct-attached models to complex networked topologies. It introduces the information lifecycle management (ILM) strategy, which aligns the information technology (IT) infrastructure with business priorities.

1.1 Information Storage

Businesses use data to derive information that is critical to their day-to-day operations. Storage is a repository that enables users to store and retrieve this digital data.

1.1.1 Data

Data is a collection of raw facts from which conclusions may be drawn. Handwritten letters, a printed book, a family photograph, a movie on video tape, printed and duly signed copies of mortgage papers, a bank's ledgers, and an account holder's passbooks are all examples of data.

Before the advent of computers, the procedures and methods adopted for data creation and sharing were limited to fewer forms, such as paper and film. Today, the same data can be converted into more convenient forms such as an e-mail message, an e-book, a bitmapped image, or a digital movie. This data can be generated using a computer and stored in strings of 0s and 1s, as shown in Figure 1-2. Data in this form is called *digital data* and is accessible by the user only after it is processed by a computer.

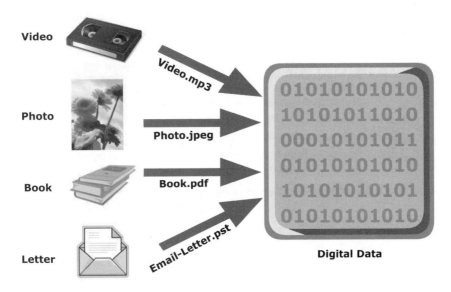

Figure 1-2: Digital data

With the advancement of computer and communication technologies, the rate of data generation and sharing has increased exponentially. The following is a list of some of the factors that have contributed to the growth of digital data:

- **Increase in data processing capabilities:** Modern-day computers provide a significant increase in processing and storage capabilities. This enables the conversion of various types of content and media from conventional forms to digital formats.

- **Lower cost of digital storage:** Technological advances and decrease in the cost of storage devices have provided low-cost solutions and encouraged the development of less expensive data storage devices. This cost benefit has increased the rate at which data is being generated and stored.

- **Affordable and faster communication technology:** The rate of sharing digital data is now much faster than traditional approaches. A handwritten letter may take a week to reach its destination, whereas it only takes a few seconds for an e-mail message to reach its recipient.

Inexpensive and easier ways to create, collect, and store all types of data, coupled with increasing individual and business needs, have led to accelerated data growth, popularly termed the *data explosion*. Data has different purposes and criticality, so both individuals and businesses have contributed in varied proportions to this data explosion.

The importance and the criticality of data vary with time. Most of the data created holds significance in the short-term but becomes less valuable over time. This governs the type of data storage solutions used. Individuals store data on a variety of storage devices, such as hard disks, CDs, DVDs, or Universal Serial Bus (USB) flash drives.

EXAMPLE OF RESEARCH AND BUSINESS DATA

- **Seismology:** Involves collecting data related to various sources and parameters of earthquakes, and other relevant data that needs to be processed to derive meaningful information.

- **Product data:** Includes data related to various aspects of a product, such as inventory, description, pricing, availability, and sales.

- **Customer data:** A combination of data related to a company's customers, such as order details, shipping addresses, and purchase history.

- **Medical data:** Data related to the health care industry, such as patient history, radiological images, details of medication and other treatment, and insurance information.

Businesses generate vast amounts of data and then extract meaningful information from this data to derive economic benefits. Therefore, businesses need to maintain data and ensure its availability over a longer period.

Furthermore, the data can vary in criticality and may require special handling. For example, legal and regulatory requirements mandate that banks maintain account information for their customers accurately and securely. Some businesses handle data for millions of customers, and ensures the security and integrity of data over a long period of time. This requires high-capacity storage devices with enhanced security features that can retain data for a long period.

1.1.2 Types of Data

Data can be classified as structured or unstructured (see Figure 1-3) based on how it is stored and managed. Structured data is organized in rows and columns in a rigidly defined format so that applications can retrieve and process it efficiently. Structured data is typically stored using a database management system (DBMS).

Data is unstructured if its elements cannot be stored in rows and columns, and is therefore difficult to query and retrieve by business applications. For example, customer contacts may be stored in various forms such as sticky notes, e-mail messages, business cards, or even digital format files such as .doc, .txt, and .pdf. Due its unstructured nature, it is difficult to retrieve using a customer relationship management application. Unstructured data may not have the required components to identify itself uniquely for any type of processing or interpretation. Businesses are primarily concerned with managing unstructured data because over 80 percent of enterprise data is unstructured and requires significant storage space and effort to manage.

1.1.3 Information

Data, whether structured or unstructured, does not fulfill any purpose for individuals or businesses unless it is presented in a meaningful form. Businesses need to analyze data for it to be of value. *Information* is the intelligence and knowledge derived from data.

Businesses analyze raw data in order to identify meaningful trends. On the basis of these trends, a company can plan or modify its strategy. For example, a retailer identifies customers' preferred products and brand names by analyzing their purchase patterns and maintaining an inventory of those products.

Effective data analysis not only extends its benefits to existing businesses, but also creates the potential for new business opportunities by using the information in creative ways. Job portal is an example. In order to reach a wider set of prospective employers, job seekers post their résumés on various websites offering job search facilities. These websites collect the résumés and post them on centrally accessible locations for prospective employers. In addition, companies post available positions on job search sites. Job-matching software matches keywords from résumés to keywords in job postings. In this manner, the job search engine uses data and turns it into information for employers and job seekers.

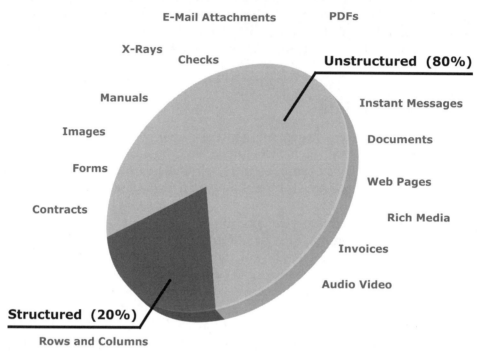

Figure 1-3: Types of data

Because information is critical to the success of a business, there is an ever-present concern about its availability and protection. Legal, regulatory, and contractual obligations regarding the availability and protection of data only add to these concerns. Outages in key industries, such as financial services, telecommunications, manufacturing, retail, and energy cost millions of U.S. dollars per hour.

1.1.4 Storage

Data created by individuals or businesses must be stored so that it is easily accessible for further processing. In a computing environment, devices designed for storing data are termed *storage devices* or simply *storage*. The type of storage used varies based on the type of data and the rate at which it is created and used. Devices such as memory in a cell phone or digital camera, DVDs, CD-ROMs, and hard disks in personal computers are examples of storage devices.

Businesses have several options available for storing data including internal hard disks, external disk arrays and tapes.

1.2 Evolution of Storage Technology and Architecture

Historically, organizations had centralized computers (mainframe) and information storage devices (tape reels and disk packs) in their data center. The evolution of open systems and the affordability and ease of deployment that they offer made it possible for business units/departments to have their own servers and storage. In earlier implementations of open systems, the storage was typically internal to the server.

The proliferation of departmental servers in an enterprise resulted in unprotected, unmanaged, fragmented islands of information and increased operating cost. Originally, there were very limited policies and processes for managing these servers and the data created. To overcome these challenges, storage technology evolved from non-intelligent internal storage to intelligent networked storage (see Figure 1-4). Highlights of this technology evolution include:

- **Redundant Array of Independent Disks (RAID):** This technology was developed to address the cost, performance, and availability requirements of data. It continues to evolve today and is used in all storage architectures such as DAS, SAN, and so on.

- **Direct-attached storage (DAS):** This type of storage connects directly to a server (host) or a group of servers in a cluster. Storage can be either internal or external to the server. External DAS alleviated the challenges of limited internal storage capacity.

- **Storage area network (SAN):** This is a dedicated, high-performance *Fibre Channel (FC)* network to facilitate *block-level* communication between servers and storage. Storage is partitioned and assigned to a server for accessing its data. SAN offers scalability, availability, performance, and cost benefits compared to DAS.

- **Network-attached storage (NAS):** This is dedicated storage for *file serving* applications. Unlike a SAN, it connects to an existing communication network (LAN) and provides file access to heterogeneous clients. Because it is purposely built for providing storage to file server applications, it offers higher scalability, availability, performance, and cost benefits compared to general purpose file servers.

- **Internet Protocol SAN (IP-SAN):** One of the latest evolutions in storage architecture, IP-SAN is a convergence of technologies used in SAN and NAS. IP-SAN provides block-level communication across a local or wide area network (LAN or WAN), resulting in greater consolidation and availability of data.

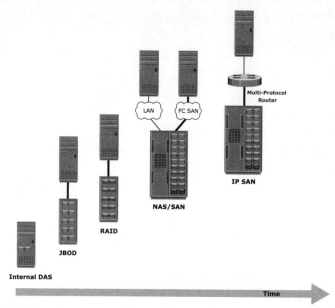

Figure 1-4: Evolution of storage architectures

Storage technology and architecture continues to evolve, which enables organizations to consolidate, protect, optimize, and leverage their data to achieve the highest return on information assets.

1.3 Data Center Infrastructure

Organizations maintain data centers to provide centralized data processing capabilities across the enterprise. Data centers store and manage large amounts of mission-critical data. The data center infrastructure includes computers, storage systems, network devices, dedicated power backups, and environmental controls (such as air conditioning and fire suppression).

Large organizations often maintain more than one data center to distribute data processing workloads and provide backups in the event of a disaster. The storage requirements of a data center are met by a combination of various storage architectures.

1.3.1 Core Elements

Five core elements are essential for the basic functionality of a data center:

- **Application:** An application is a computer program that provides the logic for computing operations. Applications, such as an order processing system, can be layered on a database, which in turn uses operating system services to perform read/write operations to storage devices.

- **Database:** More commonly, a database management system (DBMS) provides a structured way to store data in logically organized tables that are interrelated. A DBMS optimizes the storage and retrieval of data.

- **Server and operating system:** A computing platform that runs applications and databases.

- **Network:** A data path that facilitates communication between clients and servers or between servers and storage.

- **Storage array:** A device that stores data persistently for subsequent use.

These core elements are typically viewed and managed as separate entities, but all the elements must work together to address data processing requirements.

Figure 1-5 shows an example of an order processing system that involves the five core elements of a data center and illustrates their functionality in a business process.

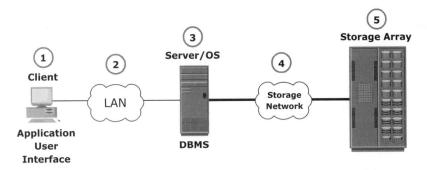

(1) A customer places an order through the AUI of the order processing application software located on the client computer.

(2) The client connects to the server over the LAN and accesses the DBMS located on the server to update the relevant information such as the customer name, address, payment method, products ordered, and quantity ordered.

(3) The DBMS uses the server operating system to read and write this data to the database located on physical disks in the storage array.

(4) The Storage Network provides the communication link between the server and the storage array and transports the read or write commands between them.

(5) The storage array, after receiving the read or write commands from the server, performs the necessary operations to store the data on physical disks.

Figure 1-5: Example of an order processing system

1.3.2 Key Requirements for Data Center Elements

Uninterrupted operation of data centers is critical to the survival and success of a business. It is necessary to have a reliable infrastructure that ensures data is accessible at all times. While the requirements, shown in Figure 1-6, are applicable to all elements of the data center infrastructure, our focus here is on storage systems. The various technologies and solutions to meet these requirements are covered in this book.

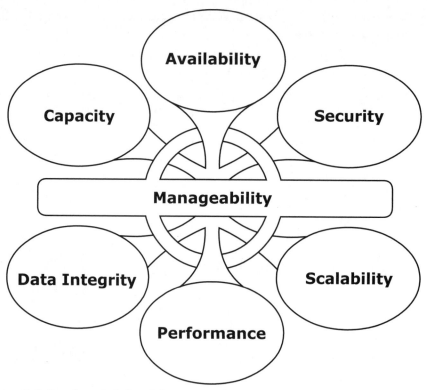

Figure 1-6: Key characteristics of data center elements

- **Availability:** All data center elements should be designed to ensure accessibility. The inability of users to access data can have a significant negative impact on a business.

- **Security:** Polices, procedures, and proper integration of the data center core elements that will prevent unauthorized access to information must be established. In addition to the security measures for client access, specific mechanisms must enable servers to access only their allocated resources on storage arrays.

- **Scalability:** Data center operations should be able to allocate additional processing capabilities or storage on demand, without interrupting business operations. Business growth often requires deploying more servers, new applications, and additional databases. The storage solution should be able to grow with the business.

- **Performance:** All the core elements of the data center should be able to provide optimal performance and service all processing requests at high speed. The infrastructure should be able to support performance requirements.

- **Data integrity:** Data integrity refers to mechanisms such as error correction codes or parity bits which ensure that data is written to disk exactly as it was received. Any variation in data during its retrieval implies corruption, which may affect the operations of the organization.

- **Capacity:** Data center operations require adequate resources to store and process large amounts of data efficiently. When capacity requirements increase, the data center must be able to provide additional capacity without interrupting availability, or, at the very least, with minimal disruption. Capacity may be managed by reallocation of existing resources, rather than by adding new resources.

- **Manageability:** A data center should perform all operations and activities in the most efficient manner. Manageability can be achieved through automation and the reduction of human (manual) intervention in common tasks.

1.3.3 Managing Storage Infrastructure

Managing a modern, complex data center involves many tasks. Key management activities include:

- *Monitoring* is the continuous collection of information and the review of the entire data center infrastructure. The aspects of a data center that are monitored include security, performance, accessibility, and capacity.

- *Reporting* is done periodically on resource performance, capacity, and utilization. Reporting tasks help to establish business justifications and chargeback of costs associated with data center operations.

- *Provisioning* is the process of providing the hardware, software, and other resources needed to run a data center. Provisioning activities include capacity and resource planning. *Capacity planning* ensures that the user's and the application's future needs will be addressed in the most cost-effective and controlled manner. *Resource planning* is the process of evaluating and identifying required resources, such as personnel, the facility (site), and the technology. Resource planning ensures that adequate resources are available to meet user and application requirements.

For example, the utilization of an application's allocated storage capacity may be monitored. As soon as utilization of the storage capacity reaches a critical value, additional storage capacity may be provisioned to the application. If utilization of the storage capacity is properly monitored and reported, business growth can be understood and future capacity requirements can be anticipated. This helps to frame a proactive data management policy.

1.4 Key Challenges in Managing Information

In order to frame an effective information management policy, businesses need to consider the following key challenges of information management:

- **Exploding digital universe:** The rate of information growth is increasing exponentially. Duplication of data to ensure high availability and repurposing has also contributed to the multifold increase of information growth.

- **Increasing dependency on information:** The strategic use of information plays an important role in determining the success of a business and provides competitive advantages in the marketplace.

- **Changing value of information:** Information that is valuable today may become less important tomorrow. The value of information often changes over time.

Framing a policy to meet these challenges involves understanding the value of information over its lifecycle.

1.5 Information Lifecycle

The *information lifecycle* is the "change in the value of information" over time. When data is first created, it often has the highest value and is used frequently. As data ages, it is accessed less frequently and is of less value to the organization. Understanding the information lifecycle helps to deploy appropriate storage infrastructure, according to the changing value of information.

For example, in a sales order application, the value of the information changes from the time the order is placed until the time that the warranty becomes void (see Figure 1-7). The value of the information is highest when a company receives a new sales order and processes it to deliver the product. After order fulfillment, the customer or order data need not be available for real-time access. The company can transfer this data to less expensive secondary storage with lower accessibility and availability requirements unless or until a warranty claim or another event triggers its need. After the warranty becomes void, the company can archive or dispose of data to create space for other high-value information.

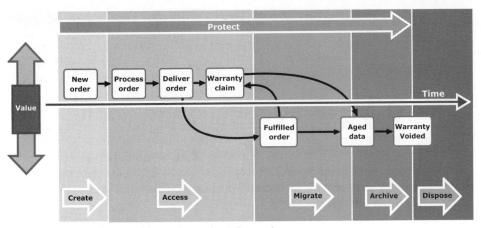

Figure 1-7: Changing value of sales order information

1.5.1 Information Lifecycle Management

Today's business requires data to be protected and available 24 × 7. Data centers can accomplish this with the optimal and appropriate use of storage infrastructure. An effective information management policy is required to support this infrastructure and leverage its benefits.

Information lifecycle management (ILM) is a proactive strategy that enables an IT organization to effectively manage the data throughout its lifecycle, based on predefined business policies. This allows an IT organization to optimize the storage infrastructure for maximum return on investment. An ILM strategy should include the following characteristics:

- **Business-centric:** It should be integrated with key processes, applications, and initiatives of the business to meet both current and future growth in information.

- **Centrally managed:** All the information assets of a business should be under the purview of the ILM strategy.

- **Policy-based:** The implementation of ILM should not be restricted to a few departments. ILM should be implemented as a policy and encompass all business applications, processes, and resources.

- **Heterogeneous:** An ILM strategy should take into account all types of storage platforms and operating systems.

- **Optimized:** Because the value of information varies, an ILM strategy should consider the different storage requirements and allocate storage resources based on the information's value to the business.

TIERED STORAGE

Tiered storage is an approach to define different storage levels in order to reduce total storage cost. Each tier has different levels of protection, performance, data access frequency, and other considerations. Information is stored and moved between different tiers based on its value over time. For example, mission-critical, most accessed information may be stored on Tier 1 storage, which consists of high performance media with a highest level of protection. Medium accessed and other important data is stored on Tier 2 storage, which may be on less expensive media with moderate performance and protection. Rarely accessed or event specific information may be stored on lower tiers of storage.

1.5.2 ILM Implementation

The process of developing an ILM strategy includes four activities—classifying, implementing, managing, and organizing:

- *Classifying* data and applications on the basis of business rules and policies to enable differentiated treatment of information

- *Implementing* policies by using information management tools, starting from the creation of data and ending with its disposal

- *Managing* the environment by using integrated tools to reduce operational complexity

- *Organizing* storage resources in tiers to align the resources with data classes, and storing information in the right type of infrastructure based on the information's current value

Implementing ILM across an enterprise is an ongoing process. Figure 1-8 illustrates a three-step road map to enterprise-wide ILM.

Steps 1 and 2 are aimed at implementing ILM in a limited way across a few enterprise-critical applications. In Step 1, the goal is to implement a storage networking environment. Storage architectures offer varying levels of protection and performance and this acts as a foundation for future policy-based information management in Steps 2 and 3. The value of tiered storage platforms can be exploited by allocating appropriate storage resources to the applications based on the value of the information processed.

Step 2 takes ILM to the next level, with detailed application or data classification and linkage of the storage infrastructure to business policies. These classifications and the resultant policies can be automatically executed using tools for one or more applications, resulting in better management and optimal allocation of storage resources.

Step 3 of the implementation is to automate more of the applications or data classification and policy management activities in order to scale to a wider set of enterprise applications.

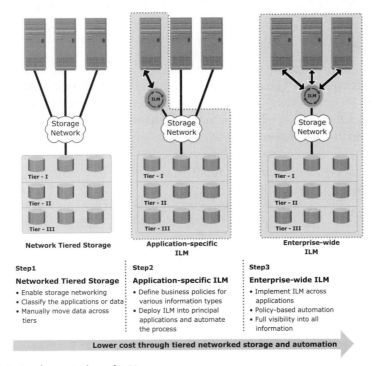

Figure 1-8: Implementation of ILM

1.5.3 ILM Benefits

Implementing an ILM strategy has the following key benefits that directly address the challenges of information management:

- *Improved utilization* by using tiered storage platforms and increased visibility of all enterprise information.
- *Simplified management* by integrating process steps and interfaces with individual tools and by increasing automation.
- *A wider range of options* for backup, and recovery to balance the need for business continuity.
- *Maintaining compliance* by knowing what data needs to be protected for what length of time.

■ *Lower Total Cost of Ownership* (TCO) by aligning the infrastructure and management costs with information value. As a result, resources are not wasted, and complexity is not introduced by managing low-value data at the expense of high-value data.

Summary

This chapter described the importance of data, information, and storage infrastructure. Meeting today's storage needs begins with understanding the type of data, its value, and key management requirements of a storage system.

This chapter also emphasized the importance of the ILM strategy, which businesses are adopting to manage information effectively across the enterprise. ILM is enabling businesses to gain competitive advantage by classifying, protecting, and leveraging information.

The evolution of storage architectures and the core elements of a data center covered in this chapter provided the foundation on information storage. The next chapter discusses storage system environment.

EXERCISES

1. A hospital uses an application that stores patient X-ray data in the form of large binary objects in an Oracle database. The application is hosted on a UNIX server, and the hospital staff accesses the X-ray records through a Gigabit Ethernet backbone. Storage array provides storage to the UNIX server, which has 6 terabytes of usable capacity.

   ▪ Explain the core elements of the data center. What are the typical challenges the storage management team may face in meeting the service-level demands of the hospital staff?

   ▪ Describe how the value of this patient data might change over time.

2. An engineering design department of a large company maintains over 600,000 engineering drawings that its designers access and reuse in their current projects, modifying or updating them as required. The design team wants instant access to the drawings for its current projects, but is currently constrained by an infrastructure that is not able to scale to meet the response time requirements. The team has classified the drawings as "most frequently accessed," "frequently accessed," "occasionally accessed," and "archive."

   ▪ Suggest a strategy for design department that optimizes the storage infrastructure by using ILM.

   ▪ Explain how you will use "tiered storage" based on access frequency.

   ▪ Detail the hardware and software components you will need to implement your strategy.

   ▪ Research products and solutions currently available to meet the solution you are proposing.

3. The marketing department at a mid size firm is expanding. New hires are being added to the department and they are given network access to the department's files. IT has given marketing a networked drive on the LAN, but it keeps reaching capacity every third week. Current capacity is 500 gigabytes (and growing), with hundreds of files. Users are complaining about LAN response times and capacity. As the IT manager, what could you recommend to improve the situation?

4. A large company is considering a storage infrastructure—one that is scalable and provides high availability. More importantly, the company also needs performance for its mission-critical applications. Which storage topology would you recommend (SAN, NAS, IP SAN) and why?

Chapter 2
Storage System Environment

Storage, as one of the core elements of a data center, is recognized as a distinct resource and it needs focus and specialization for its implementation and management. The data flows from an application to storage through various components collectively referred as a *storage system environment*. The three main components in this environment are the host, connectivity, and storage. These entities, along with their physical and logical components, facilitate data access.

This chapter details the storage system environment and focuses primarily on storage. It provides details on various hardware components of a disk drive, disk geometry, and the fundamental laws that govern disk performance. The connectivity between the host and storage facilitated by bus technology and interface protocols is also explained.

This chapter provides an understanding of various logical components of hosts such as file systems, volume managers, and operating systems, and their role in the storage system environment.

KEY CONCEPTS

Host, Connectivity, and Storage

Block-Level and File-Level Access

File System and Volume Manager

Storage Media and Devices

Disk Components

Zoned Bit Recording

Logical Block Addressing

Little's Law and the Utilization Law

2.1 Components of a Storage System Environment

The three main components in a storage system environment — the host, connectivity, and storage — are described in this section.

2.1.1 Host

Users store and retrieve data through applications. The computers on which these applications run are referred to as *hosts*. Hosts can range from simple laptops to complex clusters of servers. A host consists of physical components (hardware devices) that communicate with one another using logical components (software and protocols). Access to data and the overall performance of the storage system environment depend on both the physical and logical components of a host. The logical components of the host are detailed in Section 2.5 of this chapter.

Physical Components

A host has three key physical components:

- Central processing unit (CPU)
- Storage, such as internal memory and disk devices
- Input/Output (I/O) devices

The physical components communicate with one another by using a communication pathway called a *bus*. A bus connects the CPU to other components, such as storage and I/O devices.

CPU

The CPU consists of four main components:

- **Arithmetic Logic Unit (ALU):** This is the fundamental building block of the CPU. It performs arithmetical and logical operations such as addition, subtraction, and Boolean functions (AND, OR, and NOT).

- **Control Unit:** A digital circuit that controls CPU operations and coordinates the functionality of the CPU.

- **Register:** A collection of high-speed storage locations. The registers store intermediate data that is required by the CPU to execute an instruction and provide fast access because of their proximity to the ALU. CPUs typically have a small number of registers.

- **Level 1 (L1) cache:** Found on modern day CPUs, it holds data and program instructions that are likely to be needed by the CPU in the near future. The L1 cache is slower than registers, but provides more storage space.

Storage

Memory and storage media are used to store data, either persistently or temporarily. Memory modules are implemented using semiconductor chips, whereas storage devices use either magnetic or optical media. Memory modules enable data access at a higher speed than the storage media. Generally, there are two types of memory on a host:

- **Random Access Memory (RAM):** This allows direct access to any memory location and can have data written into it or read from it. RAM is volatile; this type of memory requires a constant supply of power to maintain memory cell content. Data is erased when the system's power is turned off or interrupted.

- **Read-Only Memory (ROM):** Non-volatile and only allows data to be read from it. ROM holds data for execution of internal routines, such as system startup.

Storage devices are less expensive than semiconductor memory. Examples of storage devices are as follows:

- Hard disk (magnetic)
- CD-ROM or DVD-ROM (optical)
- Floppy disk (magnetic)
- Tape drive (magnetic)

I/O Devices

I/O devices enable sending and receiving data to and from a host. This communication may be one of the following types:

- **User to host communications:** Handled by basic I/O devices, such as the keyboard, mouse, and monitor. These devices enable users to enter data and view the results of operations.

- **Host to host communications:** Enabled using devices such as a Network Interface Card (NIC) or modem.

- **Host to storage device communications:** Handled by a *Host Bus Adaptor (HBA)*. HBA is an application-specific integrated circuit (ASIC) board that performs I/O interface functions between the host and the storage, relieving the CPU from additional I/O processing workload. HBAs also provide connectivity outlets known as *ports* to connect the host to the storage device. A host may have multiple HBAs.

2.1.2 Connectivity

Connectivity refers to the interconnection between hosts or between a host and any other peripheral devices, such as printers or storage devices. The discussion here focuses on the connectivity between the host and the storage device. The components of connectivity in a storage system environment can be classified as physical and logical. The *physical components* are the hardware elements that connect the host to storage and the *logical components* of connectivity are the protocols used for communication between the host and storage. The communication protocols are covered in Chapter 5.

Physical Components of Connectivity

The three physical components of connectivity between the host and storage are Bus, Port, and Cable (Figure 2-1).

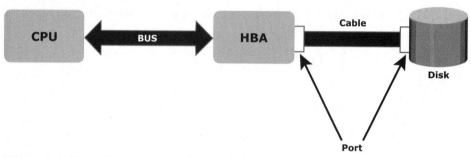

Figure 2-1: Physical components of connectivity

The *bus* is the collection of paths that facilitates data transmission from one part of a computer to another, such as from the CPU to the memory. The *port* is a specialized outlet that enables connectivity between the host and external devices. *Cables* connect hosts to internal or external devices using copper or fiber optic media.

Physical components communicate across a bus by sending bits (control, data, and address) of data between devices. These bits are transmitted through the bus in either of the following ways:

- **Serially:** Bits are transmitted sequentially along a single path. This transmission can be unidirectional or bidirectional.

- **In parallel:** Bits are transmitted along multiple paths simultaneously. Parallel can also be bidirectional.

The size of a bus, known as its width, determines the amount of data that can be transmitted through the bus at one time. The width of a bus can be compared to the number of lanes on a highway. For example, a 32-bit bus can transmit 32 bits of data and a 64-bit bus can transmit 64 bits of data simultaneously. Every bus has a clock speed measured in MHz (megahertz). These represent the data transfer rate between the end points of the bus. A fast bus allows faster transfer of data, which enables applications to run faster.

Buses, as conduits of data transfer on the computer system, can be classified as follows:

- **System bus:** The bus that carries data from the processor to memory.
- **Local or I/O bus:** A high-speed pathway that connects directly to the processor and carries data between the peripheral devices, such as storage devices and the processor.

Logical Components of Connectivity

The popular interface protocol used for the local bus to connect to a peripheral device is *peripheral component interconnect (PCI)*. The interface protocols that connect to disk systems are *Integrated Device Electronics/Advanced Technology Attachment (IDE/ATA)* and *Small Computer System Interface (SCSI)*.

PCI

PCI is a specification that standardizes how PCI expansion cards, such as network cards or modems, exchange information with the CPU. PCI provides the interconnection between the CPU and attached devices. The plug-and-play functionality of PCI enables the host to easily recognize and configure new cards and devices. The width of a PCI bus can be 32 bits or 64 bits. A 32-bit PCI bus can provide a throughput of 133 MB/s. *PCI Express* is an enhanced version of PCI bus with considerably higher throughput and clock speed.

IDE/ATA

IDE/ATA is the most popular interface protocol used on modern disks. This protocol offers excellent performance at relatively low cost. Details of IDE/ATA are provided in Chapter 5.

SCSI

SCSI has emerged as a preferred protocol in high-end computers. This interface is far less commonly used than IDE/ATA on personal computers due to its higher cost. SCSI was initially used as a parallel interface, enabling the connection of devices to a host. SCSI has been enhanced and now includes a wide variety of related technologies and standards. Chapter 5 provides details of SCSI.

2.1.3 Storage

The storage device is the most important component in the storage system environment. A storage device uses magnetic or solid state media. Disks, tapes, and diskettes use magnetic media. CD-ROM is an example of a storage device that uses optical media, and removable flash memory card is an example of solid state media.

Tapes are a popular storage media used for backup because of their relatively low cost. In the past, data centers hosted a large number of tape drives and processed several thousand reels of tape. However, tape has the following limitations:

- Data is stored on the tape linearly along the length of the tape. Search and retrieval of data is done sequentially, invariably taking several seconds to access the data. As a result, random data access is slow and time con- suming. This limits tapes as a viable option for applications that require real-time, rapid access to data.

- In a shared computing environment, data stored on tape cannot be accessed by multiple applications simultaneously, restricting its use to one application at a time.

- On a tape drive, the read/write head touches the tape surface, so the tape degrades or wears out after repeated use.

- The storage and retrieval requirements of data from tape and the overhead associated with managing tape media are significant.

In spite of its limitations, tape is widely deployed for its cost effectiveness and mobility. Continued development of tape technology is resulting in high capac- ity medias and high speed drives. Modern tape libraries come with additional memory (cache) and / or disk drives to increase data throughput. With these and added intelligence, today's tapes are part of an end-to-end data management solution, especially as a low-cost solution for storing infrequently accessed data and as long-term data storage.

Optical disk storage is popular in small, single-user computing environments. It is frequently used by individuals to store photos or as a backup medium on personal/laptop computers. It is also used as a distribution medium for single applications, such as games, or as a means of transferring small amounts of data from one self-contained system to another. Optical disks have limited capacity and speed, which limits the use of optical media as a business data storage solution.

The capability to write once and read many (WORM) is one advantage of optical disk storage. A CD-ROM is an example of a WORM device. Optical disks, to some degree, guarantee that the content has not been altered, so they can be used as low-cost alternatives for long-term storage of relatively small amounts of fixed content that will not change after it is created. Collections of optical disks in an array, called *jukeboxes*, are still used as a fixed-content storage solution. Other forms of optical disks include CD-RW and variations of DVD.

Disk drives are the most popular storage medium used in modern computers for storing and accessing data for performance-intensive, online applications. Disks support rapid access to random data locations. This means that data can be written or retrieved quickly for a large number of simultaneous users or applications. In addition, disks have a large capacity. Disk storage arrays are configured with multiple disks to provide increased capacity and enhanced performance.

2.2 Disk Drive Components

A disk drive uses a rapidly moving arm to read and write data across a flat platter coated with magnetic particles. Data is transferred from the magnetic platter through the R/W head to the computer. Several platters are assembled together with the R/W head and controller, most commonly referred to as a *hard disk drive (HDD)*. Data can be recorded and erased on a magnetic disk any number of times. This section details the different components of the disk, the mechanism for organizing and storing data on disks, and the factors that affect disk performance.

Key components of a disk drive are *platter, spindle, read/write head, actuator arm assembly, and controller* (Figure 2-2):

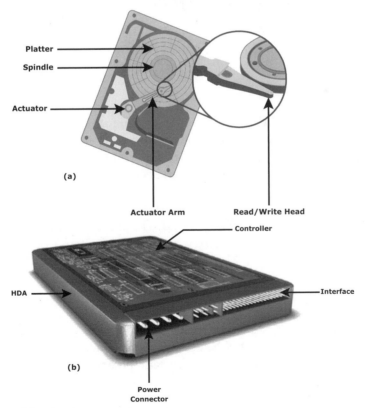

Figure 2-2: Disk Drive Components

2.2.1 Platter

A typical HDD consists of one or more flat circular disks called *platters* (Figure 2-3). The data is recorded on these platters in binary codes (0s and 1s). The set of rotating platters is sealed in a case, called a *Head Disk Assembly (HDA)*. A platter is a rigid, round disk coated with magnetic material on both surfaces (top and bottom). The data is encoded by polarizing the magnetic area, or domains, of the disk surface. Data can be written to or read from both surfaces of the platter. The number of platters and the storage capacity of each platter determine the total capacity of the drive.

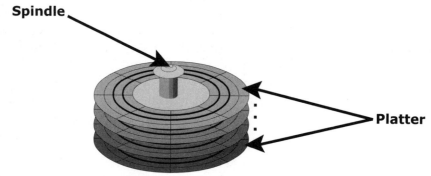

Figure 2-3: Spindle and platter

2.2.2 Spindle

A spindle connects all the platters, as shown in Figure 2-3, and is connected to a motor. The motor of the spindle rotates with a constant speed.

The disk platter spins at a speed of several thousands of revolutions per minute (rpm). Disk drives have spindle speeds of 7,200 rpm, 10,000 rpm, or 15,000 rpm. Disks used on current storage systems have a platter diameter of 3.5" (90 mm). When the platter spins at 15,000 rpm, the outer edge is moving at around 25 percent of the speed of sound. The speed of the platter is increasing with improvements in technology, although the extent to which it can be improved is limited.

2.2.3 Read/Write Head

Read/Write (R/W) heads, shown in Figure 2-4, read and write data from or to a platter. Drives have two R/W heads per platter, one for each surface of the platter. The R/W head changes the magnetic polarization on the surface of the platter when writing data. While reading data, this head detects magnetic polarization on the surface of the platter. During reads and writes, the R/W head senses the magnetic polarization and never touches the surface of the platter. When the spindle is rotating, there is a microscopic air gap between the R/W heads and the platters, known as the *head flying height*. This air gap is removed when the spindle stops rotating and the R/W head rests on a special area on the platter near the spindle. This area is called the *landing zone*. The landing zone is coated with a lubricant to reduce friction between the head and the platter.

The logic on the disk drive ensures that heads are moved to the landing zone before they touch the surface. If the drive malfunctions and the R/W head accidentally touches the surface of the platter outside the landing zone, a *head crash* occurs. In a head crash, the magnetic coating on the platter is scratched and may cause damage to the R/W head. A head crash generally results in data loss.

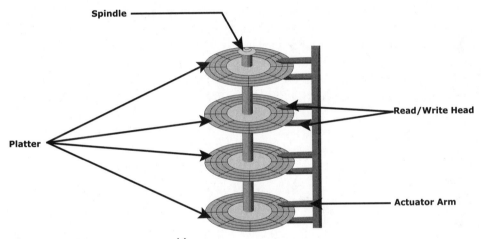

Figure 2-4: Actuator arm assembly

2.2.4 Actuator Arm Assembly

The R/W heads are mounted on the *actuator arm assembly* (refer to Figure 2-2 [a]), which positions the R/W head at the location on the platter where the data needs to be written or read. The R/W heads for all platters on a drive are attached to one actuator arm assembly and move across the platters simultaneously. Note that there are two R/W heads per platter, one for each surface, as shown in Figure 2-4.

2.2.5 Controller

The *controller* (see Figure 2-2 [b]) is a printed circuit board, mounted at the bottom of a disk drive. It consists of a microprocessor, internal memory, circuitry, and firmware. The firmware controls power to the spindle motor and the speed of the motor. It also manages communication between the drive and the host. In addition, it controls the R/W operations by moving the actuator arm and switching between different R/W heads, and performs the optimization of data access.

2.2.6 Physical Disk Structure

Data on the disk is recorded on *tracks*, which are concentric rings on the platter around the spindle, as shown in Figure 2-5. The tracks are numbered, starting from zero, from the outer edge of the platter. The number of *tracks per inch (TPI)* on the platter (or the *track density*) measures how tightly the tracks are packed on a platter.

Each track is divided into smaller units called *sectors*. A sector is the smallest, individually addressable unit of storage. The track and sector structure is written on the platter by the drive manufacturer using a formatting operation. The number of sectors per track varies according to the specific drive. The first personal computer disks had 17 sectors per track. Recent disks have a much larger number of sectors on a single track. There can be thousands of tracks on a platter, depending on the physical dimensions and recording density of the platter.

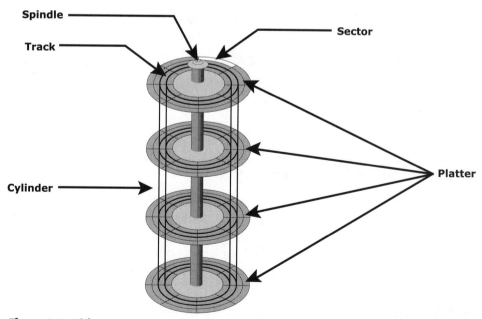

Figure 2-5: Disk structure: sectors, tracks, and cylinders

Typically, a sector holds 512 bytes of user data, although some disks can be formatted with larger sector sizes. In addition to user data, a sector also stores other information, such as sector number, head number or platter number, and track number. This information helps the controller to locate the data on the drive, but storing this information consumes space on the disk. Consequently, there is a difference between the capacity of an unformatted disk and a formatted one. Drive manufacturers generally advertise the unformatted capacity — for example, a disk advertised as being 500GB will only hold 465.7GB of user data, and the remaining 34.3GB is used for *metadata*.

A cylinder is the set of identical tracks on both surfaces of each drive platter. The location of drive heads is referred to by cylinder number, not by track number.

2.2.7 Zoned Bit Recording

Because the platters are made of concentric tracks, the outer tracks can hold more data than the inner tracks, because the outer tracks are physically longer than the inner tracks, as shown in Figure 2-6 (a). On older disk drives, the outer tracks had the same number of sectors as the inner tracks, so data density was low on the outer tracks. This was an inefficient use of available space.

Zone bit recording utilizes the disk efficiently. As shown in Figure 2-6 (b), this mechanism groups tracks into zones based on their distance from the center of the disk. The zones are numbered, with the outermost zone being zone 0. An appropriate number of sectors per track are assigned to each zone, so a zone near the center of the platter has fewer sectors per track than a zone on the outer edge. However, tracks within a particular zone have the same number of sectors.

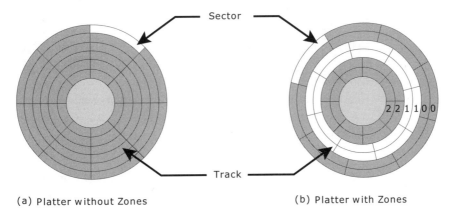

(a) Platter without Zones   (b) Platter with Zones

Figure 2-6: Zoned bit recording

The data transfer rate drops while accessing data from zones closer to the center of the platter. Applications that demand high performance should have their data on the outer zones of the platter.

2.2.8 Logical Block Addressing

Earlier drives used physical addresses consisting of the *cylinder, head, and sector (CHS)* number to refer to specific locations on the disk, as shown in Figure 2-7 (a), and the host operating system had to be aware of the geometry of each disk being used. *Logical block addressing (LBA)*, shown in Figure 2-7 (b), simplifies addressing by using a linear address to access physical blocks of data. The disk controller translates LBA to a CHS address, and the host only needs to know the size of the disk drive in terms of the number of blocks. The logical blocks are mapped to physical sectors on a 1:1 basis.

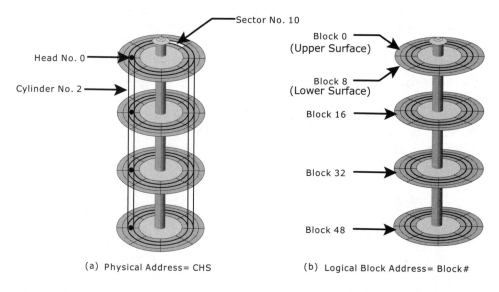

(a) Physical Address = CHS   (b) Logical Block Address = Block#

Figure 2-7: Physical address and logical block address

In Figure 2-7 (b), the drive shows eight sectors per track, eight heads, and four cylinders. This means a total of 8 × 8 × 4 = 256 blocks, so the block number ranges from 0 to 255. Each block has its own unique address. Assuming that the sector holds 512 bytes, a 500 GB drive with a formatted capacity of 465.7 GB will have in excess of 976,000,000 blocks.

2.3 Disk Drive Performance

A disk drive is an electromechanical device that governs the overall performance of the storage system environment. The various factors that affect the performance of disk drives are discussed in this section.

2.3.1 Disk Service Time

Disk service time is the time taken by a disk to complete an I/O request. Components that contribute to service time on a disk drive are *seek time, rotational latency,* and *data transfer rate.*

Seek Time

The *seek time* (also called *access time*) describes the time taken to position the R/W heads across the platter with a radial movement (moving along the radius of the platter). In other words, it is the time taken to reposition and settle the arm and the head over the correct track. The lower the seek time, the faster the I/O operation. Disk vendors publish the following seek time specifications:

- **Full Stroke:** The time taken by the R/W head to move across the entire width of the disk, from the innermost track to the outermost track.
- **Average:** The average time taken by the R/W head to move from one random track to another, normally listed as the time for one-third of a full stroke.
- **Track-to-Track:** The time taken by the R/W head to move between adjacent tracks.

Each of these specifications is measured in milliseconds. The average seek time on a modern disk is typically in the range of 3 to 15 milliseconds. Seek time has more impact on the read operation of random tracks rather than adjacent tracks. To minimize the seek time, data can be written to only a subset of the available cylinders. This results in lower usable capacity than the actual capacity of the drive. For example, a 500 GB disk drive is set up to use only the first 40 percent of the cylinders and is effectively treated as a 200 GB drive. This is known as *short-stroking* the drive.

Rotational Latency

To access data, the actuator arm moves the R/W head over the platter to a particular track while the platter spins to position the requested sector under the R/W head. The time taken by the platter to rotate and position the data under the R/W head is called *rotational latency*. This latency depends on the rotation speed of the spindle and is measured in milliseconds. The average rotational latency is one-half of the time taken for a full rotation. Similar to the seek time, rotational latency has more impact on the reading/writing of random sectors on the disk than on the same operations on adjacent sectors.

Average rotational latency is around 5.5 ms for a 5,400-rpm drive, and around 2.0 ms for a 15,000-rpm drive.

Data Transfer Rate

The *data transfer rate* (also called *transfer rate*) refers to the average amount of data per unit time that the drive can deliver to the HBA. It is important to first understand the process of read and write operations in order to calculate data transfer rates. In a *read operation*, the data first moves from disk platters to R/W heads, and then it moves to the drive's internal *buffer*. Finally, data moves from the buffer through the interface to the host HBA. In a *write operation*, the data moves from the HBA to the internal buffer of the disk drive through the drive's interface. The data then moves from the buffer to the R/W heads. Finally, it moves from the R/W heads to the platters.

The data transfer rates during the R/W operations are measured in terms of internal and external transfer rates, as shown in Figure 2-8.

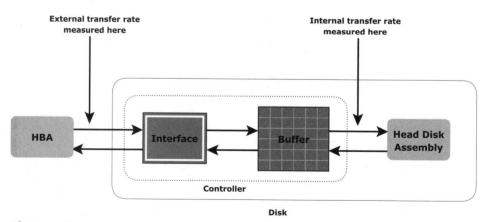

Figure 2-8: Data transfer rate

Internal transfer rate is the speed at which data moves from a single track of a platter's surface to internal buffer (cache) of the disk. Internal transfer rate takes into account factors such as the seek time. *External transfer rate* is the rate at which data can be moved through the interface to the HBA. External transfer rate is generally the advertised speed of the interface, such as 133 MB/s for ATA. The sustained external transfer rate is lower than the interface speed.

2.4 Fundamental Laws Governing Disk Performance

To understand the laws of disk performance, a disk can be viewed as a black box consisting of two elements:

- **Queue:** The location where an I/O request waits before it is processed by the I/O controller.

- **Disk I/O Controller:** Processes I/Os that are waiting in the queue one by one.

The I/O requests arrive at the controller at the rate generated by the application. This rate is also called the *arrival rate*. These requests are held in the I/O queue, and the I/O controller processes them one by one, as shown in Figure 2-9. The I/O arrival rate, the queue length, and the time taken by the I/O controller to process each request determines the performance of the disk system, which is measured in terms of response time.

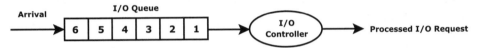

Figure 2-9: I/O processing

Little's Law is a fundamental law describing the relationship between the number of requests in a queue and the response time. The law states the following relation (numbers in parentheses indicate the equation number for cross-referencing):

$$N = a \times R \quad (1)$$

where

"N" is the total number of requests in the queuing system (requests in the queue + requests in the I/O controller)

"a" is the arrival rate, or the number of I/O requests that arrive to the system per unit of time

"R" is the average response time or the turnaround time for an I/O request — the total time from arrival to departure from the system

The *utilization law* is another important law that defines the I/O controller utilization. This law states the relation:

$$U = a \times R_S \quad (2)$$

where

"U" is the I/O controller utilization

"R_S" is the *service time*, or the average time spent by a request on the controller. $1/R_S$ is the *service rate*.

From the arrival rate "a", the average inter-arrival time, R_a, can be computed as:

$R_a = 1/a$ (3)

Consequently, *utilization* can be defined as the ratio of the service time to the average inter-arrival time, and is expressed as:

$U = R_S/R_a$ (4)

The value of this ratio varies between 0 and 1.

Here, it is important to realize that in a single controller system, the arrival rate must be smaller than the service rate. In other words, the service time must be smaller than the average inter-arrival time; otherwise, I/O requests will arrive into the system faster than the I/O controller can process them.

With the help of these two fundamental laws, a number of important measures of disk performance, such as average response time, average queue length, and time spent by a request in a queue can be derived.

In the following equation, the term average response rate (S) can be defined as the reciprocal of the average response time (R), and is derived as follows:

S = service rate – arrival rate

Consequently,

R = 1/ (service rate – arrival rate)

$R = 1/(1/R_S - 1/R_a)$

  $= 1/(1/R_S - a)$ (from eq. 3)

  $= R_S/(1 - a \times R_S)$

$R = R_S/(1-U)$ (5) (from eq. 2)

As a result,

Average response time (R) = service time/(1 – utilization)
(from equation 2)

As utilization reaches 1 — that is, as the I/O controller saturates — the response time is closer to infinity. In essence, the saturated component, or the bottleneck, forces the serialization of I/O requests, meaning each I/O request has to wait for the completion of the I/O requests that preceded it.

Utilization (U) can also be used to represent the average number of I/O requests on the controller, as shown in the following:

Number of requests in the queue (N_Q) = Number of requests in the system (N) – Number of requests on the controller or utilization (U). Number of requests in a queue is also referred to as *average queue size*.

$N_Q = N - U$

$\quad = a \times R - U \quad$ (from eq. 1)

$\quad = a \times (R_S / (1 - U)) - U \quad$ (from eq. 5)

$\quad = (R_S / R_a) / (1 - U) - U \quad$ (from eq. 3)

$\quad = U / (1 - U) - U \quad$ (from eq. 4)

$\quad = U (1 / (1 - U) - 1)$

$\quad = \mathbf{U^2 / (1-U)} \quad$ (6)

The time spent by a request in the queue is equal to the time spent by a request in the system, or the average response time minus the time spent by a request on the controller for processing:

$\quad = R_s / (1 - U) - R_s \quad$ (from eq. 5)

$\quad = U \times R_S / (1 - U)$

$\quad = U \times$ avg. response time

$\quad = \mathbf{Utilization \times R} \quad$ (7)

Consider a disk I/O system in which an I/O request arrives at a rate of 100 I/Os per second. The service time, R_S, is 8 ms. The following measures of disk performance can be computed using the relationships developed above — utilization of I/O controller (U), total response time (R), average queue size [$U^2 / (1 - U)$] and total time spent by a request in a queue ($U \times R$), as follows:

Arrival rate (a) = 100 I/O/s; consequently, the arrival time

$R_a = 1/a = 10$ ms

$R_S = 8$ ms (given)

1. Utilization (U) = $R_S / R_a = 8 / 10 = 0.8$ or 80%
2. Response time (R) = $R_S /(1 - U) = 8 / (1 - 0.8) = 40$ ms
3. Average queue size = $U^2 / (1 - U) = (0.8)^2 / (1 - 0.8) = 3.2$
4. Time spent by a request in a queue = $U \times R$, or the total response time-service time = 32 ms

Now, if controller power is doubled, the service time is halved; consequently, $R_S = 4$ ms in this scenario.

1. Utilization (U) = $4 / 10 = 0.4$ or 40%
2. Response time (R) = $4 / (1 - 0.4) = 6.67$ ms
3. Average queue size = $(0.4)^2 / (1 - 0.4) = 0.26$
4. Time spent by a request in a queue = $0.4 \times 6.67 = 2.67$ ms

As a result, it can be concluded that by reducing the service time (the sum of seek time, latency, and internal transfer rate) or utilization by half, the response time can be reduced drastically (almost six times in the preceding example). The relationship between utilization and response time is shown in Figure 2-10.

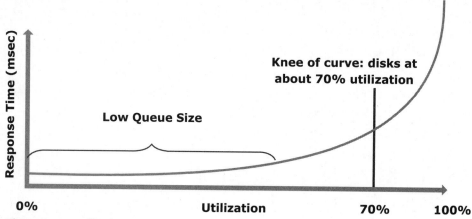

Figure 2-10: Utilization vs. Response time

Response time changes are nonlinear as utilization increases. When the average queue sizes are low, response time remains low. Response time increases slowly with added load on the queue, and increases exponentially when utilization exceeds 70 percent.

2.5 Logical Components of the Host

The logical components of a host consist of the software applications and protocols that enable data communication with the user as well as the physical components. Following are the logical components of a host:

- Operating system
- Device drivers
- Volume manager
- File system
- Application

2.5.1 Operating System

An *operating system* controls all aspects of the computing environment. It works between the application and physical components of the computer system. One of the services it provides to the application is data access. The operating system also monitors and responds to user actions and the environment. It organizes and controls hardware components and manages the allocation of hardware resources. It provides basic security for the access and usage of all managed resources. An operating system also performs basic storage management tasks while managing other underlying components, such as the file system, volume manager, and device drivers.

2.5.2 Device Driver

A *device driver* is special software that permits the operating system to interact with a specific device, such as a printer, a mouse, or a hard drive. A device driver enables the operating system to recognize the device and to use a standard interface (provided as an *application programming interface*, or *API*) to access and control devices. Device drivers are hardware dependent and operating system specific.

2.5.3 Volume Manager

In the early days, an HDD appeared to the operating system as a number of continuous disk blocks. The entire HDD would be allocated for the file system or other data entity used by the operating system or application. The disadvantage was lack of flexibility: As an HDD ran out of space, there was no easy way to extend the file system's size. As the storage capacity of the HDD increased, allocating the entire HDD for the file system often resulted in underutilization of storage capacity.

Disk partitioning was introduced to improve the flexibility and utilization of HDDs. In partitioning, an HDD is divided into logical containers called *logical volumes (LVs)* (see Figure 2-11). For example, a large physical drive can be partitioned into multiple LVs to maintain data according to the file system's and applications' requirements. The partitions are created from groups of contiguous cylinders when the hard disk is initially set up on the host. The host's file system accesses the partitions without any knowledge of partitioning and the physical structure of the disk.

Concatenation is the process of grouping several smaller physical drives and presenting them to the host as one logical drive (see Figure 2-11).

The evolution of *Logical Volume Managers (LVMs)* enabled the dynamic extension of file system capacity and efficient storage management. LVM is software that runs on the host computer and manages the logical and physical storage. LVM is an optional, intermediate layer between the file system and the physical disk. It can aggregate several smaller disks to form a larger virtual disk or to partition a larger-capacity disk into virtual, smaller-capacity disks, which are then presented to applications. The LVM provides optimized storage access and simplifies storage resource management. It hides details about the physical disk and the location of data on the disk; and it enables administrators to change the storage allocation without changing the hardware, even when the application is running.

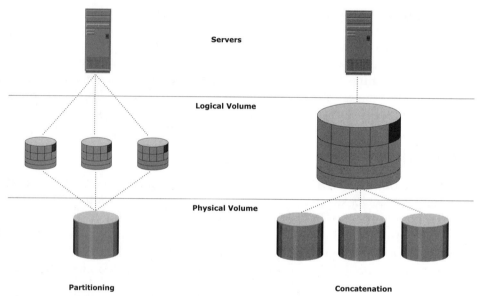

Figure 2-11: Disk partitioning and concatenation

The basic LVM components are the *physical volumes, volume groups,* and *logical volumes.* In LVM terminology, each physical disk connected to the host system is a *physical volume (PV).* LVM converts the physical storage provided by the physical volumes to a logical view of storage, which is then used by the operating system and applications. A *volume group* is created by grouping together one or more physical volumes. A unique *physical volume identifier (PVID)* is assigned to each physical volume when it is initialized for use by the LVM. Physical volumes can be added or removed from a volume group dynamically. They cannot be shared between volume groups; the entire physical volume becomes part of a volume group. Each physical volume is partitioned into equal-sized data blocks called *physical extents* when the volume group is created.

Logical volumes are created within a given volume group. A logical volume can be thought of as a virtual disk partition, while the volume group itself can be thought of as a disk. A volume group can have a number of logical volumes. The size of a logical volume is based on a multiple of the physical extents.

The logical volume appears as a physical device to the operating system. A logical volume can be made up of noncontiguous physical partitions and can span multiple physical volumes. A file system can be created on a logical volume; and logical volumes can be configured for optimal performance to the application and can be mirrored to provide enhanced data availability.

2.5.4 File System

A *file* is a collection of related records or data stored as a unit with a name. A *file system* is a hierarchical structure of files. File systems enable easy access to data files residing within a disk drive, a disk partition, or a logical volume. A file system needs host-based logical structures and software routines that control access to files. It provides users with the functionality to create, modify, delete, and access files. Access to the files on the disks is controlled by the permissions given to the file by the owner, which are also maintained by the file system.

A file system organizes data in a structured hierarchical manner via the use of directories, which are containers for storing pointers to multiple files. All file systems maintain a pointer map to the directories, subdirectories, and files that are part of the file system. Some of the common file systems are as follows:

- FAT 32 (File Allocation Table) for Microsoft Windows
- NT File System (NTFS) for Microsoft Windows
- UNIX File System (UFS) for UNIX
- Extended File System (EXT2/3) for Linux

Apart from the files and directories, the file system also includes a number of other related records, which are collectively called the *metadata*. For example, metadata in a UNIX environment consists of the *superblock*, the *inodes*, and the list of data blocks free and in use. The metadata of a file system has to be consistent in order for the file system to be considered healthy. A superblock contains important information about the file system, such as the file system type, creation and modification dates, size and layout, the count of available resources (such as number of free blocks, inodes, etc.), and a flag indicating the mount status of the file system. An inode is associated with every file and directory and contains information about file length, ownership, access privileges, time of last access/modification, number of links, and the addresses for finding the location on the physical disk where the actual data is stored.

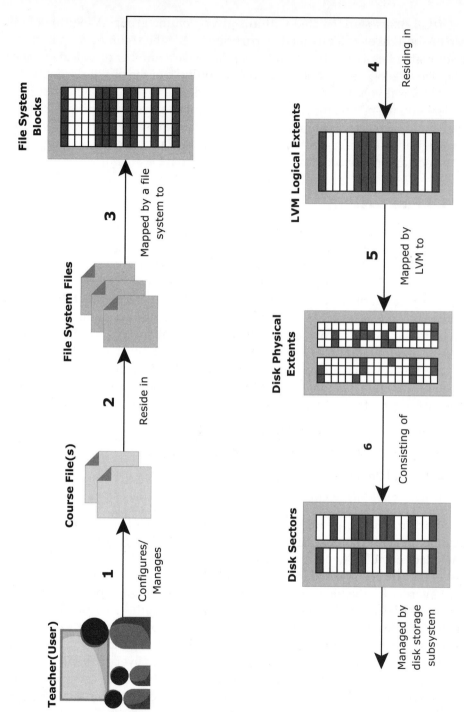

Figure 2-12: Process of mapping user files to disk storage

A file system *block* is the smallest "container" of physical disk space allocated for data. Each file system block is a contiguous area on the physical disk. The block size of a file system is fixed at the time of its creation. File system size depends on block size and the total number of blocks of data stored. A file can span multiple file system blocks because most files are larger than the predefined block size of the file system. File system blocks cease to be contiguous (i.e., become fragmented) when new blocks are added or deleted. Over time, as files grow larger, the file system becomes increasingly fragmented.

Figure 2-12 shows the following process of mapping user files to the disk storage subsystem with an LVM:

1. Files are created and managed by users and applications.

2. These files reside in the file systems.

3. The file systems are then mapped to units of data, or file system blocks.

4. The file system blocks are mapped to logical extents.

5. These in turn are mapped to disk physical extents either by the operating system or by the LVM.

6. These physical extents are mapped to the disk storage subsystem.

If there is no LVM, then there are no logical extents. Without LVM, file system blocks are directly mapped to disk sectors.

The *file system tree* starts with the *root directory*. The root directory has a number of *subdirectories*. A file system should be mounted before it can be used.

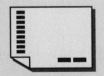 The system utility `fsck` is run to check file system consistency in a UNIX host. An example of the file system in an inconsistent state is when the file system has outstanding changes and the computer system crashes before the changes are committed to disk. At the time of booting, the `fsck` command first checks for consistency of file systems critical for a successful boot. If the critical file systems are found to be consistent, the command checks the consistency of all other file systems. If any file system is found to be inconsistent, it is not mounted. The inconsistent file system can sometimes be repaired automatically by the `fsck` command or may require user interaction for, and confirmation of, corrective actions to be taken.

A file system can be either a journaling file system or a nonjournaling file system. *Nonjournaling file systems* create a potential for lost files because they may use many separate writes to update their data and metadata. If the system crashes during the write process, metadata or data may be lost or corrupted.

When the system reboots, the file system attempts to update the metadata structures by examining and repairing them. This operation takes a long time on large file systems. If there is insufficient information to recreate the desired or original structure, files may be misplaced or lost, resulting in corrupted file systems.

A *journaling file system* uses a separate area called a *log*, or *journal*. This journal may contain all the data to be written (*physical journal*), or it may contain only the metadata to be updated (*logical journal*). Before changes are made to the file system, they are written to this separate area. Once the journal has been updated, the operation on the file system can be performed. If the system crashes during the operation, there is enough information in the log to "replay" the log record and complete the operation. Journaling results in a very quick file system check because it only looks at the active, most recently accessed parts of a large file system. In addition, because information about the pending operation is saved, the risk of files being lost is reduced.

A disadvantage of journaling file systems is that they are slower than other file systems. This slowdown is the result of the extra operations that have to be performed on the journal each time the file system is changed. However, the much shortened time for file system checks and the file system integrity provided by journaling far outweighs this disadvantage. Nearly all file system implementations today use journaling.

Dedicated file servers may be installed to manage and share a large number of files over a network. These file servers support multiple file systems and they use file sharing protocols specific to the operating system — for example, NFS and CIFS. These protocols are detailed in Chapter 7.

2.5.5 Application

An *application* is a computer program that provides the logic for computing operations. It provides an interface between the user and the host and among multiple hosts. Conventional business applications using databases have a three-tiered architecture — the application user interface forms the front-end tier; the computing logic forms, or the application itself is, the middle tier; and the underlying databases that organize the data form the back-end tier. The application sends requests to the underlying operating system to perform read/write (R/W) operations on the storage devices. Applications can be layered on the database, which in turn uses the OS services to perform R/W operations to storage devices. These R/W operations (I/O operations) enable transactions between the front-end and back-end tiers.

Data access can be classified as block-level or file-level depending on whether the application uses a logical block address or the file name and a file record identifier to read from and write to a disk.

Block-Level Access

Block-level access is the basic mechanism for disk access. In this type of access, data is stored and retrieved from disks by specifying the logical block address. The block address is derived based on the geometric configuration of the disks. Block size defines the basic unit of data storage and retrieval by an application. Databases, such as Oracle and SQL Server, define the block size for data access and the location of the data on the disk in terms of the logical block address when an I/O operation is performed.

File-Level Access

File-level access is an abstraction of block-level access. File-level access to data is provided by specifying the name and path of the file. It uses the underlying block-level access to storage and hides the complexities of logical block addressing (LBA) from the application and the DBMS.

OBJECT-LEVEL ACCESS

Object-level access is an intelligent evolution of data access whereby objects are the fundamental unit for data storage and access from storage. Data belonging to certain objects is grouped or organized and identified with a unique object identifier. Applications use this identifier to store and retrieve the data.

2.6 Application Requirements and Disk Performance

The analysis of application storage requirements conventionally begins with determining storage capacity. This can be easily estimated by the size and number of file systems and database components that will be used by applications. The application I/O size and the number of I/Os the application generates are two important measures affecting disk performance and response time.

Consequently, the storage design and layout for an application commences with the following:

1. Analyzing the number of I/Os generated at peak workload
2. Documenting the application I/O size or block size

The block size depends on the file system and database on which the application is built. Block sizes in a database environment are controlled by the underlying database engine and the environment variables set.

Consider an example of a SCSI controller (SCSI interface) with a throughput of 160 MB/s and disk service time $R_S = 0.3$ ms. The computation of the rate $(1 / [R_S +$ Transfer time]) at which I/Os are serviced in a typical database I/O with block sizes 4 KB, 8 KB, 16 KB, 32 KB, and 64 KB are shown in Table 2-1. The rate at which the application I/Os are serviced is termed I/Os per second (IOPS).

Table 2-1: Maximum IOPS Performed by SCSI Controller

BLOCK SIZE	TRANSFER TIME (MS)	IOPS= 1/(R$_S$ + TRANSFER TIME)
4 KB	4 KB / 160 MB = 0.025	1 / (0.3 + 0.025) = 3,076
8 KB	8 KB / 160 MB = 0.05	1 / (0.3 + 0.05) = 2,857
16 KB	16 KB / 160 MB = 0.1	1 / (0.3 + 0.1) = 2,500
32 KB	32 KB / 160 MB = 0.2	1 / (0.3 + 0.2) = 2,000
64 KB	64 KB / 160 MB = 0.4	1 / (0.3 + 0.4) = 1,428

As a result, the number of IOPS per controller depends on the I/O block size and ranges from 1,400 (for 64 KB) to 3,100 (for 4 KB).

The disk service time (R_S) is a key measure of disk performance; R_S along with disk utilization rate (U) determines the I/O response time for applications.

As shown earlier in this chapter, the total disk service time (R_S) is the sum of seek time (E), rotational latency (L), and the internal transfer time (X):

$$R_S = E + L + X$$

E is determined based on the randomness of the I/O request. L and X are measures provided by disk vendors as technical specifications of the disk. Consider an example with the following specifications provided for a disk:

- Average seek time of 5 ms in a random I/O environment, or E = 5 ms.

- Disk rotation speed of 15,000 rpm — from which rotational latency (L) can be determined, which is one half of the time taken for a full rotation or L = (0.5 / 15,000 rpm expressed in ms).

- 40 MB/s internal data transfer rate, from which the internal transfer time (X) is derived based on the block size of the I/O — for example, an I/O with a block size of 32 KB or X = 32 KB / 40 MB.

Consequently, $R_S = 5$ ms + (0.5 / 15,000) + 32 KB / 40 MB = 7.8 ms.

The maximum number of I/Os serviced per second or IOPS = 1/ R_S.

In other words, for an I/O with a block size of 32 KB and $R_S = 7.8$ ms, the maximum IOPS will be $1 / (7.8 \times 10^{-3}) = 128$ IOPS.

Table 2-2 lists the maximum IOPS that can be serviced for different block sizes.

Table 2-2: Maximum IOPS Performed by Disk Drive

BLOCK SIZE	RS = E+L+X	IOPS = 1/RS
4 KB	5 ms + (0.5 / 15,000 rpm) + 4K / 40MB = 5 + 2 + 0.1 = 7.1	140
8 KB	5 ms + (0.5 / 15,000 rpm) + 8K / 40MB = 5 + 2 + 0.2 = 7.2	139
16 KB	5 ms + (0.5 / 15,000 rpm) + 16K / 40MB = 5 + 2 + 0.4 = 7.4	135
32 KB	5 ms + (0.5 / 15,000 rpm) + 32K / 40MB = 5 + 2 + 0.8 = 7.8	128
64 KB	5 ms + (0.5 / 15,000 rpm) + 64K / 40MB = 5 + 2+ 1.6 = 8.6	116

Table 2-2 shows that the value of E, the seek time, is still the largest component of R_S. It contributes 5 ms out of 7.1 ms to 8.6 ms (58–70 percent) of the disk service time.

The IOPS ranging from 116 to 140 for different block sizes represents the IOPS that could be achieved at potentially very high levels of utilization (close to 100 percent). As shown in Section 2.4, the application response time, R, increases with an increase in utilization or the IOPS.

For the example in Table 2-2, the I/O response time (R) for an I/O with a block size of 64 KB will be approximately 215 ms when the controller works close to 96 percent utilization, as shown here:

$$R = R_S \ / \ (1- \ U)$$

$$= 8.6 \ / \ (1\text{-}0.96)$$

$$= 215 \text{ ms}$$

If an application demands a faster response time, then the utilization for the disks should be maintained below 70 percent, or the knee of the curve, after which the response time increases exponentially.

Considering another example from Table 2-2, with a block size of 8 KB and the utilization near 100 percent, a maximum of 139 IOPS could be achieved. However, at U = 97 percent the IOPS in the system will be approximately 134, and the response time, R, for each I/O will be 240 ms.

Similarly, the response time for 105 IOPS (U = 75%) will be 29.5 ms; for 75 IOPS (54% utilization), it will be 15.7 ms; and for 45 IOPS (32% utilization), it will be 10.6 ms.

Considering a block size of 64 KB, at U = 100 percent, the maximum IOPS that can be sustained will be 116. The application will not be able to sustain 135 IOPS for the block size and performance specifications used in this example. For 64KB I/O at 105 IOPS (U = 91%), R = 88.6 ms, and at 45 IOPS (U = 39%), R = 14.6 ms.

Storage requirements for an application are specified in terms of both capacity and the IOPS that should be met for the application. If an application needs 200GB of disk space, then this capacity could currently be provided with a single disk. However, if the application I/O demands are high, then it will result in performance degradation because one disk cannot provide the required response time for I/O operations.

The total number of disks required (N) for an application is computed as follows:

If C is the number of disks required to meet the capacity and I is the number of disks required for meeting IOPS, then

$$N = Max (C, I)$$

Disk vendors publish the disk potential in terms of IOPS based on the benchmark they carry out for different block sizes and application environments.

Consider an example in which the capacity requirements for an application are 1.46 TB. The peak workload generated by the application is estimated at 9,000 IOPS. The vendor specifies that a 146 GB, 15,000-rpm drive is capable of a maximum of 180 IOPS (U = 70%).

In this example, the number of disks required to meet the capacity requirements will be only 1.46 TB / 146 GB = 10 disks. To meet 9,000 IOPS, 50 disks will be required (9,000 / 180). As a result, the number of disks required to meet the application demand will be Max (10, 50) = 50 disks.

In many application environments, more disks are configured to meet the IOPS requirements than to meet the storage capacity requirements. For response-time-sensitive applications, the number of drives required is also calculated based on the IOPS that a single disk can sustain at less than 70 percent utilization level to provide a better response time.

Summary

This chapter detailed the storage system environment — the host, connectivity, and storage. The data flows from an application to storage through these components. Physical and logical components of these entities affect the overall performance of the storage system environment.

Storage is the most important component in the storage system environment. The hard disk drive (HDD) is the most popular storage device that uses magnetic media for accessing and storing data for performance-intensive applications. Logically, the HDD can be viewed in sectors, tracks, and cylinders, which form the basis of disk addressing. This chapter detailed the fundamental laws that govern HDD performance. Overall performance depends on disk response time, which consists of seek time, rotational latency, and disk service time.

Modern disk storage systems use multiple disks and techniques such as RAID to meet the capacity and performance requirements of applications, as described in the next chapter.

EXERCISES

1. What are the benefits of using multiple HBAs on a host?

2. An application specifies a requirement of 200 GB to host a database and other files. It also specifies that the storage environment should support 5,000 IOPS during its peak processing cycle. The disks available for configuration provide 66 GB of usable capacity, and the manufacturer specifies that they can support a maximum of 140 IOPS. The application is response time sensitive and disk utilization beyond 60 percent will not meet the response time requirements of the application. Compute and explain the theoretical basis for the minimum number of disks that should be configured to meet the requirements of the application.

3. Which components constitute the disk service time? Which component contributes the largest percentage of the disk service time in a random I/O operation?

4. Why do formatted disks have less capacity than unformatted disks?

5. The average I/O size of an application is 64 KB. The following specifications are available from the disk manufacturer: average seek time = 5 ms, 7,200 RPM, transfer rate = 40 MB/s. Determine the maximum IOPS that could be performed with this disk for this application. Taking this case as an example, explain the relationship between disk utilization and IOPS.

6. Consider a disk I/O system in which an I/O request arrives at the rate of 80 IOPS. The disk service time is 6 ms.

   a. Compute the following:

      Utilization of I/O controller

      Total response time

      Average queue size

      Total time spent by a request in a queue

   b. Compute the preceding parameter if the service time is halved.

7. Refer to Question 6 and plot a graph showing the response time and utilization, considering 20 percent, 40 percent, 60 percent, 80 percent, and 100 percent utilization of the I/O controller. Describe the conclusion that could be derived from the graph.

8. The Storage Networking Industry Association (SNIA) shared storage model is a simple and powerful model for describing the shared storage architecture. This model is detailed at www.snia.org/education/storage_networking_primer/shared_storage_model/SNIA-SSM-text-2003-04-13.pdf. Study this model and prepare a report explaining how the elements detailed in this chapter are represented in the SNIA model.

Chapter 3
Data Protection: RAID

I n the late 1980s, rapid adoption of computers for business processes stimulated the growth of new applications and databases, significantly increasing the demand for storage capacity. At that time, data was stored on a single large, expensive disk drive called *Single Large Expensive Drive (SLED)*. Use of single disks could not meet the required performance levels, due to their inherent limitations (detailed in Chapter 2, Section 2.4, "Fundamental Laws Governing Disk Performance").

KEY CONCEPTS

Hardware and Software RAID

Striping, Mirroring, and Parity

RAID Write Penalty

Hot Spares

HDDs are susceptible to failures due to mechanical wear and tear and other environmental factors. An HDD failure may result in data loss. The solutions available during the 1980s were not able to meet the availability and performance demands of applications.

An HDD has a projected life expectancy before it fails. *Mean Time Between Failure (MTBF)* measures (in hours) the average life expectancy of an HDD. Today, data centers deploy thousands of HDDs in their storage infrastructures. The greater the number of HDDs in a storage array, the greater the probability of a disk failure in the array. For example, consider a storage array of 100 HDDs, each with an MTBF of 750,000 hours. The MTBF of this collection of HDDs in the array, therefore, is 750,000/100 or 7,500 hours. This means that a HDD in this array is likely to fail at least once in 7,500 hours.

RAID is an enabling technology that leverages multiple disks as part of a set, which provides data protection against HDD failures. In general, RAID implementations also improve the I/O performance of storage systems by storing data across multiple HDDs.

In 1987, Patterson, Gibson, and Katz at the University of California, Berkeley, published a paper titled "A Case for Redundant Arrays of Inexpensive Disks

(RAID)." This paper described the use of small-capacity, inexpensive disk drives as an alternative to large-capacity drives common on mainframe computers. The term *RAID* has been redefined to refer to *independent* disks, to reflect advances in the storage technology. RAID storage has now grown from an academic concept to an industry standard.

This chapter details RAID technology, RAID levels, and different types of RAID implementations and their benefits.

3.1 Implementation of RAID

There are two types of RAID implementation, hardware and software. Both have their merits and demerits and are discussed in this section.

3.1.1 Software RAID

Software RAID uses host-based software to provide RAID functions. It is implemented at the operating-system level and does not use a dedicated hardware controller to manage the RAID array.

Software RAID implementations offer cost and simplicity benefits when compared with hardware RAID. However, they have the following limitations:

- **Performance:** Software RAID affects overall system performance. This is due to the additional CPU cycles required to perform RAID calculations. The performance impact is more pronounced for complex implementations of RAID, as detailed later in this chapter.

- **Supported features:** Software RAID does not support all RAID levels.

- **Operating system compatibility:** Software RAID is tied to the host operating system hence upgrades to software RAID or to the operating system should be validated for compatibility. This leads to inflexibility in the data processing environment.

3.1.2 Hardware RAID

In *hardware RAID* implementations, a specialized hardware controller is implemented either on the host or on the array. These implementations vary in the way the storage array interacts with the host.

Controller card RAID is host-based hardware RAID implementation in which a specialized RAID controller is installed in the host and HDDs are connected to it. The RAID Controller interacts with the hard disks using a PCI bus. Manufacturers also integrate RAID controllers on motherboards. This integration reduces the overall cost of the system, but does not provide the flexibility required for high-end storage systems.

The external RAID controller is an array-based hardware RAID. It acts as an interface between the host and disks. It presents storage volumes to the host, which manage the drives using the supported protocol. Key functions of RAID controllers are:

- Management and control of disk aggregations
- Translation of I/O requests between logical disks and physical disks
- Data regeneration in the event of disk failures

3.2 RAID Array Components

A *RAID array* is an enclosure that contains a number of HDDs and the supporting hardware and software to implement RAID. HDDs inside a RAID array are usually contained in smaller sub-enclosures. These sub-enclosures, or *physical arrays*, hold a fixed number of HDDs, and may also include other supporting hardware, such as power supplies. A subset of disks within a RAID array can be grouped to form logical associations called *logical arrays*, also known as a *RAID set* or a *RAID group* (see Figure 3-1).

Logical arrays are comprised of logical volumes (LV). The operating system recognizes the LVs as if they are physical HDDs managed by the RAID controller. The number of HDDs in a logical array depends on the RAID level used. Configurations could have a logical array with multiple physical arrays or a physical array with multiple logical arrays.

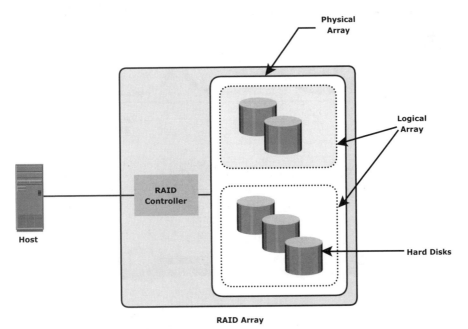

Figure 3-1: Components of RAID array

3.3 RAID Levels

RAID levels (see Table 3-1) are defined on the basis of striping, mirroring, and parity techniques. These techniques determine the data availability and performance characteristics of an array. Some RAID arrays use one technique, whereas others use a combination of techniques. Application performance and data availability requirements determine the RAID level selection.

3.3.1 Striping

A RAID set is a group of disks. Within each disk, a predefined number of contiguously addressable disk blocks are defined as *strips*. The set of aligned strips that spans across all the disks within the RAID set is called a *stripe*. Figure 3-2 shows physical and logical representations of a striped RAID set.

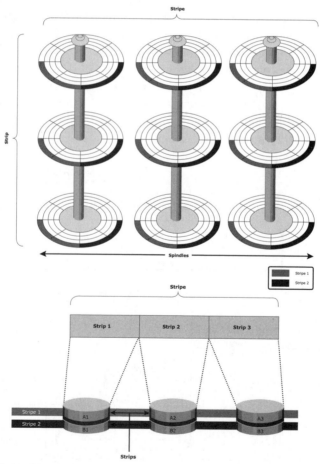

Figure 3-2: Striped RAID set

Strip size (also called *stripe depth*) describes the number of blocks in a *strip*, and is the maximum amount of data that can be written to or read from a single HDD in the set before the next HDD is accessed, assuming that the accessed data starts at the beginning of the strip. Note that all strips in a stripe have the same number of blocks, and decreasing strip size means that data is broken into smaller pieces when spread across the disks.

Stripe size is a multiple of strip size by the number of HDDs in the RAID set. *Stripe width* refers to the number of data strips in a stripe.

Striped RAID does not protect data unless parity or mirroring is used. However, striping may significantly improve I/O performance. Depending on the type of RAID implementation, the RAID controller can be configured to access data across multiple HDDs simultaneously.

3.3.2 Mirroring

Mirroring is a technique whereby data is stored on two different HDDs, yielding two copies of data. In the event of one HDD failure, the data is intact on the surviving HDD (see Figure 3-3) and the controller continues to service the host's data requests from the surviving disk of a mirrored pair.

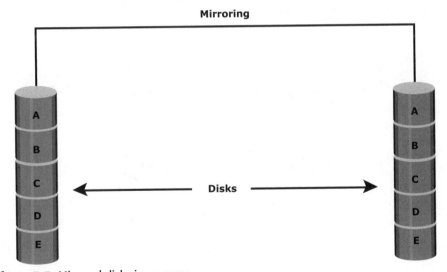

Figure 3-3: Mirrored disks in an array

When the failed disk is replaced with a new disk, the controller copies the data from the surviving disk of the mirrored pair. This activity is transparent to the host.

In addition to providing complete data redundancy, mirroring enables faster recovery from disk failure. However, disk mirroring provides only data protection and is not a substitute for data backup. Mirroring constantly captures changes in the data, whereas a backup captures point-in-time images of data.

Mirroring involves duplication of data — the amount of storage capacity needed is twice the amount of data being stored. Therefore, mirroring is considered expensive and is preferred for mission-critical applications that cannot afford data loss. Mirroring improves read performance because read requests can be serviced by both disks. However, write performance deteriorates, as each write request manifests as two writes on the HDDs. In other words, mirroring does not deliver the same levels of write performance as a striped RAID.

3.3.3 Parity

Parity is a method of protecting striped data from HDD failure without the cost of mirroring. An additional HDD is added to the stripe width to hold parity, a mathematical construct that allows re-creation of the missing data. Parity is a redundancy check that ensures full protection of data without maintaining a full set of duplicate data.

Parity information can be stored on separate, dedicated HDDs or distributed across all the drives in a RAID set. Figure 3-4 shows a parity RAID. The first four disks, labeled *D*, contain the data. The fifth disk, labeled *P*, stores the parity information, which in this case is the sum of the elements in each row. Now, if one of the *D*s fails, the missing value can be calculated by subtracting the sum of the rest of the elements from the parity value.

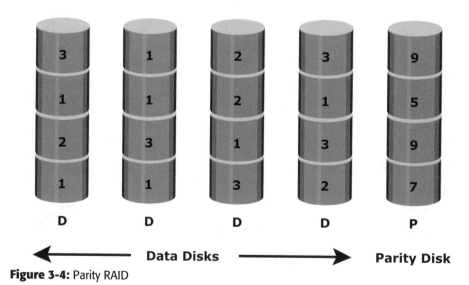

Figure 3-4: Parity RAID

In Figure 3-4, the computation of parity is represented as a simple arithmetic operation on the data. However, parity calculation is a *bitwise XOR* operation. Calculation of parity is a function of the RAID controller.

Compared to mirroring, parity implementation considerably reduces the cost associated with data protection. Consider a RAID configuration with five disks. Four of these disks hold data, and the fifth holds parity information. Parity requires 25 percent extra disk space compared to mirroring, which requires 100 percent extra disk space. However, there are some disadvantages of using parity. Parity information is generated from data on the data disk. Therefore, parity is recalculated every time there is a change in data. This recalculation is time-consuming and affects the performance of the RAID controller.

Table 3-1: Raid Levels

LEVELS	BRIEF DESCRIPTION
RAID 0	Striped array with no fault tolerance
RAID 1	Disk mirroring
RAID 3	Parallel access array with dedicated parity disk
RAID 4	Striped array with independent disks and a dedicated parity disk
RAID 5	Striped array with independent disks and distributed parity
RAID 6	Striped array with independent disks and dual distributed parity
Nested	Combinations of RAID levels. Example: RAID 1 + RAID 0

3.3.4 RAID 0

In a RAID 0 configuration, data is striped across the HDDs in a RAID set. It utilizes the full storage capacity by distributing strips of data over multiple HDDs in a RAID set. To read data, all the strips are put back together by the controller. The stripe size is specified at a host level for software RAID and is vendor specific for hardware RAID. Figure 3-5 shows RAID 0 on a storage array in which data is striped across 5 disks. When the number of drives in the array increases, performance improves because more data can be read or written simultaneously. RAID 0 is used in applications that need high I/O throughput. However, if these applications require high availability, RAID 0 does not provide data protection and availability in the event of drive failures.

3.3.5 RAID 1

In a RAID 1 configuration, data is mirrored to improve fault tolerance (see Figure 3-6). A RAID 1 group consists of at least two HDDs. As explained in mirroring, every write is written to both disks, which is transparent to the host in a hardware RAID implementation. In the event of disk failure, the impact on data recovery is the least among all RAID implementations. This is because the RAID controller uses the mirror drive for data recovery and continuous operation. RAID 1 is suitable for applications that require high availability.

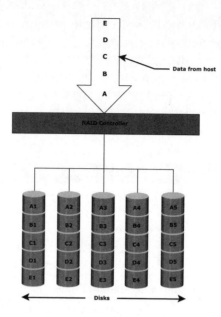

Figure 3-5: RAID 0

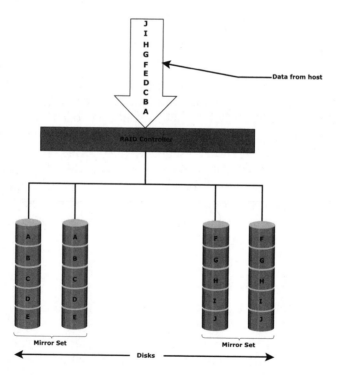

Figure 3-6: RAID 1

3.3.6 Nested RAID

Most data centers require data redundancy and performance from their RAID arrays. RAID 0+1 and RAID 1+0 combine the performance benefits of RAID 0 with the redundancy benefits of RAID 1. They use striping and mirroring techniques and combine their benefits. These types of RAID require an even number of disks, the minimum being four (see Figure 3-7).

RAID 1+0 is also known as RAID 10 (Ten) or RAID 1/0. Similarly, RAID 0+1 is also known as RAID 01 or RAID 0/1. RAID 1+0 performs well for workloads that use small, random, write-intensive I/O. Some applications that benefit from RAID 1+0 include the following:

- High transaction rate Online Transaction Processing (OLTP)
- Large messaging installations
- Database applications that require high I/O rate, random access, and high availability

A common misconception is that RAID 1+0 and RAID 0+1 are the same. Under normal conditions, RAID levels 1+0 and 0+1 offer identical benefits. However, rebuild operations in the case of disk failure differ between the two.

RAID 1+0 is also called *striped mirror*. The basic element of RAID 1+0 is a mirrored pair, which means that data is first mirrored and then both copies of data are striped across multiple HDDs in a RAID set. When replacing a failed drive, only the mirror is rebuilt. In other words, the disk array controller uses the surviving drive in the mirrored pair for data recovery and continuous operation. Data from the surviving disk is copied to the replacement disk.

RAID 0+1 is also called *mirrored stripe*. The basic element of RAID 0+1 is a stripe. This means that the process of striping data across HDDs is performed initially and then the entire stripe is mirrored. If one drive fails, then the entire stripe is faulted. A rebuild operation copies the entire stripe, copying data from each disk in the healthy stripe to an equivalent disk in the failed stripe. This causes increased and unnecessary I/O load on the surviving disks and makes the RAID set more vulnerable to a second disk failure.

3.3.7 RAID 3

RAID 3 stripes data for high performance and uses parity for improved fault tolerance. Parity information is stored on a dedicated drive so that data can be reconstructed if a drive fails. For example, of five disks, four are used for data and one is used for parity. Therefore, the total disk space required is 1.25 times the size of the data disks. RAID 3 **always** reads and writes complete stripes of data across all disks, as the drives operate in parallel. There are no partial writes that update one out of many strips in a stripe. Figure 3-8 illustrates the RAID 3 implementation.

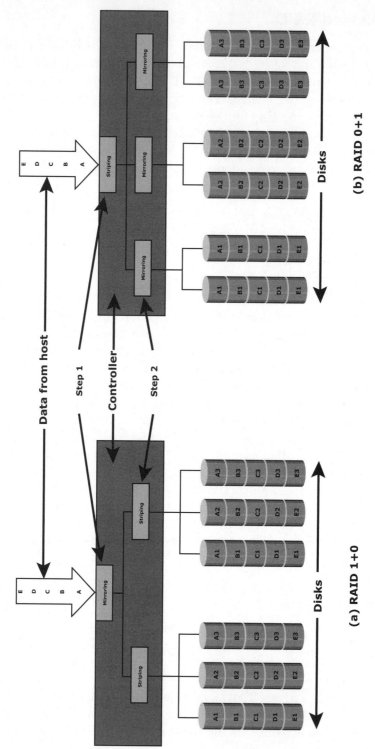

Figure 3-7: Nested RAID

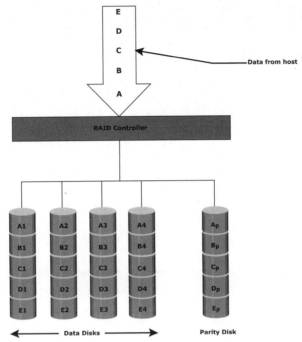

Figure 3-8: RAID 3

RAID 3 provides good bandwidth for the transfer of large volumes of data. RAID 3 is used in applications that involve large sequential data access, such as video streaming.

3.3.8 RAID 4

Similar to RAID 3, RAID 4 stripes data for high performance and uses parity for improved fault tolerance (refer to Figure 3-8). Data is striped across all disks except the parity disk in the array. Parity information is stored on a dedicated disk so that the data can be rebuilt if a drive fails. Striping is done at the block level.

Unlike RAID 3, data disks in RAID 4 can be accessed independently so that specific data elements can be read or written on single disk without read or write of an entire stripe. RAID 4 provides good read throughput and reasonable write throughput.

3.3.9 RAID 5

RAID 5 is a very versatile RAID implementation. It is similar to RAID 4 because it uses striping and the drives (strips) are independently accessible. The difference between RAID 4 and RAID 5 is the parity location. In RAID 4, parity is written to a dedicated drive, creating a write bottleneck for the parity disk. In RAID 5, parity is distributed across all disks. The distribution of parity in RAID 5 overcomes the write bottleneck. Figure 3-9 illustrates the RAID 5 implementation.

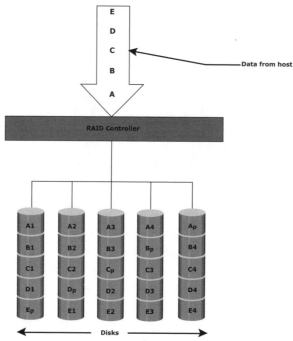

Figure 3-9: RAID 5

RAID 5 is preferred for messaging, data mining, medium-performance media serving, and relational database management system (RDBMS) implementations in which database administrators (DBAs) optimize data access.

3.3.10 RAID 6

RAID 6 works the same way as RAID 5 except that RAID 6 includes a second parity element to enable survival in the event of the failure of two disks in a

RAID group (see Figure 3-10). Therefore, a RAID 6 implementation requires at least four disks. RAID 6 distributes the parity across all the disks. The write penalty in RAID 6 is more than that in RAID 5; therefore, RAID 5 writes perform better than RAID 6. The rebuild operation in RAID 6 may take longer than that in RAID 5 due to the presence of two parity sets.

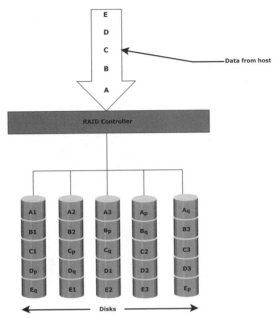

Figure 3-10: RAID 6

3.4 RAID Comparison

Table 3-2 compares the different types of RAID.

Table 3-2: Comparison of Different RAID Types

RAID	MIN. DISKS	STORAGE EFFICIENCY %	COST	READ PERFORMANCE	WRITE PERFORMANCE	WRITE PENALTY
0	2	100	Low	Very good for both random and sequential read	Very good	No
1	2	50	High	Good. Better than a single disk.	Good. Slower than a single disk, as every write must be committed to all disks.	Moderate
3	3	(n-1)*100/n where n= number of disks	Moderate	Good for random reads and very good for sequential reads.	Poor to fair for small random writes. Good for large, sequential writes.	High
4	3	(n-1)*100/n where n= number of disks	Moderate	Very good for random reads. Good to very good for sequential writes.	Poor to fair for random writes. Fair to good for sequential writes.	High

Continued

Table 3-2 (continued)

RAID	MIN. DISKS	STORAGE EFFICIENCY %	COST	READ PERFORMANCE	WRITE PERFORMANCE	WRITE PENALTY
5	3	$(n-1)*100/n$ where n= number of disks	Moderate	Very good for random reads. Good for sequential reads	Fair for random writes. Slower due to parity overhead. Fair to good for sequential writes.	High
6	4	$(n-2)*100/n$ where n= number of disks	Moderate but more than RAID 5	Very good for random reads. Good for sequential reads.	Good for small, random writes (has write penalty).	Very High
1+0 and 0+1	4	50	High	Very good	Good	Moderate

3.5 RAID Impact on Disk Performance

When choosing a RAID type, it is imperative to consider the impact to disk performance and application IOPS.

In both mirrored and parity RAID configurations, every write operation translates into more I/O overhead for the disks which is referred to as *write penalty*. In a RAID 1 implementation, every write operation must be performed on two disks configured as a mirrored pair while in a RAID 5 implementation, a write operation may manifest as four I/O operations. When performing small I/Os to a disk configured with RAID 5, the controller has to read, calculate, and write a parity segment for every data write operation.

Figure 3-11 illustrates a single write operation on RAID 5 that contains a group of five disks. Four of these disks are used for data and one is used for parity.

The parity (P) at the controller is calculated as follows:

$$E_p = E_1 + E_2 + E_3 + E_4 \text{ (XOR operations)}$$

Here, D1 to D4 is striped data across the RAID group of five disks.

Whenever the controller performs a write I/O, parity must be computed by reading the old parity ($E_{p\,old}$) and the old data ($E_{4\,old}$) from the disk, which means two read I/Os. The new parity ($E_{p\,new}$) is computed as follows:

$$E_{p\,new} = E_{p\,old} - E_{4\,old} + E_{4\,new} \text{ (XOR operations)}$$

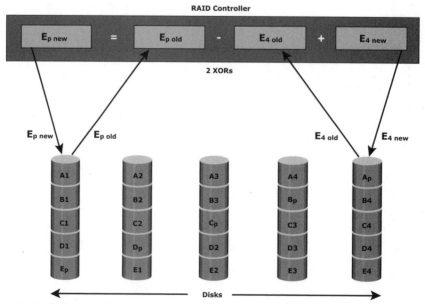

Figure 3-11: Write penalty in RAID 5

After computing the new parity, the controller completes the write I/O by writing the new data and the new parity onto the disks, amounting to two write I/Os. Therefore, the controller performs two disk reads and two disk writes for every write operation, and the write penalty in RAID 5 implementations is 4.

In RAID 6, which maintains dual parity, a disk write requires three read operations: for $E_{p1\ old}$, $E_{p2\ old}$, and $E_{4\ old}$. After calculating $E_{p1\ new}$ and $E_{p2\ new}$, the controller performs three write I/O operations for $E_{p1\ new}$, $E_{p2\ new}$ and $E_{4\ new}$. Therefore, in a RAID 6 implementation, the controller performs six I/O operations for each write I/O, and the write penalty is 6.

3.5.1 Application IOPS and RAID Configurations

When deciding the number of disks required for an application, it is important to consider the impact of RAID based on IOPS generated by the application. The total disk load should be computed by considering the type of RAID configuration and the ratio of read compared to write from the host.

The following example illustrates the method of computing the disk load in different types of RAID.

Consider an application that generates 5,200 IOPS, with 60 percent of them being reads.

The disk load in RAID 5 is calculated as follows:

RAID 5 disk load = 0.6 × 5,200 + **4** × (0.4 × 5,200) [because the write penalty for RAID 5 is 4]

$$= 3,120 + 4 \times 2,080$$

$$= 3,120 + 8,320$$

$$= 11,440 \text{ IOPS}$$

The disk load in RAID 1 is calculated as follows:

RAID 1 disk load = 0.6 × 5,200 + **2** × (0.4 × 5,200) [because every write manifests as two writes to the disks]

$$= 3,120 + 2 \times 2,080$$

$$= 3,120 + 4,160$$

$$= 7,280 \text{ IOPS}$$

The computed disk load determines the number of disks required for the application. If in this example an HDD with a specification of a maximum 180 IOPS for the application needs to be used, the number of disks required to meet the workload for the RAID configuration would be as follows:

■ RAID 5: 11,440 / 180 = 64 disks

■ RAID 1: 7,280 / 180 = 42 disks (approximated to the nearest even number)

3.6 Hot Spares

A *hot spare* refers to a spare HDD in a RAID array that temporarily replaces a failed HDD of a RAID set. A hot spare takes the identity of the failed HDD in the array. One of the following methods of data recovery is performed depending on the RAID implementation:

- If parity RAID is used, then the data is rebuilt onto the hot spare from the parity and the data on the surviving HDDs in the RAID set.

- If mirroring is used, then the data from the surviving mirror is used to copy the data.

When the failed HDD is replaced with a new HDD, one of the following takes place:

- The hot spare replaces the new HDD permanently. This means that it is no longer a hot spare, and a new hot spare must be configured on the array.

- When a new HDD is added to the system, data from the hot spare is copied to it. The hot spare returns to its idle state, ready to replace the next failed drive.

A hot spare should be large enough to accommodate data from a failed drive. Some systems implement multiple hot spares to improve data availability.

A hot spare can be configured as *automatic* or *user initiated,* which specifies how it will be used in the event of disk failure. In an automatic configuration, when the recoverable error rates for a disk exceed a predetermined threshold, the disk subsystem tries to copy data from the failing disk to the hot spare automatically. If this task is completed before the damaged disk fails, then the subsystem switches to the hot spare and marks the failing disk as unusable. Otherwise, it uses parity or the mirrored disk to recover the data. In the case of a user-initiated configuration, the administrator has control of the rebuild process. For example, the rebuild could occur overnight to prevent any degradation of system performance. However, the system is vulnerable to another failure if a hot spare is unavailable.

Summary

Individual disks are prone to failures and pose the threat of data unavailability for applications. RAID addresses data availability requirements by using mirroring and parity techniques. RAID implementations with striping enhance I/O performance by spreading data across multiple HDDs in addition to redundancy benefits.

This chapter explained the fundamental constructs of striping, mirroring, and parity, which form the basis for various RAID levels. Implementation of RAID levels depends on application requirements for performance and data protection.

RAID is the cornerstone technology for several advancements in storage. The next generation of storage systems are intelligent storage systems that implement RAID along with a specialized operating environment that offers high performance and availability. Intelligent storage systems are detailed in the next chapter.

EXERCISES

1. Why is RAID 1 not a substitute for a backup?

2. Why is RAID 0 not an option for data protection and high availability?

3. Explain the process of data recovery in case of a drive failure in RAID 5.

4. What are the benefits of using RAID 3 in a backup application?

5. Discuss the impact of random and sequential I/O in different RAID configurations.

6. An application has 1,000 heavy users at a peak of 2 IOPS each and 2,000 typical users at a peak of 1 IOPS each, with a read/write ratio of 2:1. It is estimated that the application also experiences an overhead of 20 percent for other workloads. Calculate the IOPS requirement for RAID 1, RAID 3, RAID 5, and RAID 6.

7. For Question 7, compute the number of drives required to support the application in different RAID environments if 10K RPM drives with a rating of 130 IOPS per drive were used.

Chapter 4
Intelligent Storage System

Business-critical applications require high levels of performance, availability, security, and scalability. A hard disk drive is a core element of storage that governs the performance of any storage system. Some of the older disk array technologies could not overcome performance constraints due to the limitations of a hard disk and its mechanical components. RAID technology made an important contribution to enhancing storage performance and reliability, but hard disk drives even with a RAID implementation could not meet performance requirements of today's applications.

KEY CONCEPTS

Intelligent Storage System

Front-End Command Queuing

Cache Mirroring and Vaulting

Logical Unit Number

LUN Masking

High-end Storage System

Midrange Storage System

With advancements in technology, a new breed of storage solutions known as an *intelligent storage system* has evolved. The intelligent storage systems detailed in this chapter are the feature-rich RAID arrays that provide highly optimized I/O processing capabilities. These arrays have an operating environment that controls the management, allocation, and utilization of storage resources. These storage systems are configured with large amounts of memory called *cache* and use sophisticated algorithms to meet the I/O requirements of performance-sensitive applications.

4.1 Components of an Intelligent Storage System

An intelligent storage system consists of four key components: *front end, cache, back end,* and *physical disks.* Figure 4-1 illustrates these components and their interconnections. An I/O request received from the host at the front-end port is processed through cache and the back end, to enable storage and retrieval of data from the physical disk. A read request can be serviced directly from cache if the requested data is found in cache.

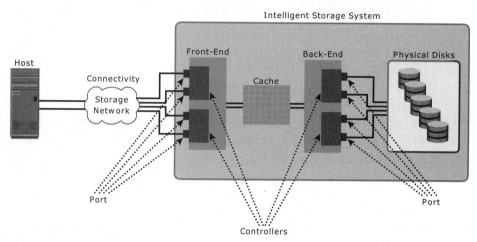

Figure 4-1: Components of an intelligent storage system

4.1.1 Front End

The front end provides the interface between the storage system and the host. It consists of two components: front-end ports and front-end controllers. The *front-end ports* enable hosts to connect to the intelligent storage system. Each front-end port has processing logic that executes the appropriate transport protocol, such as SCSI, Fibre Channel, or iSCSI, for storage connections. Redundant ports are provided on the front end for high availability.

Front-end controllers route data to and from cache via the internal data bus. When cache receives write data, the controller sends an acknowledgment message back to the host. Controllers optimize I/O processing by using command queuing algorithms.

Front-End Command Queuing

Command queuing is a technique implemented on front-end controllers. It determines the execution order of received commands and can reduce unnecessary drive head movements and improve disk performance. When a command is received for execution, the command queuing algorithms assigns a tag that defines a sequence in which commands should be executed. With command queuing, multiple commands can be executed concurrently based on the organization of data on the disk, regardless of the order in which the commands were received.

The most commonly used command queuing algorithms are as follows:

- **First In First Out** (FIFO): This is the default algorithm where commands are executed in the order in which they are received (Figure 4-2 [a]). There is no reordering of requests for optimization; therefore, it is inefficient in terms of performance.

- **Seek Time Optimization:** Commands are executed based on optimizing read/write head movements, which may result in reordering of commands. Without seek time optimization, the commands are executed in the order they are received. For example, as shown in Figure 4-2(a), the commands are executed in the order A, B, C and D. The radial movement required by the head to execute C immediately after A is less than what would be required to execute B. With seek time optimization, the command execution sequence would be A, C, B and D, as shown in Figure 4-2(b).

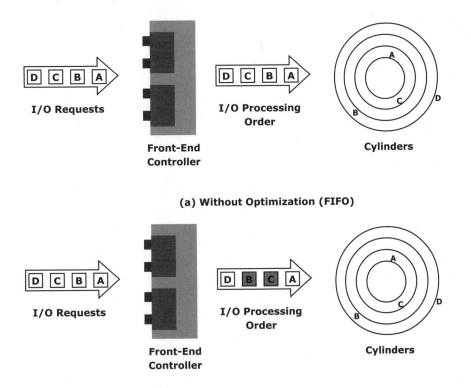

(a) Without Optimization (FIFO)

(b) With Seek Time Optimization

Figure 4-2: Front-end command queuing

▪ **Access Time Optimization:** Commands are executed based on the combination of seek time optimization and an analysis of rotational latency for optimal performance.

Command queuing can also be implemented on disk controllers and this may further supplement the command queuing implemented on the front-end controllers. Some models of SCSI and Fibre Channel drives have command queuing implemented on their controllers.

4.1.2 Cache

Cache is an important component that enhances the I/O performance in an intelligent storage system. Cache is semiconductor memory where data is placed temporarily to reduce the time required to service I/O requests from the host.

Cache improves storage system performance by isolating hosts from the mechanical delays associated with physical disks, which are the slowest components of an intelligent storage system. Accessing data from a physical disk usually takes a few milliseconds because of seek times and rotational latency. If a disk has to be accessed by the host for every I/O operation, requests are queued, which results in a delayed response. Accessing data from cache takes less than a millisecond. Write data is placed in cache and then written to disk. After the data is securely placed in cache, the host is acknowledged immediately.

Structure of Cache

Cache is organized into pages or slots, which is the smallest unit of cache allocation. The size of a cache page is configured according to the application I/O size. Cache consists of the *data store* and *tag RAM.* The data store holds the data while tag RAM tracks the location of the data in the data store (see Figure 4-3) and in disk.

Entries in tag RAM indicate where data is found in cache and where the data belongs on the disk. Tag RAM includes a *dirty bit* flag, which indicates whether the data in cache has been committed to the disk or not. It also contains time-based information, such as the time of last access, which is used to identify cached information that has not been accessed for a long period and may be freed up.

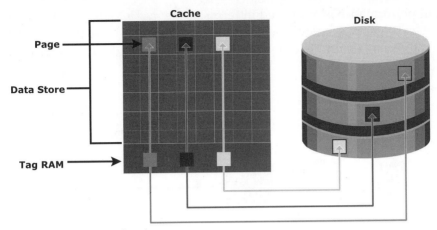

Figure 4-3: Structure of cache

Read Operation with Cache

When a host issues a read request, the front-end controller accesses the tag RAM to determine whether the required data is available in cache. If the requested data is found in the cache, it is called a *read cache hit* or *read hit* and data is sent directly to the host, without any disk operation (see Figure 4-4[a]). This provides a fast response time to the host (about a millisecond). If the requested data is not found in cache, it is called a *cache miss* and the data must be read from the disk (see Figure 4-4[b]). The back-end controller accesses the appropriate disk and retrieves the requested data. Data is then placed in cache and is finally sent to the host through the front-end controller. Cache misses increase I/O response time.

A *pre-fetch*, or *read-ahead*, algorithm is used when read requests are sequential. In a sequential read request, a contiguous set of associated blocks is retrieved. Several other blocks that have not yet been requested by the host can be read from the disk and placed into cache in advance. When the host subsequently requests these blocks, the read operations will be read hits. This process significantly improves the response time experienced by the host. The intelligent storage system offers fixed and variable pre-fetch sizes. In *fixed pre-fetch*, the intelligent storage system pre-fetches a fixed amount of data. It is most suitable when I/O sizes are uniform. In *variable pre-fetch*, the storage system pre-fetches an amount of data in multiples of the size of the host request. Maximum pre-fetch limits the number of data blocks that can be pre-fetched to prevent the disks from being rendered busy with pre-fetch at the expense of other I/O.

Read performance is measured in terms of the *read hit ratio,* or the *hit rate,* usually expressed as a percentage. This ratio is the number of read hits with respect to the total number of read requests. A higher read hit ratio improves the read performance.

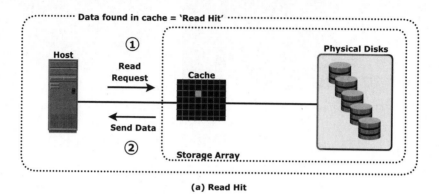

(a) Read Hit

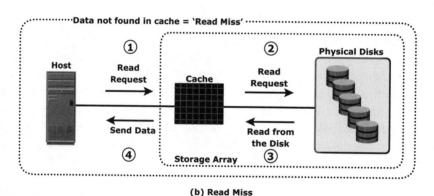

(b) Read Miss

Figure 4-4: Read hit and read miss

Write Operation with Cache

Write operations with cache provide performance advantages over writing directly to disks. When an I/O is written to cache and acknowledged, it is completed in far less time (from the host's perspective) than it would take to write directly to disk. Sequential writes also offer opportunities for optimization because many smaller writes can be coalesced for larger transfers to disk drives with the use of cache.

A write operation with cache is implemented in the following ways:

▪ **Write-back cache:** Data is placed in cache and an acknowledgment is sent to the host immediately. Later, data from several writes are committed (de-staged) to the disk. Write response times are much faster, as the write operations are isolated from the mechanical delays of the disk. However, uncommitted data is at risk of loss in the event of cache failures.

- **Write-through cache:** Data is placed in the cache and immediately written to the disk, and an acknowledgment is sent to the host. Because data is committed to disk as it arrives, the risks of data loss are low but write response time is longer because of the disk operations.

Cache can be bypassed under certain conditions, such as very large size write I/O. In this implementation, if the size of an I/O request exceeds the predefined size, called *write aside size*, writes are sent to the disk directly to reduce the impact of large writes consuming a large cache area. This is particularly useful in an environment where cache resources are constrained and must be made available for small random I/Os.

Cache Implementation

Cache can be implemented as either dedicated cache or global cache. With dedicated cache, separate sets of memory locations are reserved for reads and writes. In global cache, both reads and writes can use any of the available memory addresses. Cache management is more efficient in a global cache implementation, as only one global set of addresses has to be managed.

Global cache may allow users to specify the percentages of cache available for reads and writes in cache management. Typically, the read cache is small, but it should be increased if the application being used is read intensive. In other global cache implementations, the ratio of cache available for reads versus writes is dynamically adjusted based on the workloads.

Cache Management

Cache is a finite and expensive resource that needs proper management. Even though intelligent storage systems can be configured with large amounts of cache, when all cache pages are filled, some pages have to be freed up to accommodate new data and avoid performance degradation. Various cache management algorithms are implemented in intelligent storage systems to proactively maintain a set of free pages and a list of pages that can be potentially freed up whenever required:

- **Least Recently Used (LRU):** An algorithm that continuously monitors data access in cache and identifies the cache pages that have not been accessed for a long time. LRU either frees up these pages or marks them for reuse. This algorithm is based on the assumption that data which hasn't been accessed for a while will not be requested by the host. However, if a page contains write data that has not yet been committed to disk, data will first be written to disk before the page is reused.

■ **Most Recently Used (MRU):** An algorithm that is the converse of LRU. In MRU, the pages that have been accessed most recently are freed up or marked for reuse. This algorithm is based on the assumption that recently accessed data may not be required for a while.

As cache fills, the storage system must take action to flush dirty pages (data written into the cahce but not yet written to the disk) in order to manage its availability. Flushing is the process of committing data from cache to the disk. On the basis of the I/O access rate and pattern, high and low levels called *watermarks* are set in cache to manage the flushing process. *High watermark (HWM)* is the cache utilization level at which the storage system starts high-speed flushing of cache data. *Low watermark (LWM)* is the point at which the storage system stops the high-speed or forced flushing and returns to idle flush behavior. The cache utilization level, as shown in Figure 4-5, drives the mode of flushing to be used:

■ **Idle flushing:** Occurs continuously, at a modest rate, when the cache utilization level is between the high and low watermark.

■ **High watermark flushing:** Activated when cache utilization hits the high watermark. The storage system dedicates some additional resources to flushing. This type of flushing has minimal impact on host I/O processing.

■ **Forced flushing:** Occurs in the event of a large I/O burst when cache reaches 100 percent of its capacity, which significantly affects the I/O response time. In forced flushing, dirty pages are forcibly flushed to disk.

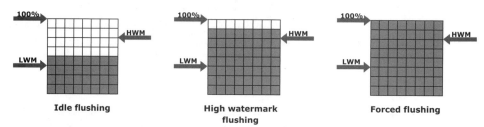

Figure 4-5: Types of flushing

Cache Data Protection

Cache is volatile memory, so a power failure or any kind of cache failure will cause the loss of data not yet committed to the disk. This risk of losing uncommitted data held in cache can be mitigated using *cache mirroring* and *cache vaulting*:

■ **Cache mirroring:** Each write to cache is held in two different memory locations on two independent memory cards. In the event of a cache failure, the write data will still be safe in the mirrored location and can be committed to the disk. Reads are staged from the disk to the cache;

therefore, in the event of a cache failure, the data can still be accessed from the disk. As only writes are mirrored, this method results in better utilization of the available cache.

In cache mirroring approaches, the problem of maintaining *cache coherency* is introduced. Cache coherency means that data in two different cache locations must be identical at all times. It is the responsibility of the array operating environment to ensure coherency.

■ **Cache vaulting:** Cache is exposed to the risk of uncommitted data loss due to power failure. This problem can be addressed in various ways: powering the memory with a battery until AC power is restored or using battery power to write the cache content to the disk. In the event of extended power failure, using batteries is not a viable option because in intelligent storage systems, large amounts of data may need to be committed to numerous disks and batteries may not provide power for sufficient time to write each piece of data to its intended disk. Therefore, storage vendors use a set of physical disks to dump the contents of cache during power failure. This is called cache vaulting and the disks are called vault drives. When power is restored, data from these disks is written back to write cache and then written to the intended disks.

4.1.3 Back End

The *back end* provides an interface between cache and the physical disks. It consists of two components: back-end ports and back-end controllers. The back end controls data transfers between cache and the physical disks. From cache, data is sent to the back end and then routed to the destination disk. Physical disks are connected to ports on the back end. The back end controller communicates with the disks when performing reads and writes and also provides additional, but limited, temporary data storage. The algorithms implemented on back-end controllers provide error detection and correction, along with RAID functionality.

For high data protection and availability, storage systems are configured with dual controllers with multiple ports. Such configurations provide an alternate path to physical disks in the event of a controller or port failure. This reliability is further enhanced if the disks are also dual-ported. In that case, each disk port can connect to a separate controller. Multiple controllers also facilitate load balancing.

4.1.4 Physical Disk

A physical disk stores data persistently. Disks are connected to the back-end with either SCSI or a Fibre Channel interface (discussed in subsequent chapters). An intelligent storage system enables the use of a mixture of SCSI or Fibre Channel drives and IDE/ATA drives.

SOLID-STATE DRIVES

 Flash-based solid-state drives (SSDs) are a recent innovation for delivering ultra-high performance for mission-critical applications. Solid-state Flash drives utilize Flash memory to store and retrieve data. Unlike FC or SATA drives, Flash drives have no moving parts, and leverage semiconductor-based block storage devices, resulting in minimized response time and less power requirements to run. Flash drives are constructed with nonvolatile semiconductor memory to support persistent storage and they use either single-level cell (SLC) or multi-level cell (MLC) to store bits on each memory cell. SLC stores one bit per cell and is used in high-performance memory cards. MLC memory cards store more bits per cell and provide slower transfer speeds. The advantage of MLC over SLC memory cards is the lower manufacturing cost.

Flash drives that use SLC technology combined with sophisticated controllers can behave like virtual HDDs through a traditional storage interface (such as Fibre Channel) to achieve ultra-fast read/write performance, high reliability, and data integrity. Flash drives have been tested and qualified to withstand the intense workloads of high-end enterprise storage applications.

Flash storage technology is ideally suited to support applications that need to process massive amounts of information very quickly, such as currency exchange and electronic trading systems, real time data feed processing, mainframe transaction processing, and many others. Storage systems with enterprise-class Flash drives can deliver single-millisecond application response times, up to 10 times faster than those with traditional 15K RPM Fibre Channel disk drives.

In a storage array, Flash drives can store a terabyte of data using 38 percent less energy than traditional mechanical disk drives. It would take 30 15K RPM Fibre Channel disk drives to deliver the same performance as a single Flash drive, which translates into a 98 percent reduction in power consumption in a transaction-per-second comparison.

Logical Unit Number

Physical drives or groups of RAID protected drives can be logically split into volumes known as logical volumes, commonly referred to as *Logical Unit Numbers* (LUNs). The use of LUNs improves disk utilization. For example, without the use of LUNs, a host requiring only 200 GB could be allocated an entire 1TB physical disk. Using LUNs, only the required 200 GB would be allocated to the host, allowing the remaining 800 GB to be allocated to other hosts.

In the case of RAID protected drives, these logical units are slices of RAID sets and are spread across all the physical disks belonging to that set. The logical units can also be seen as a logical partition of a RAID set that is presented to a host as a physical disk. For example, Figure 4-6 shows a RAID set consisting of five disks that have been sliced, or partitioned, into several LUNs. LUNs 0 and 1 are shown in the figure.

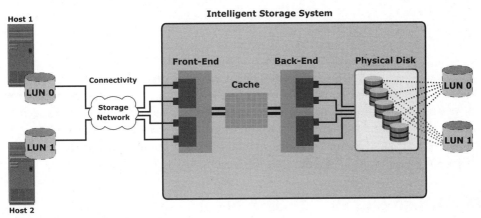

Figure 4-6: Logical unit number

Note how a portion of each LUN resides on each physical disk in the RAID set. LUNs 0 and 1 are presented to hosts 1 and 2, respectively, as physical volumes for storing and retrieving data. Usable capacity of the physical volumes is determined by the RAID type of the RAID set.

The capacity of a LUN can be expanded by aggregating other LUNs with it. The result of this aggregation is a larger capacity LUN, known as a *meta-LUN*. The mapping of LUNs to their physical location on the drives is managed by the operating environment of an intelligent storage system.

LUN Masking

LUN masking is a process that provides data access control by defining which LUNs a host can access. LUN masking function is typically implemented at the front end controller. This ensures that volume access by servers is controlled appropriately, preventing unauthorized or accidental use in a distributed environment.

For example, consider a storage array with two LUNs that store data of the sales and finance departments. Without LUN masking, both departments can easily see and modify each other's data, posing a high risk to data integrity and security. With LUN masking, LUNs are accessible only to the designated hosts.

4.2 Intelligent Storage Array

Intelligent storage systems generally fall into one of the following two categories:

- High-end storage systems
- Midrange storage systems

Traditionally, high-end storage systems have been implemented with *active-active arrays,* whereas midrange *storage systems* used typically in small- and medium-sized enterprises have been implemented with *active-passive arrays.* Active-passive arrays provide optimal storage solutions at lower costs. Enterprises make use of this cost advantage and implement active-passive arrays to meet specific application requirements such as performance, availability, and scalability. The distinctions between these two implementations are becoming increasingly insignificant.

4.2.1 High-end Storage Systems

High-end storage systems, referred to as *active-active arrays,* are generally aimed at large enterprises for centralizing corporate data. These arrays are designed with a large number of controllers and cache memory. An active-active array implies that the host can perform I/Os to its LUNs across any of the available paths (see Figure 4-7).

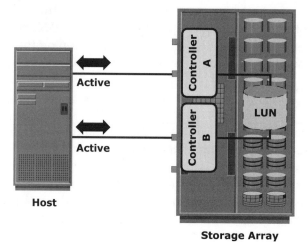

Figure 4-7: Active-active configuration

To address the enterprise storage needs, these arrays provide the following capabilities:

- Large storage capacity
- Large amounts of cache to service host I/Os optimally
- Fault tolerance architecture to improve data availability
- Connectivity to mainframe computers and open systems hosts
- Availability of multiple front-end ports and interface protocols to serve a large number of hosts
- Availability of multiple back-end Fibre Channel or SCSI RAID controllers to manage disk processing
- Scalability to support increased connectivity, performance, and storage capacity requirements
- Ability to handle large amounts of concurrent I/Os from a number of servers and applications
- Support for array-based local and remote replication

In addition to these features, high-end arrays possess some unique features and functionals that are required for mission-critical applications in large enterprises.

4.2.2 Midrange Storage System

Midrange storage systems are also referred to as *active-passive arrays* and they are best suited for small- and medium-sized enterprises. In an active-passive array, a host can perform I/Os to a LUN only through the paths to the owning controller of that LUN. These paths are called *active paths*. The other paths are passive with respect to this LUN. As shown in Figure 4-8, the host can perform reads or writes to the LUN only through the path to controller A, as controller A is the owner of that LUN. The path to controller B remains passive and no I/O activity is performed through this path.

Midrange storage systems are typically designed with two controllers, each of which contains host interfaces, cache, RAID controllers, and disk drive interfaces.

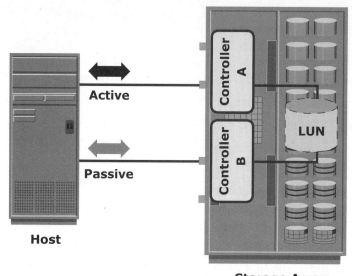

Figure 4-8: Active-passive configuration

Midrange arrays are designed to meet the requirements of small and medium enterprises; therefore, they host less storage capacity and global cache than active-active arrays. There are also fewer front-end ports for connection to servers. However, they ensure high redundancy and high performance for applications with predictable workloads. They also support array-based local and remote replication.

4.3 Concepts in Practice: EMC CLARiiON and Symmetrix

To illustrate the concepts just discussed, this section covers the EMC implementation of intelligent storage arrays.

The EMC CLARiiON storage array is an active-passive array implementation. It is the EMC midrange networked storage offering that delivers enterprise-quality features and functionality. It is ideally suited for applications with predictable workloads that need moderate to high response time and throughput.

The EMC Symmetrix networked storage array is an active-active array implementation. Symmetrix is a solution for customers who require an uncompromising level of service, performance, as well as the most advanced business continuity solution to support large and unpredictable application workloads. Symmetrix also provides built-in, advanced-level security features and offers the most efficient use of power and cooling to support enterprise-level data storage requirements.

For the latest information on CLARiiON and Symmetrix, please refer to http://education.EMC.com/ismbook.

4.3.1 CLARiiON Storage Array

The CX4 series is the fourth generation CLARiiON CX storage platform. Each generation has added enhancements to performance, availability, and scalability over the previous generation while the high-level architecture remains the same. Figure 4-9 shows an EMC CLARiiON storage array.

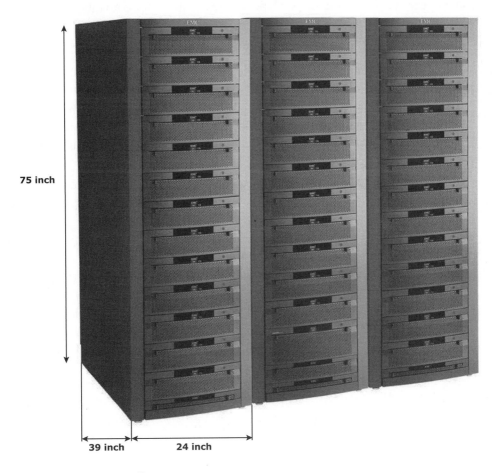

75 inch

39 inch   24 inch

Figure 4-9: EMC CLARiiON

CLARiiON is built with modular building blocks and no single point of failure. CLARiiON CX4 is first midrange storage array that supports flash drives with 30 times more IOPS capability. The other features of CLARiiON are as follows:

- *UltraFlex* technology for dual protocol connectivity, online expansion via IO modules, and readiness for future technologies—such as 8 Gb/s Fibre Channel and 10 Gb/s iSCSI.

- Scalable up to 960 disks

- Supports different types and sizes of drives, and RAID types (0, 1, 1+0, 3, 5, 6)

- Supports up to 16 GB of available cache memory per controller (Storage Processor)

- Enhances availability with nondisruptive upgrade and failover

- Ensures data protection through mirrored write cache and cache vaulting

- Provides data integrity through disk scrubbing. The background verification process runs continually and reads all sectors of all the disks. If a block is unreadable, the back-end error handling recovers the bad sectors from parity or mirror data.

- Supports storage-based local and remote data replication for backup and disaster recovery through SnapView and MirrorView software.

4.3.2 CLARiiON CX4 Architecture

The *Storage Processor Enclosure (SPE)* and the *Disk Array Enclosure (DAE)* are the key modular building blocks of a CLARiiON. A DAE enclosure contains up to 15 disk drives, two link control cards (LCCs), two power supplies, and two fan modules. An SPE contains two storage processors, each consisting of one CPU module and slots for I/O modules. Figure 4-10 shows the CLARiiON CX4 architecture.

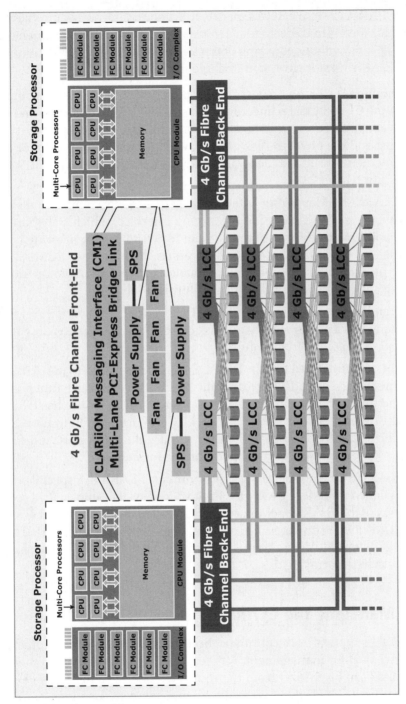

Figure 4-10: CLARiiON architecture

The CLARiiON architecture supports fully redundant, hot swappable components. This means that the system can survive with a failed component, which can be replaced without powering down the system. The important components of the CLARiiON storage system include the following:

- **Intelligent storage processor (SP):** Intelligent SP is the main component of the CLARiiON architecture. SP are configured in pairs for maximum availability. SP provide both front-end and back-end connectivity to the host and the physical disk, respectively. SP also include memory, most of which is used for cache. Depending on the model, each SP includes one or two CPUs.

- **CLARiiON Messaging Interface (CMI):** The SPs communicate to each other over the CLARiiON Messaging Interface, which transports commands, status information, and data for write cache mirroring between the SPs. CLARiiON uses PCI-Express as the high-speed CMI. The PCI Express architecture delivers high bandwidth per pin, has superior routing characteristics, and provides improved reliability.

- **Standby Power Supply (SPS):** In the event of a power failure, the SPS maintains a power supply to the cache for long enough to allow the content to be copied to the vault.

- **Link Control Card (LCC):** The LCC provides services to the drive enclosure, which includes the capability to control enclosure functionalities and monitor environmental status. Each drive enclosure has two LCCs. The other functions performed by LCCs are loop configuration control, failover control, marker LED control, individual disk port control, drive presence detection, and voltage status information.

- **FLARE Storage Operating Environment:** FLARE is a special software designed for EMC CLARiiON. Each storage system ships with a complete copy of the FLARE operating system installed on its first four disks. When CLARiiON is powered up, each SP boots and runs the FLARE operating system. FLARE performs resource allocation and other management tasks in the array.

4.3.3 Managing the CLARiiON

CLARiiON supports both command-line interface (CLI) and graphical user interface (GUI) for management. *Naviseccli* is a CLI-based management tool. Commands can be entered from the connected host system or from a remote server through Telnet/SSH to perform all management functions.

Navisphere management software is a GUI-based suite of tools that enables centralized management of CLARiiON storage systems. These tools are used to monitor, configure, and manage CLARiiON storage arrays. The Navisphere management suite includes the following:

- **Navisphere Manager:** A GUI-based tool for centralized storage system management that is used to configure and manage CLARiiON. It is a web-based user interface that helps to securely manage CLARiiON storage systems locally or remotely over the IP connection, using a common browser. Navisphere Manager provides the flexibility to manage single or multiple systems.

- **Navisphere Analyzer:** A performance analysis tool for CLARiiON hardware components.

- **Navisphere Agent:** A host-residing tool that provides a management communication path to the system and enables CLI access.

4.3.4 Symmetrix Storage Array

The EMC Symmetrix establishes the highest standards for performance and capacity for an enterprise information storage solution and is recognized as the industry's most trusted storage platform. Figure 4-11 shows the EMC Symmetrix DMX-4 storage array.

EMC Symmetrix uses the Direct Matrix Architecture and incorporates a fault-tolerant design. Other features of the Symmetrix are as follows:

- Incrementally scalable up to 2,400 disks

- Supports Flash-based solid-state drives

- Dynamic global cache memory (16 GB–512 GB)

- Advanced processing power (up to 130 PowerPC)

- Large number of concurrent data paths available (32–128 data paths) for I/O processing

- High data processing bandwidth (up to 128 GB/s)

- Data protection with RAID 1, 1+0 (also known as 10 for mainframe), 5, and 6

- Storage-based local and remote replication for business continuity through TimeFinder and SRDF software

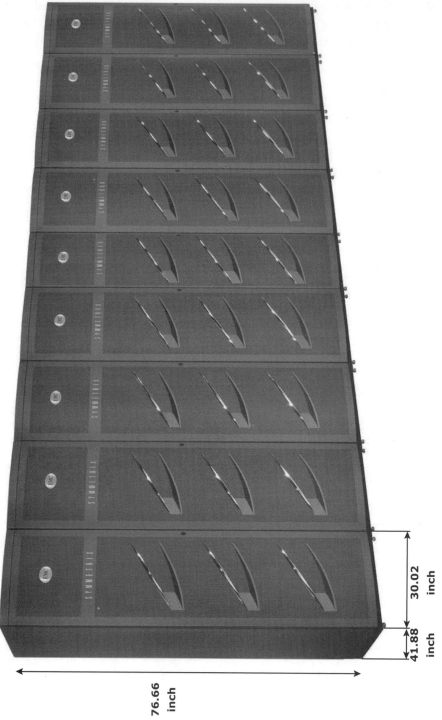

Figure 4-11: EMC Symmetrix

4.3.5 Symmetrix Component Overview

Figure 4-12 shows the basic block diagram of Symmetrix components.

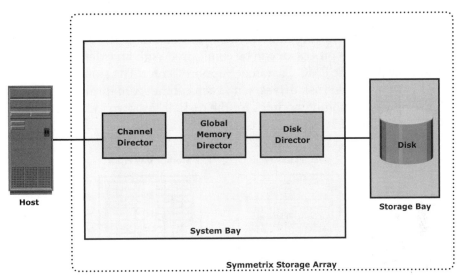

Figure 4-12: Basic building blocks of Symmetrix

The Symmetrix system bay consists of front-end controllers (called *Channel Directors*) for host connectivity, large amounts of global cache (called *Global Memory Director [GMD]*), and back-end controllers (called *Disk Directors*) for disk connectivity. The storage bay is a disk enclosure that can house 240 drives in a cabinet. Figure 4-13 shows the components of the Symmetrix system bay and storage bay.

The system bay consists of a card cage structure whereby controller cards are inserted in cage slots. The 24 slots at the front contain the GMD, disk director, and channel director cards. The rear slots contain channel adapters, disk adapters, and environmental control module cards.

The system bay contains up to 12 front-end channel directors and adapters. Channel directors provide connectivity options for Fibre Channel, ESCON, FICON, iSCSI, or GigE connectivity to the host or the network.

The Symmetrix DMX-4 system also comprises up to eight GMD cards in the card cage. Individual memory directors are available from 2 GB to 64 GB. Symmetrix uses Double Data Rate Synchronous Dynamic Random-Access Memory (DDR SDRAM), the latest generation of the SDRAM chip technology.

Up to eight disk directors/adapters, in pairs, provide back-end 2 GB/s connectivity to the Fibre Channel disk drives. Each disk director can support a maximum of 240 drives.

Two communication and environmental control modules, also called *cross communication modules* (XCMs), are provided for configuration and other communication purposes. The XCMs contain the Ethernet interface between the directors (channel, memory, and disk) and the service processor.

The service processor contains a keyboard, a video display, a mouse, and a server that connects to the Symmetrix subsystem through the private Ethernet interface. The service processor can be configured with an external modem to communicate with the EMC Customer Support Center. The storage bay is configured with up to 240 disk drives, with each cabinet containing a redundant power supply and cooling modules for the disk drives, two LCCs, and 4 to 15 Fibre Channel disk drives per enclosure.

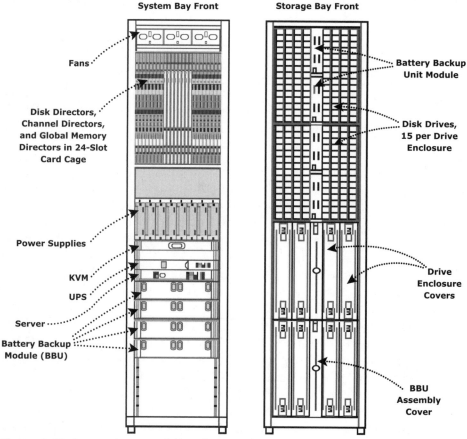

Figure 4-13: Symmetrix system bay and storage bay

4.3.6 Direct Matrix Architecture

Symmetrix uses the Direct Matrix Architecture consisting of dedicated paths for data transfer between the front end, global memory, and the back end. Key components of Symmetrix DMX are as follows:

- **Front end:** The host connects to Symmetrix via a front-end port on the channel director. Multiple directors are configured, each with multiple ports to provide host connectivity and redundancy. Each Symmetrix channel director supports eight internal links to global memory. Data transfers between host and global memory can execute concurrently across multiple ports on a director (refer to Figure 4-14).

- **Back end:** Back end disk directors manage the interface to the disk drives and are responsible for data movement between the disk drives and global memory. Each disk director on a Symmetrix system supports 8 internal links to global memory.

- **Global Memory:** The Symmetrix global memory is its most important component. All read and write operations are performed through global memory. Host I/Os are received at the front end and processed through global memory at much greater electronic speeds than transfers involving disks. The global memory directors work in pairs. The hardware writes to the one global memory director first and then writes are mirrored to the secondary global memory director, for data protection. Each global memory director has 16 ports with full-duplex serial connections between the global memory director and the channel or disk directors (a total of 16 directors) through the *direct matrix*. Each of the 8 director ports on the 16 directors connects to one of the 16 memory ports on each of the 8 global memory directors, as shown in Figure 4-14. These 128 individual point-to-point connections facilitate up to 128 concurrent cache operations in the system, providing ultra-high bandwidth for I/O processing.

- **XCM:** XCM is the communication agent between the service processor and all the processing nodes (channel, disk, and memory director) within the system. External connections to the service processor provide dial-home capability for remote monitoring and diagnostics. The XCM also has the capability to issue remote commands to the director boards, global memory directors, and itself. These commands can be issued from the service processor or remotely, by the EMC Customer Support Center, providing a rich set of intelligent serviceability functions.

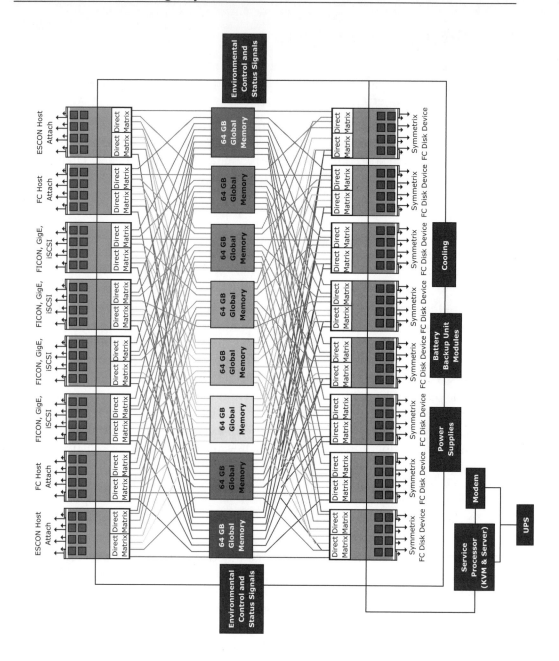

Figure 4-14: Direct matrix architecture

▪ **Symmetrix Enginuity:** This is the operating environment for EMC Symmetrix. Enginuity manages and ensures the optimal flow and integrity of information through the various hardware components of the Symmetrix system. It manages all Symmetrix operations and system resources to optimize performance intelligently. Enginuity ensures system availability through advanced fault monitoring, detection, and correction capabilities and provides concurrent maintenance and serviceability features. It also offers a foundation for specific software features for disaster recovery, business continuance, and storage management.

Summary

This chapter detailed the features and components of the intelligent storage system — front end, cache, back end, and physical disks. The active-active and active-passive implementations of intelligent storage systems were also described. An intelligent storage system provides the following benefits to an organization:

▪ Increased capacity

▪ Improved performance

▪ Easier storage management

▪ Improved data availability

▪ Improved scalability and flexibility

▪ Improved business continuity

▪ Improved security and access control

An intelligent storage system is now an integral part of every mission-critical data center. Although a high-end intelligent storage system addresses information storage requirements, it poses a challenge for administrators to share information easily and securely across the enterprise.

Storage networking is a flexible information-centric strategy that extends the reach of intelligent storage systems throughout an enterprise. It provides a common way to manage, share, and protect information. Storage networking is detailed in the next section.

EXERCISES

1. Consider a scenario in which an I/O request from track 1 is followed by an I/O request from track 2 on a sector that is 180 degrees away from the first request. A third request is from a sector on track 3, which is adjacent to the sector on which the first request is made. Discuss the advantages and disadvantages of using the command queuing algorithm in this scenario.

2. Which type of application benefits the most by bypassing write cache? Why?

3. An Oracle database uses a block size of 4 KB for its I/O operation. The application that uses this database primarily performs a sequential read operation. Suggest and explain the appropriate values for the following cache parameters: cache page size, cache allocation (read versus write), pre-fetch type, and write aside cache.

4. Download Navisphere Simulator and the lab guide from `http://education.EMC.com/ismbook` and perform the tasks listed.

Section

II

Storage Networking Technologies and Virtualization

In This Section

Chapter 5
Direct-Attached Storage and Introduction to SCSI

Direct-Attached Storage (DAS) is an architecture where storage connects directly to servers. Applications access data from DAS using block-level access protocols. The internal HDD of a host, tape libraries, and directly connected external HDD packs are some examples of DAS.

KEY CONCEPTS
Internal and External DAS
SCSI Architecture
SCSI Addressing

Although the implementation of storage networking technologies are gaining popularity, DAS has remained ideal for localized data access and sharing in environments that have a small number of servers. For example, small businesses, departments, and workgroups that do not share information across enterprises find DAS to be an appropriate solution. Medium-size companies use DAS for file serving and e-mail, while larger enterprises leverage DAS in conjunction with SAN and NAS.

This chapter details the two types of DAS along with their benefits and limitations. A major part of this chapter is devoted to detailing the types of storage devices used in DAS environments and SCSI—the most prominent protocol used in DAS.

5.1 Types of DAS

DAS is classified as internal or external, based on the location of the storage device with respect to the host.

5.1.1 Internal DAS

In *internal DAS* architectures, the storage device is internally connected to the host by a serial or parallel bus. The physical bus has distance limitations and can only be sustained over a shorter distance for high-speed connectivity. In addition, most internal buses can support only a limited number of devices, and they occupy a large amount of space inside the host, making maintenance of other components difficult.

5.1.2 External DAS

In *external DAS* architectures, the server connects directly to the external storage device (see Figure 5-1). In most cases, communication between the host and the storage device takes place over SCSI or FC protocol. Compared to internal DAS, an external DAS overcomes the distance and device count limitations and provides centralized management of storage devices.

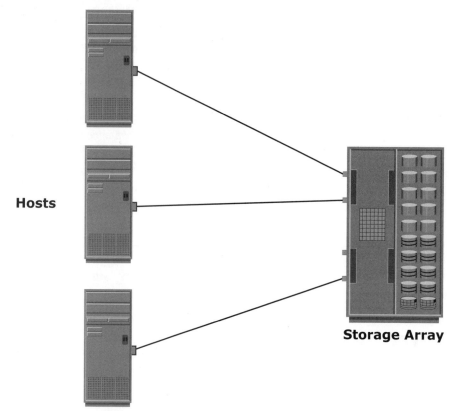

Figure 5-1: External DAS architecture

5.2 DAS Benefits and Limitations

DAS requires a relatively lower initial investment than storage networking. Storage networking architectures are discussed later in this book. DAS configuration is simple and can be deployed easily and rapidly. Setup is managed using host-based tools, such as the host OS, which makes storage management tasks easy for small and medium enterprises. DAS is the simplest solution when compared to other storage networking models and requires fewer management tasks, and less hardware and software elements to set up and operate.

However, DAS does not scale well. A storage device has a limited number of ports, which restricts the number of hosts that can directly connect to the storage. A limited bandwidth in DAS restricts the available I/O processing capability. When capacities are being reached, the service availability may be compromised, and this has a ripple effect on the performance of all hosts attached to that specific device or array. The distance limitations associated with implementing DAS because of direct connectivity requirements can be addressed by using Fibre Channel connectivity. DAS does not make optimal use of resources due to its limited ability to share front end ports. In DAS environments, unused resources cannot be easily re-allocated, resulting in islands of over-utilized and under-utilized storage pools.

Disk utilization, throughput, and cache memory of a storage device, along with virtual memory of a host govern the performance of DAS. RAID-level configurations, storage controller protocols, and the efficiency of the bus are additional factors that affect the performance of DAS. The absence of storage interconnects and network latency provide DAS with the potential to outperform other storage networking configurations.

5.3 Disk Drive Interfaces

The host and the storage device in DAS communicate with each other by using predefined protocols such as IDE/ATA, SATA, SAS, SCSI, and FC. These protocols are implemented on the HDD controller. Therefore, a storage device is also known by the name of the protocol it supports. This section describes each of these storage devices in detail.

5.3.1 IDE/ATA

An Integrated Device Electronics/Advanced Technology Attachment (IDE/ATA) disk supports the IDE protocol. The term IDE/ATA conveys the dual-naming conventions for various generations and variants of this interface. The IDE component in IDE/ATA provides the specification for the controllers connected to the computer's motherboard for communicating with the device attached. The ATA component is the interface for connecting storage devices, such as CD-ROMs, floppy disk drives, and HDDs, to the motherboard.

IDE/ATA has a variety of standards and names, such as ATA, ATA/ATAPI, EIDE, ATA-2, Fast ATA, ATA-3, Ultra ATA, and Ultra DMA. The latest version of ATA—Ultra DMA/133—supports a throughput of 133 MB per second.

In a master-slave configuration, an ATA interface supports two storage devices per connector. However, if the performance of the drive is important, sharing a port between two devices is not recommended.

Figure 5-2 shows two commonly used IDE connectors attached to their cables. A 40-pin connector is used to connect ATA disks to the motherboard, and a 34-pin connector is used to connect floppy disk drives to the motherboard.

An IDE/ATA disk offers excellent performance at low cost, making it a popular and commonly used hard disk.

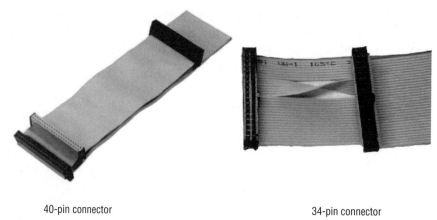

40-pin connector   34-pin connector

Figure 5-2: Common IDE connectors

5.3.2 SATA

A SATA (Serial ATA) is a serial version of the IDE/ATA specification. SATA is a disk-interface technology that was developed by a group of the industry's leading vendors with the aim of replacing parallel ATA.

A SATA provides point-to-point connectivity up to a distance of one meter and enables data transfer at a speed of 150 MB/s. Enhancements to the SATA have increased the data transfer speed up to 600 MB/s.

A SATA bus directly connects each storage device to the host through a dedicated link, making use of *low-voltage differential signaling (LVDS)*. LVDS is an electrical signaling system that can provide high-speed connectivity over low-cost, twisted-pair copper cables. For data transfer, a SATA bus uses LVDS with a voltage of 250 mV.

A SATA bus uses a small 7-pin connector and a thin cable for connectivity. A SATA port uses 4 signal pins, which improves its pin efficiency compared to the parallel ATA that uses 26 signal pins, for connecting an 80-conductor ribbon cable to a 40-pin header connector.

SATA devices are *hot-pluggable,* which means that they can be connected or removed while the host is up and running. A SATA port permits single-device connectivity. Connecting multiple SATA drives to a host requires multiple ports to be present on the host. Single-device connectivity enforced in SATA, eliminates the performance problems caused by cable or port sharing in IDE/ATA.

5.3.3 Parallel SCSI

SCSI is available in a variety of interfaces. Parallel SCSI (referred to as SCSI) is one of the oldest and most popular forms of storage interface used in hosts. SCSI is a set of standards used for connecting a peripheral device to a computer and transferring data between them. Often, SCSI is used to connect HDDs and tapes to a host. SCSI can also connect a wide variety of other devices such as scanners and printers. Communication between the hosts and the storage devices uses the SCSI command set, described later in this chapter.

Since its inception, SCSI has undergone rapid revisions, resulting in continuous performance improvements. The oldest SCSI variant, called SCSI-1 provided data transfer rate of 5 MB/s; SCSI Ultra 320 provides data transfer speeds of 320 MB/s. Other variants of SCSI and transfer speeds are listed in Table 5-2.

Table 5-1 provides a comparison between the features of IDE/ATA and SCSI, the two most popular hard disk interfaces.

Table 5-1: Comparison of IDE/ATA with SCSI

FEATURE	IDE/ATA	SCSI
Speed	100, 133, 150 MB/s	320 MB/s
Connectivity	Internal	Internal and external
Cost	Low	Moderate to high
Hot-pluggable	No	Yes
Performance	Moderate to low	High
Ease of configuration	High	Low to moderate
Maximum number of devices supported	2	16

SERIAL ATTACHED SCSI DISKS

Serial Attached SCSI (SAS) is the evolution of SCSI beyond SCSI Ultra 320. SAS addresses the scalability, performance, reliability, and manageability requirements of a data center while leveraging a common electrical and physical connection interface with SATA. SAS uses SCSI commands for communication and is pin compatible with SATA. SAS supports data transfer rate of 3 Gb/s (SAS 300). It supports dual porting, full-duplex, device addressing, and uses a simplified protocol to minimize interoperability issues between controllers and drives. It also enables connectivity to multiple devices through expanders and is commonly preferred over SCSI in high-end servers for faster disk access.

5.4 Introduction to Parallel SCSI

Shugart Associates and NCR developed a system interface in 1981 and named it Shugart Associates System Interface (SASI). SASI was developed to build a proprietary, high-performance standard primarily for use by these two companies. However, to increase the acceptance of SASI in the industry, the standard was updated to a more robust interface and renamed SCSI. In 1986, the American National Standards Institution (ANSI) acknowledged the new SCSI as an industry standard.

SCSI, first developed for hard disks, is often compared to IDE/ATA. SCSI offers improved performance and expandability and compatibility options, making it suitable for high-end computers. However, the high cost associated with SCSI limits its popularity among home or business desktop users.

FC DISKS

FC disks use the FC-AL topology (FC-AL2 over copper). FC is the specification in storage networking for gigabit speed network technology. Although FC disks are used extensively with SAN technology, they can also be implemented for DAS. Faster access speeds of Fibre Channel (8.5 Gb/s) for 8 GFC (Gigabit Fibre Channel) are used in high-end storage system.

5.4.1 Evolution of SCSI

Prior to the development of SCSI, the interfaces used to communicate with devices varied with each device. For example, an HDD interface could only be used with a hard disk drive. SCSI was developed to provide a device-independent mechanism for attaching to and accessing host computers. SCSI also provided an efficient peer-to-peer I/O bus that supported multiple devices. Today, SCSI is commonly used as a hard disk interface. However, SCSI can be used to add devices, such as tape drives and optical media drives, to the host computer without modifying the system hardware or software. Over the years, SCSI has undergone radical changes and has evolved into a robust industry standard. Various SCSI standards are detailed in this section.

SCSI-1

SCSI-1, renamed to distinguish it from other SCSI versions, is the original standard that the ANSI approved. SCSI-1 defined the basics of the first SCSI bus, including cable length, signaling characteristics, commands, and transfer modes. SCSI-1 devices supported only single-ended transmission and *passive termination*. SCSI-1 used a narrow 8-bit bus, which offered a maximum data transfer rate of 5 MB/s.

SCSI-1 implementations resulted in incompatible devices and several subsets of standards. Due to these issues, work on improving the SCSI-1 standard began in 1985, a year before its formal approval.

SCSI-2

To control the various problems caused by the nonstandard implementation of the original SCSI, a working paper was created to define a set of standard commands for a SCSI device. This set of standards, called the *common command set (CCS)*, formed the basis of the SCSI-2 standard.

SCSI-2 was focused on improving performance, enhancing reliability, and adding additional features to the SCSI-1 interface, in addition to standardizing and formalizing the SCSI commands. The ANSI withdrew the SCSI-1 standard and, in 1994, approved SCSI-2 as one large document: X3.131-1994. The transition from SCSI-1 to SCSI-2 did not raise much concern because SCSI-2 offered backward compatibility with SCSI-1.

SCSI-3

In 1993, work began on developing the next version of the SCSI standard, SCSI-3. Unlike SCSI-2, the SCSI-3 standard document is comprised different but related standards, rather than one large document.

5.4.2 SCSI Interfaces

Along with the evolving SCSI standards, SCSI interfaces underwent several improvements. Parallel SCSI, or SCSI parallel interface (SPI), was the original

SCSI interface (Table 5-2 lists some of the available parallel SCSI interfaces). The SCSI design is now making a transition into Serial Attached SCSI (SAS), which is based on a serial point-to-point design, while retaining the other aspects of the SCSI technology.

In addition to the interfaces listed in Table 5-2, many interfaces are not complete SCSI standards, but still implement the SCSI command model.

Table 5-2: SCSI Interfaces

INTERFACE	STANDARD	BUS WIDTH	CLOCK SPEED	MAX THROUGHPUT	MAX DEVICES
SCSI-1	SCSI-1	8	5 MHz	5 MB/s	8
Fast SCSI	SCSI-2	8	10 MHz	10 MB/s	8
Fast Wide SCSI	SCSI-2; SCSI-3 SPI	16	10 MHz	20 MB/s	16
Ultra SCSI	SCSI-3 SPI	8	20 MHz	20 MB/s	8
Ultra Wide SCSI	SCSI-3 SPI	16	20 MHz	40 MB/s	16
Ultra2 SCSI	SCSI-3 SPI-2	8	40 MHz	40 MB/s	8
Ultra2 Wide SCSI	SCSI-3 SPI-2	16	40 MHz	80 MB/s	16
Ultra3 SCSI	SCSI-3 SPI-3	16	40 MHz DDR	160 MB/s	16
Ultra320 SCSI	SCSI-3 SPI-4	16	80 MHz DDR	320 MB/s	16
Ultra640 SCSI	SCSI-3 SPI-5	16	160 MHz DDR	640 MB/s	16

FIBRE CHANNEL PROTOCOL

FCP (Fibre Channel Protocol) is the implementation of SCSI-3 over Fibre Channel networks. A new SCSI design, iSCSI, implements the SCSI-3 standard over Internet Protocol (IP) and uses TCP as a transport mechanism.

5.4.3 SCSI-3 Architecture

The SCSI-3 architecture defines and categorizes various SCSI-3 standards and requirements for SCSI-3 implementations. (For more information, see Technical Committee T10 "SCSI Architecture Model-3 (SAM-3)" document from www.t10.org.) The SCSI-3 architecture was approved and published as the standard X.3.270-1996 by the ANSI. This architecture helps developers, hardware designers, and users to understand and effectively utilize SCSI. The three major components of a SCSI architectural model are as follows:

- **SCSI-3 command protocol:** This consists of primary commands that are common to all devices as well as device-specific commands that are unique to a given class of devices.

- **Transport layer protocols:** These are a standard set of rules by which devices communicate and share information.

- **Physical layer interconnects:** These are interface details such as electrical signaling methods and data transfer modes.

Common access methods are the ANSI software interfaces for SCSI devices. Figure 5-3 shows the SCSI-3 standards architecture with interrelated groups of other standards within SCSI-3.

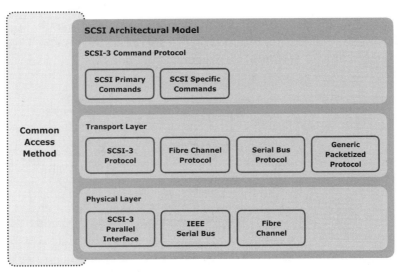

Figure 5-3: SCSI-3 standards architecture

SCSI-3 Client-Server Model

SCSI-3 architecture derives its base from the client-server relationship, in which a client directs a service request to a server, which then fulfills the client's request. In a SCSI environment, an initiator-target concept represents the client-server model. In a SCSI-3 client-server model, a particular SCSI device acts as a SCSI target device, a SCSI initiator device, or a SCSI target/initiator device. Each device performs the following functions:

- **SCSI initiator device:** Issues a command to the SCSI target device, to perform a task. A SCSI host adaptor is an example of an initiator.

- **SCSI target device:** Executes commands to perform the task received from a SCSI initiator. Typically a SCSI peripheral device acts as a target device. However, in certain implementations, the host adaptor can also be a target device.

Figure 5-4 displays the SCSI-3 client-server model, in which a SCSI initiator, or a client, sends a request to a SCSI target, or a server. The target performs the tasks requested and sends the output to the initiator, using the protocol service interface.

A SCSI target device contains one or more logical units. A logical unit is an object that implements one of the device functional models as described in the SCSI command standards. The logical unit processes the commands sent by a SCSI initiator. A logical unit has two components, a *device server* and a *task manager*, as shown in Figure 5-4. The device server addresses client requests, and the task manager performs management functions.

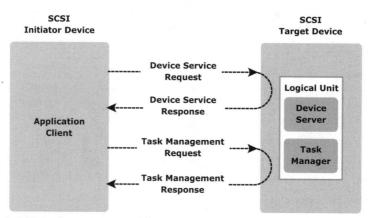

Figure 5-4: SCSI-3 client-server model

The SCSI initiator device is comprised of an application client and task management function, which initiates device service and task management requests. Each device service request contains a *Command Descriptor Block (CDB)*. The CDB defines the command to be executed and lists command-specific inputs and other parameters specifying how to process the command. The application client also creates tasks, objects within the logical unit, representing the work associated with a command or a series of linked commands. A task persists until either the "task complete response" is sent or the task management function or exception condition ends it.

The SCSI devices are identified by a specific number called a SCSI ID. In narrow SCSI (bus width=8), the devices are numbered 0 through 7; in wide (bus width=16) SCSI, the devices are numbered 0 through 15. These ID numbers set the device priorities on the SCSI bus. In narrow SCSI, 7 has the highest priority and 0 has the lowest priority. In wide SCSI, the device IDs from 8 to 15 have the highest priority, but the entire sequence of wide SCSI IDs has lower priority than narrow SCSI IDs. Therefore, the overall priority sequence for a wide SCSI is 7, 6, 5, 4, 3, 2, 1, 0, 15, 14, 13, 12, 11, 10, 9, and 8.

When a device is initialized, SCSI allows for automatic assignment of device IDs on the bus, which prevents two or more devices from using the same SCSI ID.

SCSI Ports

SCSI ports are the physical connectors that the SCSI cable plugs into for communication with a SCSI device. A SCSI device may contain target ports, initiator ports, target/initiator ports, or a target with multiple ports. Based on the port combinations, a SCSI device can be classified as an initiator model, a target model, a combined model, or a target model with multiple ports (see Figure 5-5).

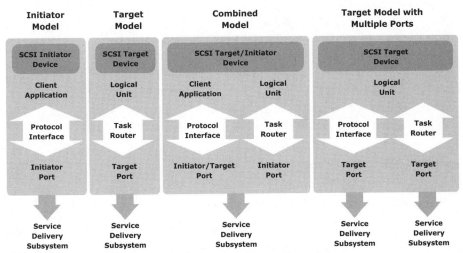

Figure 5-5: SCSI device models with different port configurations

In an initiator model, the SCSI initiator device has only initiator ports. Therefore, the application client can only initiate requests to the service delivery subsystem and receive confirmation. This device cannot serve any requests, and therefore does not contain a logical unit.

Similarly, a SCSI target device with only a target port can serve requests but cannot initiate them. The SCSI target/initiator device has a target/initiator port that can switch orientations depending on the role it plays while participating in an I/O operation. To cater to service requests from multiple devices, a SCSI device may also have multiple ports of the same orientation (target).

SCSI Communication Model

A SCSI communication model (see Figure 5-6) is comprised of three interconnecting layers as defined in the SAM-3 and is similar to the OSI seven-layer model. Lower-level layers render their services to the upper-level layers. A high-level layer communicates with a low-level layer by invoking the services that the low-level layer provides. The protocol at each layer defines the communication between peer layer entities.

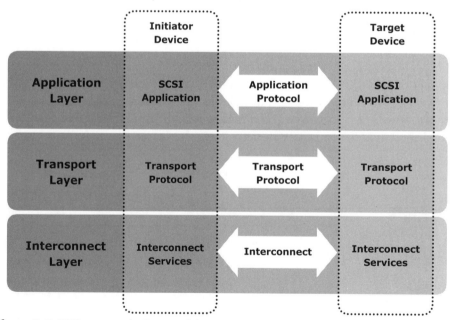

Figure 5-6: SCSI communication model

There are three layers in the SCSI communication model:

- **SCSI application layer (SAL):** This layer contains both client and server applications that initiate and process SCSI I/O operations using a SCSI application protocol.

- **SCSI transport protocol layer (STPL):** This layer contains the services and protocols that allow communication between an initiator and targets.

- **Interconnect layer:** This layer facilitates data transfer between the initiator and targets. The interconnect layer is also known as the *service delivery subsystem* and comprises the services, signalling mechanisms, and interconnects for data transfer.

5.4.4 Parallel SCSI Addressing

In the Parallel SCSI Initiator-Target communication (see Figure 5-7), an initiator ID uniquely identifies the initiator and is used as an originating address. This ID is in the range of 0 to 15, with the range 0 to 7 being the most common. A target ID uniquely identifies a target and is used as the address for exchanging commands and status information with initiators. The target ID is in the range of 0 to 15.

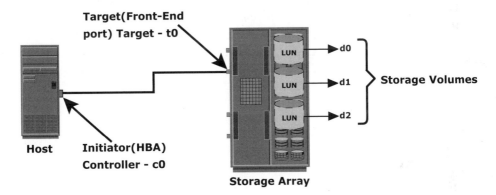

Host Addressing :
Storage Volume 1 - c0 t0 d0
Storage Volume 2 - c0 t0 d1
Storage Volume 3 - c0 t0 d2

Figure 5-7: SCSI Initiator-Target communication

SCSI addressing is used to identify hosts and devices. In this addressing, the UNIX naming convention is used to identify a disk and the three identifiers—initiator ID, target ID, and a LUN—in the cn|tn|dn format, which is also referred as *ctd addressing*. Here, cn is the initiator ID, commonly referred to as the controller ID; tn is the target ID of the device, such as t0, t1, t2, and so on; and dn is the device number reflecting the actual address of the device unit, such as d0, d1, and d2. A LUN identifies a specific logical unit in a target. The implementation of SCSI addressing may differ from one vendor to another. Figure 5-7 shows ctd addressing in the SCSI architecture.

5.5 SCSI Command Model

In the SCSI communication model (regardless of interface type: Parallel SCSI, SAS, or FC-AL2), the initiator and the target communicate with each other using a command protocol standard. The original SCSI command architecture was defined for parallel SCSI buses and later adopted for iSCSI and serial SCSI with minimal changes. Some of the other technologies that use the SCSI command set include ATA Packet Interface, USB Mass Storage class, and FireWire SBP-2. The SCSI command model is defined with the CDB. The CDB structure is detailed next.

5.5.1 CDB Structure

The initiator sends a command to the target in a CDB structure. The CDB defines the operation that corresponds to the initiator's request to be performed by the device server. The CDB consists of a 1-byte *operation code* followed by 5 or more bytes containing *command-specific parameters* and ending with a 1-byte *control field* (see Figure 5-8). The command specification is less than or equal to 16 bytes. The length of a CDB varies depending on the command and its parameters.

Byte \ Bit	7	6	5	4	3	2	1	0
0	Operation Code
1	Command-Specific Parameters
n-1	
n	Control

Figure 5-8: CDB structure

5.5.2 Operation Code

The operation code consists of group and command code fields (see Figure 5-9).

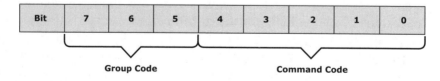

Figure 5-9: Operation code field

The *group code field* is a 3-bit field that specifies the length of the command-specific parameters shown in Table 5-3.

Table 5-3: Group Codes

GROUP CODE	COMMAND-SPECIFIC PARAMETERS
0	6 bytes
1 and 2	10 bytes
3	Reserved
4	16 bytes
5	12 bytes
6 and 7	Vendor specific

The *command code field* is a 5-bit field that allows 32 command codes in each group, for a total of 256 possible operation codes (refer to Figure 5-9). However, there are only about 60 different SCSI commands that facilitate communication between an initiator and a target. Some of the commonly used SCSI commands are shown in Table 5-4.

Table 5-4: Common SCSI Commands

COMMAND	DESCRIPTION
READ	Reads data from a device
WRITE	Writes data to a device
TEST UNIT READY	Queries the device to check whether it is ready for data transfer
INQUIRY	Returns basic information, which is also used to ping the device
REPORT LUNS	Lists the logical unit numbers
SEND AND RECEIVE DIAGNOSTIC RESULTS	Runs a simple self-test or a specialized test defined in a diagnostic page
FORMAT UNIT	Sets all sectors to all zeroes and allocates logical blocks, avoiding defective sectors
LOG SENSE	Returns current information from log pages
LOG SELECT	Used to modify data in the log pages of a SCSI target device
MODE SENSE	Returns current device parameters from mode pages
MODE SELECT	Sets device parameters on a mode page

5.5.3 Control Field

The *control field* is a 1-byte field and is the last byte of every CDB. The control field implements the *Normal Auto Contingent Allegiance (NACA)* and *link bits.* The control field structure is shown in Figure 5-10.

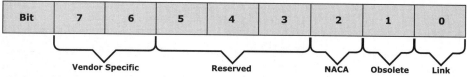

Figure 5-10: Control field

The NACA bit and associated ACA mechanism are almost never used. The NACA bit specifies whether an *auto contingent allegiance (ACA)* is established if the command returns with CHECK CONDITION status.

The link bit is unused in practice. This bit can be used to continue the task across multiple commands. A link bit of 1 indicates that the initiator has requested continuation of the task across two or more SCSI commands. Bits 3 to 5 are reserved and the last two bits are vendor-specific bits.

5.5.4 Status

After command execution, the logical unit sends the status along with the flag to the application client. The status, except INTERMEDIATE or INTERMEDIATE-CONDITION MET, indicates the end of the task. Table 5-5 shows the hexadecimal (h) codes and the associated status.

Table 5-5: SCSI Status Codes

STATUS BYTE CODES	STATUS
0h	GOOD
2h	CHECK CONDITION
4h	CONDITION MET
8h	BUSY
10h	INTERMEDIATE
14h	INTERMEDIATE-CONDITION MET
18h	RESERVATION CONFLICT
22h	COMMAND TERMINATED
28h	TASK SET FULL
30h	ACA ACTIVE
All other codes	Reserved

Summary

DAS offers several advantages, such as simplicity, ease of configuration, and manageability, but its limitations in scalability and availability restrict its use as an enterprise storage solution. DAS is still used in small and medium enterprises for localized data access and sharing and in environments that leverage DAS in conjunction with SAN and NAS. Storage devices such as IDE/ATA disks are popularly used to build DAS. SATA, SAS, SCSI, and FC are other protocols implemented on disk controllers also used in DAS environments.

SAN and NAS are preferred storage solutions for enterprises due to the limitations of DAS. The SCSI protocol is the basic building block of SAN. SCSI as a client-server model communicates between the initiator and the target using SCSI commands and SCSI port addresses. FCP (Fibre Channel Protocol), used in SAN, is an implementation of SCSI-3 over FC. NAS uses TCP/IP as a transport protocol between the hosts and NAS devices. The next chapter describes the storage networking technology architectures based on SCSI.

EXERCISES

1. DAS provides an economically viable alternative to other storage networking solutions. Justify this statement.

2. How is the priority sequence established in a wide SCSI environment?

3. Why is SCSI performance superior to that of IDE/ATA? Explain the reasons from an architectural perspective.

4. Research blade server architecture and discuss the limitations of DAS for this architecture.

5. What would you consider while choosing serial or parallel data transfer in a DAS implementation? Explain your answer and justify your choice.

6. If three hard disk drives are connected in a daisy chain and communicate over SCSI, explain how the CPU will perform I/O operations with a particular device.

7. A UNIX host has a path to a storage device that shows as c0 t1 d3. Draw a diagram to show the path and explain what it means.

Summary

Chapter 6
Storage Area Networks

O rganizations are experiencing an explosive growth in information. This information needs to be stored, protected,
optimized, and managed efficiently. Data center
managers are burdened with the challenging
task of providing low-cost, high-performance
information management solutions. An effective
information management solution must provide
the following:

KEY CONCEPTS

Storage Consolidation

Fibre Channel (FC) Architecture

Fibre Channel Protocol Stack

Fibre Channel Ports

Fibre Channel Addressing

World Wide Names

Zoning

Fibre Channel Topologies

- **Just-in-time information to business users:**
  Information must be available to business
  users when they need it. The explosive
  growth in online storage, proliferation of
  new servers and applications, spread of
  mission-critical data throughout enterprises, and demand for 24 × 7 data
  availability are some of the challenges that need to be addressed.

- **Integration of information infrastructure with business processes:** The
  storage infrastructure should be integrated with various business processes without compromising its security and integrity.

- **Flexible and resilient storage architecture:** The storage infrastructure
  must provide flexibility and resilience that aligns with changing business
  requirements. Storage should scale without compromising performance
  requirements of the applications and, at the same time, the total cost of
  managing information must be low.

Direct-attached storage (DAS) is often referred to as a stovepiped storage environment. Hosts "own" the storage and it is difficult to manage and share resources on these isolated storage devices. Efforts to organize this dispersed data led to the emergence of the storage area network (SAN). SAN is a high-speed, dedicated network of servers and shared storage devices. Traditionally connected over Fibre Channel (FC) networks, a SAN forms a single-storage pool and facilitates data centralization and consolidation. SAN meets the storage demands efficiently with better economies of scale. A SAN also provides effective maintenance and protection of data.

This chapter provides detailed insight into the FC technology on which a SAN is deployed and also reviews SAN design and management fundamentals.

6.1 Fibre Channel: Overview

The FC architecture forms the fundamental construct of the SAN infrastructure. *Fibre Channel* is a high-speed network technology that runs on high-speed optical fiber cables (preferred for front-end SAN connectivity) and serial copper cables (preferred for back-end disk connectivity). The FC technology was created to meet the demand for increased speeds of data transfer among computers, servers, and mass storage subsystems. Although FC networking was introduced in 1988, the FC standardization process began when the American National Standards Institute (ANSI) chartered the Fibre Channel Working Group (FCWG). By 1994, the new high-speed computer interconnection standard was developed and the Fibre Channel Association (FCA) was founded with 70 charter member companies. Technical Committee T11, which is the committee within INCITS (International Committee for Information Technology Standards), is responsible for Fibre Channel interfaces. T11 (previously known as X3T9.3) has been producing interface standards for high performance and mass storage applications since the 1970s.

Higher data transmission speeds are an important feature of the FC networking technology. The initial implementation offered throughput of 100 MB/s (equivalent to raw bit rate of 1Gb/s i.e. 1062.5 Mb/s in Fibre Channel), which was greater than the speeds of Ultra SCSI (20 MB/s) commonly used in DAS environments. FC in full-duplex mode could sustain throughput of 200 MB/s. In comparison with Ultra-SCSI, FC is a significant leap in storage networking technology. Latest FC implementations of 8 GFC (Fibre Channel) offers throughput of 1600 MB/s (raw bit rates of 8.5 Gb/s), whereas Ultra320 SCSI is available with a throughput of 320 MB/s. The FC architecture is highly scalable and theoretically a single FC network can accommodate approximately 15 million nodes.

6.2 The SAN and Its Evolution

A *storage area network (SAN)* carries data between servers (also known as *hosts*) and storage devices through fibre channel switches (see Figure 6-1). A SAN enables storage consolidation and allows storage to be shared across multiple servers. It enables organizations to connect geographically dispersed servers and storage.

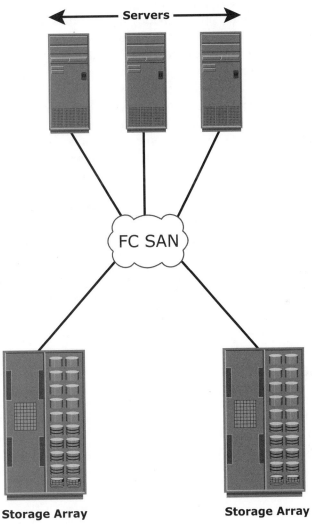

Figure 6-1: SAN implementation

A SAN provides the physical communication infrastructure and enables secure and robust communication between host and storage devices. The SAN management interface organizes connections and manages storage elements and hosts.

In its earliest implementation, the SAN was a simple grouping of hosts and the associated storage that was connected to a network using a hub as a connectivity device. This configuration of a SAN is known as a *Fibre Channel Arbitrated Loop (FC-AL)*, which is detailed later in the chapter. Use of hubs resulted in isolated FC-AL SAN islands because hubs provide limited connectivity and bandwidth.

The inherent limitations associated with hubs gave way to high-performance FC *switches*. The switched fabric topologies improved connectivity and performance, which enabled SANs to be highly scalable. This enhanced data accessibility to applications across the enterprise. FC-AL has been abandoned for SANs due to its limitations, but still survives as a disk-drive interface. Figure 6-2 illustrates the FC SAN evolution from FC-AL to enterprise SANs.

Today, Internet Protocol (IP) has become an option to interconnect geographically separated SANs. Two popular protocols that extend block-level access to applications over IP are iSCSI and Fibre Channel over IP (FCIP). These protocols are detailed in Chapter 8.

6.3 Components of SAN

A SAN consists of three basic components: servers, network infrastructure, and storage. These components can be further broken down into the following key elements: node ports, cabling, interconnecting devices (such as FC switches or hubs), storage arrays, and SAN management software.

6.3.1 Node Ports

In fibre channel, devices such as hosts, storage and tape libraries are all referred to as *nodes*. Each node is a source or destination of information for one or more nodes. Each node requires one or more ports to provide a physical interface for communicating with other nodes. These ports are integral components of an HBA and the storage front-end adapters. A port operates in full-duplex data transmission mode with a *transmit (Tx)* link and a *receive (Rx)* link (see Figure 6-3).

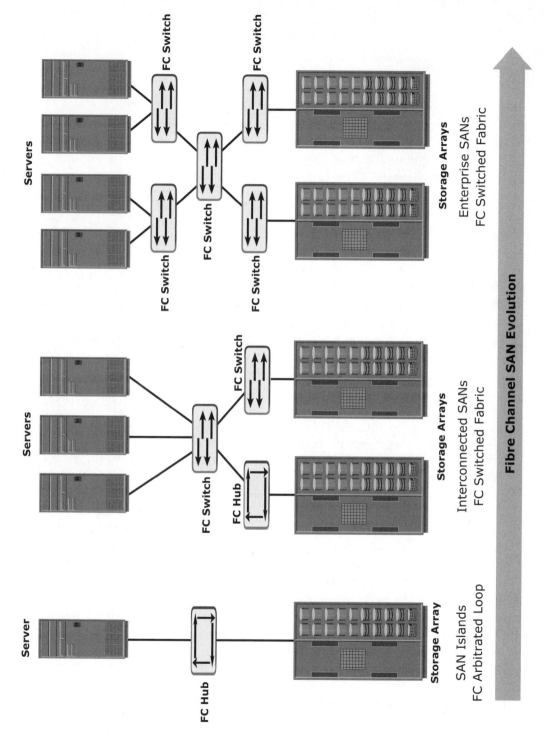

Figure 6-2: FC SAN evolution

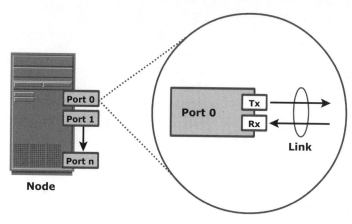

Figure 6-3: Nodes, ports, and links

6.3.2 Cabling

SAN implementations use optical fiber cabling. Copper can be used for shorter distances for back-end connectivity, as it provides a better signal-to-noise ratio for distances up to 30 meters. Optical fiber cables carry data in the form of light. There are two types of optical cables, multi-mode and single-mode.

Multi-mode fiber (MMF) cable carries multiple beams of light projected at different angles simultaneously onto the core of the cable (see Figure 6-4 (a)). Based on the bandwidth, multi-mode fibers are classified as OM1 (62.5μm), OM2 (50μm) and laser optimized OM3 (50μm). In an MMF transmission, multiple light beams traveling inside the cable tend to disperse and collide. This collision weakens the signal strength after it travels a certain distance — a process known as *modal dispersion*. An MMF cable is usually used for distances of up to 500 meters because of signal degradation (attenuation) due to modal dispersion.

Single-mode fiber (SMF) carries a single ray of light projected at the center of the core (see Figure 6-4 (b)). These cables are available in diameters of 7–11 microns; the most common size is 9 microns. In an SMF transmission, a single light beam travels in a straight line through the core of the fiber. The small core and the single light wave limits modal dispersion. Among all types of fibre cables, single-mode provides minimum signal attenuation over maximum distance (up to 10 km). A single-mode cable is used for long-distance cable runs, limited only by the power of the laser at the transmitter and sensitivity of the receiver.

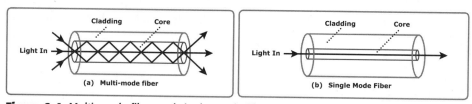

Figure 6-4: Multi-mode fiber and single-mode fiber

MMFs are generally used within data centers for shorter distance runs, while SMFs are used for longer distances. MMF transceivers are less expensive as compared to SMF transceivers.

A Standard connector (SC) (see Figure 6-5 (a)) and a Lucent connector (LC) (see Figure 6-5 (b)) are two commonly used connectors for fiber optic cables. An SC is used for data transmission speeds up to 1 Gb/s, whereas an LC is used for speeds up to 4 Gb/s. Figure 6-6 depicts a Lucent connector and a Standard connector.

A *Straight Tip (ST)* is a fiber optic connector with a plug and a socket that is locked with a half-twisted bayonet lock (see Figure 6-5 (c)). In the early days of FC deployment, fiber optic cabling predominantly used ST connectors. This connector is often used with Fibre Channel patch panels.

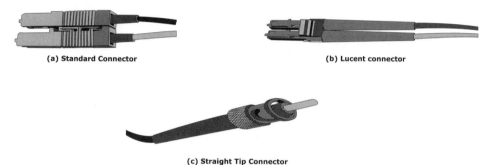

(a) Standard Connector   (b) Lucent connector

(c) Straight Tip Connector

Figure 6-5: SC, LC, and ST connectors

The Small Form-factor Pluggable (SFP) is an optical transceiver used in optical communication. The standard SFP+ transceivers support data rates up to 10 Gb/s.

6.3.3 Interconnect Devices

Hubs, switches, and directors are the interconnect devices commonly used in SAN.

Hubs are used as communication devices in FC-AL implementations. Hubs physically connect nodes in a logical loop or a physical star topology. All the nodes must share the bandwidth because data travels through all the connection points. Because of availability of low cost and high performance switches, hubs are no longer used in SANs.

Switches are more intelligent than hubs and directly route data from one physical port to another. Therefore, nodes do not share the bandwidth. Instead, each node has a dedicated communication path, resulting in bandwidth aggregation.

Directors are larger than switches and are deployed for data center implementations. The function of directors is similar to that of FC switches, but directors have higher port count and fault tolerance capabilities.

6.3.4 Storage Arrays

The fundamental purpose of a SAN is to provide host access to storage resources. The capabilities of intelligent storage arrays are detailed in Chapter 4. The large storage capacities offered by modern storage arrays have been exploited in SAN environments for storage consolidation and centralization. SAN implementations complement the standard features of storage arrays by providing high availability and redundancy, improved performance, business continuity, and multiple host connectivity.

6.3.5 SAN Management Software

SAN management software manages the interfaces between hosts, interconnect devices, and storage arrays. The software provides a view of the SAN environment and enables management of various resources from one central console.

It provides key management functions, including mapping of storage devices, switches, and servers, monitoring and generating alerts for discovered devices, and logical partitioning of the SAN, called *zoning*. In addition, the software provides management of typical SAN components such as HBAs, storage components, and interconnecting devices.

FC SWITCH VERSUS FC HUB

Scalability and performance are the primary differences between switches and hubs. A switched fabric uses 24-bit addressing, which supports over 15 million devices, whereas the FC-AL implemented in hubs supports only a maximum of 126 nodes.

Fabric switches provide full bandwidth between multiple pairs of ports in a fabric, resulting in a scalable architecture that can simultaneously support multiple communications.

Hubs provide shared bandwidth, and can support only single communication. They provide a low-cost connectivity expansion solution. Switches, conversely, can be used to build dynamic, high-performance fabrics through which multiple communications can take place simultaneously. Switches are more expensive than hubs.

6.4 FC Connectivity

The FC architecture supports three basic interconnectivity options: point-to-point, arbitrated loop (FC-AL), and fabric connect.

6.4.1 Point-to-Point

Point-to-point is the simplest FC configuration — two devices are connected directly to each other, as shown in Figure 6-6. This configuration provides a dedicated connection for data transmission between nodes. However, the point-to-point configuration offers limited connectivity, as only two devices can communicate with each other at a given time. Moreover, it cannot be scaled to accommodate a large number of network devices. Standard DAS usess point-to-point connectivity.

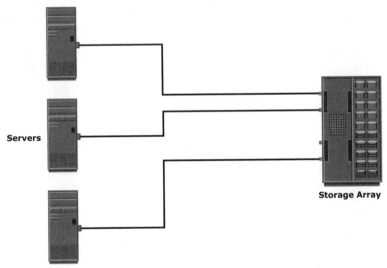

Figure 6-6: Point-to-point topology

6.4.2 Fibre Channel Arbitrated Loop

In the FC-AL configuration, devices are attached to a shared loop, as shown in Figure 6-7. FC-AL has the characteristics of a token ring topology and a physical star topology. In FC-AL, each device contends with other devices to perform I/O operations. Devices on the loop must "arbitrate" to gain control of the loop. At any given time, only one device can perform I/O operations on the loop.

As a loop configuration, FC-AL can be implemented without any interconnecting devices by directly connecting one device to another in a ring through cables.

However, FC-AL implementations may also use hubs whereby the arbitrated loop is physically connected in a star topology.

The FC-AL configuration has the following limitations in terms of scalability:

- FC-AL shares the bandwidth in the loop. Only one device can perform I/O operations at a time. Because each device in a loop has to wait for its turn to process an I/O request, the speed of data transmission is low in an FC-AL topology.

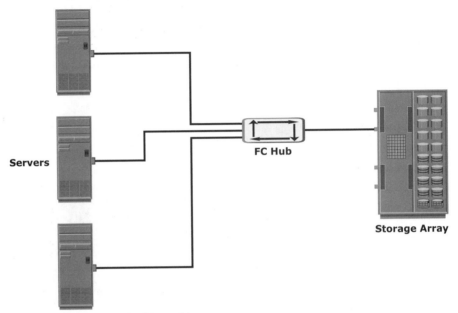

Figure 6-7: Fibre Channel arbitrated loop

- FC-AL uses 8-bit addressing. It can support up to 127 devices on a loop.
- Adding or removing a device results in loop re-initialization, which can cause a momentary pause in loop traffic.

FC-AL Transmission

When a node in the FC-AL topology attempts to transmit data, the node sends an *arbitration (ARB)* frame to each node on the loop. If two nodes simultaneously attempt to gain control of the loop, the node with the highest priority is allowed to communicate with another node. This priority is determined on the basis of Arbitrated Loop Physical Address (AL-PA) and Loop ID, described later in this chapter.

When the initiator node receives the ARB request it sent, it gains control of the loop. The initiator then transmits data to the node with which it has established a virtual connection. Figure 6-8 illustrates the process of data transmission in an FC-AL configuration.

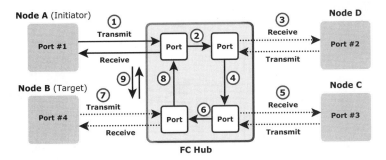

Node A want to communicate with Node B

① High priority initiator, Node A inserts the ARB frame in the loop.

② ARB frame is passed to the next node (Node D) in the loop.

③ Node D receives high priority ARB, therefore remains idle.

④ ARB is forwarded to next node (Node C) in the loop.

⑤ Node C receives high priority ARB, therefore remains idle.

⑥ ARB is forwarded to next node (Node B) in the loop.

⑦ Node B receives high priority ARB, therefore remains idle and

⑧ ARB is forwarded to next node (Node A) in the loop.

⑨ Node A receives ARB back; now it gains control of the loop and can start communicating with target Node B.

Figure 6-8: Data transmission in FC-AL

6.4.3 Fibre Channel Switched Fabric

Unlike a loop configuration, a Fibre Channel switched fabric (FC-SW) network provides interconnected devices, dedicated bandwidth, and scalability. The addition or removal of a device in a switched fabric is minimally disruptive; it does not affect the ongoing traffic between other devices.

FC-SW is also referred to as *fabric connect*. A fabric is a logical space in which all nodes communicate with one another in a network. This virtual space can be created with a switch or a network of switches. Each switch in a fabric contains a unique domain identifier, which is part of the fabric's addressing scheme. In FC-SW, nodes do not share a loop; instead, data is transferred through a dedicated path between the nodes. Each port in a fabric has a unique 24-bit fibre channel address for communication. Figure 6-9 shows an example of FC-SW.

A fabric topology can be described by the number of tiers it contains. The number of tiers in a fabric is based on the number of switches traversed between two points that are farthest from each other. However, note that this number is based on the infrastructure constructed by the fabric topology; it disregards how the storage and server are connected across the switches.

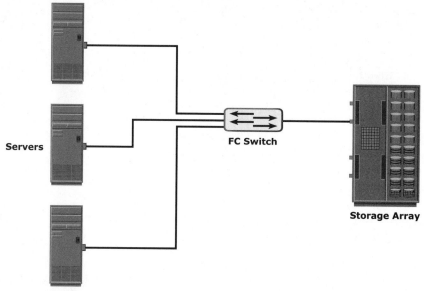

Figure 6-9: Fibre Channel switched fabric

When the number of tiers in a fabric increases, the distance that a fabric management message must travel to reach each switch in the fabric also increases. The increase in the distance also increases the time taken to propagate and complete a fabric reconfiguration event, such as the addition of a new switch, or a zone set propagation event (detailed later in this chapter). Figure 6-10 illustrates two-tier and three-tier fabric architecture.

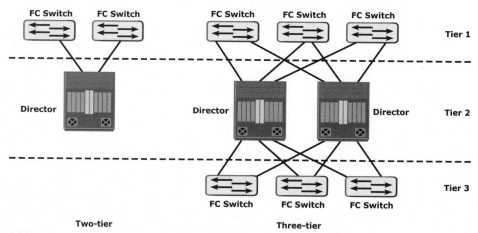

Figure 6-10: Tiered structure of FC-SW topology

FC-SW Transmission

FC-SW uses switches that are intelligent devices. They can switch data traffic from an initiator node to a target node directly through switch ports. Frames are routed between source and destination by the fabric.

As shown in Figure 6-11, if node B wants to communicate with node D, Nodes should individually login first and then transmit data via the FC-SW. This link is considered a dedicated connection between the initiator and the target.

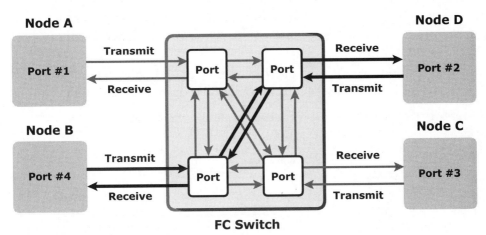

Figure 6-11: Data tansmission in FC-SW topology

6.5 Fibre Channel Ports

Ports are the basic building blocks of an FC network. Ports on the switch can be one of the following types:

- **N_port:** An end point in the fabric. This port is also known as the *node port*. Typically, it is a host port (HBA) or a storage array port that is connected to a switch in a switched fabric.

- **NL_port:** A node port that supports the arbitrated loop topology. This port is also known as the *node loop port*.

- **E_port:** An FC port that forms the connection between two FC switches. This port is also known as the *expansion port*. The E_port on an FC switch connects to the E_port of another FC switch in the fabric through a link, which is called an *Inter-Switch Link (ISL)*. ISLs are used to transfer host-to-storage data as well as the fabric management traffic from one switch to another. ISL is also one of the scaling mechanisms in SAN connectivity.

▪ **F_port:** A port on a switch that connects an N_port. It is also known as a *fabric port* and cannot participate in FC-AL.

▪ **FL_port:** A fabric port that participates in FC-AL. This port is connected to the NL_ports on an FC-AL loop. A FL_port also connects a loop to a switch in a switched fabric. As a result, all NL_ports in the loop can participate in FC-SW. This configuration is referred to as a *public loop*. In contrast, an arbitrated loop without any switches is referred to as a *private loop*. A private loop contains nodes with NL_ports, and does not contain FL_port.

▪ **G_port:** A generic port that can operate as an E_port or an F_port and determines its functionality automatically during initialization.

Figure 6-12 shows various FC ports located in the fabric.

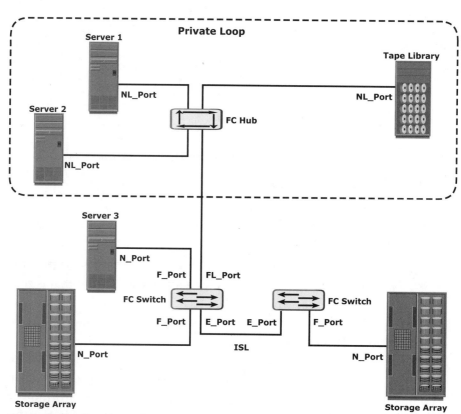

Figure 6-12: Fibre channel ports

6.6 Fibre Channel Architecture

The FC architecture represents true channel/network integration with standard interconnecting devices. Connections in a SAN are accomplished using FC. Traditionally, transmissions from host to storage devices are carried out over channel connections such as a parallel bus. Channel technologies provide high levels of performance with low protocol overheads. Such performance is due to the static nature of channels and the high level of hardware and software integration provided by the channel technologies. However, these technologies suffer from inherent limitations in terms of the number of devices that can be connected and the distance between these devices.

Fibre Channel Protocol (FCP) is the implementation of serial SCSI-3 over an FC network. In the FCP architecture, all external and remote storage devices attached to the SAN appear as local devices to the host operating system. The key advantages of FCP are as follows:

- Sustained transmission bandwidth over long distances.

- Support for a larger number of addressable devices over a network. Theoretically, FC can support over 15 million device addresses on a network.

- Exhibits the characteristics of channel transport and provides speeds up to 8.5 Gb/s (8 GFC).

FICON

Mainframe SANs use *FICON (Fibre Connectivity)* for a low-latency, high-bandwidth connection to the storage controller. FICON is an FC-4 type technology, and its place in the FC architecture is analogous to FCP. FICON was designed as a replacement for *ESCON (Enterprise System Connection)* to support mainframe attached storage systems.

FCP is specified by standards produced by T10; FCP-3 is the last issued standard, and FCP-4 is under development. FCP defines a Fibre Channel mapping layer (FC-4) that uses the services defined by ANS X3.230-199X, Fibre Channel—Physical and Signaling Interface (FC-PH) to transmit SCSI commands, data, and status information between SCSI initiator and SCSI target. FCP defines Fibre Channel information units in accordance with the SCSI architecture model. FCP also defines how the Fibre Channel services are used to perform the services defined by the SCSI architecture model.

The FC standard enables mapping several existing *Upper Layer Protocols (ULPs)* to FC frames for transmission, including SCSI, IP, High Performance Parallel Interface (HIPPI), Enterprise System Connection (ESCON), and Asynchronous Transfer Mode (ATM).

6.6.1 Fibre Channel Protocol Stack

It is easier to understand a communication protocol by viewing it as a structure of independent layers. FCP defines the communication protocol in five layers: FC-0 through FC-4 (except FC-3 layer, which is not implemented). In a layered communication model, the peer layers on each node talk to each other through defined protocols. Figure 6-13 illustrates the fibre channel protocol stack.

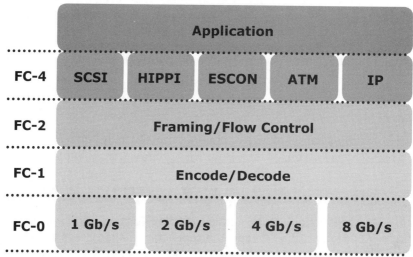

Figure 6-13: Fibre channel protocol stack

FC-4 Upper Layer Protocol

FC-4 is the uppermost layer in the FCP stack. This layer defines the application interfaces and the way Upper Layer Protocols (ULPs) are mapped to the lower FC layers. The FC standard defines several protocols that can operate on the FC-4 layer (see Figure 6-7). Some of the protocols include SCSI, HIPPI Framing Protocol, Enterprise Storage Connectivity (ESCON), ATM, and IP.

FC-2 Transport Layer

The FC-2 is the transport layer that contains the payload, addresses of the source and destination ports, and link control information. The FC-2 layer provides Fibre Channel addressing, structure, and organization of data (frames, sequences, and exchanges). It also defines fabric services, classes of service, flow control, and routing.

FC-1 Transmission Protocol

This layer defines the transmission protocol that includes serial encoding and decoding rules, special characters used, and error control. At the transmitter node, an 8-bit character is encoded into a 10-bit transmissions character. This character is then transmitted to the receiver node. At the receiver node, the 10-bit character is passed to the FC-1 layer, which decodes the 10-bit character into the original 8-bit character.

FC-0 Physical Interface

FC-0 is the lowest layer in the FCP stack. This layer defines the physical interface, media, and transmission of raw bits. The FC-0 specification includes cables, connectors, and optical and electrical parameters for a variety of data rates. The FC transmission can use both electrical and optical media.

6.6.2 Fibre Channel Addressing

An FC address is dynamically assigned when a port logs on to the fabric. The FC address has a distinct format that varies according to the type of node port in the fabric. These ports can be an N_port and an NL_port in a public loop, or an NL_port in a private loop.

The first field of the FC address of an N_port contains the domain ID of the switch (see Figure 6-14). This is an 8-bit field. Out of the possible 256 domain IDs, 239 are available for use; the remaining 17 addresses are reserved for specific services. For example, FFFFFC is reserved for the name server, and FFFFFE is reserved for the fabric login service. The maximum possible number of N_ports in a switched fabric is calculated as 239 domains × 256 areas × 256 ports = 15,663,104 Fibre Channel addresses.

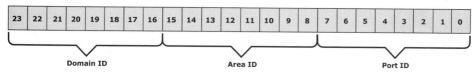

Figure 6-14: 24-bit FC address of N_port

The area ID is used to identify a group of F_ports. An example of a group of F_ports would be a card on the switch with more than one port on it. The last field in the FC address identifies the F_port within the group.

FC Address of an NL_port

The FC addressing scheme for an NL_port differs from other ports. The two upper bytes in the FC addresses of the NL_ports in a private loop are assigned zero values. However, when an arbitrated loop is connected to a fabric through an FL_port, it becomes a public loop. In this case, an NL_port supports a fabric login. The two upper bytes of this NL_port are then assigned a positive value, called a *loop identifier*, by the switch. The loop identifier is the same for all NL_ports on a given loop.

Figure 6-15 illustrates the FC address of an NL_port in both a public loop and a private loop. The last field in the FC addresses of the NL_ports, in both public and private loops, identifies the AL-PA. There are 127 allowable AL-PA addresses; one address is reserved for the FL_port on the switch.

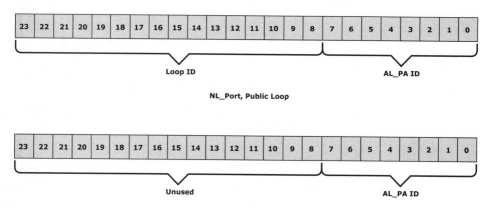

Figure 6-15: 24-bit FC address of NL_port

N_PORT ID VISUALIZATION (NPIV)

NPIV is a Fibre Channel configuration that enables multiple N_port IDs to share a single physical N_port.

World Wide Names

Each device in the FC environment is assigned a 64-bit unique identifier called the *World Wide Name* (WWN). The Fibre Channel environment uses two types of WWNs: World Wide Node Name (WWNN) and World Wide Port Name (WWPN). Unlike an FC address, which is assigned dynamically, a WWN is a static name for each device on an FC network. WWNs are similar to the Media Access Control (MAC) addresses used in IP networking. WWNs are *burned* into the hardware or assigned through software. Several configuration definitions in a SAN use WWN for identifying storage devices and HBAs. The name server in an FC environment keeps the association of WWNs to the dynamically created FC addresses for nodes. Figure 6-16 illustrates the WWN structure for an array and the HBA.

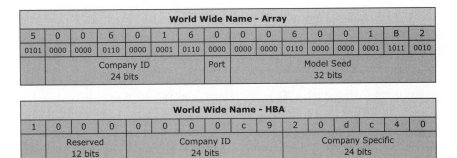

Figure 6-16: World Wide Names

6.6.3 FC Frame

An FC frame (Figure 6-17) consists of five parts: *start of frame (SOF), frame header, data field, cyclic redundancy check (CRC)*, and *end of frame (EOF)*.

The SOF and EOF act as delimiters. In addition to this role, the SOF is a flag that indicates whether the frame is the first frame in a sequence of frames.

The frame header is 24 bytes long and contains addressing information for the frame. It includes the following information: Source ID (S_ID), Destination ID (D_ID), Sequence ID (SEQ_ID), Sequence Count (SEQ_CNT), Originating Exchange ID (OX_ID), and Responder Exchange ID (RX_ID), in addition to some control fields.

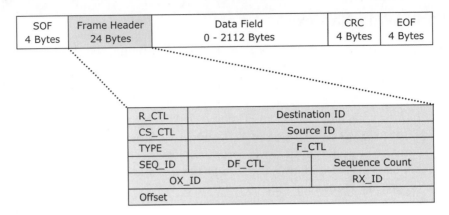

Figure 6-17: FC frame

The S_ID and D_ID are standard FC addresses for the source port and the destination port, respectively. The SEQ_ID and OX_ID identify the frame as a component of a specific sequence and exchange, respectively.

The frame header also defines the following fields:

- **Routing Control (R_CTL)**: This field denotes whether the frame is a link control frame or a data frame. Link control frames are nondata frames that do not carry any payload. These frames are used for setup and messaging. In contrast, data frames carry the payload and are used for data transmission.

- **Class Specific Control (CS_CTL)**: This field specifies link speeds for class 1 and class 4 data transmission.

- **TYPE**: This field describes the upper layer protocol (ULP) to be carried on the frame if it is a data frame. However, if it is a link control frame, this field is used to signal an event such as "fabric busy." For example, if the TYPE is 08, and the frame is a data frame, it means that the SCSI will be carried on an FC.

- **Data Field Control (DF_CTL)**: A 1-byte field that indicates the existence of any optional headers at the beginning of the data payload. It is a mechanism to extend header information into the payload.

- **Frame Control (F_CTL)**: A 3-byte field that contains control information related to frame content. For example, one of the bits in this field indicates whether this is the first sequence of the exchange.

The data field in an FC frame contains the data payload, up to 2,112 bytes of original data — in most cases, SCSI data. The biggest possible payload an FC frame can deliver is 2,112 bytes of data with 36 bytes of fixed overhead. A link control frame, by definition, has a payload of 0 bytes. Only data frames carry a payload.

The CRC checksum facilitates error detection for the content of the frame. This checksum verifies data integrity by checking whether the content of the frames was received correctly. The CRC checksum is calculated by the sender before encoding at the FC-1 layer. Similarly, it is calculated by the receiver after decoding at the FC-1 layer.

6.6.4. Structure and Organization of FC Data

In an FC network, data transport is analogous to a conversation between two people, whereby a frame represents a word, a sequence represents a sentence, and an exchange represents a conversation.

- **Exchange operation:** An exchange operation enables two N_ports to identify and manage a set of information units. This unit maps to a sequence. Sequences can be both unidirectional and bidirectional depending upon the type of data sequence exchanged between the initiator and the target.

- **Sequence:** A sequence refers to a contiguous set of frames that are sent from one port to another. A sequence corresponds to an information unit, as defined by the ULP.

- **Frame:** A frame is the fundamental unit of data transfer at Layer 2. Each frame can contain up to 2,112 bytes of payload.

6.6.5 Flow Control

Flow control defines the pace of the flow of data frames during data transmission. FC technology uses two flow-control mechanisms: buffer-to-buffer credit (BB_Credit) and end-to-end credit (EE_Credit).

BB_Credit

FC uses the *BB_Credit* mechanism for hardware-based flow control. BB_Credit controls the maximum number of frames that can be present over the link at any given point in time. In a switched fabric, BB_Credit management may take place between any two FC ports. The transmitting port maintains a count of free receiver buffers and continues to send frames if the count is greater than 0. The BB_Credit mechanism provides frame acknowledgment through the *Receiver Ready (R_RDY)* primitive.

EE_Credit

The function of end-to-end credit, known as EE_Credit, is similar to that of BB_Credit. When an initiator and a target establish themselves as nodes communicating with each other, they exchange the EE_Credit parameters (part of Port Login).

The EE_Credit mechanism affects the flow control for class 1 and class 2 traffic only.

6.6.6 Classes of Service

The FC standards define different classes of service to meet the requirements of a wide range of applications. The table below shows three classes of services and their features (Table 6-1).

Table 6-1: FC Class of Services

	CLASS 1	**CLASS 2**	**CLASS 3**
Communication type	Dedicated connection	Nondedicated connection	Nondedicated connection
Flow control	End-to-end credit	End-to-end credit B-to-B credit	B-to-B credit
Frame delivery	In order delivery	Order not guaranteed	Order not guaranteed
Frame acknowledgement	Acknowledged	Acknowledged	Not acknowledged
Multiplexing	No	Yes	Yes
Bandwidth utilization	Poor	Moderate	High

Another class of services is *class F,* which is intended for use by the switches communicating through ISLs. Class F is similar to Class 2, and it provides notification of nondelivery of frames. Other defined Classes 4, 5, and 6 are used for specific applications. Currently, these services are not in common use.

6.7 Zoning

Zoning is an FC switch function that enables nodes within the fabric to be logically segmented into groups that can communicate with each other (see Figure 6-18). When a device (host or storage array) logs onto a fabric, it is registered with the name server. When a port logs onto the fabric, it goes through a device discovery process with other devices registered in the name server. The zoning function controls this process by allowing only the members in the same zone to establish these link-level services.

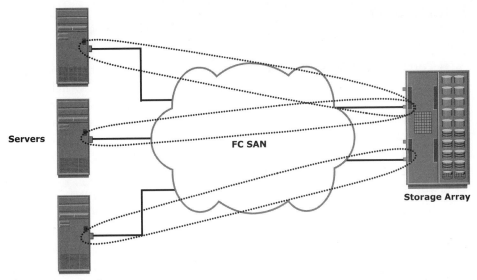

Figure 6-18: Zoning

Multiple zone sets may be defined in a fabric, but only one zone set can be active at a time. A zone set is a set of zones and a zone is a set of members. A member may be in multiple zones. Members, zones, and zone sets form the hierarchy defined in the zoning process (see Figure 6-19). *Members* are nodes within the SAN that can be included in a zone. *Zones* comprise a set of members that have access to one another. A port or a node can be a member of multiple zones. *Zone sets* comprise a group of zones that can be activated or deactivated as a single entity in a fabric. Only one zone set per fabric can be active at a time. Zone sets are also referred to as *zone configurations*.

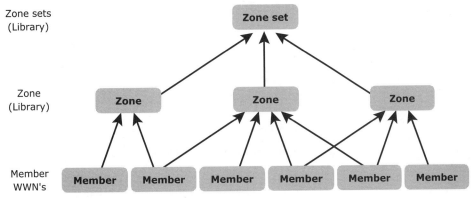

Figure 6-19: Members, zones, and zone sets

Types of Zoning

Zoning can be categorized into three types:

- **Port zoning:** It uses the FC addresses of the physical ports to define zones. In port zoning, access to data is determined by the physical switch port to which a node is connected. The FC address is dynamically assigned when the port logs on to the fabric. Therefore, any change in the fabric configuration affects zoning. Port zoning is also called *hard zoning*. Although this method is secure, it requires updating of zoning configuration information in the event of fabric reconfiguration.

- **WWN zoning:** It uses World Wide Names to define zones. WWN zoning is also referred to as *soft zoning*. A major advantage of WWN zoning is its flexibility. It allows the SAN to be recabled without reconfiguring the zone information. This is possible because the WWN is static to the node port.

- **Mixed zoning:** It combines the qualities of both WWN zoning and port zoning. Using mixed zoning enables a specific port to be tied to the WWN of a node.

Figure 6-20 shows the three types of zoning on an FC network.

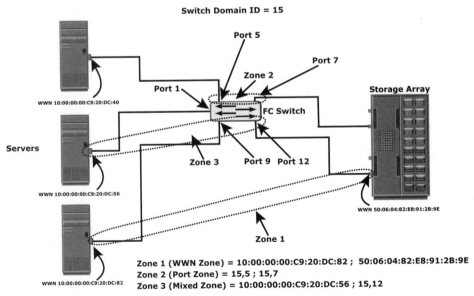

Figure 6-20: Types of zoning

Zoning is used in conjunction with LUN masking for controlling server access to storage. However, these are two different activities. Zoning takes place at the fabric level and LUN masking is done at the array level.

6.8 Fibre Channel Login Types

Fabric services define three login types:

- Fabric login (FLOGI) is performed between an N_port and an F_port. To log on to the fabric, a device sends a FLOGI frame with the World Wide Node Name (WWNN) and World Wide Port Name (WWPN) parameters to the login service at the well-known FC address FFFFFE. In turn, the switch accepts the login and returns an Accept (ACC) frame with the assigned FC address for the device. Immediately after the FLOGI, the N_port registers itself with the local name server on the switch, indicating its WWNN, WWPN, and assigned FC address.

- Port login (PLOGI) is performed between an N_port and another N_port to establish a session. The initiator N_port sends a PLOGI request frame to the target N_port, which accepts it. The target N_port returns an ACC to the initiator N_port. Next, the N_ports exchange service parameters relevant to the session.

- Process login (PRLI) is also performed between an N_port and another N_port. This login relates to the FC-4 ULPs such as SCSI. N_ports exchange SCSI-3-related service parameters. N_ports share information about the FC-4 type in use, the SCSI initiator, or the target.

FAN-OUT AND FAN-IN

Fan-out enables multiple server ports to communicate to a single storage port. A four server connection to a single storage port results in a fan-out ratio of 4. Typically, there is an architectural limit based on the array's capability to record and manage several initiators that connect to a port, as the hardware capabilities determine the possible aggregate IOPS and MB/s per port.

Fan-in specifies accessibility of a host port to storage ports on multiple arrays. Like fan-out, the restrictions on fan-in are also based on an architectural limit.

6.9 FC Topologies

Fabric design follows standard topologies to connect devices. Core-edge fabric is one of the popular topology designs. Variations of core-edge fabric and mesh topologies are most commonly deployed in SAN implementations.

6.9.1 Core-Edge Fabric

In the *core-edge fabric* topology, there are two types of switch tiers in this fabric. The *edge tier* usually comprises switches and offers an inexpensive approach to adding more hosts in a fabric. The tier at the edge fans out from the tier at the core. The nodes on the edge can communicate with each other.

The *core tier* usually comprises enterprise directors that ensure high fabric availability. Additionally all traffic has to either traverse through or terminate at this tier. In a two-tier configuration, all storage devices are connected to the core tier, facilitating fan-out. The host-to-storage traffic has to traverse one and two ISLs in a two-tier and three-tier configuration, respectively. Hosts used for mission-critical applications can be connected directly to the core tier and consequently avoid traveling through the ISLs to process I/O requests from these hosts.

The core-edge fabric topology increases connectivity within the SAN while conserving overall port utilization. If expansion is required, an additional edge switch can be connected to the core. This topology can have different variations. In a *single-core topology,* all hosts are connected to the edge tier and all storage is connected to the core tier. Figure 6-21 depicts the core and edge switches in a single-core topology.

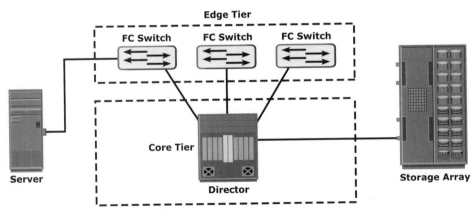

Figure 6-21: Single core topology

A *dual-core topology* can be expanded to include more core switches. However, to maintain the topology, it is essential that new ISLs are created to connect each edge switch to the new core switch that is added. Figure 6-22 illustrates the core and edge switches in a dual-core topology.

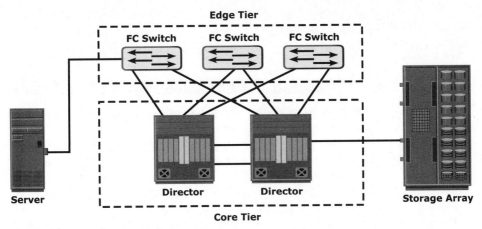

Figure 6-22: Dual-core topology

Benefits and Limitations of Core-Edge Fabric

The core-edge fabric provides one-hop storage access to all storage in the system. Because traffic travels in a deterministic pattern (from the edge to the core), a core-edge provides easier calculation of ISL loading and traffic patterns. Because each tier's switch is used for either storage or hosts, one can easily identify which resources are approaching their capacity, making it easier to develop a set of rules for scaling and apportioning.

A well-defined, easily reproducible building-block approach makes rolling out new fabrics easier. Core-edge fabrics can be scaled to larger environments by linking core switches, adding more core switches, or adding more edge switches. This method can be used to extend the existing simple core-edge model or to expand the fabric into a compound or complex core-edge model.

However, the core-edge fabric may lead to some performance-related problems because scaling a core-edge topology involves increasing the number of ISLs in the fabric. As more edge switches are added, the domain count in the fabric increases. A common best practice is to keep the number of host-to-storage hops unchanged, at one hop, in a core-edge. Hop count represents the total number of devices a given piece of data (packet) passes through. Generally a large hop count means greater the transmission delay between data traverse from its source to destination.

As the number of cores increases, it may be prohibitive to continue to maintain ISLs from each core to each edge switch. When this happens, the fabric design can be changed to a compound or complex core-edge design.

BLADE SERVER

Blade server architecture deployment has rapidly increased server count in modern data centers.

In blade server architecture, the backplane hosts the server blades and the I/O modules. High-end blade servers have up to 16 server blades and 8 I/O modules configured. The server blades are hot pluggable. The FC switch module in the chassis takes the place of the edge switch in standard core-edge fabrics, which also reduces the required cable count. Blade servers use mezzanine cards instead of HBAs for FC connectivity. The mezzanine cards connect the internal ports on the switch module through the backplane.

6.9.2 Mesh Topology

In a *mesh topology*, each switch is directly connected to other switches by using ISLs. This topology promotes enhanced connectivity within the SAN. When the number of ports on a network increases, the number of nodes that can participate and communicate also increases.

A mesh topology may be one of the two types: full mesh or partial mesh. In a *full mesh*, every switch is connected to every other switch in the topology. Full mesh topology may be appropriate when the number of switches involved is small. A typical deployment would involve up to four switches or directors, with each of them servicing highly localized host-to-storage traffic. In a full mesh topology, a maximum of one ISL or hop is required for host-to-storage traffic.

In a *partial mesh* topology, several hops or ISLs may be required for the traffic to reach its destination. Hosts and storage can be located anywhere in the fabric, and storage can be localized to a director or a switch in both mesh topologies.

A full mesh topology with a symmetric design results in an even number of switches, whereas a partial mesh has an asymmetric design and may result in an odd number of switches. Figure 6-23 depicts both a full mesh and a partial mesh topology.

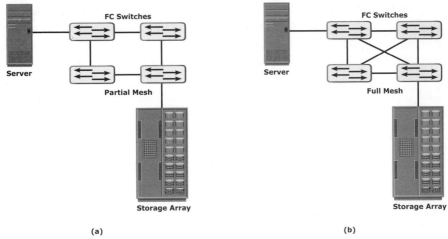

Figure 6-23: Partial mesh and full mesh topologies

6.10 Concepts in Practice: EMC Connectrix

This section discusses the Connectrix connectivity products offered by EMC that provide connectivity in large-scale, workgroup, mid-tier, and mixed iSCSI and FC environments. For the latest information, visit http://education.EMC .com/ismbook.

FC switches and directors are key components of the SAN environment. EMC offers the following connectivity products under the Connectrix brand (see Figure 6-24):

- Enterprise directors
- Departmental switches
- Multiprotocol routers

Enterprise Director   **Departmental Switches**   **Multiprotocol Router**

Figure 6-24: EMC Connectrix

Enterprise directors are ideal for large enterprise connectivity. They offer high port density and high component redundancy. Enterprise directors are deployed in high-availability or large-scale environments. Connectrix directors offer several hundred ports per domain. Departmental switches are best suited for workgroup, mid-tier environments. Multiprotocol routers support mixed iSCSI and FC environments. They can bridge FC SAN and IP SAN, a feature that enables these routers to provide connectivity between iSCSI host initiators and FC storage targets. They can extend FC SAN over long distances through IP networks.

In addition to FC ports, Connectrix switches and directors have Ethernet ports and serial ports for communication and switch management functions. Connectrix management software enables configuration, monitoring, and management of Connectrix switches.

6.10.1 Connectrix Switches

B-series and MDS make up the Connectrix family of switches offered by EMC. These switches offer scalability up to 80 ports and are designed to meet workgroup, department-level, and enterprise-level requirements. They are designed with a nonblocking architecture and can operate in heterogeneous environments. The features of these switches that ensure their high availability are their nondisruptive software, port upgrade, redundant, and hot-swappable components. These switches can be managed through CLI, Web Tools, and Fabric Manager.

6.10.2 Connectrix Directors

EMC offers the high-end Connectrix family of directors. Their modular architectural design offers scalability up to 528 ports. They are suitable for server and storage consolidation across enterprises. These directors have redundant components for high availability and they provide multi-protocol connectivity for both mainframe and open system environments. Connectrix directors offer high speeds (up to 10 Gb/s) and high system bandwidth (up to 2.2 Tb/s). They also support ISL trunking and in-band and out-of-band management functionality. The connectrix director also offers a virtual SAN feature for fabric management and security. Like switches, directors can be managed through CLI or other GUI tools.

6.10.3 Connectrix Management Tools

There are several ways to monitor and manage FC switches in a fabric. Individual switch management is accomplished through the console port, using CLI or browser-based tools.

Command-line utilities such as Telnet and SSH may be used to log on to the switch over IP and issue CLI commands. The primary purpose of the CLI is to automate the management of a large number of switches or directors with the use of scripts. The third option is to use browser-based tools that provide GUIs. These Java-based tools can also display the topology map.

Fabricwide management and monitoring is accomplished by using vendor-specific tools and Simple Network Management Protocol (SNMP)-based, third-party software.

EMC ControlCenter SAN Manager provides a single interface for managing Storage Area Network. With SAN Manager one can discover, monitor, manage, and configure complex heterogeneous SAN environments faster and easier. It streamlines and centralizes SAN management operations across multi-vendor storage networks and storage devices. It enables storage administrators to manage SAN zones and LUN masking consistently across multi-vendor SAN arrays and switches. EMC ControlCenter SAN Manager also supports virtual environments including VMware, Symmetrix Virtual Provisioning, and Virtual SANs.

Figure 6-25 illustrates EMC ControlCenter SAN Manager interface.

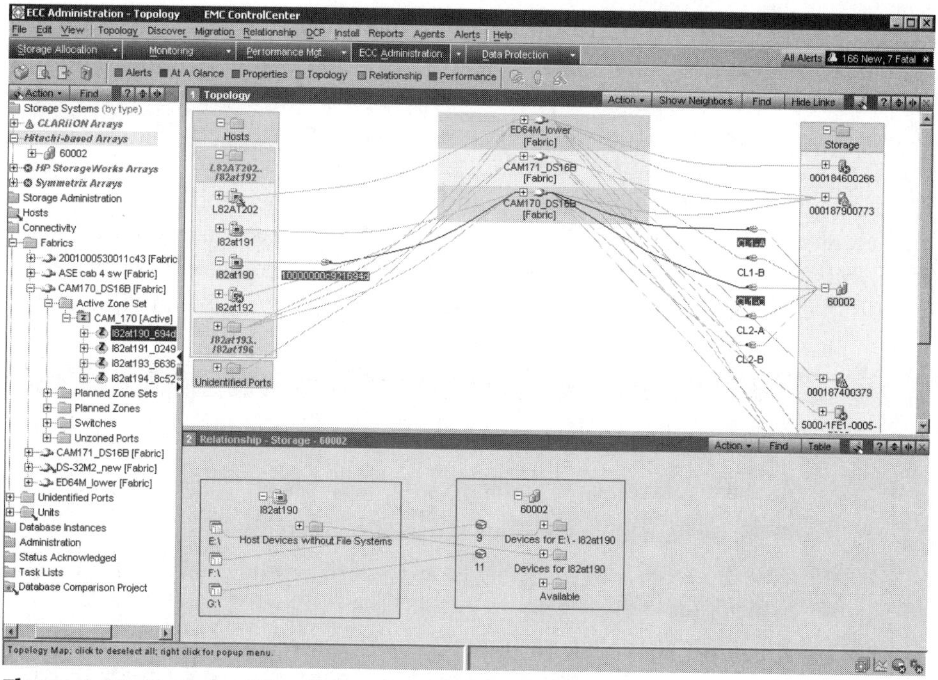

Figure 6-25: Managing FC switches through SAN Manager

Summary

The SAN has enabled the consolidation of storage and benefited organizations by lowering the cost of storage service delivery. SAN reduces overall operational cost and downtime and enables faster application deployment.

SANs and tools that have emerged for SANs enable data centers to allocate storage to an application and migrate workloads between different servers and storage devices dynamically. This significantly increases server utilization.

SANs simplify the business-continuity process because organizations are able to logically connect different data centers over long distances and provide cost-effective, disaster recovery services that can be effectively tested.

The adoption of SANs has increased with the decline of hardware prices and has enhanced the maturity of storage network standards. Small and medium-size enterprises and departments that initially resisted shared storage pools have now begun to adopt SANs.

This chapter detailed the components of a SAN and the FC technology that forms its backbone. FC meets today's demands for reliable, high-performance, and low-cost applications.

The interoperability between FC switches from different vendors has enhanced significantly compared to early SAN deployments. The standards published by a dedicated study group within T11 on SAN routing, and the new product offerings from vendors, are now revolutionizing the way SANs are deployed and operated.

Although SANs have eliminated islands of storage, their initial implementation created islands of SANs in an enterprise. The emergence of the iSCSI and FCIP technologies, detailed in Chapter 8, has pushed the convergence of the SAN with IP technology, providing more benefits to using storage technologies.

EXERCISES

1. What is zoning? Discuss a scenario,

    (i) where soft zoning is preferred over hard zoning.

    (ii) where hard zoning is preferred over soft zoning.

2. Describe the process of assigning FC address to a node when logging in to the network for the first time.

3. Seventeen switches, with 16 ports each, are connected in a mesh topology. How many ports are available for host and storage connectivity if you create a high-availability solution?

4. Discuss the advantage of FC-SW over FC-AL.

5. How flow control works in FC network.

6. Why is class 3 service most preferred for FC communication?

Chapter 7
Network-Attached Storage

N*etwork-attached storage (NAS)* is an IP-based file-sharing device attached to a local area network. NAS provides the advantages of server consolidation by eliminating the need for multiple file servers. It provides storage consolidation through file-level data access and sharing. NAS is a preferred storage solution that enables clients to share files quickly and directly with minimum storage management overhead. NAS also helps to eliminate bottlenecks that users face when accessing files from a general-purpose server.

KEY CONCEPTS

NAS Device

Remote File Sharing

NAS Connectivity and Protocols

NAS Performance and Availability

MTU and Jumbo Frames

NAS uses network and file-sharing protocols to perform filing and storage functions. These protocols include TCP/IP for data transfer and CIFS and NFS for remote file service. NAS enables both UNIX and Microsoft Windows users to share the same data seamlessly. To enable data sharing, NAS typically uses NFS for UNIX, CIFS for Windows, and File Transfer Protocol (FTP) and other protocols for both environments. Recent advancements in networking technology have enabled NAS to scale up to enterprise requirements for improved performance and reliability in accessing data.

A NAS device is a dedicated, high-performance, high-speed, single-purpose file serving and storage system. NAS serves a mix of clients and servers over an IP network. Most NAS devices support multiple interfaces and networks.

A NAS device uses its own operating system and integrated hardware, software components to meet specific file service needs. Its operating system is optimized for file I/O and, therefore, performs file I/O better than a general-purpose server. As a result, a NAS device can serve more clients than traditional file servers, providing the benefit of server consolidation.

This chapter describes the components of NAS, different types of NAS implementations, the file-sharing protocols, and the transport and network layer protocols used in NAS implementations. The chapter also explains NAS design considerations and factors that affect NAS performance.

7.1 General-Purpose Servers vs. NAS Devices

A NAS device is optimized for file-serving functions such as storing, retrieving, and accessing files for applications and clients. As shown in Figure 7-1, a general-purpose server can be used to host any application, as it runs a generic operating system. Unlike a general-purpose server, a NAS device is dedicated to file-serving. It has a real-time operating system dedicated to file serving by using open-standard protocols. Some NAS vendors support features such as native clustering for high availability.

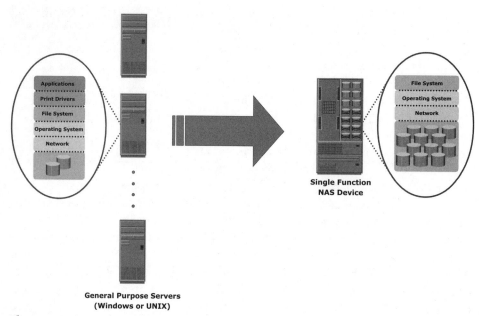

Figure 7-1: General purpose server vs. NAS device

7.2 Benefits of NAS

NAS offers the following benefits:

- **Supports comprehensive access to information:** Enables efficient file sharing and supports many-to-one and one-to-many configurations. The many-to-one configuration enables a NAS device to serve many clients simultaneously. The one-to-many configuration enables one client to connect with many NAS devices simultaneously.

- **Improved efficiency:** Eliminates bottlenecks that occur during file access from a general-purpose file server because NAS uses an operating system specialized for file serving. It improves the utilization of general-purpose servers by relieving them of file-server operations.

- **Improved flexibility:** Compatible for clients on both UNIX and Windows platforms using industry-standard protocols. NAS is flexible and can serve requests from different types of clients from the same source.

- **Centralized storage:** Centralizes data storage to minimize data duplication on client workstations, simplify data management, and ensures greater data protection.

- **Simplified management:** Provides a centralized console that makes it possible to manage file systems efficiently.

- **Scalability:** Scales well in accordance with different utilization profiles and types of business applications because of the high performance and low-latency design.

- **High availability:** Offers efficient replication and recovery options, enabling high data availability. NAS uses redundant networking components that provide maximum connectivity options. A NAS device can use clustering technology for failover.

- **Security:** Ensures security, user authentication, and file locking in conjunction with industry-standard security schemas.

7.3 NAS File I/O

NAS uses file-level access for all of its I/O operations. File I/O is a high-level request that specifies the file to be accessed, but does not specify its logical block address. For example, a file I/O request from a client may specify reading 256 bytes from byte number 1152 onward in a specific file. Unlike block I/O, there is no disk volume or disk sector information in a file I/O request. The NAS operating system keeps track of the location of files on the disk volume and converts client file I/O into block-level I/O to retrieve data.

The NAS operating system issues a block I/O request to fulfill the file read and write requests that it receives. The retrieved data is again converted to file-level I/O for applications and clients.

7.3.1 File Systems and Remote File Sharing

A file system is a structured way of storing and organizing data files. Many file systems maintain a file access table to simplify the process of finding and accessing files.

7.3.2 Accessing a File System

A file system must be mounted before it can be used. In most cases, the operating system mounts a local file system during the boot process. The mount process creates a link between the file system and the operating system. When mounting a file system, the operating system organizes files and directories in a tree-like structure and grants the user the privilege of accessing this structure. The tree is rooted at a mount point that is named using operating system conventions. Users and applications can traverse the entire tree from the root to the leaf nodes. Files are located at leaf nodes, and directories and subdirectories are located at intermediate roots. The relationship between the user and the file system terminates when the file system is unmounted. Figure 7-2 shows an example of the UNIX directory structure under UNIX operating environments.

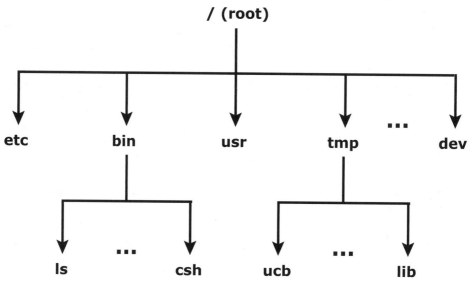

Figure 7-2: UNIX directory structure

7.3.3 File Sharing

File sharing refers to storing and accessing data files over a network. In a file-sharing environment, a user who creates the file (the creator or owner of a file) determines the type of access to be given to other users (read, write, execute, append, delete, and list) and controls changes to the file. When multiple users try to access a shared file at the same time, a protection scheme is required to maintain data integrity and, at the same time, make this sharing possible.

File Transfer Protocol (FTP), distributed file systems, and a client/server model that uses a file-sharing protocol are some examples of implementations of file-sharing environments.

FTP is a client/server protocol that enables data transfer over a network. An FTP server and an FTP client communicate with each other using TCP as the transport protocol. FTP, as defined by the standard, is not a secure method of data transfer because it uses unencrypted data transfer over a network. FTP over Secure Shell (SSH) adds security to the original FTP specification.

A *distributed file system (DFS)* is a file system that is distributed across several hosts. A DFS can provide hosts with direct access to the entire file system, while ensuring efficient management and data security.

The traditional *client/server model*, which is implemented with file-sharing protocols, is another mechanism for remote file sharing. In this model, the clients mount remote file systems that are available on dedicated file servers. The standard client/server file-sharing protocols are NFS for UNIX and CIFS for Windows. NFS and CIFS enable the owner of a file to set the required type of access, such as read-only or read-write, for a particular user or group of users.

In both of these implementations, users are unaware of the location of the file system. In addition, a *name service*, such as Domain Name System (DNS), Lightweight Directory Access Protocol (LDAP), and Network Information Services (NIS), helps users identify and access a unique resource over the network. A *naming service protocol* creates a namespace, which holds the unique name of every network resource and helps recognize resources on the network.

7.4 Components of NAS

A NAS device has the following components (see Figure 7-3):

■ NAS head (CPU and Memory)

■ One or more network interface cards (NICs), which provide connectivity to the network. Examples of NICs include Gigabit Ethernet, Fast Ethernet, ATM, and Fiber Distributed Data Interface (FDDI).

■ An optimized operating system for managing NAS functionality

■ NFS and CIFS protocols for file sharing

■ Industry-standard storage protocols to connect and manage physical disk resources, such as ATA, SCSI, or FC

The NAS environment includes clients accessing a NAS device over an IP network using standard protocols.

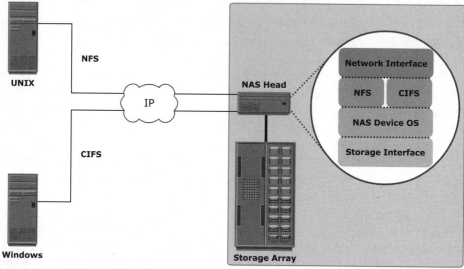

Figure 7-3: Components of NAS

7.5 NAS Implementations

As mentioned earlier, there are two types of NAS implementations: integrated and gateway. The *integrated NAS* device has all of its components and storage system in a single enclosure. In *gateway* implementation, NAS head shares its storage with SAN environment.

7.5.1 Integrated NAS

An integrated NAS device has all the components of NAS, such as the NAS head and storage, in a single enclosure, or frame. This makes the integrated NAS a self-contained environment. The NAS head connects to the IP network to provide connectivity to the clients and service the file I/O requests. The storage consists of a number of disks that can range from low-cost ATA to high-throughput FC disk drives. Management software manages the NAS head and storage configurations.

An integrated NAS solution ranges from a low-end device, which is a single enclosure, to a high-end solution that can have an externally connected storage array.

A low-end appliance-type NAS solution is suitable for applications that a small department may use, where the primary need is consolidation of storage, rather than high performance or advanced features such as disaster recovery and business continuity. This solution is fixed in capacity and might not be upgradable beyond its original configuration. To expand the capacity, the solution must be scaled by deploying additional units, a task that increases management overhead because multiple devices have to be administered.

In a high-end NAS solution, external and dedicated storage can be used. This enables independent scaling of the capacity in terms of NAS heads or storage. However, there is a limit to scalability of this solution.

7.5.2 Gateway NAS

A gateway NAS device consists of an independent NAS head and one or more storage arrays. The NAS head performs the same functions that it does in the integrated solution; while the storage is shared with other applications that require block-level I/O. Management functions in this type of solution are more complex than those in an integrated environment because there are separate administrative tasks for the NAS head and the storage. In addition to the components that are explicitly tied to the NAS solution, a gateway solution can also utilize the FC infrastructure, such as switches, directors, or direct-attached storage arrays.

The gateway NAS is the most scalable because NAS heads and storage arrays can be independently scaled up when required. Adding processing capacity to the NAS gateway is an example of scaling. When the storage limit is reached, it can scale up, adding capacity on the SAN independently of the NAS head. Administrators can increase performance and I/O processing capabilities for their environments without purchasing additional interconnect devices and storage. Gateway NAS enables high utilization of storage capacity by sharing it with SAN environment.

7.5.3 Integrated NAS Connectivity

An integrated solution is self-contained and can connect into a standard IP network. Although the specifics of how devices are connected within a NAS implementation vary by vendor and model. In some cases, storage is embedded within a NAS device and is connected to the NAS head through internal connections, such as ATA or SCSI controllers. In others, the storage may be external but connected by using SCSI controllers. In a high-end integrated NAS model, external storage can be directly connected by FC HBAs or by dedicated FC switches. In the case of a low-end integrated NAS model, backup traffic is shared on the same public IP network along with the regular client access traffic. In the case of a high-end integrated NAS model, an isolated backup network can be used to segment the traffic from impeding client access. More complex solutions may include an intelligent storage subsystem, enabling faster backup and larger capacities while simultaneously enhancing performance. Figure 7-4 illustrates an example of integrated NAS connectivity.

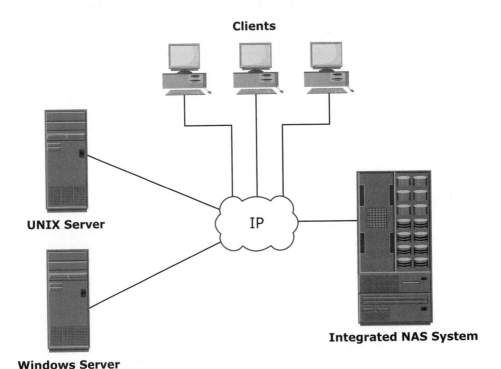

Figure 7-4: Integrated NAS connectivity

7.5.4 Gateway NAS Connectivity

In a gateway solution, front-end connectivity is similar to that in an integrated solution. An integrated environment has a fixed number of NAS heads, making it relatively easy to determine IP networking requirements. In contrast, networking requirements in a gateway environment are complex to determine due to scalability options. Adding more NAS heads may require additional networking connectivity and bandwidth.

Communication between the NAS gateway and the storage system in a gateway solution is achieved through a traditional FC SAN. To deploy a stable NAS solution, factors such as multiple paths for data, redundant fabrics, and load distribution must be considered. Figure 7-5 illustrates an example of gateway NAS connectivity.

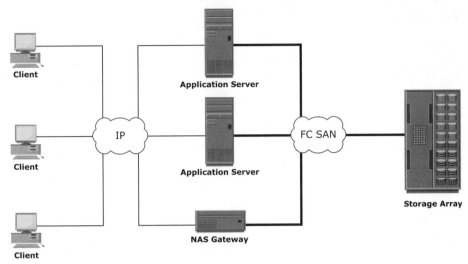

Figure 7-5: Gateway NAS connectivity

Implementation of a NAS gateway solution requires analysis of current SAN environment. This analysis is required to determine the feasibility of introducing a NAS workload to the existing SAN. Analyze the SAN to determine whether the workload is primarily read or write, or random or sequential. Determine the predominant I/O size in use. In general, sequential workloads have large I/Os. Typically, NAS workloads are random with small I/O size. Introducing sequential workload with random workloads can be disruptive to the sequential workload. Therefore, it is recommended to separate the NAS and SAN disks. Also, determine whether the NAS workload performs adequately with the configured cache in the storage subsystem.

7.6 NAS File-Sharing Protocols

Most NAS devices support multiple file service protocols to handle file I/O requests to a remote file system. As mentioned earlier, NFS and CIFS are the common protocols for file sharing. NFS is predominantly used in UNIX-based operating environments; CIFS is used in Microsoft Windows–based operating environments.

These file sharing protocols enable users to share file data across different operating environments and provide a means for users to migrate transparently from one operating system to another.

7.6.1 NFS

NFS is a client/server protocol for file sharing that is most commonly used on UNIX systems. NFS was originally based on the connectionless *User Datagram Protocol* (UDP). It uses a machine-independent model to represent user data. It also uses Remote Procedure Call (RPC) as a method of interprocess communication between two computers. The NFS protocol provides a set of RPCs to access a remote file system for the following operations:

- Searching files and directories
- Opening, reading, writing to, and closing a file
- Changing file attributes
- Modifying file links and directories

NFS uses the mount protocol to create a connection between the client and the remote system to transfer data. NFS (NFSv3 and earlier) is a *stateless* protocol, which means that it does not maintain any kind of table to store information about open files and associated pointers. Therefore, each call provides a full set of arguments to access files on the server. These arguments include a file name and a location, a particular position to read or write, and the versions of NFS.

Currently, three versions of NFS are in use:

- **NFS version 2 (NFSv2):** Uses UDP to provide a stateless network connection between a client and a server. Features such as locking are handled outside the protocol.

- **NFS version 3 (NFSv3):** The most commonly used version, it uses UDP or TCP, and is based on the stateless protocol design. It includes some new features, such as a 64-bit file size, asynchronous writes, and additional file attributes to reduce re-fetching.

- **NFS version 4 (NFSv4):** This version uses TCP and is based on a stateful protocol design. It offers enhanced security.

7.6.2 CIFS

CIFS is a client/server application protocol that enables client programs to make requests for files and services on remote computers over TCP/IP. It is a public, or open, variation of Server Message Block (SMB) protocol.

The CIFS protocol enables remote clients to gain access to files that are on a server. CIFS enables file sharing with other clients by using special locks.

File names in CIFS are encoded using unicode characters. CIFS provides the following features to ensure data integrity:

- It uses file and record locking to prevent users from overwriting the work of another user on a file or a record.

- It runs over TCP.

- It supports fault tolerance and can automatically restore connections and reopen files that were open prior to interruption. The fault tolerance features of CIFS depend on whether an application is written to take advantage of these features. Moreover, CIFS is a stateful protocol because the CIFS server maintains connection information regarding every connected client. In the event of a network failure or CIFS server failure, the client receives a disconnection notification. User disruption is minimized if the application has the embedded intelligence to restore the connection. However, if the embedded intelligence is missing, the user has to take steps to reestablish the CIFS connection.

  Users refer to remote file systems with an easy-to-use file naming scheme:

  `\\server\share or \\servername.domain.suffix\share.`

7.7 NAS I/O Operations

The NFS and CIFS protocols handle file I/O requests to a remote file system, which is managed by the NAS device. The process of NAS I/O is as follows:

1. The requestor packages an I/O request into TCP/IP and forwards it through the network stack. The NAS device receives this request from the network.

2. The NAS device converts the I/O request into an appropriate physical storage request, which is a block-level I/O, and then performs the operation against the physical storage pool.

3. When the data is returned from the physical storage pool, the NAS device processes and repackages the data into an appropriate file protocol response.

4. The NAS device packages this response into TCP/IP again and forwards it to the client through the network.

Figure 7-6 illustrates this process.

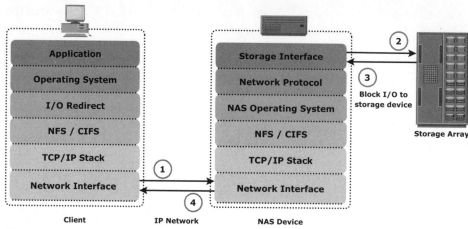

Figure 7-6: NAS I/O operation

7.7.1 Hosting and Accessing Files on NAS

Following are the steps required to host files and permit users to access the hosted files on a NAS device:

1. **Create storage array volumes:** Create volumes on the storage array and assign Logical Unit Numbers (LUN) to the volumes. Present the newly created volumes to the NAS device.

2. **Create NAS Volumes:** Perform a discovery operation on the NAS device, to recognize the new array-volumes and create NAS Volumes (logical volumes). Multiple volumes from the storage array may be combined to form large NAS volumes.

3. **Create NAS file systems:** Create NAS file systems on the NAS volumes.

4. **Mount file systems:** Mount the created NAS file system on the NAS device.

5. **Access the file systems:** Publish the mounted file systems on the network using NFS or CIFS for client access.

7.8 Factors Affecting NAS Performance and Availability

As NAS uses IP network, bandwidth and latency issues associated with IP affect NAS performance. Network congestion is one of the most significant sources of latency (Figure 7-7) in a NAS environment. Other factors that affect NAS performance at different levels are:

1. **Number of hops:** A large number of hops can increase latency because IP processing is required at each hop, adding to the delay caused at the router.

2. **Authentication with a directory service such as LDAP, Active Directory, or NIS:** The authentication service must be available on the network, with adequate bandwidth, and must have enough resources to accommodate the authentication load. Otherwise, a large number of authentication requests are presented to the servers, increasing latency. Authentication adds to latency only when authentication occurs.

3. **Retransmission:** Link errors, buffer overflows, and flow control mechanisms can result in retransmission. This causes packets that have not reached the specified destination to be resent. Care must be taken when configuring parameters for speed and duplex settings on the network devices and the NAS heads so that they match. Improper configuration may result in errors and retransmission, adding to latency.

4. **Overutilized routers and switches:** The amount of time that an overutilized device in a network takes to respond is always more than the response time of an optimally utilized or underutilized device. Network administrators can view vendor-specific statistics to determine the utilization of switches and routers in a network. Additional devices should be added if the current devices are overutilized.

5. **File/directory lookup and metadata requests:** NAS clients access files on NAS devices. The processing required before reaching the appropriate file or directory can cause delays. Sometimes a delay is caused by deep directory structures and can be resolved by flattening the directory structure. Poor file system layout and an overutilized disk system can also degrade performance.

6. **Overutilized NAS devices:** Clients accessing multiple files can cause high utilization levels on a NAS device which can be determined by viewing utilization statistics. High utilization levels can be caused by a poor file system structure or insufficient resources in a storage subsystem.

7. **Overutilized clients:** The client accessing CIFS or NFS data may also be overutilized. An overutilized client requires longer time to process the responses received from the server, increasing latency. Specific performance-monitoring tools are available for various operating systems to help determine the utilization of client resources.

Configuring VLANs and setting proper Maximum Transmission Unit (MTU) and TCP window size can improve NAS performance. Link aggregation and redundant network configurations ensure high availability.

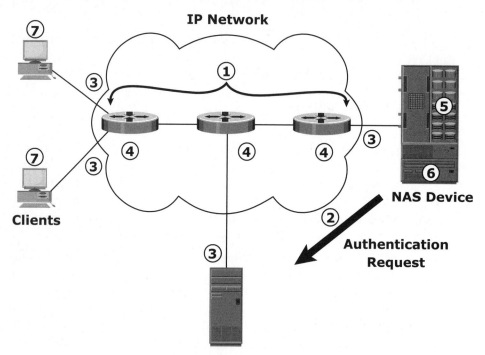

Figure 7-7: Causes of latency

A *virtual LAN (VLAN)* is a switched network that is logically segmented by functions, project teams, or applications, regardless of the user's physical location. A VLAN is similar to a physical LAN except that the VLAN enables the grouping of end stations even if they are not physically located on the same network segment. VLAN is a layer 2 (data link layer) construct. A network switch can be divided among multiple VLANs, enabling better utilization of port density and reducing the overall cost of deploying a network infrastructure.

A VLAN can control the overall broadcast traffic. The broadcast traffic on one VLAN is not transmitted outside that VLAN, which substantially reduces broadcast overhead, makes bandwidth available for applications, and reduces the network's vulnerability to broadcast storms.

VLANs are also used to provide security firewalls, restrict individual user access, flag network intrusions, and control the size and composition of the broadcast domain.

The *MTU* setting determines the size of the largest packet that can be transmitted without data fragmentation. *Path maximum transmission unit discovery* is the process of discovering the maximum size of a packet that can be sent across a network without fragmentation. The default MTU settings are specific for each protocol and depend on the type of NIC installed. The default MTU setting for an Ethernet interface card is 1,500 bytes. A feature called *jumbo frames* is used to send, receive, or transport Ethernet frames with an MTU of more than 1,500 bytes. The most common deployments of jumbo frames have an MTU of 9,000 bytes. Servers send and receive larger frames more efficiently than smaller ones in heavy network traffic conditions. Jumbo frames ensure increased efficiency because it takes fewer, larger frames to transfer the same amount of data, just as with existing Ethernet packets. Larger packets also reduce the amount of raw network bandwidth being consumed for the same amount of payload. Larger frames also help smooth the sudden I/O bursts.

The *TCP window size* is the maximum amount of data that can be on the network at any time for a connection. For example, if a pair of hosts is talking over a TCP connection that has a TCP window size of 64 KB, the sender can send only 64 KB of data and must then wait for an acknowledgment from the receiver. If the receiver acknowledges that all the data has been received, then the sender is free to send another 64 KB of data. If the sender receives an acknowledgment from the receiver that only the first 32 KB of data has been received, which can happen only if another 32 KB of data is in transit or was lost, the sender can only send another 32 KB of data because the transmission cannot have more than 64 KB of unacknowledged data outstanding.

In theory, the TCP window size should be set to the product of the available bandwidth of the network and the round-trip time of data sent over the network. For example, if a network has a bandwidth of 100 Mbps and the round-trip time is 5 milliseconds, the TCP window should be as follows:

100 Mb/s × .005 seconds = 524,288 bits

524,288 bits / 8 bits/byte = 65,536 bytes

The size of TCP window field that controls the flow of data is between 2 bytes and 65,535 bytes.

Link aggregation is the process of combining two or more network interfaces into a logical network interface, enabling higher throughput, load sharing or load balancing, transparent path failover, and scalability. Link aggregation in a NAS device combines channels to achieve redundancy of network connectivity. Due to link aggregation, multiple active Ethernet connections to the same switch appear as one link. If a connection or a port in the aggregation is lost, then all the network traffic on that link is redistributed across the remaining active connections. The primary purpose of the aggregation is high availability.

7.9 Concepts in Practice: EMC Celerra

EMC offers NAS solutions with the Celerra family of products. Celerra is available in either a gateway or an integrated configuration. EMC Celerra provides a dedicated, high-performance, high-speed communication infrastructure for file level I/Os. It uses a significantly streamlined or tuned operating system. It supports Network Data Management Protocol (NDMP) for backup, CIFS, NFS, FTP, and iSCSI. Celerra supports Fast Ethernet Channel by using PAgP or IEEE 802.3ad LACP to combine two or more data channels into one data channel for high availability. Visit `http://education.EMC.com/ismbook` for the latest information.

7.9.1 Architecture

Celerra consists of a Control Station and NAS heads (Data Movers). The *Data Mover* is a network and storage interface device and the *control station* is a management interface device.

Data Mover

The Data Mover is an independent, autonomous file server that transfers requested files to clients. Figure 7-8 shows the NS40 and NSX blade Data Movers. *Data Access in Real Time (DART)* is Celerra's specialized operating system, which runs on the Data Mover. This operating system is optimized for performing file operations to move data from the storage array to the network. DART supports standard network file access protocols, such as NFS, CIFS, and FTP.

Celerra can be configured as a network fail-safe device; DART minimizes disruption to data access caused by network failures. A logical device is created using physical ports or logical ports combined together to create redundant groups of ports. The logically grouped Data Mover network ports monitor network traffic on the ports. Celerra also contains an active fail-safe device port, which can sense traffic disruption. The standby or non-active port assumes the IP address and the MAC address, minimizing disruption to data access. Features of the Celerra Data Mover include the following:

- Dual Intel processors
- PCI or PCI-X support
- High-memory capacity
- Multiport network cards
- Fibre Channel connectivity to storage arrays
- A highly specialized operating system (DART)

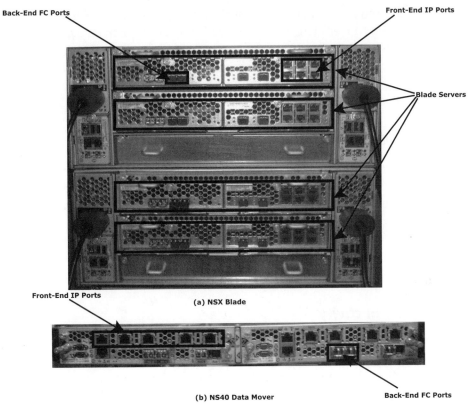

Back-End FC Ports

Front-End IP Ports

Blade Servers

Front-End IP Ports

(a) NSX Blade

(b) NS40 Data Mover

Back-End FC Ports

Figure 7-8: Celerra Data Mover

Creating and accessing a file system are the two important *client access functions* of the Celerra Data Mover. Creation of file systems is accomplished either manually or by using Automatic Volume Management (AVM). Accessing file systems is accomplished by performing an export in the UNIX environment or by publishing a share in the Microsoft Windows environment.

The Data Mover enables creation of multiple *virtual Data Movers* on a single physical Data Mover. A virtual Data Mover creates multiple virtual CIFS servers on each virtual Data Mover. The virtual Data Mover consolidates the file-serving functionality of multiple servers onto a Data Mover because each virtual Data Mover can maintain isolated CIFS servers with their own root file system environments. The virtual Data Mover also enables entire virtual environments to be loaded, unloaded, or even replicated between physical Data Movers.

The Celerra Data Mover offers two configuration options for NAS environments: a primary Data Mover or a standby Data Mover. A standby Data Mover can be configured as a primary Data Mover for high availability configurations. A standby Data Mover is also provided for a group of primary Data Movers. Celerra Data Movers operate in one of the three modes, which affect the process of failover. In *Automatic mode,* the failover process occurs without first trying recovery; in *Retry mode,* the Data Mover is rebooted before failover; and in *Manual mode,* the failover is done manually.

Control Station

The *control station* provides dedicated processing capabilities to control, manage, and configure a NAS solution. The control station hosts the Linux operating system that is used to install, manage, and configure Data Movers and monitor the environmental conditions and performance of all components. The control station also provides high-availability features such as fault monitoring, fault recovery, fault reporting, call home, and remote diagnostics. Administrative functions are also accessible through the local console, SSH, or a Web browser.

Storage Connectivity

Celerra data movers connect to storage in two ways: integrated and gateway. In the integrated configuration, dedicated storage is assigned to Celerra (see Figure 7-9[a]). In this configuration, the control station is connected to the Data Movers via a private, internal IP network. Each Data Mover is directly connected to the storage array through dual Fibre Channel connections. The Data Movers provide an interface for the control station through both an internal Ethernet and a serial connection.

After DART is loaded, the Data Movers can be connected to the client network. The Data Movers are connected to the control station for remote management. The physical disks on the storage array are then partitioned through commands from the control station to create system volumes and data volumes for client access.

In a gateway configuration, Celerra is assigned separately provisioned storage within a shared storage array. Any capacity remaining within the array can be assigned to the conventional SAN hosts that are connected to the Fibre Switch (see Figure 7-9[b]) after appropriate zoning and LUN masking is performed. Each Data Mover is dual-connected to the storage array for redundancy through one or more Fibre Channel switches in the gateway configuration.

Client access and configuration steps are similar to that of an integrated connect.

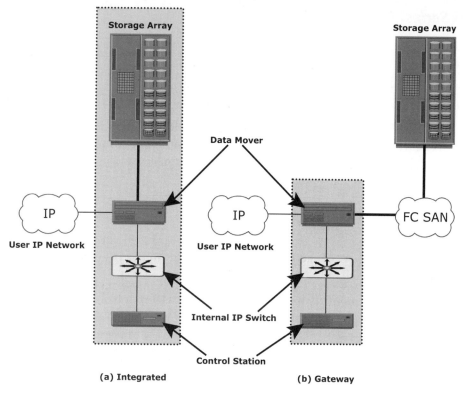

Figure 7-9: Celerra integrated and gateway connect

7.9.2 Celerra Product Family

This section describes some of the integrated and gateway NAS products available from EMC.

NS Series: Integrated

The back-end storage is directly connected to Celerra in the NS Series. The following models are offered:

- **NS20:** The NS20 comes in either an NS20 or an NS20FC configuration, and can have one or two X-Blade (Data Movers), and a single control station.

- **NS40:** This has a single or dual X-Blade configuration. This series provides high performance and capacity.

NS Series: Gateway

Gateway Data Movers share the back-end storage with the SAN hosts. The following models are offered:

- **NS40G:** This is an entry-level gateway, which delivers high performance, provides high availability, and requires simple management.
- **NSX:** The NSX system is the most highly redundant model in the Celerra family of products. It supports 4–8 X-Blades that come in an X-Blade Enclosure, and provides redundant management switches in each enclosure and dual control stations.

7.9.3 Celerra Management Software

EMC Celerra can be managed through either a command-line interface or the Celerra Manager GUI.

- **CLI Management:** This can be accessed from the control station through the SSH (secure shell) interface tool, or PUTTY. CLI can be used for scripting common repetitive tasks that may run on a predetermined schedule to ease administrative burdens. It has approximately 80 UNIX-like commands.
- **GUI Management—Celerra Manager:** GUI management through the Celerra Manager has the following two options—*Celerra Manager Basic Edition,* or *Celerra Manager Advanced Edition,* which is licensed separately and provides advanced features.

Summary

Decisions regarding storage infrastructure are based on maintaining the balance between cost and performance. Organizations look for the performance and scalability of SAN combined with the ease of use and lower total cost of ownership of NAS solutions. The convergence of SAN and NAS is inevitable because of advances in storage networking technology. Both SAN and NAS have enjoyed unique advantages in enterprises, and the advances in IP technology have scaled NAS solutions to meet the demands of performance-sensitive applications.

Cost and ease of use drive the application's needs in terms of performance and capacity. Although NAS invariably imposes higher protocol overhead, NAS applications tend to be most efficient for file-sharing tasks, such as NFS in UNIX, and CIFS in Microsoft Windows. Network-based locking at the file level provides a high level of concurrent access protection. NAS can also be optimized to deliver file information to many clients with file-level protection. Two common applications that utilize the effectiveness of NAS include hosting home directories and providing a data store for static Web pages that are accessed by different Web servers. In certain situations, organizations can deploy NAS solutions for database applications in a limited manner. These situations are usually limited to applications for which the majority of data access is read-only, the databases are small, access volume is low, and predictable performance is not mandatory. In this type of situation, NAS solutions can reduce overall storage costs.

Careful evaluation of emerging trends in the networking and storage industry is imperative when selecting the appropriate technology. Along with the need for high performance, ease of management and sharing of data are also increasing. The choice of technology should balance these requirements; consider the complexity and maturity of the technology that is deployed. IP-SAN, detailed in the following chapter, is an emerging technology that has matured to meet enterprise demands.

EXERCISES

1. List and explain the considerations for capacity design for both CPU and storage in a NAS environment.

2. SAN is configured for a backup to disk environment, and the storage configuration has additional capacity available. Can you have a NAS gateway configuration use this SAN? Discuss the implications of sharing the backup-to-disk SAN environment with NAS.

3. Explain how the performance of NAS can be affected if the TCP window size at the sender and the receiver are not synchronized.

4. Research the use of baby jumbo frames and how it affects NAS performance.

5. Research the file sharing features of the NFS protocol.

6. A NAS implementation configured jumbo frames on the NAS head, with 9,000 as its MTU. However, the implementers did not see any performance improvement and actually experienced performance degradation. What could be the cause? Research the end-to-end jumbo frame support requirements in a network.

7. Acme Corporation is trying to decide between an integrated or a gateway NAS solution. The existing SAN at Acme will provide capacity and scalability. The IT department is considering a NAS solution for the Training department at Acme for training videos. The videos would only be used by the training department for evaluation of instructors. Pick a NAS solution and explain the reasons for your choice.

Chapter 8
IP SAN

Traditional SAN environments allow block I/O over Fibre Channel, whereas NAS environments allow file I/O over IP-based networks. Organizations need the performance and scalability of SAN plus the ease of use and lower TCO of NAS solutions. The emergence of IP technology that supports block I/O over IP has positioned IP for storage solutions.

KEY CONCEPTS
iSCSI Protocol
Native and Bridged iSCSI
FCIP Protocol

IP offers easier management and better interoperability. When block I/O is run over IP, the existing network infrastructure can be leveraged, which is more economical than investing in new SAN hardware and software. Many long-distance, disaster recovery (DR) solutions are already leveraging IP-based networks. In addition, many robust and mature security options are now available for IP networks. With the advent of block storage technology that leverages IP networks (the result is often referred to as IP SAN), organizations can extend the geographical reach of their storage infrastructure.

IP SAN technologies can be used in a variety of situations. Figure 8-1 illustrates the co-existence of FC and IP storage technologies in an organization where mission-critical applications are serviced through FC, and business-critical applications and remote office applications make use of IP SAN. Disaster recovery solutions can also be implemented using both of these technologies.

Two primary protocols that leverage IP as the transport mechanism are iSCSI and Fibre Channel over IP (FCIP).

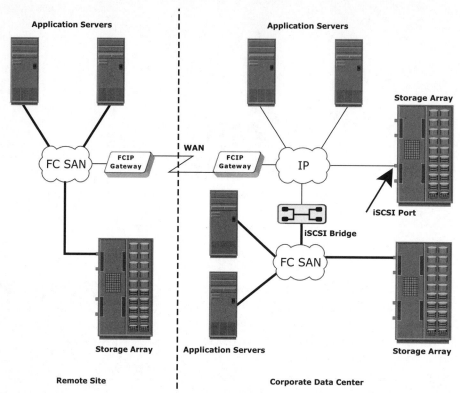

Figure 8-1: Co-existance of FC and IP storage technologies

iSCSI is the host-based encapsulation of SCSI I/O over IP using an Ethernet NIC card or an iSCSI HBA in the host. As illustrated in Figure 8-2 (a), IP traffic is routed over a network either to a gateway device that extracts the SCSI I/O from the IP packets or to an iSCSI storage array. The gateway can then send the SCSI I/O to an FC-based external storage array, whereas an iSCSI storage array can handle the extraction and I/O natively.

FCIP uses a pair of bridges (FCIP gateways) communicating over TCP/IP as the transport protocol. FCIP is used to extend FC networks over distances and/or an existing IP-based infrastructure, as illustrated in Figure 8-2 (b).

Today, iSCSI is widely adopted for connecting servers to storage because it is relatively inexpensive and easy to implement, especially in environments where an FC SAN does not exist. FCIP is extensively used in disaster-recovery implementations, where data is duplicated on disk or tape to an alternate site. This chapter describes iSCSI and FCIP protocols, components and topologies in detail.

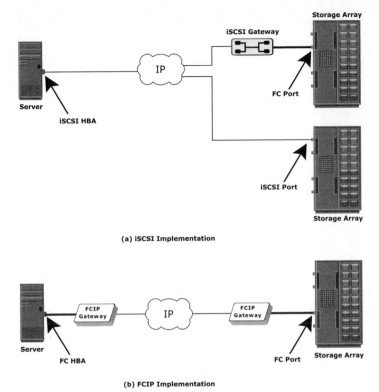

Figure 8-2: iSCSI and FCIP implementation

8.1 iSCSI

iSCSI is an IP-based protocol that establishes and manages connections between storage, hosts, and bridging devices over IP. iSCSI carries block-level data over IP-based networks, including Ethernet networks and the Internet. iSCSI is built on the SCSI protocol by encapsulating SCSI commands and data in order to allow these encapsulated commands and data blocks to be transported using TCP/IP packets.

8.1.1 Components of iSCSI

Host (initiators), targets, and an IP-based network are the principal iSCSI components. The simplest iSCSI implementation does not require any FC components. If an iSCSI-capable storage array is deployed, a host itself can act as an iSCSI initiator, and directly communicate with the storage over an IP network. However, in complex implementations that use an existing FC array for iSCSI connectivity, iSCSI gateways or routers are used to connect the existing FC SAN. These devices perform protocol translation from IP packets to FC packets and vice-versa, thereby bridging connectivity between the IP and FC environments.

8.1.2 iSCSI Host Connectivity

iSCSI host connectivity requires a hardware component, such as a NIC with a software component (iSCSI initiator) or an iSCSI HBA. In order to use the iSCSI protocol, a software initiator or a translator must be installed to route the SCSI commands to the TCP/IP stack.

A standard NIC, a TCP/IP offload engine (TOE) NIC card, and an iSCSI HBA are the three physical iSCSI connectivity options.

A standard NIC is the simplest and least expensive connectivity option. It is easy to implement because most servers come with at least one, and in many cases two, embedded NICs. It requires only a software initiator for iSCSI functionality. However, the NIC provides no external processing power, which places additional overhead on the host CPU because it is required to perform all the TCP/IP and iSCSI processing.

If a standard NIC is used in heavy I/O load situations, the host CPU may become a bottleneck. *TOE NIC* help alleviate this burden. A TOE NIC offloads the TCP management functions from the host and leaves iSCSI functionality to the host processor. The host passes the iSCSI information to the TOE card and the TOE card sends the information to the destination using TCP/IP. Although this solution improves performance, the iSCSI functionality is still handled by a software initiator, requiring host CPU cycles.

An *iSCSI HBA* is capable of providing performance benefits, as it offloads the entire iSCSI and TCP/IP protocol stack from the host processor. Use of an iSCSI HBA is also the simplest way for implementing a boot from SAN environment via iSCSI. If there is no iSCSI HBA, modifications have to be made to the basic operating system to boot a host from the storage devices because the NIC needs to obtain an IP address before the operating system loads. The functionality of an iSCSI HBA is very similar to the functionality of an FC HBA, but it is the most expensive option.

A fault-tolerant host connectivity solution can be implemented using host-based multipathing software (e.g., EMC PowerPath) regardless of the type of physical connectivity. Multiple NICs can also be combined via link aggregation technologies to provide failover or load balancing. Complex solutions may also include the use of vendor-specific storage-array software that enables the iSCSI host to connect to multiple ports on the array with multiple NICs or HBAs.

8.1.3 Topologies for iSCSI Connectivity

The topologies used to implement iSCSI can be categorized into two classes: native and bridged. *Native topologies* do not have any FC components; they perform all communication over IP. The initiators may be either directly attached to targets or connected using standard IP routers and switches. *Bridged topologies* enable the co-existence of FC with IP by providing iSCSI-to-FC bridging functionality. For example, the initiators can exist in an IP environment while the storage remains in an FC SAN.

Native iSCSI Connectivity

If an iSCSI-enabled array is deployed, FC components are not needed for iSCSI connectivity in the native topology. In the example shown in Figure 8-3 (a), the array has one or more Ethernet NICs that are connected to a standard Ethernet switch and configured with an IP address and listening port. Once a client/initiator is configured with the appropriate target information, it connects to the array and requests a list of available LUNs. A single array port can service multiple hosts or initiators as long as the array can handle the amount of storage traffic that the hosts generate.

Many arrays provide more than one interface so that they can be configured in a highly available design or have multiple targets configured on the initiator. Some NAS devices are also capable of functioning as iSCSI targets, enabling file-level and block-level access to centralized storage. This offers additional storage options for environments with integrated NAS devices or environments that don't have an iSCSI/FC bridge.

Bridged iSCSI Connectivity

A bridged iSCSI implementation includes FC components in its configuration. Figure 8-3 (b) illustrates an existing FC storage array used to service hosts connected through iSCSI.

The array does not have any native iSCSI capabilities—that is, it does not have any Ethernet ports. Therefore, an external device, called a bridge, router, gateway, or a multi-protocol router, must be used to bridge the communication from the IP network to the FC SAN. These devices can be a stand-alone unit, or in many cases are integrated with an existing FC switch. In this configuration, the bridge device has Ethernet ports connected to the IP network, and FC ports connected to the storage. These ports are assigned IP addresses, similar to the ports on an iSCSI-enabled array.

The iSCSI initiator/host is configured with the bridge's IP address as its target destination. The bridge is also configured with an FC initiator or multiple initiators. These are called *virtual initiators* because there is no physical device, such as an HBA, to generate the initiator record.

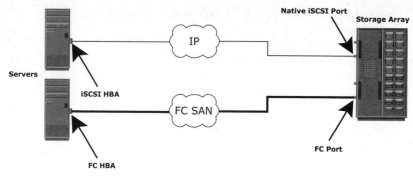

(a) Native iSCSI Connectivity

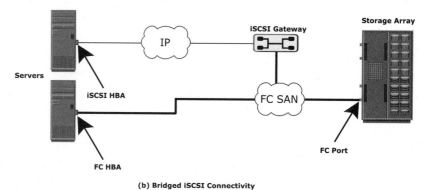

(b) Bridged iSCSI Connectivity

Figure 8-3: Native and bridged iSCSI connectivity

Combining FCP and Native iSCSI Connectivity

A combination topology can also be implemented. In this case, a storage array capable of connecting the FC and iSCSI hosts without the need for external bridging devices is needed (see Figure 8-3 [a]). These solutions reduce complexity, as they remove the need for configuring bridges. However, additional processing requirements are placed on the storage array because it has to accommodate the iSCSI traffic along with the standard FC traffic.

8.1.4 iSCSI Protocol Stack

The architecture of iSCSI is based on the client/server model. Figure 8-4 displays a model of the iSCSI protocol layers and depicts the encapsulation order of SCSI commands for their delivery through a physical carrier.

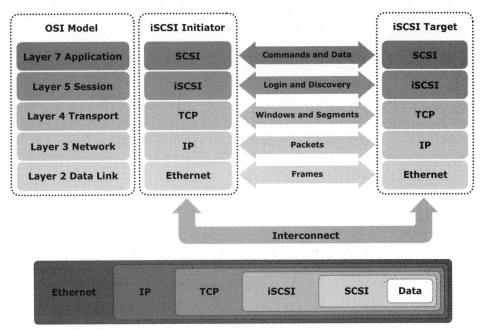

Figure 8-4: iSCSI protocol stack

SCSI is the command protocol that works at the application layer of the OSI model. The initiators and targets use SCSI commands and responses to talk to each other. The SCSI command descriptor blocks, data, and status messages are encapsulated into TCP/IP and transmitted across the network between initiators and targets.

iSCSI is the session-layer protocol that initiates a reliable session between a device that recognizes SCSI commands and TCP/IP. The iSCSI session-layer interface is responsible for handling login, authentication, target discovery, and session management. TCP is used with iSCSI at the transport layer to provide reliable service.

TCP is used to control message flow, windowing, error recovery, and retransmission. It relies upon the network layer of the OSI model to provide global addressing and connectivity. The layer-2 protocols at the data link layer of this model enable node-to-node communication for each hop through a separate physical network.

Communication between an iSCSI initiator and target is detailed next.

8.1.5 iSCSI Discovery

An initiator must discover the location of the target on a network, and the names of the targets available to it before it can establish a session. This discovery can take place in two ways: *SendTargets discovery* and *internet Storage Name Service (iSNS)*.

In SendTargets discovery, the initiator is manually configured with the target's network portal, which it uses to establish a discovery session with the iSCSI service on the target. The initiator issues the `SendTargets` command, and the target responds with the names and addresses of the targets available to the host.

iSNS (see Figure 8-5) enables the automatic discovery of iSCSI devices on an IP network. The initiators and targets can be configured to automatically register themselves with the iSNS server. Whenever an initiator wants to know the targets that it can access, it can query the iSNS server for a list of available targets.

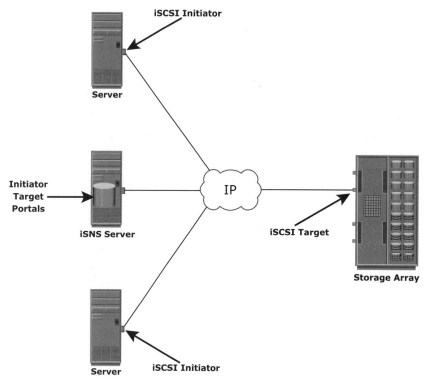

Figure 8-5: Discovery using iSNS

Discovery can also take place by using Service Location Protocol (SLP). However, this is less commonly used than `SendTargets` discovery and iSNS.

8.1.6 iSCSI Names

A unique worldwide iSCSI identifier, known as an *iSCSI name*, is used to name the initiators and targets within an iSCSI network to facilitate communication. The unique identifier can be a combination of department, application, manufacturer name, serial number, asset number, or any tag that can be used to recognize and manage a storage resource. There are two types of iSCSI names:

- **iSCSI Qualified Name (IQN):** An organization must own a registered domain name in order to generate iSCSI Qualified Names. This domain name does not have to be active or resolve to an address. It just needs to be reserved to prevent other organizations from using the same domain name to generate iSCSI names. A date is included in the name to avoid potential conflicts caused by transfer of domain names; the organization is required to have owned the domain name on that date. An example of an IQN is

  `iqn.2008-02.com.example:optional_string`

  The `optional_string` provides a serial number, an asset number, or any of the storage device identifiers.

- **Extended Unique Identifier (EUI):** An EUI is a globally unique identifier based on the IEEE EUI-64 naming standard. An EUI comprises the eui prefix followed by a 16-character hexadecimal name, such as `eui.0300732A32598D26`.

  The 16-character part of the name includes 24 bits for the company name assigned by IEEE and 40 bits for a unique ID, such as a serial number. This allows for a more streamlined, although less user-friendly, name string because the resulting iSCSI name is simply eui followed by the hexadecimal WWN.

In either format, the allowed special characters are dots, dashes, and blank spaces. The iSCSI Qualified Name enables storage administrators to assign meaningful names to storage devices, and therefore manage those devices more easily.

Network Address Authority (NAA) is an additional iSCSI node name type to enable worldwide naming format as defined by the InterNational Committee for Information Technology Standards (INCITS) T11 - Fibre Channel (FC) protocols and used by Serial Attached SCSI (SAS). This format enables SCSI storage devices containing both iSCSI ports and SAS ports to use the same NAA-based SCSI device name. This format is defined by RFC3980, "T11 Network Address Authority (NAA) Naming Format for iSCSI Node Names."

8.1.7 iSCSI Session

An iSCSI session is established between an initiator and a target. A session ID (SSID), which includes an initiator ID (ISID) and a target ID (TSID), identifies a session. The session can be intended for one of the following:

▪ Discovery of available targets to the initiator and the location of a specific target on a network

▪ Normal operation of iSCSI (transferring data between initiators and targets)

TCP connections may be added and removed within a session. Each iSCSI connection within the session has a unique connection ID (CID).

8.1.8 iSCSI PDU

iSCSI initiators and targets communicate using iSCSI Protocol Data Units (PDUs). All iSCSI PDUs contain one or more header segments followed by zero or more data segments. The PDU is then encapsulated into an IP packet to facilitate the transport.

A PDU includes the components shown in Figure 8-6. The IP header provides packet-routing information that is used to move the packet across a network. The TCP header contains the information needed to guarantee the packet's delivery to the target. The iSCSI header describes how to extract SCSI commands and data for the target. iSCSI adds an optional CRC, known as the *digest*, beyond the TCP checksum and Ethernet CRC to ensure datagram integrity. The header and the data digests are optionally used in the PDU to validate integrity, data placement, and correct operation.

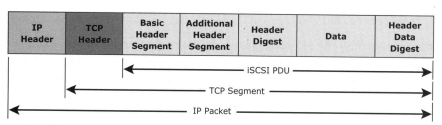

Figure 8-6: iSCSI PDU encapsulated in an IP packet

A message that is transmitted on a network is divided into a number of packets. If necessary, each packet can be sent by a different route across the network. Packets can arrive in a different order than the order in which they were sent. IP just delivers them. It's up to TCP to put them back in the right sequence. The target extracts the SCSI commands and data on the basis of information in the iSCSI header.

As shown in Figure 8-7, each iSCSI PDU does not correspond in a 1:1 relationship with an IP packet. Depending on its size, an iSCSI PDU can span an IP packet or even coexist with another PDU in the same packet. Therefore, each IP packet and Ethernet frame can be used more efficiently because fewer packets and frames are required to transmit the SCSI information.

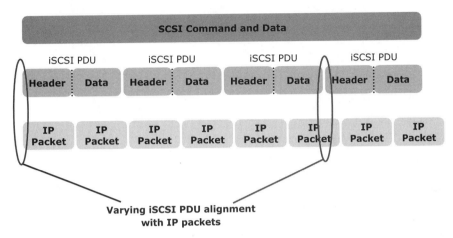

Figure 8-7: Alignment of iSCSI PDUs with IP packets

8.1.9 Ordering and Numbering

iSCSI communication between initiators and targets is based on the request-response command sequences. A command sequence may generate multiple PDUs. A *command sequence number (CmdSN)* within an iSCSI session is used to number all initiator-to-target command PDUs belonging to the session. This number is used to ensure that every command is delivered in the same order in which it is transmitted, regardless of the TCP connection that carries the command in the session.

Command sequencing begins with the first login command and the CmdSN is incremented by one for each subsequent command. The iSCSI target layer is responsible for delivering the commands to the SCSI layer in the order of their CmdSN. This ensures the correct order of data and commands at a target even when there are multiple TCP connections between an initiator and the target using portal groups.

Similar to command numbering, a *status sequence number (StatSN)* is used to sequentially number status responses, as shown in Figure 8-8. These unique numbers are established at the level of the TCP connection.

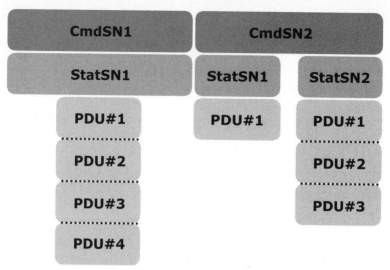

Figure 8-8: Command and status sequence number

A target sends the *request-to-transfer (R2T)* PDUs to the initiator when it is ready to accept data. *Data sequence number (DataSN)* is used to ensure in-order delivery of data within the same command. The DataSN and R2T sequence numbers are used to sequence data PDUs and R2Ts, respectively. Each of these sequence numbers is stored locally as an unsigned 32-bit integer counter defined by iSCSI. These numbers are communicated between the initiator and target in the appropriate iSCSI PDU fields during command, status, and data exchanges.

In the case of read operations, the DataSN begins at zero and is incremented by one for each subsequent data PDU in that command sequence. In the case of a write operation, the first unsolicited data PDU or the first data PDU in response to an R2T begins with a DataSN of zero and increments by one for each subsequent data PDU. R2TSN is set to zero at the initiation of the command and incremented by one for each subsequent R2T sent by the target for that command.

8.1.10 iSCSI Error Handling and Security

The iSCSI protocol addresses errors in IP data delivery. Command sequencing is used for flow control, the missing commands, and responses, and data blocks are detected using sequence numbers. Use of the optional digest improves communication integrity in addition to TCP checksum and Ethernet CRC.

The error detection and recovery in iSCSI can be classified into three levels: Level 0 = Session Recovery, Level 1 = Digest Failure Recovery and Level 2 = Connection Recovery. The error-recovery level is negotiated during login.

- **Level 0:** If an iSCSI session is damaged, all TCP connections need to be closed and all tasks and unfulfilled SCSI commands should be completed. Then, the session should be restarted via the repeated login.

- **Level 1:** Each node should be able to selectively recover a lost or damaged PDU within a session for recovery of data transfer. At this level, identification of an error and data recovery at the SCSI task level is performed, and an attempt to repeat the transfer of a lost or damaged PDU is made.

- **Level 2:** New TCP connections are opened to replace a failed connection. The new connection picks up where the old one failed.

iSCSI may be exposed to the security vulnerabilities of an unprotected IP network. Some of the security methods that can be used are IPSec and authentication solutions such as Kerberos and CHAP (challenge-handshake authentication protocol).

8.2 FCIP

Organizations are now looking for new ways to transport data throughout the enterprise, locally over the SAN as well as over longer distances, to ensure that data reaches all the users who need it. One of the best ways to achieve this goal is to interconnect geographically dispersed SANs through reliable, high-speed links. This approach involves transporting FC block data over the existing IP infrastructure used throughout the enterprise.

The FCIP standard has rapidly gained acceptance as a manageable, cost-effective way to blend the best of two worlds: FC block-data storage and the proven, widely deployed IP infrastructure. FCIP is a tunneling protocol that enables distributed FC SAN islands to be transparently interconnected over existing IP-based local, metropolitan, and wide-area networks. As a result, organizations now have a better way to protect, store, and move their data while leveraging investments in existing technology.

FCIP uses TCP/IP as its underlying protocol. In FCIP, the FC frames are encapsulated onto the IP payload, as shown in Figure 8-9. FCIP does not manipulate FC frames (translating FC IDs for transmission).

When SAN islands are connected using FCIP, each interconnection is called an *FCIP link*. A successful FCIP link between two SAN islands results in a fully merged FC fabric.

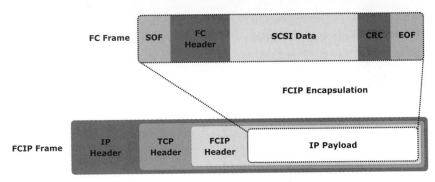

Figure 8-9: FCIP encapsulation

 FCIP may require high network bandwidth when merging SANs or replicating or backing up data. FCIP does not handle data traffic throttling or flow control; these are controlled by the communicating FC switches and devices within the fabric.

8.2.1 FCIP Topology

An FCIP environment functions as if it is a single cohesive SAN environment. Before geographically dispersed SANs are merged, a fully functional layer 2 network exists on the SANs. This layer 2 network is a standard SAN fabric. These physically independent fabrics are merged into a single fabric with an IP link between them.

An FCIP gateway router is connected to each fabric via a standard FC connection (see Figure 8-10). The fabric treats these routers like layer 2 fabric switches. The other port on the router is connected to an IP network and an IP address is assigned to that port. This is similar to the method of assigning an IP address to an iSCSI port on a gateway. Once IP connectivity is established, the two independent fabrics are merged into a single fabric. When merging the two fabrics, all the switches and routers must have unique domain IDs, and the fabrics must contain unique zone set names. Failure to ensure these requirements will result in a segmented fabric. The FC addresses on each side of the link are exposed to the other side, and zoning or masking can be done to any entity in the new environment.

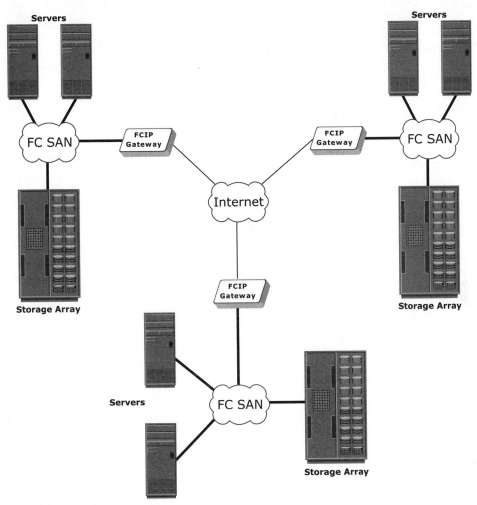

Figure 8-10: FCIP topology

8.2.2 FCIP Performance and Security

Performance, reliability, and security should always be taken into consideration when implementing storage solutions. The implementation of FCIP is also subject to the same consideration.

From the perspective of performance, multiple paths to multiple FCIP gateways from different switches in the layer 2 fabric eliminates single points of failure and provides increased bandwidth. In a scenario of extended distance, the IP network may be a bottleneck if sufficient bandwidth is not available. In addition, because FCIP creates a unified fabric, disruption in the underlying IP network can cause instabilities in the SAN environment. These include a segmented fabric, excessive RSCNs, and host timeouts.

The vendors of FC switches have recognized some of the drawbacks related to FCIP and have implemented features to provide additional stability, such as the capability to segregate FCIP traffic into a separate virtual fabric.

Security is also a consideration in an FCIP solution because the data is transmitted over public IP channels. Various security options are available to protect the data based on the router's support. IPSec is one such security measure that can be implemented in the FCIP environment.

FIBRE CHANNEL OVER ETHERNET (FCOE)

FCoE is a mapping of FC frames over Gigabit Ethernet networks. Ethernet is used as the physical interface for carrying FC frames. Multi-function network/storage adapters are used for FC-to-Ethernet mapping.

FCoE maps FC natively over Ethernet while being independent of the Ethernet forwarding scheme, as shown in the following figure.

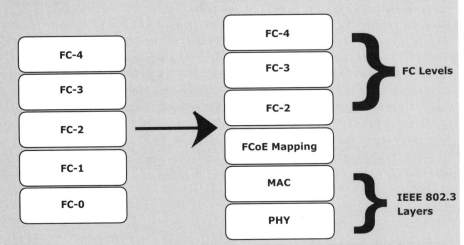

The FCoE protocol specification replaces the FC0 and FC1 layers of the FC stack with Ethernet. By retaining the native FC constructs, FCoE allows a seamless integration with existing FC networks and management software. For more information, visit http://www.fcoe.com.

Summary

iSCSI has enabled IT organizations to gain the benefits of storage networking architecture at reasonable costs. Storage networks can now be geographically distributed with the help of hybrid IP SAN technology, which enhances storage utilization across enterprises. FCIP has emerged as a solution for implementing viable business continuity across enterprises.

Because IP SANs are based on standard Ethernet protocols, the concepts, security mechanisms, and management tools are familiar to administrators. This has enabled the rapid adoption of IP SAN in organizations. The block-level I/O requirements of certain applications that cannot be made with NAS can be targeted for implementation with iSCSI.

This chapter detailed the two IP SAN technologies, iSCSI and FCIP. The next chapter focuses on CAS, another important storage networking technology that addresses the online storage and retrieval of content and long-term archives.

EXERCISES

1. How does iSCSI handle the process of authentication? Research the available options.

2. List some of the data storage applications that could benefit from an IP SAN solution.

4. What are the major performance considerations for FCIP?

5. Research the multipathing software available for an iSCSI environment. Write a technical note on the features and functionality of EMC PowerPath support for iSCSI.

6. Research the iSCSI capabilities in a NAS device; provide use case examples.

7. A company is considering implementing storage. They do not have a current storage infrastructure to use, but they have a network that gives them good performance. Discuss whether native or bridged iSCSI should be used and explain your recommendation.

8. The IP bandwidth provided for FCIP connectivity seems to be constrained. Discuss its implications if the SANs that are merged are fairly large, with 500 ports on each side, and the SANs at both ends are constantly reconfigured.

9. Compared to a standard IP frame, what percentage of reduction can be realized in protocol overhead in an iSCSI configured to use jumbo frames with an MTU value of 9,000 bytes?

10. Why should an MTU value of at least 2,500 bytes be configured in a bridged iSCSI environment?

Chapter 9
Content-Addressed Storage

I n the life cycle of information, data is actively created, accessed, edited, and changed. As data ages, it becomes less likely to change and eventually becomes "fixed" but continues to be accessed by multiple applications and users. This data is called *fixed content*.

> **KEY CONCEPTS**
>
> Fixed Content and Archives
>
> Single-Instance Storage
>
> Object Storage and Retrieval
>
> Content Authenticity

Traditionally, fixed content was not treated as a specialized form of data and was stored using a variety of storage media, ranging from optical disks to tapes to magnetic disks. While these traditional technologies store content, none of them provide all of the unique requirements for storing and accessing fixed content.

Accumulations of fixed content such as documents, e-mail messages, web pages, and digital media throughout an organization have resulted in an unprecedented growth in the amount of data. It has also introduced the challenge of managing fixed content. Furthermore, users demand assurance that stored content has not changed and require an immediate online access to fixed content. These requirements resulted in the development of Content-Addressed Storage (CAS).

CAS is an *object-based system* that has been purposely built for storing fixed content data. It is designed for secure online storage and retrieval of fixed content. Unlike file-level and block-level data access that use file names and the physical location of data for storage and retrieval, CAS stores user data and its attributes as separate objects. The stored object is assigned a globally unique address known as a *content address (CA)*. This address is derived from the object's binary representation. CAS provides an optimized and centrally managed storage solution that can support *single-instance storage (SiS)* to eliminate multiple copies of the same data.

This chapter describes fixed content and archives, traditional solutions deployed for archives and their limitations, the features and benefits of CAS, CAS architecture, storage and retrieval in a CAS environment, and examples of CAS solutions.

9.1 Fixed Content and Archives

Data is accessed and modified at varying frequencies between the time it is created and discarded. Some data frequently changes, for example, data accessed by an Online Transaction Processing (OLTP) application. Some data that does not typically change, but is allowed to change if required is, for example, bill of material and design documents.

Another category of data is fixed content, which defines data that cannot be changed. X-rays and pictures are examples of fixed content data. It is mandatary for all organizations to retain some data for an extended period of time due to government regulations and legal/contractual obligations. Fixed data, which is retained for future reference or business value, is referred to as fixed content asset. Some examples of fixed content asset include electronic documents, e-mail messages, Web pages, and digital media (see Figure 9-1).

Organizations make use of these digital assets to generate new revenues, improve service levels, and leverage historical value. This demands frequent and quick retrieval of the fixed contents at multiple locations. An *archive* is a repository where fixed content is placed. Online data availability in the archive can further increase the business value of the referenced information.

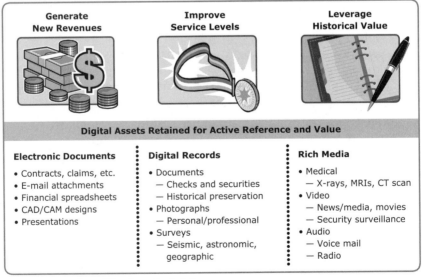

Figure 9-1: Examples of fixed content data

9.2 Types of Archives

An electronic data archive is a repository for data that has fewer access requirements. It can be implemented as online, nearline, or offline based on the means of access:

- **Online archive:** The storage device is directly connected to the host to make the data immediately available. This is best suited for active archives.

- **Nearline archive:** The storage device is connected to the host and information is local, but the device must be mounted or loaded to access the information.

- **Offline archive:** The storage device is not directly connected, mounted, or loaded. Manual intervention is required to provide this service before information can be accessed.

An archive is often stored on a *write once read many (WORM)* device, such as a CD-ROM. These devices protect the original file from being overwritten. Some tape devices also provide this functionality by implementing file-locking capabilities in the hardware or software. Although these devices are inexpensive, they involve operational, management, and maintenance overhead.

Requirements to retain archives have caused corporate archives to grow at a rate of 50 percent or more per year. At the same time, organizations must reduce costs while maintaining required service-level agreements (SLAs). Therefore, it is essential to find a solution that minimizes the fixed costs of the archive's operations and management.

Archives implemented using tape devices and optical disks involve many hidden costs. The traditional archival process using optical disks and tapes is not optimized to recognize the content, so the same content could be archived several times. Additional costs are involved in offsite storage of media and media management. Tapes and optical media are also susceptible to wear and tear. Frequent changes in these device technologies lead to the overhead of converting the media into new formats to enable access and retrieval.

Government agencies and industry regulators are establishing new laws and regulations to enforce the protection of archives from unauthorized destruction and modification. These regulations and standards affect all businesses and have established new requirements for preserving the integrity of information in the archives. These requirements have exposed the hidden costs and shortcomings of the traditional tape and optical media archive solutions.

COMPLIANCE REQUIREMENTS

Businesses such as banking, finance, and health care have to comply with standards enforced by regulators for archived data. These rules detail the regulatory requirements for maintaining the authenticity, integrity, and availability of all business records, contracts, legal documents, and business communications in electronic data formats. These regulations may also state that all businesses are required to inform their customers when their electronic data is compromised.

SEC Rule 17a-3 and 17a-4 of the Securities Exchange Act of 1934, the Sarbanes-Oxley Act, and the Health Insurance Portability and Accountability Act (HIPAA) are some examples of these regulations.

9.3 Features and Benefits of CAS

CAS has emerged as an alternative to tape and optical solutions because it overcomes many of their obvious deficiencies. CAS also meets the demand to improve data accessibility and to properly protect, dispose of, and ensure service-level agreements for archived data. The features and benefits of CAS include the following:

- **Content authenticity:** It assures the genuineness of stored content. This is achieved by generating a unique content address and automating the process of continuously checking and recalculating the content address for stored objects. Content authenticity is assured because the address assigned to each piece of fixed content is as unique as a fingerprint. Every time an object is read, CAS uses a hashing algorithm to recalculate the object's content address as a validation step and compares the result to its original content address. If the object fails validation, it is rebuilt from its mirrored copy.

- **Content integrity:** Refers to the assurance that the stored content has not been altered. Use of hashing algorithm for content authenticity also ensures content integrity in CAS. If the fixed content is altered, CAS assigns a new address to the altered content, rather than overwrite the original fixed content, providing an audit trail and maintaining the fixed content in its original state. As an integral part of maintaining data integrity and audit trail capabilities, CAS supports parity RAID protection in addition to mirroring. Every object in a CAS system is systematically checked in the background. Over time, every object is tested, guaranteeing content integrity even in the case of hardware failure, random error, or attempts to alter the content with malicious intent.

- **Location independence:** CAS uses a unique identifier that applications can leverage to retrieve data rather than a centralized directory, path names, or URLs. Using a content address to access fixed content makes the physical location of the data irrelevant to the application requesting the data. Therefore the location from which the data is accessed is transparent to the application. This yields complete content mobility to applications across locations.

■ **Single-instance storage (SiS):** The unique signature is used to guarantee the storage of only a single instance of an object. This signature is derived from the binary representation of the object. At write time, the CAS system is polled to see if it already has an object with the same signature. If the object is already on the system, it is not stored, rather only a pointer to that object is created. SiS simplifies storage resource management tasks, especially when handling hundreds of terabytes of fixed content.

■ **Retention enforcement:** Protecting and retaining data objects is a core requirement of an archive system. CAS creates two immutable components: a data object and a meta-object for every object stored. The meta-object stores object's attributes and data handling policies. For systems that support object-retention capabilities, the retention policies are enforced until the policies expire.

■ **Record-level protection and disposition:** All fixed content is stored in CAS once and is backed up with a protection scheme. The array is composed of one or more storage clusters. Some CAS architectures provide an extra level of protection by replicating the content onto arrays located at a different location. The disposition of records also follows the stringent guidelines established by regulators for shredding and disposing of data in electronic formats.

■ **Technology independence:** The CAS system interface is impervious to technology changes. As long as the application server is able to map the original content address the data remains accessible. Although hardware changes are inevitable, the goal of CAS hardware vendors is to ensure compatibility across platforms.

■ **Fast record retrieval:** CAS maintains all content on disks that provide subsecond "time to first byte" (200 ms–400 ms) in a single cluster. Random disk access in CAS enables fast record retrieval.

9.4 CAS Architecture

The CAS architecture is shown in Figure 9-2. A client accesses the CAS-Based storage over a LAN through the server that runs the CAS API (application programming interface). The CAS API is responsible for performing functions that enable an application to store and retrieve the data.

CAS architecture is a *Redundant Array of Independent Nodes (RAIN)*. It contains storage nodes and access nodes networked as a cluster by using a private LAN that is internal to it. The internal LAN can be reconfigured automatically to detect the configuration changes such as the addition of storage or access nodes. Clients access the CAS on a separate LAN, which is used for interconnecting clients and servers to the CAS.

The nodes are configured with low-cost, high-capacity ATA HDDs. These nodes run an operating system with special software that implements the features and functionality required in a CAS system.

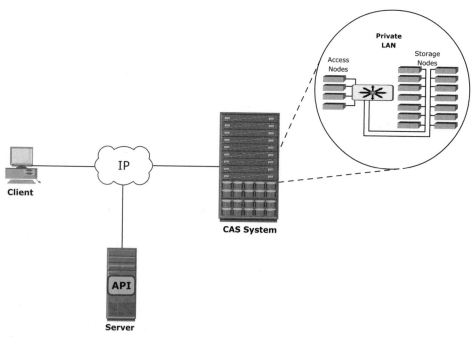

Figure 9-2: CAS Architecture

When the cluster is installed, the nodes are configured with a "role" defining the functionality they provide to the cluster. A node can be configured as a storage node, an access node, or a dual-role node. *Storage nodes* store and protect data objects. They are sometimes referred to as *back-end nodes*. *Access nodes* provide connectivity to application servers through the customer's LAN. They establish connectivity through a private LAN to the storage nodes in the cluster. The number of access nodes is determined by the amount of user required throughput from the cluster. If a node is configured solely as an "access node," its disk space cannot be used to store data objects. This configuration is generally found in older installations of CAS. Storage and retrieval requests are sent to the access node via the customer's LAN. *Dual-role nodes* provide both storage and access node capabilities. This node configuration is more typical than a pure access node configuration.

Almost all CAS products have the same features and options. Some may be implemented differently, but the following features are an essential part of any CAS solution:

- **Integrity checking:** It ensures that the content of the file matches the digital signature (hashed output or CA). The integrity checks can be done on every read or by using a background process. If problems are identified in any of the objects the nodes automatically repair or regenerate the object.

- **Data protection and node resilience:** This ensures that the content stored on the CAS system is available in the event of disk or node failure. Some CAS systems provide local replication or mirrors that copy a data object to another node in the same cluster. This decreases the total available capacity by 50 percent. Parity protection is another way to protect CAS data. It uses less capacity to store data, but takes longer to regenerate the data if corrupted. Remote replication copies data objects to a secondary storage device in a remote location. Remote replication is used as a disaster-recovery solution or for backup. Replication technologies are detailed in Chapters 13 and 14.

- **Load balancing:** Distributes data objects on multiple nodes to provide maximum throughput, availability, and capacity utilization.

- **Scalability:** Adding more nodes to the cluster without any interruption to data access and with minimum administrative overhead.

- **Self diagnosis and repair:** Automatically detects and repairs corrupted objects and alert the administrator of any potential problem. These failures can be at an object level or a node level. They are transparent to the users who access the archive. CAS systems can be configured to alert remote support teams who diagnose and make repairs remotely.

- **Report generation and event notification:** Provides on-demand reporting and event notification. A command-line interface (CLI) or a graphical user interface (GUI) can produce various types of reports. Any event notification can be communicated to the administrator through syslog, SNMP, SMTP, or e-mail.

- **Fault tolerance:** Ensures data availability if a component of the CAS system fails, through the use of redundant components and data protection schemes. If remote replication of CAS is implemented, failover to the remote CAS system occurs when the primary CAS system is unavailable.

- **Audit trails:** Enable documentation of management activity and any access and disposition of data. Audit trails are mandated by compliance requirements.

9.5 Object Storage and Retrieval in CAS

The process of storing and retrieving objects in CAS is explained in Figures 9-3 and 9-4, respectively. This process requires an understanding of the following CAS terminologies:

- **Application programming interface (API):** A high-level implementation of an interface that specifies the details of how clients can make service requests. The CAS API resides on the application server and is responsible for storing and retrieving the objects in a CAS system.

- **Access profile:** Used by access applications to authenticate to a CAS cluster and by CAS clusters to authenticate themselves to each other for replication.

- **Virtual pools:** Enable a single logical cluster to be broken up into multiple logical groupings of data.

- **Binary large object (BLOB):** The actual data without the descriptive information (metadata). The distinct bit sequence of user data represents the actual content of a file and is independent of the name and physical location.

- **Content address (CA):** An object's address, which is created by a hash algorithm run across the binary representation of the object. While generating a CA, the hash algorithm considers all aspects of the content, returning a unique content address to the user's application.

  A unique number is calculated from the sequence of bits that constitutes file content. If even a single character changes in the file, the resulting CA is different. A *hash output,* also called a *digest,* is a type of fingerprint for a variable-length data file. This output represents the file contents and is used to locate the file in a CAS system. The digest can be used to verify whether the data is authentic or has changed because of equipment failure or human intervention. When a user tries to retrieve or open a file, the server sends the CA to the CAS system with the appropriate function to read the file. The CAS system uses the CA to locate the file and passes it back to the application server.

- **C-Clip:** A virtual package that contains data (BLOB) and its associated CDF. The *C-Clip ID* is the CA that the system returns to the client application. It is also referred as a *C-Clip handle* or *C-Clip reference.*

- **C-Clip Descriptor File (CDF):** An XML file that the system creates while making a C-Clip. This file includes CAs for all referenced BLOBs and associated metadata. Metadata includes characteristics of CAS objects such as size, format, and expiration date.

Referring to Figure 9-3, the data object storage process in a CAS system is as follows:

1. End users present the data to be archived to the CAS API via an application. The application server may also interact directly with the source (e.g., an X-ray machine) that generated this fixed content.

2. The API separates the actual data (BLOB) from the metadata and the CA is calculated from the object's binary representation.

3. The content address and metadata of the object are then inserted into the C-Clip Descriptor File (CDF). The C-clip is then transferred to and stored on the CAS system.

4. The CAS system recalculates the object's CA as a validation step and stores the object. This is to ensure that the content of the object has not changed.

5. An acknowledgment is sent to the API after a mirrored copy of the CDF and a protected copy of the BLOB have been safely stored in the CAS system. After a data object is stored in the CAS system, the API is given a C-Clip ID and C-Clip ID is stored local to the application server.

6. Using the C-Clip ID, the application can read the data back from the CAS system.

   Once an object is stored successfully, it is made available to end users for retrieval and use. The content address is usually hidden from the user. A user accesses the file stored on CAS by the same file name. It is the application server that references the CA to retrieve the stored content; this process is transparent to the user. No modification is needed to the application's user interface to accommodate the CAS storage and retrieval process.

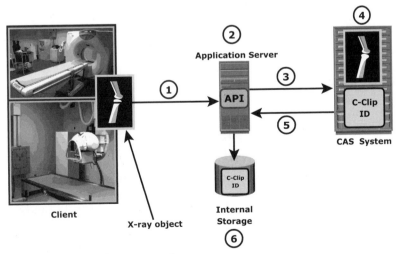

Figure 9-3: Storing data objects on CAS

The process of data retrieval from CAS follows these steps:

1. The end user or an application requests an object.

2. The application queries the local table of C-Clip IDs stored in the local storage and locates the C-Clip ID for the requested object.

3. Using the API, a retrieval request is sent along with the C-Clip ID to the CAS system.

4. The CAS system delivers the requested information to the application, which in turn delivers it to the end user.

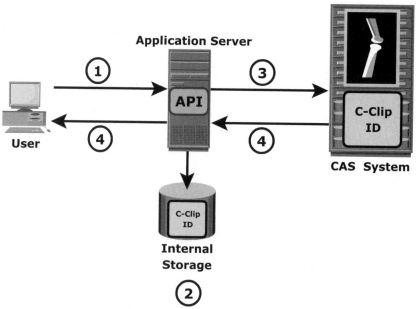

Figure 9-4: Data object retrieval from CAS system

9.6 CAS Examples

Organizations have deployed CAS solutions to solve several business problems. Two solutions are described in detail in the following sections.

9.6.1 Health Care Solution: Storing Patient Studies

A large health care center examines hundreds of patients every day and generates large volumes of medical records. Each record may be composed of one or more images that range in size from about 15 MB for standard digital X-ray images to over 1 GB for oncology studies. The patient records are stored online for a period of 60–90 days for immediate use by attending physicians. Even if a patient's record is no longer needed for any reason, HIPAA requirements stipulate that the records should be kept in the original formats for at least seven years.

Beyond 90 days, hospitals may backup images to tape or send them to an offsite archive service for long-term retention. The cost of restoring or retrieving an image in long-term storage may be five to ten times more than leaving the image online. Long-term storage may also involve extended recovery time, ranging from hours to days. Medical image solution providers offer hospitals the capability to view medical records, such as online X-ray images, with sufficient response times and resolution to enable rapid assessments of patients. Figure 9-5 illustrates the use of CAS in this scenario. The patient records are moved to the CAS system after 60-90 days. This facilitates long-term storage and at the same time when immediate access is needed, the records are available by accessing the CAS system.

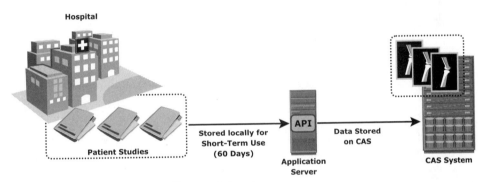

Figure 9-5: Storing patient studies on CAS system

9.6.2 Finance Solution: Storing Financial Records

In a typical banking scenario, images of checks, each about 25 KB in size, are created and sent to archive services over an IP network. A check imaging service provider may process 50–90 million check images per month. Typically, check images are actively processed in transactional systems for about five days.

For the next 60 days, check images may be requested by banks or individual consumers for verification purposes at the rate of about 0.5 percent of the total check pool, or about 250,000–450,000 requests. Beyond 60 days, access requirements drop drastically, to as few as one for every 10,000 checks. Figure 9-6 illustrates the use of CAS in this scenario. The check images are stored on a CAS system, starting at day 60 and can be held there indefinitely.

A typical check image archive can approach a size of 100 TB. Check imaging is one example of a financial service application that is best serviced with CAS. Customer transactions initiated by e-mail, contracts, and security transaction records may need to be kept online for 30 years; CAS is the preferred storage solution in such cases.

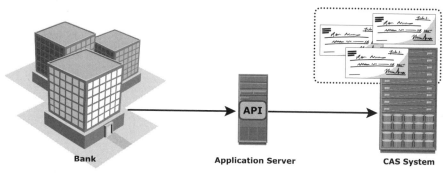

Figure 9-6: Storing finiancial records on CAS system

HIERARCHICAL STORAGE MANAGEMENT (HSM)

Business organizations need to move data between storage tiers for many reasons, including cost, protection, and compliance, depending on its value over time. HSM is a policy-based management system of file backup and archiving. The policies are established to store data on different tiers of storage based on the relevance and importance of the information. An example of a policy is if a file on a high-performance storage tier is not accessed for 120 days, it should be migrated to a low performance storage tier or archived on the CAS system. At the same time, when users need that migrated file, access to it must be provided seamlessly. HSM implements such policies and automates the process of migration and recall of data from different tiers of storage. The process of migration is completely transparent to the user. After the migration, the original file on the high-performance storage is replaced with a *stub file*, which acts as a placeholder and looks like the original file to the user.

9.7 Concepts in Practice: EMC Centera

EMC Centera is a simple, affordable, and secure repository for information archiving. EMC Centera is the first platform designed and optimized specifically to deal with the storage and retrieval of fixed content, meeting performance, compliance, and regulatory requirements. Compared to traditional archive solutions, EMC Centera provides faster record retrieval, SiS, guaranteed content authenticity, self-healing, and support for numerous industry regulatory standards. Visit `http://education.EMC.com/ismbook` for the latest information.

9.7.1 EMC Centera Models

EMC Centera is offered in three different models to meet different types of user requirements—EMC Centera Basic, EMC Centera Governance Edition, and EMC Centera Compliance Edition Plus (CE+):

- **EMC Centera Basic:** Provides all functionality without the enforcement of retention periods.

- **EMC Centera Governance Edition:** Provides the retention capabilities required by organizations to responsibly manage electronic records in addition to the features provided by EMC Centera Basic. Deploying Governance Edition enforces organizational and application policies for information retention and disposition.

- **CE+:** Provides extensive compliance capabilities. CE+ is designed to meet the requirements of the most stringent of regulated business environments for electronic storage media as established by regulations from the Securities and Exchange Commission (SEC), or other national and international regulatory groups.

9.7.2 EMC Centera Architecture

The architecture of the RAIN-based EMC Centera system is designed to be highly scalable and to store petabytes of content. While the EMC Centera cabinet can accommodate 32 nodes, the entry level configuration starts with as few as 4 nodes and 2 internal switches and is expandable in increments of 4 nodes. The nodes run a Linux operating system and CentraStar software to implement all the CAS functionality. A collection of nodes and internal switches is referred to as a cube. A cube contains two internal switches and a maximum of 16 nodes. A fully configured cabinet is comprised of two cubes, as shown in Figure 9-7.

The EMC Centera node contains four SATA HDDs and a dual-source power supply that enables EMC Centera nodes to connect to two power sources. Each power outlet on a node connects to a separate power rail.

Figure 9-8 illustrates the EMC Centera architecture. Each node contains more than 1 TB of usable capacity and can be configured as access and/or storage nodes. EMC Centera has two 24-port 2 gigabit internal switches that provide communications for up to 16 nodes within the private LAN. Several cabinets of these nodes and switches can be connected to form an EMC Centera cluster. An EMC Centera domain consists of one or more clusters. Applications may support multiple clusters within a EMC Centera domain. Each cabinet can host up to 23 TB. The usable protected capacity varies depending on whether it uses *content protection parity (CPP)* or *content protection mirrored (CPM)*.

In CPP, the data is fragmented into segments, with an additional parity segment. Each segment is on a different node, similar to a file-type RAID. If a node or a disk fails, the other nodes regenerate the missing segment on a different node.

In CPM, each data object is mirrored and each mirror resides on a different node (refer to Figure 9-8). If a node or a disk fails, the EMC Centera software automatically broadcasts to the node with the mirrored copy to regenerate another copy to a different node so that two copies are always available.

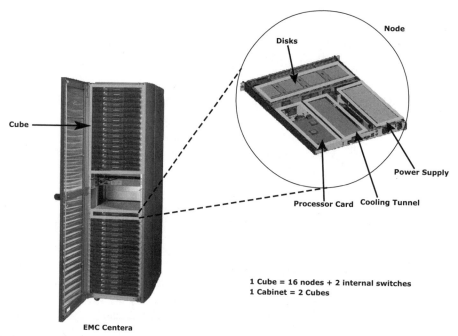

1 Cube = 16 nodes + 2 internal switches
1 Cabinet = 2 Cubes

Figure 9-7: EMC Centera configuration

Both CPP and CPM provide total protection against failure using EMC Centera's unique *self-healing* functions. With the self-healing feature, if any component in the node or the entire node fails, data is regenerated to a different part of the cluster, ensuring that data is always protected. In addition to this "organic regeneration" process, there are other processes that run continuously in the background, verifying objects by scrubbing and ensuring that objects are not corrupted. The self-managing and configuring functionality enable rapid installation and implementation of EMC Centera.

EMC Centera protects users from technology changes by allowing various generations to coexist in a single CAS cluster.

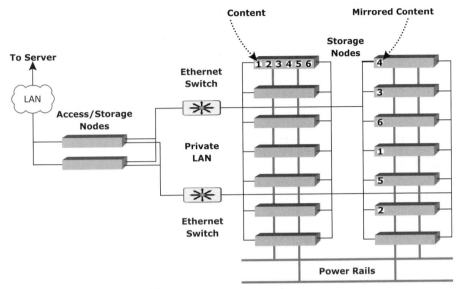

Figure 9-8: EMC Centera architecture

9.7.3 Centera Tools

A group of tools are available to users and service personnel to manage the functions of EMC Centera. They include EMC Centera Viewer, EMC Centera Monitor, EMC Centera Console, and EMC Centera Health Reporting:

- **EMC Centera Viewer:** It is a GUI that is loaded to a client that has network access to EMC Centera. The tool provides a simple means of displaying EMC Centera's capacity utilization and operational performance. It also enables the system administrator to change any site-specific information, such as the public network information and end-user contact information. EMC Centera Viewer is commonly used by service personnel to perform maintenance and to upgrade the CentraStar code.

- **EMC Centera Monitor:** It is a tool that enables users to monitor a single cube in EMC Centera, by displaying system properties such as configuration, capacity, and software version.

- **EMC Centera Console:** It is a web-based management tool that enables system operators to view detailed information about alerts, configurations, performance, and relationships between multiple EMC Centera clusters.

- **EMC Centera Health Reporting:** It is done through an automatic e-mail message that an EMC Centera cluster periodically sends to the EMC Customer Support Center or a list of predefined recipients. The message reports the current status of the EMC Centera cluster. This enables remote monitoring, diagnosis, and support for EMC Centera hardware and software.

9.7.4 EMC Centera Universal Access

An important feature of EMC Centera, when compared to traditional archive solutions, is that the EMC Centera archive is online. In addition, the EMC Centera archive is accessible from any application or platform. EMC Centera Universal Access acts as a high-performance store and forward protocol translator. It communicates with application servers using network file protocols (NFS, CIFS, HTTP) and with an EMC Centera cluster through Centera API (see Figure 9-9).

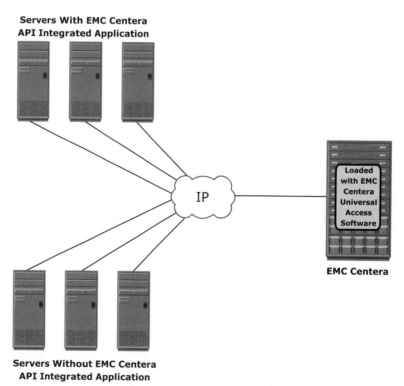

Figure 9-9: EMC Centera Universal Access

With EMC Centera Universal Access, any enterprise application that can mount a network drive or use FTP and HTTP can take advantage of EMC Centera's benefits. From home-grown applications to nonintegrated versions of applications, EMC Centera Universal Access makes it possible to utilize EMC Centera in customer environments with no change to existing applications. This greatly simplifies and accelerates deployment.

Summary

Understanding the information lifecycle enables storage designers to adopt different storage technology to meet data archival requirements. CAS offers a centrally managed networked storage solution for fixed content. CAS has enabled IT organizations to realize significant cost savings and improve operational efficiency and data protection. CAS meets stringent regulatory requirements that have helped organizations avoid penalties and issues associated with regulatory noncompliance. CAS eliminates data duplication with SiS, which reduces IT maintenance costs and increases long-term return on investment for storage systems.

This chapter outlined the challenges involved in managing fixed content, the CAS architecture and its benefits, and how CAS is deployed and managed, using EMC Centera as an example.

Storage networking technologies have provided the primary architecture that has evolved and matured to meet the business's information storage demands. As this evolution continues, organizations have started using multi-vendor and multi-generation technologies that must work together without compromising business requirements. The virtualization technologies described in the next chapter provides more flexibility and scalability to meet next-generation storage needs.

EXERCISES

1. Explain how a CAS solution fits into the ILM strategy.

2. To access data in a SAN, a host uses a physical address known as a logical block address (LBA). A host using a CAS device does not use (or need) a physical address. Why?

3. The IT department of a department store uses tape to archive data. Explain 4–5 major points you could provide to persuade the IT department to move to a CAS solution. How would your suggestions impact the IT department?

Chapter 10
Storage Virtualization

As storage networking technology matures, larger and complex implementations are becoming more common. The heterogeneous nature of storage infrastructures has further added to the complexity of managing and utilizing storage resources effectively. Specialized technologies are required to meet stringent service level agreements and to provide an adaptable infrastructure with reduced cost of management. The virtualization technologies discussed in this chapter provide enhanced productivity, asset utilization, and better management of the storage infrastructure.

KEY CONCEPTS

Memory Virtualization

Network Virtualization

Server Virtualization

Storage Virtualization

In-Band and Out-of-Band Implementations

Block-Level and File-Level Virtualization

Virtualization is the technique of masking or abstracting physical resources, which simplifies the infrastructure and accommodates the increasing pace of business and technological changes. It increases the utilization and capability of IT resources, such as servers, networks, or storage devices, beyond their physical limits. Virtualization simplifies resource management by pooling and sharing resources for maximum utilization and makes them appear as logical resources with enhanced capabilities.

10.1 Forms of Virtualization

Virtualization has existed in the IT industry for several years and in different forms, including memory virtualization, network virtualization, server virtualization, and storage virtualization.

10.1.1 Memory Virtualization

Virtual memory makes an application appear as if it has its own contiguous logical memory independent of the existing physical memory resources.

Since the beginning of the computer industry, memory has been and continues to be an expensive component of a host. It determines both the size and the number of applications that can run on a host.

With technological advancements, memory technology has changed and the cost of memory has decreased. Virtual memory managers (VMMs) have evolved, enabling multiple applications to be hosted and processed simultaneously.

In a virtual memory implementation, a memory address space is divided into contiguous blocks of fixed-size pages. A process known as *paging* saves inactive memory pages onto the disk and brings them back to physical memory when required. This enables efficient use of available physical memory among different processes. The space used by VMMs on the disk is known as a *swap file*. A swap file (also known as *page file* or *swap space*) is a portion of the hard disk that functions like physical memory (RAM) to the operating system. The operating system typically moves the least used data into the swap file so that RAM will be available for processes that are more active. Because the space allocated to the swap file is on the hard disk (which is slower than the physical memory), access to this file is slower.

10.1.2 Network Virtualization

Network virtualization creates virtual networks whereby each application sees its own logical network independent of the physical network. A *virtual LAN (VLAN)* is an example of network virtualization that provides an easy, flexible, and less expensive way to manage networks. VLANs make large networks more manageable by enabling a centralized configuration of devices located in physically diverse locations.

Consider a company in which the users of a department are separated over a metropolitan area with their resources centrally located at one office. In a typical network, each location has its own network connected to the others through routers. When network packets cross routers, latency influences network performance. With VLANs, users with similar access requirements can be grouped together into the same virtual network. This setup eliminates the need for network routing. As a result, although users are physically located at disparate locations, they appear to be at the same location accessing resources locally. In addition to improving network performance, VLANs also provide enhanced security by isolating sensitive data from the other networks and by restricting access to the resources located within the networks.

Virtual SAN (VSAN)

A *virtual SAN/virtual fabric* is a recent evolution of SAN and conceptually, functions in the same way as a VLAN.

In a VSAN, a group of hosts or storage ports communicate with each other using a virtual topology defined on the physical SAN. VSAN technology enables users to build one or more Virtual SANs on a single physical topology containing switches and ISLs. This technology improves storage area network (SAN) scalability, availability, and security. These benefits are derived from the separation of Fibre Channel services in each VSAN and isolation of traffic between VSANs. Some of the features of VSAN are:

- Fibre Channel ID (FC ID) of a host in a VSAN can be assigned to a host in another VSAN, thus improving scalability of SAN.

- Every instance of a VSAN runs all required protocols such as FSPF, domain manager, and zoning.

- Fabric-related configurations in one VSAN do not affect the traffic in another VSAN.

- Events causing traffic disruptions in one VSAN are contained within that VSAN and are not propagated to other VSANs.

10.1.3 Server Virtualization

Server virtualization enables multiple operating systems and applications to run simultaneously on different *virtual machines* created on the same physical server (or group of servers). Virtual machines provide a layer of abstraction between the operating system and the underlying hardware. Within a physical server, any number of virtual servers can be established; depending on hardware capabilities (see Figure 10-1). Each virtual server seems like a physical machine to the operating system, although all virtual servers share the same underlying physical hardware in an isolated manner. For example, the physical memory is shared between virtual servers but the address space is not. Individual virtual servers can be restarted, upgraded, or even crashed, without affecting the other virtual servers on the same physical machine.

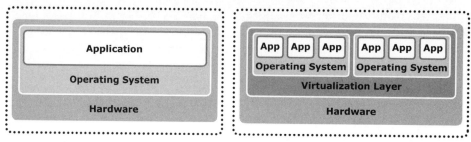

(a) Before Server Virtualization   **(b) After Server Virtualization**

Figure 10-1: Server virtualization

With changes in computing from a dedicated to a client/server model, the physical server faces resource conflict issues when two or more applications running on these servers have conflicting requirements (e.g., need different values in the same registry entry, different versions of the same DLL). These issues are further compounded with an application's high-availability requirements. As a result, the servers are limited to serve only one application at a time, as shown in Figure 10-1(a). On the other hand, many applications do not take full advantage of the hardware capabilities available to them. Consequently, resources such as processors, memory, and storage remain underutilized.

Server virtualization addresses the issues that exist in a physical server environment. The virtualization layer, shown in Figure 10-1(b), helps to overcome resource conflicts by isolating applications running on different operating systems on the same machine. In addition, server virtualization can dynamically move the underutilized hardware resources to a location where they are needed most, improving utilization of the underlying hardware resources.

10.1.4 Storage Virtualization

Storage virtualization is the process of presenting a logical view of the physical storage resources to a host. This logical storage appears and behaves as physical storage directly connected to the host. Throughout the evolution of storage technology, some form of storage virtualization has been implemented. Some examples of storage virtualization are host-based volume management, LUN creation, tape storage virtualization, and disk addressing (CHS to LBA).

The key benefits of storage virtualization include increased storage utilization, adding or deleting storage without affecting an application's availability, and nondisruptive data migration (access to files and storage while migrations are in progress).

Figure 10-2 illustrates a virtualized storage environment. At the top are four servers, each of which has one virtual volume assigned, which is currently in use by an application. These virtual volumes are mapped to the actual storage in the arrays, as shown at the bottom of the figure. When I/O is sent to a virtual volume, it is redirected through the virtualization at the storage network layer to the mapped physical array.

The discussion that follows provides details about the different types of storage virtualization, methods of implementation, the challenges associated with the implementation of storage virtualization, and examples of implementation.

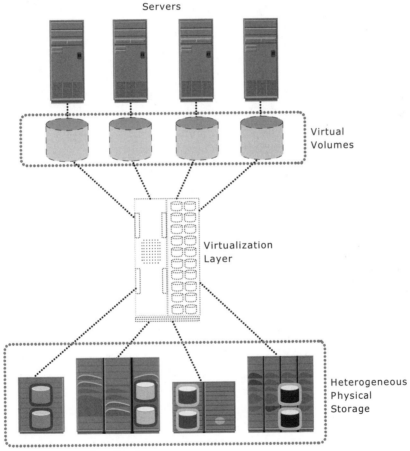

Figure 10-2: Storage virtualization

10.2 SNIA Storage Virtualization Taxonomy

The SNIA (Storage Networking Industry Association) storage virtualization taxonomy (see Figure 10-3) provides a systematic classification of storage virtualization, with three levels defining what, where, and how storage can be virtualized.

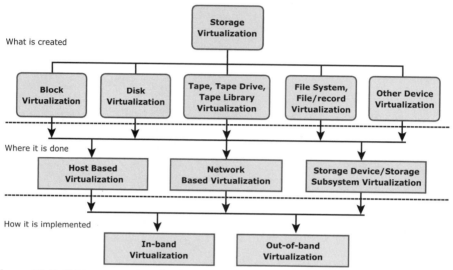

Figure 10-3: SNIA storage virtualization taxonomy

The first level of the storage virtualization taxonomy addresses "what" is created. It specifies the types of virtualization: block virtualization, file virtualization, disk virtualization, tape virtualization, or any other device virtualization. Block-level and file-level virtualization are the core focus areas covered later in this chapter.

The second level describes "where" the virtualization can take place. This requires a multilevel approach that characterizes virtualization at all three levels of the storage environment: server, storage network, and storage, as shown in Figure 10-4. An effective virtualization strategy distributes the intelligence across all three levels while centralizing the management and control functions. Data storage functions—such as RAID, caching, checksums, and hardware scanning—should remain on the array. Similarly, the host should control application-focused areas, such as clustering and application failover, and volume management of raw disks. However, path redirection, path failover, data access, and distribution or load-balancing capabilities should be moved to the switch or the network.

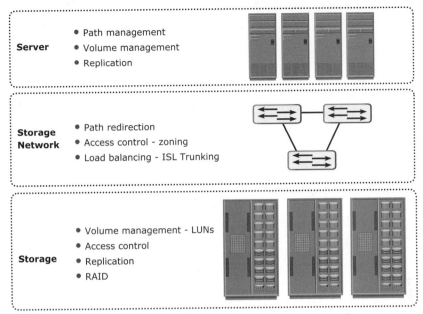

Figure 10-4: Storage virtualization at different levels of the storage environment

The third level of the storage virtualization taxonomy specifies the network level virtualization methodology, in-band or out-of-band.

10.3 Storage Virtualization Configurations

Storage virtualization at the network is implemented using either the in-band or the out-of-band methodology. In an *out-of-band* implementation, the virtualized environment configuration is stored external to the data path. As shown in Figure 10-5(a), the configuration is stored on the virtualization appliance configured external to the storage network that carries the data. This configuration is also called split-path because the control and data paths are split (the control path runs through the appliance, the data path does not). This configuration enables the environment to process data at a network speed with only minimal latency added for translation of the virtual configuration to the physical storage. The data is not cached at the virtualization appliance beyond what would normally occur in a typical SAN configuration. Since the virtualization appliance is hardware-based and optimized for Fibre Channel communication, it can be scaled significantly. In addition, because the data is unaltered in an out-of-band implementation, many of the existing array features and functions can be utilized in addition to the benefits provided by virtualization.

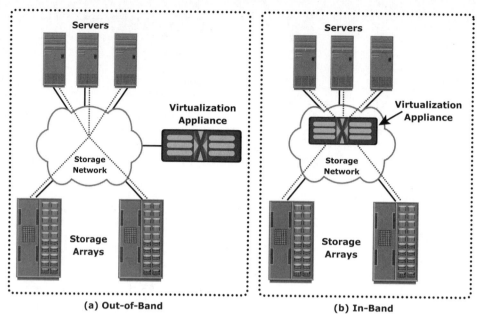

(a) Out-of-Band   **(b) In-Band**

Figure 10-5: Storage virtualization configuration

The *in-band* implementation places the virtualization function in the data path, as shown in Figure 10-5(b). General-purpose servers or appliances handle the virtualization and function as a translation engine for the virtual configuration to the physical storage. While processing, data packets are often cached by the appliance and then forwarded to the appropriate target. An in-band implementation is software-based and data storing and forwarding through the appliance results in additional latency. It introduces a delay in the application response time because the data remains in the network for some time before being committed to disk.

In terms of infrastructure, the in-band architecture increases complexity and adds a new layer of virtualization (the appliance), while limiting the ability to scale the storage infrastructure. An in-band implementation is suitable for static environments with predictable workloads.

10.4 Storage Virtualization Challenges

Storage networking and feature-rich intelligent storage arrays have addressed and provided specific solutions to business problems. As an enabler, virtualization should add value to the existing solution, but introducing virtualization into an environment adds new challenges. The storage virtualization solution must be capable of addressing issues such as scalability, functionality, manageability, and support.

10.4.1 Scalability

Consider the scalability of an environment with no virtualization. This environment may have several storage arrays that provide storage independently of each other. Each array is managed independently and meets application requirements in terms of IOPS and capacity. After virtualization, a storage array can no longer be viewed as an individual entity. The environment as a whole must now be analyzed. As a result, the infrastructure that is implemented both at a physical level and from a virtualization perspective must be able to adequately handle the workload, which may consist of different types of processing and traffic distribution. Greater care must be exercised to ensure that storage devices are performing to meet the appropriate requirements.

10.4.2 Functionality

Functionality is another challenge in storage virtualization. Currently, the storage array provides a wide range of advanced functionality necessary for meeting an application's service levels. This includes local replication, extended-distance remote replication and the capability to provide application consistency across multiple volumes and arrays. In a virtualized environment, the virtual device must provide the same or better functionality than what is currently available on the storage array, and it must continue to leverage existing functionality on the arrays. It should protect the existing investments in processes, skills, training, and human resources.

10.4.3 Manageability

The management of the storage infrastructure in a virtualized environment is an important consideration for storage administrators. A key advantage of today's storage resource management tools in an environment without virtualization is that they provide an end-to-end view, which integrates all the resources in the storage environment. They provide efficient and effective monitoring, reporting, planning, and provisioning services to the storage environment.

Introducing a virtualization device breaks the end-to-end view into three distinct domains: the server to the virtualization device, the virtualization device to the physical storage, and the virtualization device itself. The virtualized storage environment must be capable of meeting these challenges and must integrate with existing management tools to enable management of an end-to-end virtualized environment.

10.4.4 Support

Virtualization is not a stand-alone technology but something that has to work within an existing environment. This environment may include multiple vendor technologies, such as switch and storage arrays, adding to complexity. Addressing such complexities often requires multiple management tools and introduces interoperability issues. Without a virtualization solution, many companies try to consolidate products from a single vendor to ease these challenges. Introducing a virtualization solution reduces the need to standardize on a single vendor. However, supportability issues in a virtualized heterogeneous environment introduce challenges in coordination and compatibility of products and solutions from different manufacturers and vendors.

10.5 Types of Storage Virtualization

Virtual storage is about providing logical storage to hosts and applications independent of physical resources. Virtualization can be implemented in both SAN and NAS storage environments. In a SAN, virtualization is applied at the block level, whereas in NAS, it is applied at the file level.

10.5.1 Block-Level Storage Virtualization

Block-level storage virtualization provides a translation layer in the SAN, between the hosts and the storage arrays, as shown in Figure 10-6. Instead of being directed to the LUNs on the individual storage arrays, the hosts are directed to the virtualized LUNs on the virtualization device. The virtualization device translates between the virtual LUNs and the physical LUNs on the individual arrays. This facilitates the use of arrays from different vendors simultaneously, without any interoperability issues. For a host, all the arrays appear like a single target device and LUNs can be distributed or even split across multiple arrays.

Block-level storage virtualization extends storage volumes online, resolves application growth requirements, consolidates heterogeneous storage arrays, and enables transparent volume access. It also provides the advantage of non-disruptive data migration.

In traditional SAN environments, LUN migration from one array to another was an offline event because the hosts needed to be updated to reflect the new array configuration. In other instances, host CPU cycles were required to migrate data from one array to the other, especially in a multi vendor environment. With a block-level virtualization solution in place, the virtualization engine handles the back-end migration of data, which enables LUNs to remain online and accessible while data is being migrated. No physical changes are required because the host still points to the same virtual targets on the virtualization device. However, the mappings on the virtualization device should be changed. These changes can be executed dynamically and are transparent to the end user.

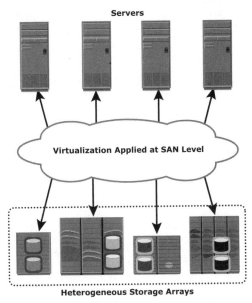

Figure 10-6: Block-level storage virtualization

Deploying heterogeneous arrays in a virtualized environment facilitates an information lifecycle management (ILM) strategy, enabling significant cost and resource optimization. Low-value data can be migrated from high- to low-performance arrays or disks. Detailed implementation of functionality and operation of block-level storage virtualization is discussed in the section "Concepts in Practice" later in this chapter.

10.5.2 File-Level Virtualization

File-level virtualization addresses the NAS challenges by eliminating the dependencies between the data accessed at the file level and the location where the files are physically stored. This provides opportunities to optimize storage utilization and server consolidation and to perform nondisruptive file migrations.

Figure 10-7 illustrates a NAS environment before and after the implementation of file-level virtualization.

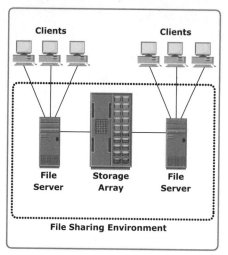
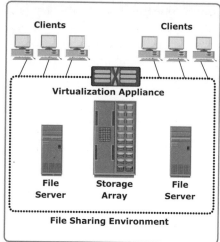

(a) Before File-Level Virtualization **(b) After File-Level Virtualization**

Figure 10-7: NAS device before and after file-level virtualization

Before virtualization, each NAS device or file server is physically and logically independent. Each host knows exactly where its file-level resources are located. Underutilized storage resources and capacity problems result because files are bound to a specific file server. It is necessary to move the files from one server to another because of performance reasons or when the file server fills up. Moving files across the environment is not easy and requires downtime for the file servers. Moreover, hosts and applications need to be reconfigured with the new path, making it difficult for storage administrators to improve storage efficiency while maintaining the required service level.

File-level virtualization simplifies file mobility. It provides user or application independence from the location where the files are stored. File-level virtualization creates a logical pool of storage, enabling users to use a logical path, rather than a physical path, to access files. File-level virtualization facilitates the movement of file systems across the online file servers. This means that while the files are being moved, clients can access their files non-disruptively. Clients can also read their files from the old location and write them back to the new location without realizing that the physical location has changed. Multiple clients connected to multiple servers can perform online movement of their files to optimize utilization of their resources. A global namespace can be used to map the logical path of a file to the physical path names. Detailed implementation of functionality and operation of file-level storage virtualization is discussed in the next section.

10.6 Concepts in Practice

EMC Invista and Rainfinity are EMC product implementations of block-level and file-level virtualization, respectively. These virtualization solutions offer improvements over traditional device-level controls in the area of capacity utilization, storage tier management, performance optimization, and data protection. For more details on Invista and Rainfinity, please refer to `http://education` `.EMC.com/ismbook`.

10.6.1 EMC Invista

EMC Invista is an out of band SAN-based block-level storage virtualization solution. It uses intelligent SAN switches with customized hardware to virtualize physical storage in a logical presentation. These switches are capable of handling data operations at network speed. They use specialized software to examine the port, logical volume, and offset to which the I/O is sent and can control the target path of I/Os to the storage devices.

Invista is physically located between the production hosts and the storage arrays, as shown in Figure 10-8. The part of Invista that is connected to the hosts is called the *front end*. The part that is connected to the storage arrays is called the *back end*. The hosts and storage are connected to the Invista hardware directly or through a SAN switch. The host and storage array connections are Fibre Channel interfaces on intelligent Fibre Channel switches within Invista.

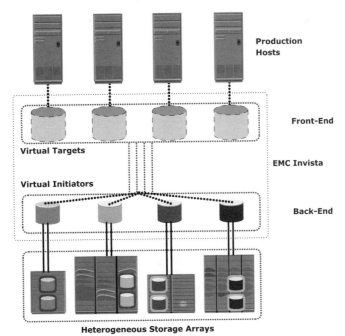

Figure 10-8: Storage virtualization with EMC Invista

Hosts see Invista as a storage device or a virtual target, whereas storage sees Invista as a host or a virtual initiator. The virtual targets are abstract entities, which are created by designating specific ports on the switch to be used as front-end ports, which become visible in the name server on the switch. Invista uses virtual targets and virtual initiators to map virtual volumes to the physical storage on back-end arrays. Invista serves as a proxy device, intercepting communications between the host and the storage by providing virtualization.

Invista Components

Figure 10-9 shows the hardware components of an Invista instance. The main hardware components are the control path cluster (CPC), the data path controller (DPC), and the Ethernet switch.

A *CPC* is a customized storage device (A dual node cluster in an active-active configuration) running Invista software. The CPC does not contain any user data; instead, it stores Invista configuration parameters, including storage device information, virtual volume information, the clone group, and information about the storage volumes belonging to the storage devices. It also performs all the control and management functions of the virtual storage.

The DPC is a special purpose SAN switch/blade. It runs special firmware and layered software that enables the creation and management of virtual initiators and targets. The DPC receives I/O from the host initiator and controls its attributes, such as target, LUN, and offset within the logical unit. The DPC performs I/O-mapping operations and redirection for read and write operations between the hosts (front end) and the storage arrays (back end). The DPC gets its configuration from the CPC.

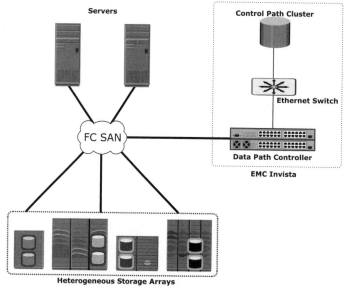

Figure 10-9: Invista's hardware components

An *Ethernet switch* connects the CPC and the DPC through a private IP network for configuration and control path traffic. The software provides dynamic volume mobility, network-based volume management, and heterogeneous point-in-time copies.

Invista Operation

When an I/O request from a host arrives at the DPC, it handles the I/O and maps it to the appropriate virtual target (or initiator), as shown in Figure 10-10. In some exceptional cases, if the command is a SCSI inquiry about the device or an I/O for which the DPC does not have mapping information, the CPC handles the request.

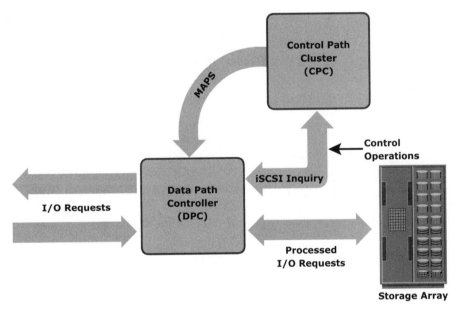

Figure 10-10: Invista operations

If a new storage array is added to the intelligent switch, the CPC discovers the new array and updates the mapping information to put that new array into use. With the mapping done, the I/O gets redirected to the new storage location.

Similarly, if an old array needs to be removed, the CPC issues another set of instructions to move the data from that old array to another array. The DPC copies the data online and the old array can be moved out nondisruptively.

Invista Advantages

EMC Invista provides block-level storage virtualization in heterogeneous storage environments. It also supports dynamic volume mobility for volume extension and data migration between different storage tiers without any downtime.

Invista supports local and remote replication functionality; and it integrates with the existing SAN infrastructure and uses the full fabric bandwidth for high-speed I/O processing. Invista provides separate data and control paths for easy management and faster I/O processing.

10.6.2 Rainfinity

Rainfinity is a dedicated hardware/software solution for file-level virtualization. The Rainfinity *Global File Virtualization (GFV)* appliance (see Figure 10-11) provides an abstraction of file-based storage transparently to users. Files can be moved from one file server to another even when clients are reading and writing their data.

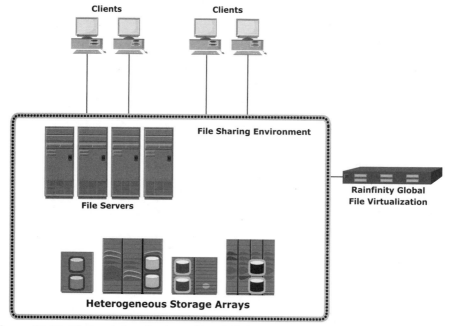

Figure 10-11: File-level virtualization with Rainfinity

A Rainfinity global namespace transparently maps the logical path names to the physical locations after the files have been moved. Therefore, users and applications are redirected to the new location without reconfiguring the physical path names. The management of the namespace can be accomplished by industry standard protocols and mechanisms, such as a Distributed File System (DFS), NIS, and LDAP. Rainfinity integrates itself with these existing industry standard namespaces.

The Rainfinity appliance integrates into the existing IP network and acts like a layer 2 bridge between the client and the file server. This enables Rainfinity to see and process the traffic between clients and file servers with minimal modification to the existing network. Rainfinity is aware of file-sharing protocols (CIFS and NFS). This application-layer intelligence enables Rainfinity to move data from one server to another without interrupting client access.

Rainfinity Components

The Rainfinity GFV appliance is a 64-bit processor with up to 16 GB of cache memory. The GFV appliance consists of two hot-swappable SCSI hard drives configured with RAID 1 to buffer all writes to the disk. It also contains a keyboard, a mouse, and a CD-ROM drive for software uploads.

Rainfinity is shipped with Rainfinity code, Windows Proxy service, and the Security ID (SID) translator. The Rainfinity code is a customized Linux-based operating system. The Windows Proxy service is installed on a separate Windows server and is required to move CIFS data. Rainfinity connects to a computer running Windows Proxy and uses it to collect performance statistics and execute administration tasks.

Rainfinity translates the security properties of the files and directories involved in a CIFS transaction with the help of the SID translator. The SID translator runs on a separate Windows server. This capability is used to assist data migrations when the access control list (ACL) is defined in terms of local groups on the source file server. When the data is migrated to the destination server, the ACL should be defined in terms of the corresponding local groups on the destination server. The rules governing such translation are defined in the SID translation tables.

Rainfinity Operations

In a NAS environment, the file servers and Rainfinity appliance are connected over an IP network. Rainfinity requires a separate VLAN in the network so that it does not interfere with the data path and clients can continue to access the storage with no disruption.

When data needs to be relocated for cost or performance optimization, the ports associated with the file servers involved in relocation are then associated with the Rainfinity VLAN. Rainfinity is in the data path for these file servers and all I/Os associated with these file servers pass through it. As Rainfinity now has control of this traffic, it can move the file system to its new location, transparently to the clients. Once the data relocation is complete, Rainfinity can update the global namespace; and the namespace, in turn, updates the clients. This update of the client namespace informs the clients about the new file system location. As clients are updated, their I/Os are now directed to the new location, removing Rainfinity from the I/O path. The new copy of the data is at the new location, and the original source reflects a point-in-time copy at the end of the data relocation.

Rainfinity treats data relocation as a transaction and has the capability to roll back transactions. During a transaction, updates to data are synchronized across the source and the new destination, eliminating the risk of data corruption. Rainfinity has an auto-complete feature that provides policy-based control on transaction completion. These policies can be framed based on the percentage of clients remapping. Rainfinity can handle multiple simultaneous transactions but performs only one active move transaction at a time, queuing up other transactions. Once the initial data copy is accomplished, multiple switching transactions are allowed.

Rainfinity uses the best characteristics of both the in-band and out-of-band method. The Rainfinity appliance remains out of band until it is required for data mobility. When Rainfinity is not performing any move or redirecting access task, all the file servers remain in the public LAN segment. When files are moved, the two file servers involved in the move must be part of the Rainfinity LAN segment (VLAN) and Rainfinity comes in-band.

Global Namespace Management

Rainfinity *Global Namespace Appliance* (GNA) allows storage administrators to remove the physical attributes associated with file storage and introduce a logical namespace in their environment. With a scalable, transparent file protocol-switching capability, a global namespace stores namespace schemes, provides directory services, and controls the file access point of CIFS and NFS clients. Commonly used operating systems include the client and server global namespace software that dynamically manages client referral and local mounts. The GFV *Global Namespace Management Application* provides an interface to view and manage file system namespaces. This application presents a unified view of global namespaces so that it is easier to understand the logical structure of the files. In addition, the application centrally manages distributed global namespaces by subscribing to and publishing namespace schemas that are stored on the DFS, NIS, and LDAP servers. The published namespaces are used by other Rainfinity applications that relocate data, while providing continuous read/write access.

The unified namespace view enables the creation of a multiprotocol global namespace that is serviced by independent CIFS and NFS global namespace servers. The Global Namespace Management Application merges the contents of namespace schemas by matching logical names, presenting a unified namespace hierarchy. In addition, the migration and consolidation application automatically updates the physical locations in both namespace schemas. These multiprotocol namespace synchronization capabilities eliminate the manual administrative tasks of maintaining separate namespaces.

Rainfinity Advantages

Like Invista, Rainfinity offers capacity management and storage consolidation. Rainfinity also provides tiered storage management support to achieve the enterprise ILM strategy. Rainfinity's primary application and advantage is transparent data mobility.

Summary

Virtualization provides flexibility while easing management of the existing infrastructure. Virtualization enables users to optimally utilize current processes, technologies, and systems. It allows for the addition, modification, or replacement of physical resources without affecting application availability. Virtualization technology offers high security and data integrity, which are mandatory for centralized computing environments. It also reduces performance degradation issues and unplanned downtime due to faults, and ensures increased availability of hardware resources.

This chapter detailed the different forms of virtualization and their benefits. It also covered block-level and file-level storage virtualization and provided associated product examples, explaining their processes. The data mobility features in virtualization ensure uninterrupted storage operation and prevent application outages due to any resource conflict or unavailability.

Resources and data are still vulnerable to natural disasters and other planned and unplanned outages, which can affect data availability. The next chapter covers business continuity and describes disaster recovery solutions that ensure high availability and uninterrupted business operations.

EXERCISES

1. What do VLANs virtualize? Discuss VLAN implementation as a virtualization technology.

2. Research SNIA's storage virtualization taxonomy and write a short technical note.

3. How can a block-level virtualization implementation be used as a data migration tool? Explain how data migration will be accomplished and discuss the advantages of using this method for storage. Compare this method to traditional migration methods.

4. Frequently, storage arrays in a data center are replaced with newer arrays to take advantage of technology advancements and cost benefits and to allow business growth. Migrating data from old arrays to a new array has now become a routinely performed activity in data centers. Do a survey of host-based, storage array–based, and virtualization appliance–based migration methods. Detail the advantages and disadvantages. Consider a migration scenario in which you are migrating from a DAS to a SAN environment.

5. Refer to question 4. Which method of migration will you use? Develop a short presentation explaining why you are recommending a particular method. Include a work breakdown structure for executing the migration with your recommended method.

Business Continuity

In This Section

Chapter 11
Introduction to
Business Continuity

KEY CONCEPTS

Business Continuity

Information Availability

Disaster Recovery

Disaster Restart

BC Planning

Business Impact Analysis

Continuous access to information is a must for the smooth functioning of business operations today, as the cost of business disruption could be catastrophic. There are many threats to information availability, such as natural disasters (e.g., flood, fire, earthquake), unplanned occurrences (e.g., cybercrime, human error, network and computer failure), and planned occurrences (e.g., upgrades, backup, restore) that result in the inaccessibility of information. It is critical for businesses to define appropriate plans that can help them overcome these crises. Business continuity is an important process to define and implement these plans.

Business continuity (BC) is an integrated and enterprisewide process that includes all activities (internal and external to IT) that a business must perform to mitigate the impact of planned and unplanned downtime. BC entails preparing for, responding to, and recovering from a system outage that adversely affects business operations. It involves proactive measures, such as business impact analysis and risk assessments, data protection, and security, and reactive countermeasures, such as disaster recovery and restart, to be invoked in the event of a failure. The goal of a business continuity solution is to ensure the "information availability" required to conduct vital business operations.

This chapter describes the factors that affect information availability. It also explains how to create an effective BC plan and design fault-tolerant mechanisms to protect against single points of failure.

11.1 Information Availability

Information availability (IA) refers to the ability of the infrastructure to function according to business expectations during its specified time of operation. Information availability ensures that people (employees, customers, suppliers, and partners) can access information whenever they need it. Information availability can be defined with the help of reliability, accessibility and timeliness.

- **Reliability:** This reflects a component's ability to function without failure, under stated conditions, for a specified amount of time.

- **Accessibility:** This is the state within which the required information is accessible at the right place, to the right user. The period of time during which the system is in an accessible state is termed *system uptime;* when it is not accessible it is termed *system downtime.*

- **Timeliness:** Defines the exact moment or the time window (a particular time of the day, week, month, and/or year as specified) during which information must be accessible. For example, if online access to an application is required between 8:00 AM and 10:00 PM each day, any disruptions to data availability outside of this time slot are not considered to affect timeliness.

11.1.1 Causes of Information Unavailability

Various planned and unplanned incidents result in data unavailability. *Planned outages* include installation/integration/maintenance of new hardware, software upgrades or patches, taking backups, application and data restores, facility operations (renovation and construction), and refresh/migration of the testing to the production environment. *Unplanned outages* include failure caused by database corruption, component failure, and human errors.

Another type of incident that may cause data unavailability is natural or man-made disasters such as flood, fire, earthquake, and contamination. As illustrated in Figure 11-1, the majority of outages are planned. Planned outages are expected and scheduled, but still cause data to be unavailable. Statistically, less than 1 percent is likely to be the result of an unforeseen disaster.

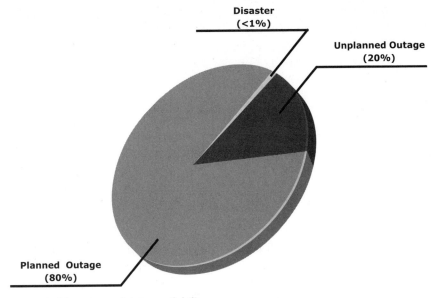

Figure 11-1: Disruptors of data availability

11.1.2 Measuring Information Availability

Information availability relies on the availability of the hardware and software components of a data center. Failure of these components might disrupt information availability. A failure is the termination of a component's ability to perform a required function. The component's ability can be restored by performing an external corrective action, such as a manual reboot, a repair, or replacement of the failed component(s). Repair involves restoring a component to a condition that enables it to perform a required function within a specified time by using procedures and resources. Proactive risk analysis performed as part of the BC planning process considers the component failure rate and average repair time, which are measured by MTBF and MTTR:

- **Mean Time Between Failure (MTBF):** It is the average time available for a system or component to perform its normal operations between failures.

- **Mean Time To Repair (MTTR):** It is the average time required to repair a failed component. While calculating MTTR, it is assumed that the fault responsible for the failure is correctly identified and that the required spares and personnel are available. Note that a fault is a physical defect at the component level, which may result in data unavailability. MTTR includes the time required to do the following: detect the fault, mobilize the maintenance team, diagnose the fault, obtain the spare parts, repair, test, and resume normal operations.

IA is the fraction of a time period that a system is in a condition to perform its intended function upon demand. It can be expressed in terms of system uptime and downtime and measured as the amount or percentage of system uptime:

IA = system uptime / (system uptime + system downtime)

In terms of MTBF and MTTR, IA could also be expressed as

IA = MTBF / (MTBF + MTTR)

Uptime per year is based on the exact timeliness requirements of the service, this calculation leads to the number of "9s" representation for availability metrics. Table 11-1 lists the approximate amount of downtime allowed for a service to achieve certain levels of 9s availability.

For example, a service that is said to be "five 9s available" is available for 99.999 percent of the scheduled time in a year ($24 \times 7 \times 365$).

Table 11-1: Availability Percentage and Allowable Downtime

UPTIME (%)	DOWNTIME (%)	DOWNTIME PER YEAR	DOWNTIME PER WEEK
98	2	7.3 days	3 hr 22 minutes
99	1	3.65 days	1 hr 41 minutes
99.8	0.2	17 hr 31 minutes	20 minutes 10 sec
99.9	0.1	8 hr 45 minutes	10 minutes 5 sec
99.99	0.01	52.5 minutes	1 minute
99.999	0.001	5.25 minutes	6 sec
99.9999	0.0001	31.5 sec	0.6 sec

11.1.3 Consequences of Downtime

Data unavailability, or downtime, results in loss of productivity, loss of revenue, poor financial performance, and damages to reputation. Loss of productivity reduces the output per unit of labor, equipment, and capital. Loss of revenue includes direct loss, compensatory payments, future revenue losses, billing losses, and investment losses. Poor financial performance affects revenue recognition, cash flow, discounts, payment guarantees, credit rating, and stock price. Damages to reputation may result in a loss of confidence or credibility with customers, suppliers, financial markets, banks, and business partners. Other possible consequences of downtime include the cost of additional equipment rental, overtime, and extra shipping.

The business impact of downtime is the sum of all losses sustained as a result of a given disruption. An important metric, *average cost of downtime per hour*, provides a key estimate in determining the appropriate BC solutions. It is calculated as follows:

> Average cost of downtime per hour = average productivity loss per hour + average revenue loss per hour
>
> Where:
>
> Productivity loss per hour = (total salaries and benefits of all employees per week) / (average number of working hours per week)
>
> Average revenue loss per hour = (total revenue of an organization per week) / (average number of hours per week that an organization is open for business)

The average downtime cost per hour may also include estimates of projected revenue loss due to other consequences such as damaged reputations and the additional cost of repairing the system.

11.2 BC Terminology

This section introduces and defines common terms related to BC operations and are used in the next few chapters to explain advanced concepts:

- **Disaster recovery:** This is the coordinated process of restoring systems, data, and the infrastructure required to support key ongoing business operations in the event of a disaster. It is the process of restoring a previous copy of the data and applying logs or other necessary processes to that copy to bring it to a known point of consistency. Once all recoveries are completed, the data is validated to ensure that it is correct.

- **Disaster restart:** This is the process of restarting business operations with mirrored consistent copies of data and applications.

- **Recovery-Point Objective (RPO):** This is the point in time to which systems and data must be recovered after an outage. It defines the amount of data loss that a business can endure. A large RPO signifies high tolerance to information loss in a business. Based on the RPO, organizations plan for the minimum frequency with which a backup or replica must be made. For example, if the RPO is six hours, backups or replicas must be made at least once in 6 hours. Figure 11-2 shows various RPOs and their corresponding ideal recovery strategies. An organization can plan for an appropriate BC technology solution on the basis of the RPO it sets. For example:

■ **RPO of 24 hours:** This ensures that backups are created on an offsite tape drive every midnight. The corresponding recovery strategy is to restore data from the set of last backup tapes.

■ **RPO of 1 hour:** This ships database logs to the remote site every hour. The corresponding recovery strategy is to recover the database at the point of the last log shipment.

■ **RPO of zero:** This mirrors mission-critical data synchronously to a remote site.

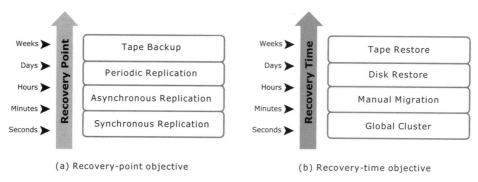

(a) Recovery-point objective   (b) Recovery-time objective

Figure 11-2: Strategies to meet RPO and RTO targets

■ **Recovery-Time Objective (RTO):** The time within which systems, applications, or functions must be recovered after an outage. It defines the amount of downtime that a business can endure and survive. Businesses can optimize disaster recovery plans after defining the RTO for a given data center or network. For example, if the RTO is two hours, then use a disk backup because it enables a faster restore than a tape backup. However, for an RTO of one week, tape backup will likely meet requirements. Some examples of RTOs and the recovery strategies to ensure data availability are listed below (refer to Figure 11-2):

■ **RTO of 72 hours:** Restore from backup tapes at a cold site.

■ **RTO of 12 hours:** Restore from tapes at a hot site.

■ **RTO of 4 hours:** Use a data vault to a hot site.

- **RTO of 1 hour:** Cluster production servers with controller-based disk mirroring.

- **RTO of a few seconds:** Cluster production servers with bidirectional mirroring, enabling the applications to run at both sites simultaneously.

▪ **Data vault:** A repository at a remote site where data can be periodically or continuously copied (either to tape drives or disks), so that there is always a copy at another site.

▪ **Hot site:** A site where an enterprise's operations can be moved in the event of disaster. It is a site with the required hardware, operating system, application, and network support to perform business operations, where the equipment is available and running at all times.

▪ **Cold site:** A site where an enterprise's operations can be moved in the event of disaster, with minimum IT infrastructure and environmental facilities in place, but not activated.

▪ **Cluster:** A group of servers and other necessary resources, coupled to operate as a single system. Clusters can ensure high availability and load balancing. Typically, in failover clusters, one server runs an application and updates the data, and another server is kept redundant to take over completely, as required. In more sophisticated clusters, multiple servers may access data, and typically one server performs coordination.

11.3 BC Planning Lifecycle

BC planning must follow a disciplined approach like any other planning process. Organizations today dedicate specialized resources to develop and maintain BC plans. From the conceptualization to the realization of the BC plan, a lifecycle of activities can be defined for the BC process. The BC planning lifecycle includes five stages (see Figure 11-3):

1. Establishing objectives

2. Analyzing

3. Designing and developing

4. Implementing

5. Training, testing, assessing, and maintaining

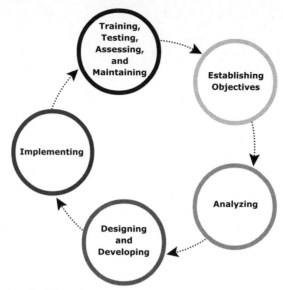

Figure 11-3: BC planning lifecycle

Several activities are performed at each stage of the BC planning lifecycle, including the following key activities:

1. Establishing objectives

    ▪ Determine BC requirements.

    ▪ Estimate the scope and budget to achieve requirements.

    ▪ Select a BC team by considering subject matter experts from all areas of the business, whether internal or external.

    ▪ Create BC policies.

2. Analyzing

    ▪ Collect information on data profiles, business processes, infrastructure support, dependencies, and frequency of using business infrastructure.

    ▪ Identify critical business needs and assign recovery priorities.

    ▪ Create a risk analysis for critical areas and mitigation strategies.

    ▪ Conduct a Business Impact Analysis (BIA).

    ▪ Create a cost and benefit analysis based on the consequences of data unavailability.

    ▪ Evaluate options.

3. Designing and developing

   - Define the team structure and assign individual roles and responsibilities. For example, different teams are formed for activities such as emergency response, damage assessment, and infrastructure and application recovery.

   - Design data protection strategies and develop infrastructure.

   - Develop contingency scenarios.

   - Develop emergency response procedures.

   - Detail recovery and restart procedures.

4. Implementing

   - Implement risk management and mitigation procedures that include backup, replication, and management of resources.

   - Prepare the disaster recovery sites that can be utilized if a disaster affects the primary data center.

   - Implement redundancy for every resource in a data center to avoid single points of failure.

5. Training, testing, assessing, and maintaining

   - Train the employees who are responsible for backup and replication of business-critical data on a regular basis or whenever there is a modification in the BC plan.

   - Train employees on emergency response procedures when disasters are declared.

   - Train the recovery team on recovery procedures based on contingency scenarios.

   - Perform damage assessment processes and review recovery plans.

   - Test the BC plan regularly to evaluate its performance and identify its limitations.

   - Assess the performance reports and identify limitations.

   - Update the BC plans and recovery/restart procedures to reflect regular changes within the data center.

11.4 Failure Analysis

Failure analysis involves analyzing the data center to identify systems that are susceptible to a single point of failure and implementing fault-tolerance mechanisms such as redundancy.

11.4.1 Single Point of Failure

A *single point of failure* refers to the failure of a component that can terminate the availability of the entire system or IT service. Figure 11-4 illustrates the possibility of a single point of failure in a system with various components: server, network, switch, and storage array. The figure depicts a system setup in which an application running on the server provides an interface to the client and performs I/O operations. The client is connected to the server through an IP network, the server is connected to the storage array through a FC connection, an HBA installed at the server sends or receives data to and from a storage array, and an FC switch connects the HBA to the storage port.

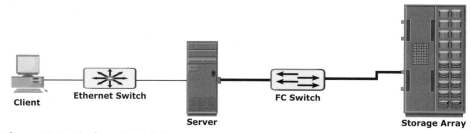

Figure 11-4: Single point of failure

In a setup where each component must function as required to ensure data availability, the failure of a single component causes the failure of the entire data center or an application, resulting in disruption of business operations. In this example, several single points of failure can be identified. The single HBA on the server, the server itself, the IP network, the FC switch, the storage array ports, or even the storage array could become potential single points of failure. To avoid single points of failure, it is essential to implement a fault-tolerant mechanism.

11.4.2 Fault Tolerance

To mitigate a single point of failure, systems are designed with redundancy, such that the system will fail only if all the components in the redundancy group fail. This ensures that the failure of a single component does not affect data availability. Figure 11-5 illustrates the fault-tolerant implementation of the system just described (and shown in Figure 11-4).

Data centers follow stringent guidelines to implement fault tolerance. Careful analysis is performed to eliminate every single point of failure. In the example shown in Figure 11-5, all enhancements in the infrastructure to mitigate single points of failures are emphasized:

- Configuration of multiple HBAs to mitigate single HBA failure.
- Configuration of multiple fabrics to account for a switch failure.
- Configuration of multiple storage array ports to enhance the storage array's availability.
- RAID configuration to ensure continuous operation in the event of disk failure.
- Implementing a storage array at a remote site to mitigate local site failure.
- Implementing server (host) clustering, a fault-tolerance mechanism whereby two or more servers in a cluster access the same set of volumes. Clustered servers exchange *heartbeats* to inform each other about their health. If one of the servers fails, the other server takes up the complete workload.

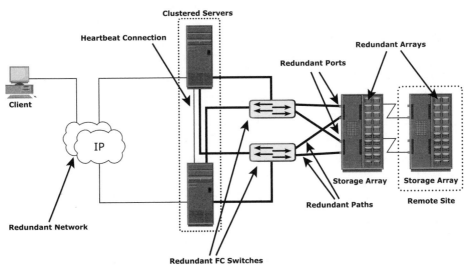

Figure 11-5: Implementation of fault tolerance

11.4.3 Multipathing Software

Configuration of multiple paths increases the data availability through path failover. If servers are configured with one I/O path to the data there will be no access to the data if that path fails. Redundant paths eliminate the path to become single points of failure. Multiple paths to data also improve I/O performance through load sharing and maximize server, storage, and data path utilization.

In practice, merely configuring multiple paths does not serve the purpose. Even with multiple paths, if one path fails, I/O will not reroute unless the system recognizes that it has an alternate path. Multipathing software provides the functionality to recognize and utilize alternate I/O path to data. Multipathing software also manages the load balancing by distributing I/Os to all available, active paths.

11.5 Business Impact Analysis

A *business impact analysis (BIA)* identifies and evaluates financial, operational, and service impacts of a disruption to essential business processes. Selected functional areas are evaluated to determine resilience of the infrastructure to support information availability. The BIA process leads to a report detailing the incidents and their impact over business functions. The impact may be specified in terms of money or in terms of time. Based on the potential impacts associated with downtime, businesses can prioritize and implement countermeasures to mitigate the likelihood of such disruptions. These are detailed in the BC plan. A BIA includes the following set of tasks:

- Identify the key business processes critical to its operation.
- Determine the attributes of the business process in terms of applications, databases, and hardware and software requirements.
- Estimate the costs of failure for each business process.
- Calculate the maximum tolerable outage and define RTO and RPO for each business process.
- Establish the minimum resources required for the operation of business processes.
- Determine recovery strategies and the cost for implementing them.

- Optimize the backup and business recovery strategy based on business priorities.
- Analyze the current state of BC readiness and optimize future BC planning.

11.6 BC Technology Solutions

After analyzing the business impact of an outage, designing appropriate solutions to recover from a failure is the next important activity. One or more copies of the original data are maintained using any of the following strategies, so that data can be recovered and business operations can be restarted using an alternate copy:

- **Backup and recovery:** Backup to tape is the predominant method of ensuring data availability. These days, low-cost, high-capacity disks are used for backup, which considerably speeds up the backup and recovery process. The frequency of backup is determined based on RPO, RTO, and the frequency of data changes.

- **Storage array-based replication (local):** Data can be replicated to a separate location within the same storage array. The replica is used independently for BC operations. Replicas can also be used for restoring operations if data corruption occurs.

- **Storage array-based replication (remote):** Data in a storage array can be replicated to another storage array located at a remote site. If the storage array is lost due to a disaster, BC operations start from the remote storage array.

- **Host-based replication:** The application software or the LVM ensures that a copy of the data managed by them is maintained either locally or at a remote site for recovery purposes.

11.7 Concept in Practice: EMC PowerPath

PowerPath is a host-based multipathing software that provides path failover and load balancing functionality. PowerPath operates between operating systems and device drivers and supports SCSI, iSCSI, and Fibre Channel environment. It prioritizes I/O bandwidth utilization by using sophisticated load balancing algorithms to ensure optimal application performance. Refer to `http://education.EMC.com/ismbook` for the latest information.

11.7.1 PowerPath Features

PowerPath provides the following features:

- **Online path configuration and management:** PowerPath provides the flexibility to define some paths to a device as "active" and some as "standby." The standby paths are used when all active paths to a logical device have failed. Paths can be dynamically added and removed by setting them in standby or active mode.

- **Dynamic load balancing across multiple paths:** PowerPath distributes the I/O requests across all available paths to the logical device. This reduces bottlenecks and improves application performance.

- **Automatic path failover:** In the event of a path failure, PowerPath fails over seamlessly to an alternative path without disrupting application operations. PowerPath redistributes I/O to the best available path to achieve optimal host performance.

- **Proactive path testing:** PowerPath uses the autoprobe and autorestore functions to proactively test the dead and restored paths, respectively. The PowerPath *autoprobe* function periodically probes inactive paths to identify failed paths before sending the application I/O. This process enables PowerPath to proactively close paths before an application experiences a timeout when sending I/O over failed paths. The PowerPath *autorestore* function runs every five minutes and tests every failed or closed path to determine whether it has been repaired.

- **Cluster support:** The deployment of PowerPath in a server cluster eliminates application downtime due to a path failure. PowerPath detects the path failure and uses an alternate path so the cluster software does not have to reconfigure the cluster to keep the applications running.

- **Interoperability:** PowerPath is supported on many operating systems, storage arrays, and storage interconnected devices, including iSCSI devices.

11.7.2 Dynamic Load Balancing

For every I/O, the PowerPath filter driver selects the path based on the load-balancing policy and failover setting for the logical device. The driver identifies all available paths that read and write to a device and builds a routing table called a volume path set for the devices. PowerPath follows any one of the following user specified load-balancing policies:

- **Round-Robin policy:** I/O requests are assigned to each available path in rotation.

- **Least I/Os policy:** I/O requests are routed to the path with the fewest queued I/O requests, regardless of the total number of I/O blocks.

- **Least Blocks policy:** I/O requests are routed to the path with the fewest queued I/O blocks, regardless of the number of requests involved.

- **Priority-Based policy:** I/O requests are balanced across multiple paths based on the composition of reads, writes, user-assigned devices, or application priorities.

I/O Operation without PowerPath

Figure 11-6 illustrates I/O operations in a storage system environment in the absence of PowerPath. The applications running on a host have four paths to the storage array. However, the applications can use only one of the paths because the LVM that is native to the host operating system allows only one path for application I/O operations.

This example illustrates how I/O throughput is unbalanced without PowerPath. Two applications are generating high I/O traffic, which overloads both paths, but the other two paths are less loaded. In this scenario, some paths may be idle or unused while other paths have multiple I/O operations queued. As a result, the applications cannot achieve optimal performance.

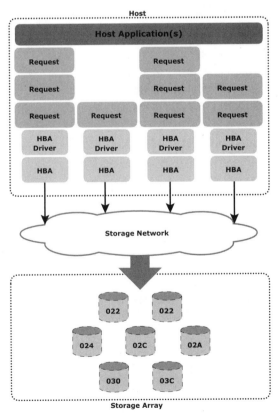

Figure 11-6: I/O without PowerPath

I/O Operation with PowerPath

Figure 11-7 shows I/O operations in a storage system environment that has PowerPath. PowerPath ensures that I/O requests are balanced across the four paths to storage, based on the load-balancing algorithm chosen. As a result, the applications can effectively utilize their resources, thereby improving their performance.

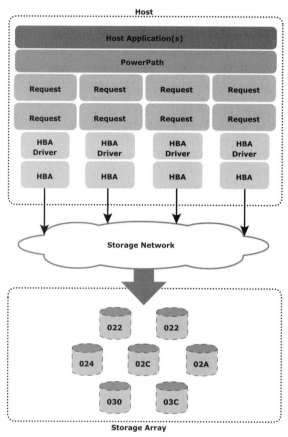

Figure 11-7: I/O with PowerPath

11.7.3 Automatic Path Failover

The next two examples demonstrate how PowerPath performs path failover operations in the event of a path failure for active-active and active-passive array configurations.

Path Failure without PowerPath

Figure 11-8 shows a scenario in which applications use only one of the four paths defined by the operating system. Without PowerPath, the loss of paths (the path failure is marked by a cross "X") due to single points of failure, such as the loss of an HBA, storage array front-end connectivity, switch port, or a failed cable, can result in an outage for one or more applications.

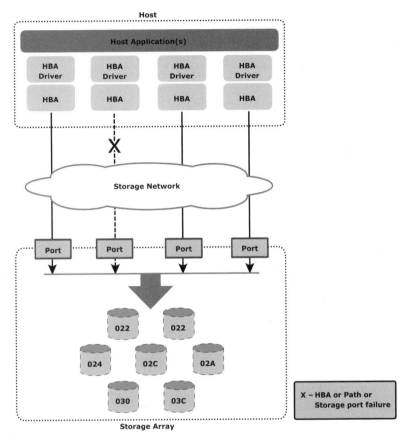

Figure 11-8: Path failure without PowerPath

Path Failover with PowerPath: Active-Active Array

Figure 11-9 shows a storage system environment in which an application uses PowerPath with an active-active array configuration to perform I/O operations. PowerPath redirects the application I/Os through an alternate active path.

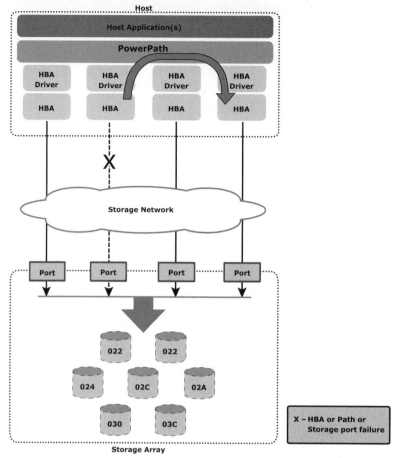

Figure 11-9: Path failover with PowerPath for an active-active array

In the event of a path failure, PowerPath performs the following operations:

1. If an HBA, cable, or storage front-end port fails, the device driver returns a timeout to PowerPath.

2. PowerPath responds by setting the path offline and redirecting the I/O through an alternate path.

3. Subsequent I/Os use alternate active path(s).

Path Failover with PowerPath: Active-Passive Array

Figure 11-10 shows a scenario in which a logical device is assigned to a storage processor B (SP B).

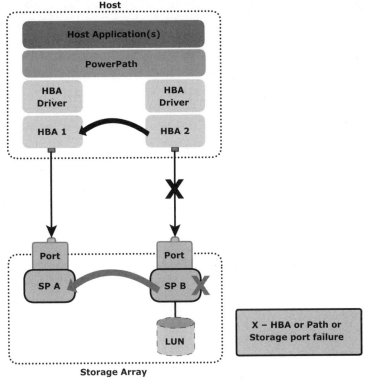

Figure 11-10: Path failover with PowerPath for an active-passive array

Path failure can occur due to a failure of the link, HBA, or storage processor (SP). In the event of a path failure, PowerPath with an active-passive configuration performs the path failover operation in the following way:

- If an active I/O path to SP B through HBA 2 fails, PowerPath uses a passive path to SP B through HBA 1.

- If HBA 2 fails, the application uses HBA 1 to access the logical device.

- If SP B fails, PowerPath stops all I/O to SP B and *trespasses* the device over to SP A. All I/O will be sent down the paths to SP A, this process is referred as *LUN trespassing*. When SP B is brought back online, PowerPath recognizes that it is available and resumes sending I/O down to SP B.

Summary

Technology innovations have led to a rich set of options in terms of storage devices and solutions to meet the needs of businesses for high availability and business continuity. The goal of any business continuity (BC) plan is to identify

and implement the most appropriate risk management and mitigation procedures to protect against possible failures. The process of analyzing the hardware
and software configuration to identify any single points of failure and their
impact on business operations is critical. A business impact analysis (BIA) helps
a company develop an appropriate BC plan to ensure that the storage infrastructure and services are designed to meet business requirements. BC provides the
framework for organizations to implement effective and cost-efficient disaster
recovery and restart procedures. In a constantly changing business environment, BC can become a demanding endeavor.

The next three chapters discuss specific BC technology solutions, backup and
recovery, local replication, and remote replication.

EXERCISES

1. A network router has a failure rate of 0.02 percent per 1,000 hours. What is the MTBF of that component?

2. The IT department of a bank promises customer access to the currency conversion rate table between 9:00 AM and 4:00 PM from Monday to Friday. It updates the table every day at 8:00 AM with a feed from the mainframe system. The update process takes 35 minutes to complete. On Thursday, due to a database corruption, the rate table could not be updated. At 9:05 AM, it was established that the table had errors. A rerun of the update was done and the table was recreated at 9:45 AM Verification was run for 15 minutes and the rate table became available to the bank branches. What was the availability of the rate table for the week in which this incident took place, assuming there were no other issues?

3. "Availability is expressed in terms of 9s." Explain the relevance of the use of 9s for availability, using examples.

4. Provide examples of planned and unplanned downtime in the context of data center operations.

5. How does clustering help to minimize RTO?

6. How is the choice of a recovery site strategy (cold and hot) determined in relation to RTO and RPO?

7. Assume the storage configuration design shown in the following figure:

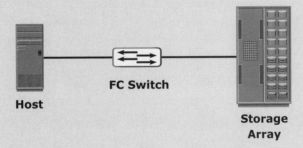

Host **FC Switch** **Storage Array**

Perform the single point of failure analysis for this configuration and provide an alternate configuration that eliminates all single points of failure.

Chapter 12
Backup and Recovery

backup is a copy of production data, created and retained for the sole purpose of recovering deleted or corrupted data. With growing business and regulatory demands for data storage, retention, and availability, organizations are faced with the task of backing up an ever-increasing amount of data. This task becomes more challenging as demand for consistent backup and quick restore of data increases throughout the enterprise — which may be spread over multiple sites. Moreover, organizations need to accomplish backup at a lower cost with minimum resources.

KEY CONCEPTS
Operational Backup
Archival
Retention Period
Bare-Metal Recovery
Backup Architecture
Backup Topologies
Virtual Tape Library

Organizations must ensure that the right data is in the right place at the right time. Evaluating backup technologies, recovery, and retention requirements for data and applications is an essential step to ensure successful implementation of the backup and recovery solution. The solution must facilitate easy recovery and retrieval from backups and archives as required by the business.

This chapter includes details about the purposes of backup, strategies for backup and recovery operations, backup methods, the backup architecture, and backup media.

12.1 Backup Purpose

Backups are performed to serve three purposes: disaster recovery, operational backup, and archival.

12.1.1 Disaster Recovery

Backups can be performed to address disaster recovery needs. The backup copies are used for restoring data at an alternate site when the primary site is incapacitated due to a disaster. Based on RPO and RTO requirements, organizations use different backup strategies for disaster recovery. When a tape-based backup method is used as a disaster recovery strategy, the backup tape media is shipped and stored at an offsite location. These tapes can be recalled for restoration at the disaster recovery site. Organizations with stringent RPO and RTO requirements use remote replication technology to replicate data to a disaster recovery site. This allows organizations to bring up production systems online in a relatively short period of time in the event of a disaster. Remote replication is covered in detail in Chapter 14.

12.1.2 Operational Backup

Data in the production environment changes with every business transaction and operation. *Operational backup* is a backup of data at a point in time and is used to restore data in the event of data loss or logical corruptions that may occur during routine processing. The majority of restore requests in most organizations fall in this category. For example, it is common for a user to accidentally delete an important e-mail or for a file to become corrupted, which can be restored from operational backup.

Operational backups are created for the active production information by using incremental or differential backup techniques, detailed later in this chapter. An example of an operational backup is a backup performed for a production database just before a bulk batch update. This ensures the availability of a clean copy of the production database if the batch update corrupts the production database.

12.1.3 Archival

Backups are also performed to address archival requirements. Although CAS has emerged as the primary solution for archives, traditional backups are still used by small and medium enterprises for long-term preservation of transaction records, e-mail messages, and other business records required for regulatory compliance.

Apart from addressing disaster recovery, archival, and operational requirements, backups serve as a protection against data loss due to physical damage of a storage device, software failures, or virus attacks. Backups can also be used to protect against accidents such as a deletion or intentional data destruction.

12.2 Backup Considerations

The amount of data loss and downtime that a business can endure in terms of RTO and RPO are the primary considerations in selecting and implementing a specific backup strategy. Another consideration is the retention period, which defines the duration for which a business needs to retain the backup copies. Some data is retained for years and some only for a few days. For example, data backed up for archival is retained for a longer period than data backed up for operational recovery.

It is also important to consider the backup media type, based on the retention period and data accessibility. Organizations must also consider the granularity of backups, explained later in this chapter. The development of a backup strategy must include a decision about the most appropriate time for performing a backup in order to minimize any disruption to production operations. Similarly, the location and time of the restore operation must be considered, along with file characteristics and data compression that influences the backup process.

Location, size, and number of files should also be considered, as they may affect the backup process. Location is an important consideration for the data to be backed up. Many organizations have dozens of heterogeneous platforms supporting complex solutions. Consider a data warehouse environment that uses backup data from many sources. The backup process must address these sources in terms of transactional and content integrity. This process must be coordinated with all heterogeneous platforms on which the data resides.

File size also influences the backup process. Backing up large-size files (example: ten 1 MB files) may use less system resources than backing up an equal amount of data comprising a large number of small-size files (example: ten thousand 1 KB files). The backup and restore operation takes more time when a file system contains many small files.

Like file size, the number of files to be backed up also influences the backup process. For example, in incremental backup, a file system containing one million files with a 10 percent daily change rate will have to create 100,000 entries in the backup catalog, which contains the table of contents for the backed up data set and information about the backup session. This large number of entries in the file system affects the performance of the backup and restore process because it takes a long time to search through a file system.

Backup performance also depends on the media used for the backup. The time-consuming operation of starting and stopping in a tape-based system affects backup performance, especially while backing up a large number of small files.

Data compression is widely used in backup systems because compression saves space on the media. Many backup devices, such as tape drives, have built-in support for hardware-based data compression. To effectively use this, it is important to understand the characteristics of the data. Some data, such as application binaries, do not compress well. Text data does compress well, whereas other data such as JPEG and ZIP files are already compressed.

12.3 Backup Granularity

Backup granularity depends on business needs and required RTO/RPO. Based on granularity, backups can be categorized as full, cumulative, and incremental. Most organizations use a combination of these three backup types to meet their backup and recovery requirements. Figure 12-1 depicts the categories of backup granularity.

Full backup is a backup of the complete data on the production volumes at a certain point in time. A full backup copy is created by copying the data on the production volumes to a secondary storage device. *Incremental backup* copies the data that has changed since the last full or incremental backup, whichever has occurred more recently. This is much faster (because the volume of data backed up is restricted to changed data), but it takes longer to restore. *Cumulative* (or *differential*) *backup* copies the data that has changed since the last full backup. This method takes longer than incremental backup but is faster to restore.

Synthetic (or *constructed*) *full backup* is another type of backup that is used in implementations where the production volume resources cannot be exclusively reserved for a backup process for extended periods to perform a full backup. It is usually created from the most recent full backup and all the incremental backups performed after that full backup. A synthetic full backup enables a full backup copy to be created offline without disrupting the I/O operation on the production volume. This also frees up network resources from the backup process, making them available for other production uses.

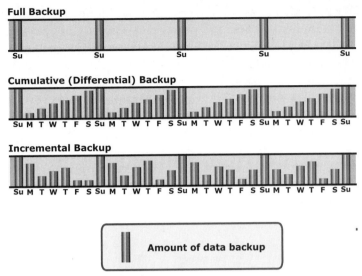

Figure 12-1: Backup granularity levels

Restore operations vary with the granularity of the backup. A full backup provides a single repository from which data can be easily restored. The process of restoration from an incremental backup requires the last full backup and all the incremental backups available until the point of restoration. A restore from a cumulative backup requires the last full backup and the most recent cumulative backup. Figure 12-2 illustrates an example of an incremental backup and restoration.

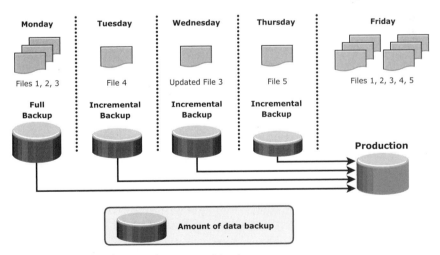

Figure 12-2: Restoring from an incremental backup

In this example, a full backup is performed on Monday evening. Each day after that, an incremental backup is performed. On Tuesday, a new file (File 4 in the figure) is added, and no other files have changed. Consequently, only File 4 is copied during the incremental backup performed on Tuesday evening. On Wednesday, no new files are added, but File 3 has been modified. Therefore, only the modified File 3 is copied during the incremental backup on Wednesday evening. Similarly, the incremental backup on Thursday copies only File 5. On Friday morning, there is data corruption, which requires data restoration from the backup. The first step toward data restoration is restoring all data from the full backup of Monday evening. The next step is applying the incremental backups of Tuesday, Wednesday, and Thursday. In this manner, data can be successfully restored to its previous state, as it existed on Thursday evening. Figure 12-3 illustrates an example of cumulative backup and restoration.

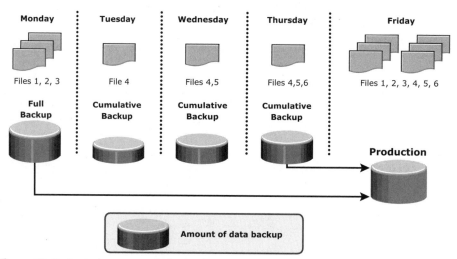

Figure 12-3: Restoring a cumulative backup

In this example, a full backup of the business data is taken on Monday evening. Each day after that, a cumulative backup is taken. On Tuesday, File 4 is added and no other data is modified since the previous full backup of Monday evening. Consequently, the cumulative backup on Tuesday evening copies only File 4. On Wednesday, File 5 is added. The cumulative backup taking place on Wednesday evening copies both File 4 and File 5 because these files have been added or modified since the last full backup. Similarly, on Thursday, File 6 is added. Therefore, the cumulative backup on Thursday evening copies all three files: File 4, File 5, and File 6.

On Friday morning, data corruption occurs that requires data restoration using backup copies. The first step in restoring data from a cumulative backup is restoring all data from the full backup of Monday evening. The next step is to apply only the latest cumulative backup — Thursday evening. In this way, the production volume data can be easily restored to its previous state on Thursday evening.

12.4 Recovery Considerations

RPO and RTO are major considerations when planning a backup strategy. RPO defines the tolerable limit of data loss for a business and specifies the time interval between two backups. In other words, the RPO determines backup frequency. For example, if application A requires an RPO of one day, it would need the data to be backed up at least once every day.

The retention period for a backup is also derived from an RPO specified for operational recovery. For example, users of application "A" may request to restore the application data from its operational backup copy, which was created a month ago. This determines the retention period for the backup. The RPO for application A can therefore range from one day to one month based on operational recovery needs. However, the organization may choose to retain the backup for a longer period of time because of internal policies or external factors, such as regulatory directives.

If short retention periods are specified for backups, it may not be possible to recover all the data needed for the requested recovery point, as some data may be older than the retention period. Long retention periods can be defined for all backups, making it possible to meet any RPO within the defined retention periods. However, this requires a large storage space, which translates into higher cost. Therefore, it is important to define the retention period based on an analysis of all the restore requests in the past and the allocated budget.

RTO relates to the time taken by the recovery process. To meet the defined RTO, the business may choose to use a combination of different backup solutions to minimize recovery time. In a backup environment, RTO influences the type of backup media that should be used. For example, recovery from data streams multiplexed in tape takes longer to complete than recovery from tapes with no multiplexing.

Organizations perform more full backups than they actually need because of recovery constraints. Cumulative and incremental backups depend on a previous full backup. When restoring from tape media, several tapes are needed to fully recover the system. With a full backup, recovery can be achieved with a lower RTO and fewer tapes.

12.5 Backup Methods

Hot backup and cold backup are the two methods deployed for backup. They are based on the state of the application when the backup is performed. In a *hot backup*, the application is up and running, with users accessing their data during the backup process. In a *cold backup*, the application is not active during the backup process.

The backup of online *production data* becomes more challenging because data is actively being used and changed. An open file is locked by the operating system and is not copied during the backup process until the user closes it. The backup application can back up open files by retrying the operation on files that were opened earlier in the backup process. During the backup process, it may be possible that files opened earlier will be closed and a retry will be successful. The maximum number of retries can be configured depending on the backup application. However, this method is not considered robust because in some environments certain files are always open.

In such situations, the backup application provides *open file agents*. These agents interact directly with the operating system and enable the creation of consistent copies of open files. In some environments, the use of open file agents is not enough. For example, a database is composed of many files of varying sizes, occupying several file systems. To ensure a consistent database backup, all files need to be backed up in the same state. That does not necessarily mean that all files need to be backed up at the same time, but they all must be synchronized so that the database can be restored with consistency.

Consistent backups of databases can also be done by using a cold backup. This requires the database to remain inactive during the backup. Of course, the disadvantage of a cold backup is that the database is inaccessible to users during the backup process.

Hot backup is used in situations where it is not possible to shut down the database. This is facilitated by *database backup agents* that can perform a backup while the database is active. The disadvantage associated with a hot backup is that the agents usually affect overall application performance.

A *point-in-time (PIT)* copy method is deployed in environments where the impact of downtime from a cold backup or the performance resulting from a hot backup is unacceptable. A pointer-based PIT copy consumes only a fraction of the storage space and can be created very quickly. A pointer-based PIT copy is implemented in a disk-based solution whereby a virtual LUN is created and holds pointers to the data stored on the production LUN or save location. In this method of backup, the database is stopped or frozen momentarily while the PIT copy is created. The PIT copy is then mounted on a secondary server and the backup occurs on the primary server. This technique is detailed in Chapter 13.

To ensure consistency, it is not enough to back up only production data for recovery. Certain attributes and properties attached to a file, such as permissions, owner, and other metadata, also need to be backed up. These attributes are as important as the data itself and must be backed up for consistency. Backup of boot sector and partition layout information is also critical for successful recovery.

In a disaster recovery environment, *bare-metal recovery (BMR)* refers to a backup in which all metadata, system information, and application configurations are appropriately backed up for a full system recovery. BMR builds the base system, which includes partitioning, the file system layout, the operating system, the applications, and all the relevant configurations. BMR recovers the base system first, before starting the recovery of data files. Some BMR technologies can recover a server onto dissimilar hardware.

12.6 Backup Process

A backup system uses client/server architecture with a backup server and multiple backup clients. The backup server manages the backup operations and maintains the backup catalog, which contains information about the backup process and backup metadata. The backup server depends on backup clients to gather the data to be backed up. The backup clients can be local to the server or they can reside on another server, presumably to back up the data visible to that server. The backup server receives backup metadata from the backup clients to perform its activities.

Figure 12-4 illustrates the backup process. The storage node is responsible for writing data to the backup device (in a backup environment, a storage node is a host that controls backup devices). Typically, the storage node is integrated with the backup server and both are hosted on the same physical platform. A backup device is attached directly to the storage node's host platform. Some backup architecture refers to the storage node as the *media server* because it connects to the storage device. Storage nodes play an important role in backup planning because they can be used to consolidate backup servers.

The backup process is based on the policies defined on the backup server, such as the time of day or completion of an event. The backup server then initiates the process by sending a request to a backup client (backups can also be initiated by a client). This request instructs the backup client to send its metadata to the backup server, and the data to be backed up to the appropriate storage node. On receiving this request, the backup client sends the metadata to the backup server. The backup server writes this metadata on its metadata catalog. The backup client also sends the data to the storage node, and the storage node writes the data to the storage device.

After all the data is backed up, the storage node closes the connection to the backup device. The backup server writes backup completion status to the metadata catalog.

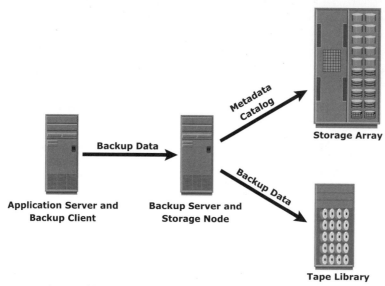

Figure 12-4: Backup architecture and process

Backup software also provides extensive reporting capabilities based on the backup catalog and the log files. These reports can include information such as the amount of data backed up, the number of completed backups, the number of incomplete backups, and the types of errors that may have occurred. Reports can be customized depending on the specific backup software used.

12.7 Backup and Restore Operations

When a backup process is initiated, significant network communication takes place between the different components of a backup infrastructure. The backup server initiates the backup process for different clients based on the backup schedule configured for them. For example, the backup process for a group of clients may be scheduled to start at 3:00 AM every day.

The backup server coordinates the backup process with all the components in a backup configuration (see Figure 12-5). The backup server maintains the information about backup clients to be contacted and storage nodes to be used in a backup operation. The backup server retrieves the backup-related information from the backup catalog and, based on this information, instructs the storage node to load the appropriate backup media into the backup devices. Simultaneously, it instructs the backup clients to start scanning the data, package it, and send it over the network to the assigned storage node. The storage node, in turn, sends metadata to the backup server to keep it updated about the media being used in the backup process. The backup server continuously updates the backup catalog with this information.

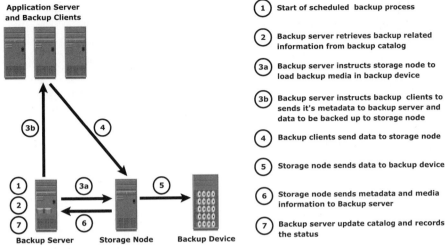

Figure 12-5: Backup operation

After the data is backed up, it can be restored when required. A restore process must be manually initiated. Some backup software has a separate application for restore operations. These restore applications are accessible only to the administrators. Figure 12-6 depicts a restore process.

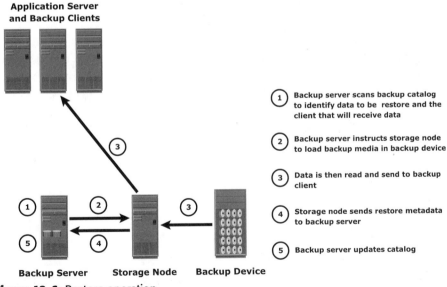

Figure 12-6: Restore operation

Upon receiving a restore request, an administrator opens the restore application to view the list of clients that have been backed up. While selecting the client for which a restore request has been made, the administrator also needs to identify the client that will receive the restored data. Data can be restored on the same client for whom the restore request has been made or on any other client. The administrator then selects the data to be restored and the specified point in time to which the data has to be restored based on the RPO. Note that because all of this information comes from the backup catalog, the restore application must also communicate to the backup server.

The administrator first selects the data to be restored and initiates the restore process. The backup server, using the appropriate storage node, then identifies the backup media that needs to be mounted on the backup devices. Data is then read and sent to the client that has been identified to receive the restored data.

Some restorations are successfully accomplished by recovering only the requested production data. For example, the recovery process of a spreadsheet is completed when the specific file is restored. In database restorations, additional data such as log files and production data must be restored. This ensures application consistency for the restored data. In these cases, the RTO is extended due to the additional steps in the restoration process.

12.8 Backup Topologies

Three basic topologies are used in a backup environment: direct attached backup, LAN based backup, and SAN based backup. A mixed topology is also used by combining LAN based and SAN based topologies.

In a *direct-attached backup*, a backup device is attached directly to the client. Only the metadata is sent to the backup server through the LAN. This configuration frees the LAN from backup traffic. The example shown in Figure 12-7 depicts use of a backup device that is not shared. As the environment grows, however, there will be a need for central management of all backup devices and to share the resources to optimize costs. An appropriate solution is to share the backup devices among multiple servers. In this example, the client also acts as a storage node that writes data on the backup device.

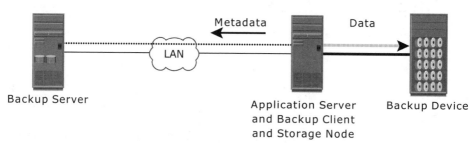

Figure 12-7: Direct-attached backup topology

In *LAN-based backup*, all servers are connected to the LAN and all storage devices are directly attached to the storage node (see Figure 12-8). The data to be backed up is transferred from the backup client (source), to the backup device (destination) over the LAN, which may affect network performance. Streaming across the LAN also affects network performance of all systems connected to the same segment as the backup server. Network resources are severely constrained when multiple clients access and share the same tape library unit (TLU).

This impact can be minimized by adopting a number of measures, such as configuring separate networks for backup and installing dedicated storage nodes for some application servers.

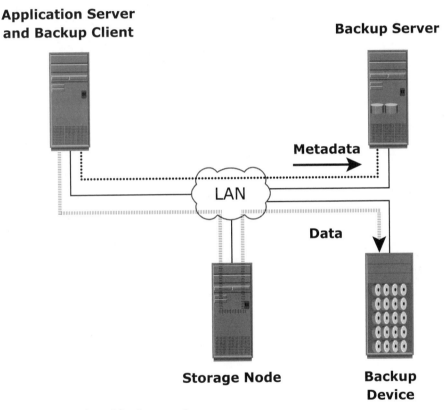

Figure 12-8: LAN-based backup topology

The *SAN-based backup* is also known as the *LAN-free backup*. Figure 12-9 illustrates a SAN-based backup. The SAN-based backup topology is the most appropriate solution when a backup device needs to be shared among the clients. In this case the backup device and clients are attached to the SAN.

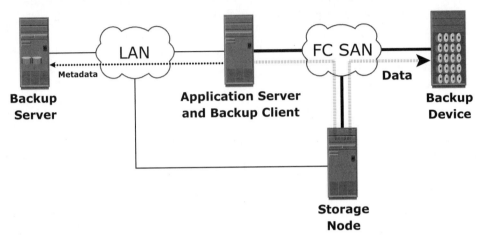

Figure 12-9: SAN-based backup topology

In this example, clients read the data from the mail servers in the SAN and write to the SAN attached backup device. The backup data traffic is restricted to the SAN, and backup metadata is transported over the LAN. However, the volume of metadata is insignificant when compared to production data. LAN performance is not degraded in this configuration.

By removing the network bottleneck, the SAN improves backup to tape performance because it frees the LAN from backup traffic. At the same time, LAN-free backups may affect the host and the application, as they consume host I/O bandwidth, memory, and CPU resources.

The emergence of low-cost disks as a backup medium has enabled disk arrays to be attached to the SAN and used as backup devices. A tape backup of these data backups on the disks can be created and shipped offsite for disaster recovery and long-term retention.

The *mixed topology* uses both the LAN-based and SAN-based topologies, as shown in Figure 12-10. This topology might be implemented for several reasons, including cost, server location, reduction in administrative overhead, and performance considerations.

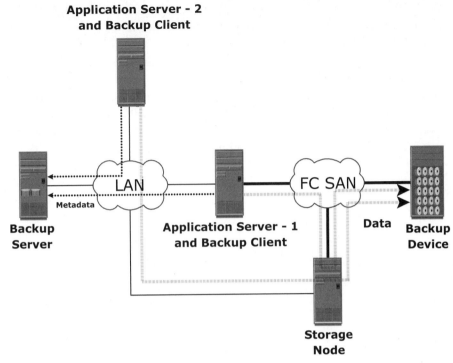

Figure 12-10: Mixed backup topology

12.8.1 Serverless Backup

Serverless backup is a LAN-free backup methodology that does not involve a backup server to copy data. The copy may be created by a network-attached controller, utilizing a SCSI extended copy or an appliance within the SAN. These backups are called serverless because they use SAN resources instead of host resources to transport backup data from its source to the backup device, reducing the impact on the application server.

Another widely used method for performing serverless backup is to leverage local and remote replication technologies. In this case, a consistent copy of the production data is replicated within the same array or the remote array, which can be moved to the backup device through the use of a storage node. Replication technologies are covered in detail in Chapter 13 and Chapter 14.

12.9 Backup in NAS Environments

The use of NAS heads imposes a new set of considerations on the backup and recovery strategy in NAS environments. NAS heads use a proprietary operating system and file system structure supporting multiple file-sharing protocols.

In the NAS environment, backups can be implemented in four different ways: server based, serverless, or using Network Data Management Protocol (NDMP) in either NDMP 2-way or NDMP 3-way.

In *application server-based backup*, the NAS head retrieves data from storage over the network and transfers it to the backup client running on the application server. The backup client sends this data to a storage node, which in turn writes the data to the backup device. This results in overloading the network with the backup data and the use of production (application) server resources to move backup data. Figure 12-11 illustrates server-based backup in the NAS environment.

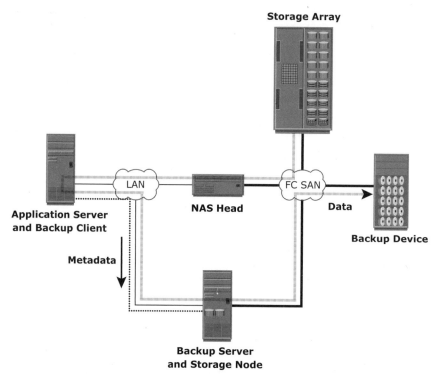

Figure 12-11: Server-based backup in NAS environment

In *serverless backup*, the network share is mounted directly on the storage node. This avoids overloading the network during the backup process and eliminates the need to use resources on the production server. Figure 12-12 illustrates serverless backup in the NAS environment. In this scenario, the storage node, which is also a backup client, reads the data from the NAS head and writes it to the backup device without involving the application server. Compared to the previous solution, this eliminates one network hop.

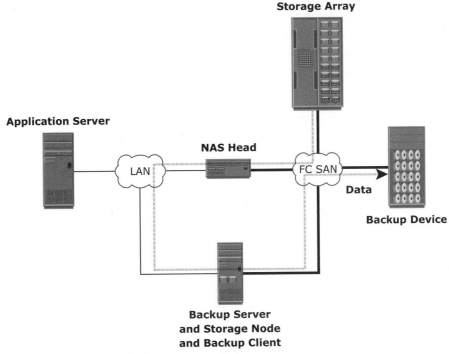

Figure 12-12: Serverless backup in NAS environment

NETWORK DATA MANAGEMENT PROTOCOL (NDMP)

NDMP is an industry-standard TCP/IP-based protocol for moving data across the network for backup and recovery. It can communicate with several interfaces for data transfer and enables vendors to use a common protocol for the backup architecture. Data can be backed up using NDMP regardless of the operating system or platform. Due to its flexibility, it is no longer necessary to transport data through the backup server, which reduces the load on the backup server and improves backup speed.

NDMP manages and transports data for robotics control of the tape library on the network. It optimizes backup and restore speeds due to the high-speed connection between the tape library and the NAS head.

In NDMP, backup data is sent directly from the NAS head to the backup device, while metadata is sent to the backup server. Figure 12-13 illustrates backup in the NAS environment using NDMP 2-way. In this model, network traffic is minimized by isolating data movement from the NAS head to the locally attached tape library. Only metadata is transported on the network. This backup solution meets the strategic need to centrally manage and control distributed data while minimizing network traffic.

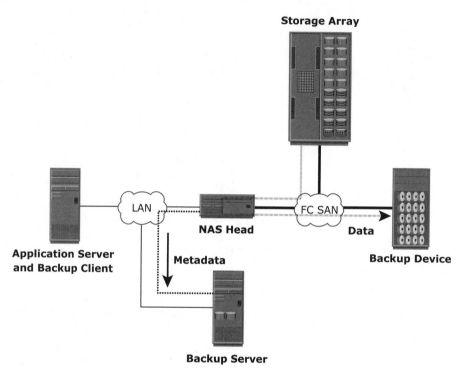

Figure 12-13: NDMP 2-way in NAS environment

In an *NDMP 3-way* file system, data is not transferred over the public network. A separate private backup network must be established between all NAS heads and the "backup" NAS head to prevent any data transfer on the public network in order to avoid any congestion or affect production operations. Metadata and NDMP control data is still transferred across the public network. Figure 12-14 depicts NDMP 3-way backup.

NDMP 3-way is useful when you have limited backup devices in the environment. It enables the NAS head to control the backup device and share it with other NAS heads by receiving backup data through NDMP.

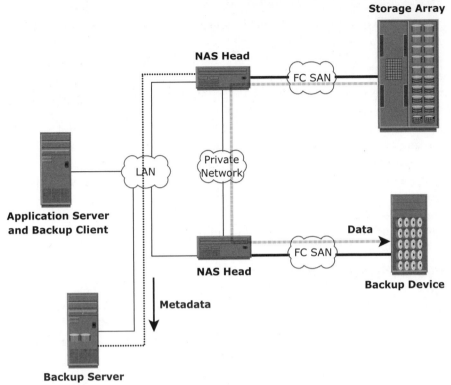

Figure 12-14: NDMP 3-way in NAS environment

12.10 Backup Technologies

A wide range of technology solutions are currently available for backup. Tapes and disks are the two most commonly used backup media. The tape technology has matured to scale to enterprise demands, whereas backup to disk is emerging as a viable option with the availability of low-cost disks. Virtual tape libraries use disks as backup medium emulating tapes, providing enhanced backup and recovery capabilities.

12.10.1 Backup to Tape

Tapes, a low-cost technology, are used extensively for backup. Tape drives are used to read/write data from/to a tape cartridge. Tape drives are referred to as sequential, or linear, access devices because the data is written or read sequentially.

Tape Mounting is the process of inserting a tape cartridge into a tape drive. The tape drive has motorized controls to move the magnetic tape around, enabling the head to read or write data.

Several types of tape cartridges are available. They vary in size, capacity, shape, number of reels, density, tape length, tape thickness, tape tracks, and supported speed. Today, a tape cartridge is composed of a magnetic tape with single or dual reels in a plastic enclosure.

A linear recording method was used in older tape drive technologies. This recording method consisted of data being written by multiple heads in parallel tracks, spanning the whole tape. Some tape drives used a helical scan method, which wrote the data diagonally. Modern tape drives use a linear serpentine method, which uses more tracks and fewer tape drive heads. Data is written in the same way as the linear method except that once the tape ends, the heads are moved and data continues to be written backward.

12.10.2 Physical Tape Library

The physical tape library provides housing and power for a number of tape drives and tape cartridges, along with a robotic arm or picker mechanism. The backup software has intelligence to manage the robotic arm and entire backup process. Figure 12-15 shows a physical tape library.

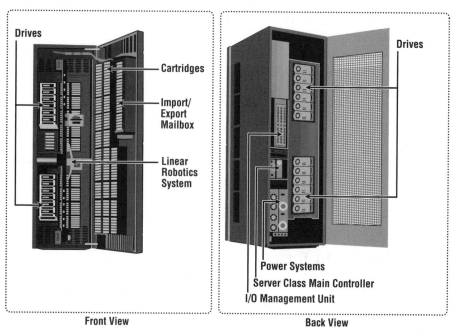

Figure 12-15: Physical tape library

Tape drives read and write data from and to a tape. Tape *cartridges* are placed in the *slots* when not in use by a tape drive. *Robotic arms* are used to move tapes around the library, such as moving a tape drive into a slot. Another type of slot called a *mail* or *import/export slot* is used to add or remove tapes from the library without opening the access doors (refer to Figure 12-15 Front View) because opening the access doors causes a library to go offline. In addition, each physical component in a tape library has an individual *element address* that is used as an addressing mechanism for moving tapes around the library.

When a backup process starts, the robotic arm is instructed to load a tape to a tape drive. This process adds to the delay to a degree depending on the type of hardware used, but it generally takes 5 to 10 seconds to mount a tape. After the tape is mounted, additional time is spent to position the heads and validate header information. This total time is called *load to ready time,* and it can vary from several seconds to minutes. The tape drive receives backup data and stores the data in its internal buffer. This backup data is then written to the tape in blocks. During this process, it is best to ensure that the tape drive is kept busy continuously to prevent gaps between the blocks. This is accomplished by buffering the data on tape drives. The speed of the tape drives can also be adjusted to match data transfer rates.

Tape drive *streaming* or *multiple streaming* writes data from multiple streams on a single tape to keep the drive busy. Shown in Figure 12-16, multiple streaming improves media performance, but it has an associated disadvantage. The backup data is interleaved because data from multiple streams is written on it. Consequently, the data recovery time is increased.

Figure 12-16: Multiple streams on tape media

Many times, even the buffering and speed adjustment features of a tape drive fail to prevent the gaps, causing the "shoe shining effect." This results in the tape drive stopping and rewinding to the appropriate point. The tape drive resumes writing only when its buffer is full, adversely affecting backup performance. When the tape operation is complete, the tape rewinds to the starting position and it is unmounted. The robotic arm is then instructed to move the unmounted tape back to the slot. *Rewind time* can range from several seconds to minutes.

When a *restore* is initiated, the backup software identifies which tapes are required. The robotic arm is instructed to move the tape from its slot to a tape drive. If the required tape is not found in the tape library, the backup software displays a message, instructing the operator to manually insert the required tape in the tape library. When a file or a group of files require restores, the tape must move sequentially to the beginning of the data before it can start reading. This process can take a significant amount of time, especially if the required files are recorded at the end of the tape.

Modern tape devices have an indexing mechanism that enables a tape to be fast forwarded to a location near the required data. The tape drive then fine-tunes the tape position to get to the data. However, before adopting a solution that uses tape drives supporting this mechanism, one must consider the benefits of data streaming performance against the cost of writing an index.

Limitations of Tape

Tapes are primarily used for long-term offsite storage because of their low cost. Tapes must be stored in locations with a controlled environment to ensure preservation of the media and prevent data corruption. Data access in a tape is sequential, which can slow backup and recovery operations. Physical transportation of the tapes to offsite locations also adds management overhead.

12.10.3 Backup to Disk

Disks have now replaced tapes as the primary device for storing backup data because of their performance advantages. Backup-to-disk systems offer ease of implementation, reduced cost, and improved quality of service. Apart from performance benefits in terms of data transfer rates, disks also offer faster recovery when compared to tapes.

Backing up to disk storage systems offers clear advantages due to their inherent random access and RAID-protection capabilities. In most backup environments, backup to disk is used as a staging area where the data is copied temporarily before transferring or staging it to tapes later. This enhances backup performance. Some backup products allow for backup images to remain on the disk for a period of time even after they have been staged. This enables a much faster restore. Figure 12-17 illustrates a recovery scenario comparing tape versus disk in a Microsoft Exchange environment that supports 800 users with a 75 MB mailbox size and a 60 GB database. As shown in the figure, a restore from disk took 24 minutes compared to the restore from a tape, which took 108 minutes for the same environment.

Recovery with a local replica, a full backup copy stored on disk and kept onsite, provides the fastest recovery solution. Using a disk enables the creation of full backups more frequently, which in turn improves RPO.

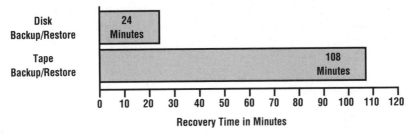

Figure 12-17: Tape versus disk restore

Backup to disk does not offer any inherent offsite capability, and is dependent on other technologies such as local and remote replication. In addition, some backup products require additional modules and licenses to support backup to disk, which may also require additional configuration steps, including creation of RAID groups and file system tuning. These activities are not usually performed by a backup administrator. Using backup to disk requires administrators to be aware of the file system's structure, fragmentation, file sizes, file system types, block size, and caching. The way the backup application interacts with the file system affects the way backup and restore occur.

For example, some backup products use very deep directory structures and group backup data in pre-allocated large files, reducing fragmentation. Other backup products use a "flat" structure, creating the backup files while the backup is running. This increases fragmentation, as more and more backup files are written to the same directory level. Therefore, it is important to understand how specific backup software operates and use the best practices provided by the storage manufacturer and the backup software vendor.

12.10.4 Virtual Tape Library

A *virtual tape library (VTL)* has the same components as that of a physical tape library except that the majority of the components are presented as virtual resources. For backup software, there is no difference between a physical tape library and a virtual tape library. Figure 12-18 shows a virtual tape library.

Virtual tape libraries use disks as backup media. Emulation software has a database with a list of virtual tapes, and each virtual tape is assigned a portion of a LUN on the disk. A virtual tape can span multiple LUNs if required. File system awareness is not required while using backup to disk because virtual tape solutions use raw devices.

Similar to a physical tape library, a robot mount is performed when a backup process starts in a virtual tape library. However, unlike a physical tape library, where this process involves some mechanical delays, in a virtual tape library it is almost instantaneous. Even the *load to ready* time is much less than in a physical tape library.

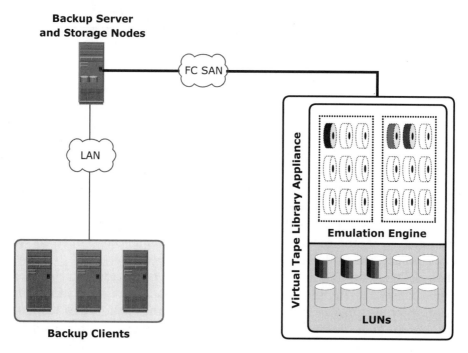

Figure 12-18: Virtual tape library

After the virtual tape is mounted and the tape drive is positioned, the virtual tape is ready to be used, and backup data can be written to it. Unlike a physical tape library, the virtual tape library is not constrained by the shoe shining effect. In most cases, data is written to the virtual tape immediately. When the operation is complete, the backup software issues a rewind command and then the tape can be unmounted. This rewind is also instantaneous. The virtual tape is then unmounted, and the virtual robotic arm is instructed to move it back to a virtual slot.

The steps to restore are similar to those in a physical tape library, but the restore operation is instantaneous. Even though virtual tapes are based on disks, which provide random access, they still emulate the tape behavior.

Virtual tape library appliances offer a number of features that are not available with physical tape libraries. Some virtual tape libraries offer *multiple emulation engines* configured in an active cluster configuration. An engine is a dedicated server with a customized operating system that makes physical disks in the VTL appear as tapes to the backup application. With this feature, one engine can pick up the virtual resources from another engine in the event of any failure and enable the clients to continue using their assigned virtual resources transparently.

Replication over IP is available with most of the virtual tape library appliances. This feature enables virtual tapes to be replicated over an inexpensive IP network to a remote site. As a result, organizations can comply with offsite requirements for backup data. It's also possible to connect the engines of a virtual tape library appliance to a physical tape library, enabling the virtual tapes to be copied onto the physical tapes, which can then be sent to a vault or shipped to an offsite location.

Using virtual tape offers several advantages over both physical tapes and disks. Compared to physical tape, virtual tape offers better single stream performance, better reliability, and random disk access characteristics. Backup and restore operations are sequential by nature, but they benefit from the disk's random access characteristics because they are always online and ready to be used, improving backup and recovery times. Virtual tape does not require the usual maintenance tasks associated with a physical tape drive, such as periodic cleaning and drive calibration. Compared to backup-to-disk devices, virtual tapes offer easy installation and administration and inherent offsite capabilities. In addition, virtual tapes do not require any additional modules or changes on the backup software.

However, virtual tapes can be used only for backup purposes because they are usually offered as an appliance. In a backup-to-disk environment, the disk systems can be used for both production and backup data. Virtual tape appliances are preconfigured from the manufacturer, facilitating easy installation and administration.

Table 12-1 shows a comparison between various backup technology options.

Table 12-1: Backup Technology Comparison

FEATURES	TAPE	DISK-AWARE BACKUP-TO-DISK	VIRTUAL TAPE
Offsite Capabilities	Yes	No	Yes
Reliability	No inherent protection methods	Yes	Yes
Performance	Subject to mechanical operations, load times	Faster single stream	Faster single stream
Use	Backup only	Multiple (backup/production)	Backup only

12.11 Concepts in Practice: EMC NetWorker

EMC backup products provide a powerful and effective way to back up and recover data. This ensures higher information protection and enables compliance with regulations and corporate policies. The EMC backup recovery portfolio consists of a broad range of products for an ever-increasing amount of backup data that presents a challenge to organizations such as demands of shorter backup windows, quicker restore responses, and de-duplication of backup data. EMC's backup products help organizations to meet these challenges through software and disk-based technologies. This section provides details of EMC NetWorker and a brief introduction about various other backup and recovery products, their major features, functionality, terminology, and processes.

Traditionally, the industry used tape backups that follow a one-size-fits-all strategy. However, tapes are challenged to meet service-level requirements. EMC NetWorker provides the capability to use disks for backup instead of tapes. The advanced backup capabilities enable the use of array-based snapshot and replication technology. These features of EMC NetWorker ensure high performance for backup and recovery. Visit `http://education.EMC.com/ismbook` for the latest information.

NetWorker enables simultaneous-access operations to a volume, for both reads and writes, as opposed to a single operation with tapes. NetWorker works within the existing framework of the hardware, operating system, software, and network communication protocols to provide protection for critical business data by centralizing, automating, and accelerating backup and recovery operations across an enterprise.

A single NetWorker server can be used to protect all clients and servers in the backup environment. NetWorker provides support for heterogeneous storage devices and platforms, and it integrates with popular databases and applications. NetWorker supports clustering technologies and open-file backup, and is compatible with tapes, disks, and virtual tape libraries. It uses the client/server model, which distributes the workload, improves backup performance, and provides network-based backup protection.

NetWorker provides advanced backup capability that leverages disk-based technologies, such as instant restore, off-host backups, and integration of backup with snapshots and full-volume mirrors. It enables meeting stringent RTO and RPO requirements.

NetWorker provides cold and hot backups, and supports a wide range of applications for hot backups with granular-level recovery. In a hot backup, NetWorker extracts data for backup using an API, and the application remains open even during the backup.

It uses 256-bit AES (advanced encryption standard) encryption authentication to provide increased security for communication between the hosts. Host machines are authenticated using the Secure Sockets Layer (SSL) protocol and self-signed certificates.

NetWorker also provides centralized management of the backup environment through a GUI, customizable reporting, and wizard-driven configuration. With the NetWorker Management Console (NMC), it can be easily administered from any host with a supported Web browser. NetWorker also provides many command-line utilities. With its various configuration points, NetWorker can be customized to meet the backup requirements of specific organizational needs. To facilitate NetWorker administration, several reports are available through the NMC reporting feature. Data maintained in the NMC server database, gathered from any or all of the NetWorker servers, is used to prepare reports on backup statistics and status, events, hosts, users, and devices.

NetWorker clients generate backups called *save sets*. NetWorker can back up multiple save sets from clients running different operating systems to any NetWorker-configured device. NetWorker can write more than one save set to a storage volume, and it supports backup to multiple devices that may be located at remote sites.

NetWorker also supports Open Tape Format (OTF), a data format that enables multiplexed, heterogeneous data to reside on the same tape. Using OTF, a NetWorker storage node can be migrated to a host running a different operating system.

12.11.1 NetWorker Backup Operation

In a NetWorker backup operation (refer to Figure 12-19), the NetWorker client pushes the backup data to the destination storage node. The client generates tracking information, including the file and directory names in the backup and the time of the backup, and sends it to the server to facilitate point-in-time recoveries. The storage node organizes the client's data and writes it to backup devices. Storage nodes also send tracking information about the save sets written during the backup to the NetWorker server. NetWorker also enables automating and scheduling the backup process.

NetWorker can initiate backup in two ways: client-initiated and server-initiated. A *client-initiated backup* is a manual/automated process that is initiated by a NetWorker client, whereas a *server-initiated backup* is initiated from the NetWorker server. The NetWorker server sends a backup request to one or more NetWorker clients. A server-initiated backup is usually configured to start automatically, but it can also be performed manually. This can be done from the NetWorker administration window or the CLI.

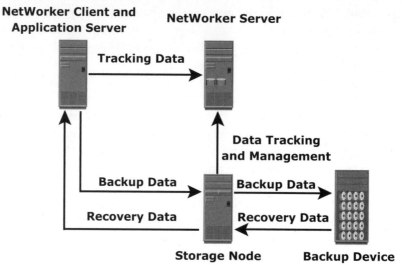

Figure 12-19: NetWorker operation

12.11.2 NetWorker Recovery

NetWorker is flexible in the way recovery operations are performed, and it maintains security to avoid recovery of data by unauthorized users. Recoverable data can include files, directories, file systems, or application data. Files can be recovered to a directory other than the directory from which they were backed up. NetWorker detects, and can be configured to automatically resolve, naming conflicts. The three types of manual recoveries — browsable, save set, and directed — are all processes initiated from a NetWorker client.

12.11.3 EmailXtender

EmailXtender is a comprehensive archive application that automatically collects, organizes, retains, and retrieves e-mail messages and attachments. It works with all major messaging environments, including Microsoft Exchange/Outlook and Lotus Domino/Notes. EmailXtender copies messages from mail servers into a dedicated archive by performing journaling on the e-mail server, preventing them from growing large enough to impact e-mail system performance. EmailXtender provides plug-in and web-based search facilities that improve storage management and operational efficiency of the messaging environment. With EmailXtender, companies can automatically enforce retention policies by periodically deleting messages from mail servers and archiving them to EmailXtender. The EmailXtract feature of EmailXtender enables removing messages from the mail server and replacing them with pointers or shortcuts to copies of the messages archived in EmailXtender. Users can seamlessly access these messages as if they were still stored on the mail server. This improves e-mail server performance, backup, and recovery performance, and reduces storage costs.

12.11.4 DiskXtender

DiskXtender is a robust storage management solution available only for the Microsoft Windows platform. DiskXtender extends the amount of space on the local NTFS (NT file system) volume. It does this by migrating files from the local drive to external media and purging files from primary storage. To a client retrieving files from the drive extended by DiskXtender, all files, whether on the extended drive or on storage media, appear to be present locally. Transfer of files to secondary storage can be controlled by a set of rules that detail migration criteria, such as a file's age, size, type, or other attributes. To avoid media-swapping delays during data request, DiskXtender intelligently queues requests for files and accesses secondary media only when necessary. To enhance availability, it can migrate a single file to as many as four different targets. Clients writing to the extended drive are unaware of the volume being extended by DiskXtender. Writing a file to a secondary media adds extended attribute information to the file on the extended drive. Purging a file removes the file data from the extended drive, leaving behind a file tag on the drive. When a file on the extended drive is requested, it is provided directly by the operating system; but if the file isn't found on the extended drive, the request is forwarded to the media storage software, which locates the appropriate media, and locates the file.

12.11.5 Avamar

Avamar is a comprehensive, client-server network backup and restore solution. Avamar differs from traditional backup and restore solutions by identifying and storing only unique sub-file data objects. Redundant data is identified at the source, drastically reducing the amount of data that travels across the network to be stored and managed by the backup host. Avamar also creates and stores "trees" that link all data objects from a single backup. These trees are used to recreate files for restore. Avamar uses standard IP network technology, so dedicated backup networks are not required. During backup, the Avamar client traverses each directory and examines the local cache to determine which files have not been previously backed up. Once an object is backed up on the server, it is never sent for backup again. This drastically reduces network traffic and enhances backup storage efficiency, guaranteeing the most effective de-duplication of the data. After an object has been stored, it cannot be deleted until the specified retention period has expired.

12.11.6 EMC Disk Library (EDL)

EDL is a dedicated virtual tape library appliance. It consists of a storage system and a Linux-based server. The server runs software that emulates tape drives and tape libraries. To the backup software, the virtual tape drives and cartridges will look and behave like physical libraries, drives, and cartridges.

Summary

Data availability is a critical requirement for information-centric businesses. Backups protect businesses from data loss and also helps to meet regulatory and compliance requirements.

This chapter detailed backup considerations, methods, technologies, and implementations in a storage networking environment. It also elaborated various backup topologies and architectures.

Although the selection of a particular backup media is driven by the defined RTO and RPO, disk-based backup has a clear advantage over tape-based backup in terms of performance, availability, faster recovery, and ease of management. These advantages are further supplemented with the use of replication technologies to achieve the highest level of service and availability requirements. Replication technologies are covered in detail in the next two chapters.

EXERCISES

1. A manufacturing corporation uses tape as its primary backup storage media throughout the organization. Full backups are performed every Sunday. Incremental backups are performed Monday through Saturday. The environment contains many backup servers, backing up different groups of servers.

   ■ The e-mail and database applications have to be shut down during the backup process. Due to the decentralized backup environment, recoverability is often compromised. There are too many tapes that need to be mounted to perform a full recovery in case of a complete failure. The time needed to recover is too lengthy.

   ■ The company would like to deploy an easy-to-manage backup environment. They want to reduce the amount of time the e-mail and database applications are unavailable, and reduce the number of tapes required to fully recover a server in case of a failure.

   ■ Propose a backup and recovery solution to address the company's needs. Justify how your solution ensures that their requirements will be met.

2. There are limited backup devices in a file sharing NAS environment. Suggest a suitable backup implementation that will minimize the network traffic, avoid any congestion, and at the same time not impact the production operations. Justify your answer.

3. Discuss the security concerns in backup environment.

4. What are the various business/technical considerations for implementing a backup solution, and how do these considerations impact the backup solution/implementation?

5. What is the purpose of performing operation backup, disaster recovery, and archiving?

6. List and explain the considerations in using tape as the backup technology. What are the challenges in this environment?

7. Describe the benefits of using "virtual tape library" over "physical tapes."

Chapter 13
Local Replication

Replication is the process of creating an exact copy of data. Creating one or more replicas of the production data is one of the ways to provide Business Continuity (BC). These replicas can be used for recovery and restart operations in the event of data loss.

KEY CONCEPTS

Data Consistency

Host-Based Local Replication

Storage Array–Based Local Replication

Copy on First Access (CoFA)

Copy on First Write (CoFW)

Restore and Restart

The primary purpose of replication is to enable users to have designated data at the right place, in a state appropriate to the recovery need. The replica should provide recoverability and restartability. Recoverability enables restoration of data from the replicas to the production volumes in the event of data loss or data corruption. It must provide minimal RPO and RTO for resuming business operations on the production volumes, while restartability must ensure consistency of data on the replica. This enables restarting business operations using the replicas.

Replication can be classified into two major categories: local and remote. Local replication refers to replicating data within the same array or the same data center. This chapter provides details about various local replication technologies, along with key steps to plan and design an appropriate local replication solution. Remote replication is covered in Chapter 14.

13.1 Source and Target

A host accessing data from one or more LUNs on the storage array is called a *production host*, and these LUNs are known as source LUNs (devices/volumes), production LUNs, or simply the *source*.

A LUN (or LUNs) on which the data is replicated is called the target LUN or simply the *target* or replica. Targets can also be accessed by hosts other than production hosts to perform operations such as backup or testing. Target data can be updated by the hosts accessing it without modifying the source. However, the source and the target are not an identical copy of each other anymore. The target can be incrementally resynchronized (copying of data that has changed since the previous synchronization) with the source to make both source and target identical.

13.2 Uses of Local Replicas

One or more local replicas of the source data can be created for various purposes, including the following:

- **Alternate source for backup:** Under normal backup operations, data is read from the production volumes (LUNs) and written to the backup device. This places additional burden on the production infrastructure, as production LUNs are simultaneously involved in production work. As the local replica contains an exact point-in-time (PIT) copy of the source data, it can be used to perform backup operations. This alleviates the backup I/O workload on the production volumes. Another benefit of using local replicas for backup is that it reduces the *backup window* to zero.

 The period during which a source is available to perform a data backup is called a *backup window*. Performing backup from the source sometimes requires the production operation to be suspended because the data being backed up is exclusively locked for the use of the backup process.

- **Fast recovery:** In the event of a partial failure of the source, or data corruption, a local replica can be used to recover lost data. In the event of a complete failure of the source, the replica can be restored to a different set of source devices. In either case, this method provides faster recovery and minimal RTO, compared to traditional restores from tape backups. In many instances business operations can be started using the source device before the data is completely copied from the replica.

- **Decision-support activities such as reporting:** Running the reports using the data on the replicas greatly reduces the I/O burden placed on the production device.

- **Testing platform:** A local replica can be used for testing critical business data or applications. For example, when planning an application upgrade, it can be tested using the local replica. If the test is successful, it can be restored to the source volumes.

- **Data migration:** Local replication can also be used for data migration. Data migration may be performed for various reasons, such as migrating from a small LUN to a larger LUN.

13.3 Data Consistency

Most file systems and databases buffer data in the host before it is written to disk. A consistent replica ensures that data buffered in the host is properly captured on the disk when the replica is created. Ensuring consistency is the primary requirement for all the replication technologies.

13.3.1 Consistency of a Replicated File System

File systems buffer data in host memory to improve application response time. The buffered information is periodically written to disk. In UNIX operating systems, the *sync daemon* is the process that flushes the buffers to disk at set intervals. In some cases, the replica may be created in between the set intervals. Hence, the host memory buffers must be flushed to ensure data consistency on the replica, prior to its creation. Figure 13-1 illustrates flushing of the buffer to its source, which is then replicated. If the host memory buffers are not flushed, data on the replica will not contain the information that was buffered in the host. If the file system is unmounted prior to the creation of the replica, the buffers would be automatically flushed and data would be consistent on the replica.

If a mounted file system is replicated, some level of recovery such as *fsck* or *log replay* would be required on the replicated file system. When the file system replication process is completed, the replica file system can be mounted for operational use.

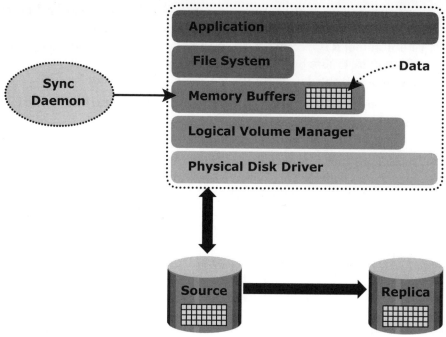

Figure 13-1: File system replication

13.3.2 Consistency of a Replicated Database

A database may be spread over numerous files, file systems, and devices. All of these must be replicated consistently to ensure that the replica is restorable and restartable. Replication can be performed with the database offline or online. If the database is offline, it is not available for I/O operations. Because no updates are occurring, the replica will be consistent.

If the database is online, it is available for I/O operations. Transactions to the database will be updating data continuously. When a database is backed up while it is online, changes made to the database at this time must be applied to the backup copy to make it consistent. Performing an online backup requires additional procedures during backup and restore. Often these procedures can be scripted to automate the process, alleviating administrative work and minimizing human error. Most databases support some form of online or hot backups. There will be increased logging activity during the time when the database is in the hot backup mode.

The sequence of operations in a hot backup mode is first to issue a database checkpoint to flush buffers to disk and place the database in hot backup mode. After taking a PIT copy, the database is taken out of hot backup mode. Logs collected are then applied to the replica to restore database consistently.

An alternate approach exploits the *dependent write I/O* principle inherent in any database management system (DBMS). According to this principle, a write I/O is not issued by an application until a prior related write I/O has completed. For example, a data write is dependent on the successful completion of the prior log write. Dependent write consistency is required for protection against power outages, loss of local channel connectivity, or storage devices. When the failure occurs a dependent write consistent image is created. A restart transforms the dependent write consistent image to a transactional consistent image — i.e., committed transactions are recovered, and in-flight transactions are discarded.

In order for a transaction to be deemed complete, databases require that a series of writes have to occur in a particular order. These writes would be recorded on the various devices/file systems. Figure 13-2, illustrates the process of flushing the buffer from host to source; I/Os 1 to 4 must complete, in order for the transaction to be considered complete. I/O 4 is dependent on I/O 3 and will occur only if I/O 3 is complete. I/O 3 is dependent on I/O 2, which in turn depends on I/O 1. Each I/O completes only after completion of the previous I/O(s).

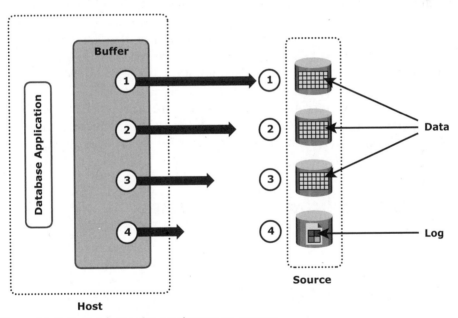

Figure 13-2: Dependent write consistency on sources

At the point in time when the replica is created, all the writes to the source devices must be captured on the replica devices to ensure data consistency. Figure 13-3 illustrates the process of replication from source to replica, I/O transactions 1 to 4 must be carried out in order for the data to be consistent on the replica.

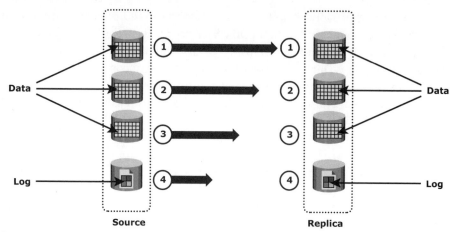

Figure 13-3: Dependent write consistency on replica

Creating a PIT copy for multiple devices happens quickly, but not instantaneously. It is possible that I/O transactions 3 and 4 were copied to the replica devices, but I/O transactions 1 and 2 were not copied. In this case, the data on the replica is inconsistent with the data on the source. If a restart were to be performed on the replica devices, I/O 4, which is available on the replica, might indicate that a particular transaction is complete, but all the data associated with the transaction will be unavailable on the replica, making the replica inconsistent.

Another way to ensure consistency is to make sure that write I/O to all source devices is held for the duration of creating the replica. This creates a consistent image on the replica. Note that databases and applications can time out if the I/O is held for too long.

13.4 Local Replication Technologies

Host-based and storage-based replications are the two major technologies adopted for local replication. File system replication and LVM-based replication are examples of host-based local replication technology. Storage array–based replication can be implemented with distinct solutions namely, full-volume mirroring, pointer-based full-volume replication, and pointer-based virtual replication.

13.4.1 Host-Based Local Replication

In host-based replication, logical volume managers (LVMs) or the file systems perform the local replication process. LVM-based replication and file system (FS) snapshot are examples of host-based local replication.

LVM-Based Replication

In LVM-based replication, logical volume manager is responsible for creating and controlling the host-level logical volume. An LVM has three components: physical volumes (physical disk), volume groups, and logical volumes. A *volume group* is created by grouping together one or more physical volumes. *Logical volumes* are created within a given volume group. A volume group can have multiple logical volumes.

In LVM-based replication, each *logical partition* in a logical volume is mapped to two physical partitions on two different physical volumes, as shown in Figure 13-4. An application write to a logical partition is written to the two physical partitions by the LVM device driver. This is also known as *LVM mirroring*. Mirrors can be split and the data contained therein can be independently accessed. LVM mirrors can be added or removed dynamically.

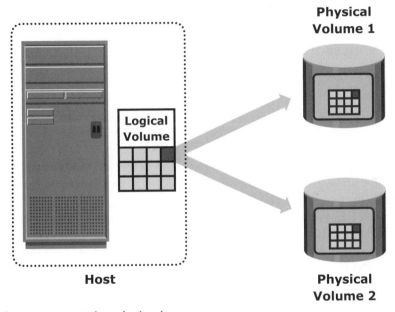

Figure 13-4: LVM-based mirroring

Advantages of LVM-Based Replication

The LVM-based replication technology is not dependent on a vendor-specific storage system. Typically, LVM is part of the operating system and no additional license is required to deploy LVM mirroring.

Limitations of LVM-Based Replication

As every write generated by an application translates into two writes on the disk, an additional burden is placed on the host CPU. This can degrade application performance. Presenting an LVM-based local replica to a second host is usually not possible because the replica will still be part of the volume group, which is usually accessed by one host at any given time.

Tracking changes to the mirrors and performing incremental synchronization operations is also a challenge as all LVMs do not support incremental resynchronization. If the devices are already protected by some level of RAID on the array, then the additional protection provided by mirroring is unnecessary. This solution does not scale to provide replicas of federated databases and applications. Both the replica and the source are stored within the same volume group. Therefore, the replica itself may become unavailable if there is an error in the volume group. If the server fails, both source and replica are unavailable until the server is brought back online.

File System Snapshot

File system (FS) snapshot is a pointer-based replica that requires a fraction of the space used by the original FS. This snapshot can be implemented by either FS itself or by LVM. It uses Copy on First Write (CoFW) principle. CoFW mechanism is discussed later in the chapter.

When the snapshot is created, a bitmap and a blockmap are created in the metadata of the Snap FS. The bitmap is used to keep track of blocks that are changed on the production FS after creation of the snap. The blockmap is used to indicate the exact address from which data is to be read when the data is accessed from the Snap FS. Immediately after creation of the snapshot all reads from the snapshot will actually be served by reading the production FS.

To read from the Snap FS, the bitmap is consulted. If the bit is 0, then the read is directed to the production FS. If the bit is 1, then the block address is obtained from the blockmap and data is read from that address. Reads from the production FS work as normal.

13.4.2 Storage Array–Based Replication

In *storage array-based local replication*, the array operating environment performs the local replication process. The host resources such as CPU and memory are not used in the replication process. Consequently, the host is not burdened by the replication operations. The replica can be accessed by an alternate host for any business operations.

In this replication, the required number of replica devices should be selected on the same array and then data is replicated between source-replica pairs. A database could be laid out over multiple physical volumes and in that case all the devices must be replicated for a consistent PIT copy of the database.

Figure 13-5 shows storage array based local replication, where source and target are in the same array and accessed by different hosts.

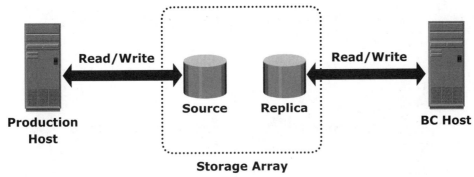

Figure 13-5: Storage array-based replication

Storage array-based local replication can be further categorized as full-volume mirroring, pointer-based full-volume replication, and pointer-based virtual replication. Replica devices are also referred as target devices, accessible by business continuity host.

Full-Volume Mirroring

In *full-volume mirroring*, the target is attached to the source and established as a mirror of the source (Figure 13-6 [a]). Existing data on the source is copied to the target. New updates to the source are also updated on the target. After all the data is copied and both the source and the target contain identical data, the target can be considered a mirror of the source.

While the target is attached to the source and the synchronization is taking place, the target remains unavailable to any other host. However, the production host can access the source.

After synchronization is complete, the target can be detached from the source and is made available for BC operations. Figure 13-6 (b) shows full-volume mirroring when the target is detached from the source. Notice that both the source and the target can be accessed for read and write operations by the production hosts.

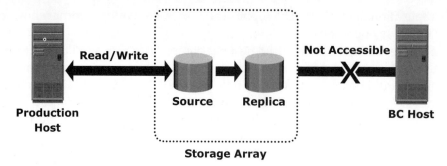

(a) Full volume mirroring with source attached to replica

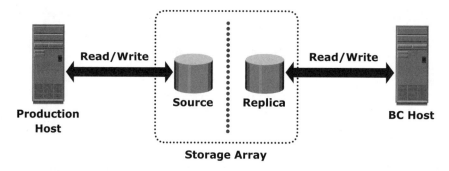

(b) Full volume mirroring with source detached from replica

Figure 13-6: Full-volume mirroring

After the split from the source, the target becomes a PIT copy of the source. The point-in-time of a replica is determined by the time when the source is detached from the target. For example, if the time of detachment is 4:00 PM, the PIT for the target is 4:00 PM

After detachment, changes made to both source and replica can be tracked at some predefined granularity. This enables incremental resynchronization (source to target) or incremental restore (target to source). The granularity of the data change can range from 512 byte blocks to 64 KB blocks. Changes are typically tracked using bitmaps, with one bit assigned for each block. If any updates occur to a particular block, the whole block is marked as changed, regardless of the size of the actual update. However, for resynchronization (or restore), only the changed blocks have to be copied, eliminating the need for a full synchronization (or restore) operation. This method reduces the time required for these operations considerably.

In full-volume mirroring, the target is inaccessible for the duration of the synchronization process, until detachment from the source. For large databases, this can take a long time.

Pointer-Based, Full-Volume Replication

An alternative to full-volume mirroring is *pointer-based full-volume replication*. Like full-volume mirroring, this technology can provide full copies of the source data on the targets. Unlike full-volume mirroring, the target is made immediately available at the activation of the replication session. Hence, one need not wait for data synchronization to, and detachment of, the target in order to access it. The time of activation defines the PIT copy of source.

Pointer-based, full-volume replication can be activated in either Copy on First Access (CoFA) mode or Full Copy mode. In either case, at the time of activation, a protection bitmap is created for all data on the source devices. Pointers are initialized to map the (currently) empty data blocks on the target to the corresponding original data blocks on the source. The granularity can range from 512 byte blocks to 64 KB blocks or higher. Data is then copied from the source to the target, based on the mode of activation.

In CoFA, after the replication session is initiated, data is copied from the source to the target when the following occurs:

- A write operation is issued to a specific address on the source for the first time (see Figure 13-7).

- A read or write operation is issued to a specific address on the target for the first time (see Figure 13-8 and Figure 13-9) .

When a write is issued to the source for the first time after session activation, original data at that address is copied to the target. After this operation, the new data is updated on the source. This ensures that original data at the point-in-time of activation is preserved on the target. This is illustrated in Figure 13-7.

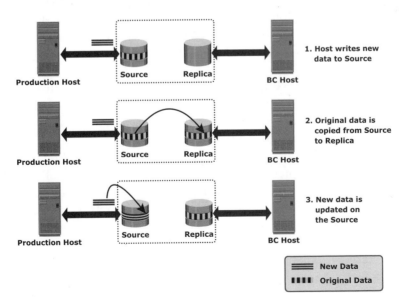

Figure 13-7: Copy on first access (CoFA) — write to source

When a read is issued to the target for the first time after session activation, the original data is copied from the source to the target and is made available to the host. This is illustrated in Figure 13-8.

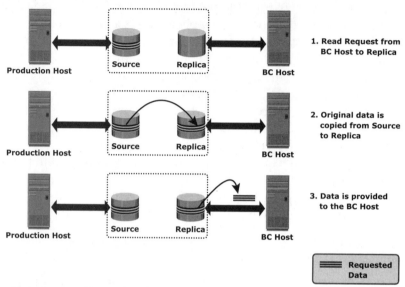

Figure 13-8: Copy on first access (CoFA) — read from target

When a write is issued to the target for the first time after session activation, the original data is copied from the source to the target. After this, the new data is updated on the target. This is illustrated in Figure 13-9.

In all cases, the protection bit for that block is reset to indicate that the original data has been copied over to the target. The pointer to the source data can now be discarded. Subsequent writes to the same data block on the source, and reads or writes to the same data blocks on the target, do not trigger a copy operation (and hence are termed Copy on First Access).

If the replication session is terminated, then the target device only has the data that was accessed until the termination, not the entire contents of the source at the point-in-time. In this case, the data on the target cannot be used for a restore, as it is not a full replica of the source.

In Full Copy mode, all data from the source is copied to the target in the background. Data is copied regardless of access. If access to a block that has not yet been copied is required, this block is preferentially copied to the target. In a complete cycle of the Full Copy mode, all data from the source is copied to the target. If the replication session is terminated now, the target will contain all the original data from the source at the point-in-time of activation. This makes the target a viable copy for recovery, restore, or other business continuity operations.

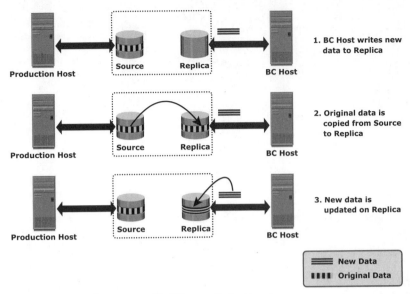

Figure 13-9: Copy on first access (CoFA) — write to target

The key difference between pointer-based, Full Copy mode and full-volume mirroring is that the target is immediately accessible on session activation in Full Copy mode. In contrast, one has to wait for synchronization and detachment to access the target in full-volume mirroring.

Both the full-volume mirroring and pointer-based full-volume replication technologies require the target devices to be at least as large as the source devices. In addition, full-volume mirroring and pointer-based full-volume replication in Full Copy mode can provide incremental resynchronization or restore capability.

Pointer-Based Virtual Replication

In *pointer-based virtual replication*, at the time of session activation, the target contains pointers to the location of data on the source. The target does not contain data, at any time. Hence, the target is known as a *virtual replica*. Similar to pointer-based full-volume replication, a protection bitmap is created for all data on the source device, and the target is immediately accessible. Granularity can range from 512 byte blocks to 64 KB blocks or greater.

When a write is issued to the source for the first time after session activation, original data at that address is copied to a predefined area in the array. This area is generally termed the *save location*. The pointer in the target is updated to point to this data address in the save location. After this, the new write is updated on the source. This process is illustrated in Figure 13-10.

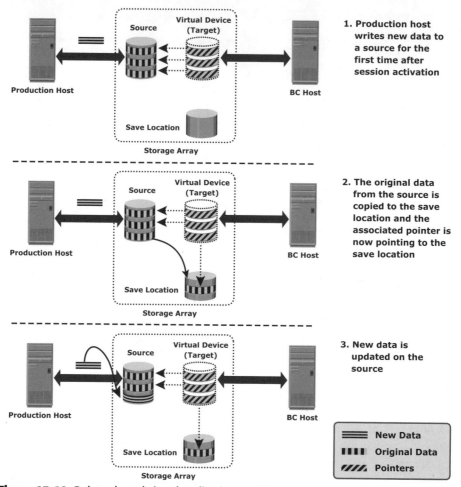

1. Production host writes new data to a source for the first time after session activation

2. The original data from the source is copied to the save location and the associated pointer is now pointing to the save location

3. New data is updated on the source

Figure 13-10: Pointer-based virtual replication – write to source

When a write is issued to the target for the first time after session activation, original data is copied from the source to the save location and similarly the pointer is updated to data in save location. Another copy of the original data is created in the save location before the new write is updated on the save location. This process is illustrated in Figure 13-11.

When reads are issued to the target, unchanged data blocks since session activation are read from the source. Original data blocks that have changed are read from the save location.

Pointer-based virtual replication uses CoFW technology. Subsequent writes to the same data block on the source or the target do not trigger a copy operation.

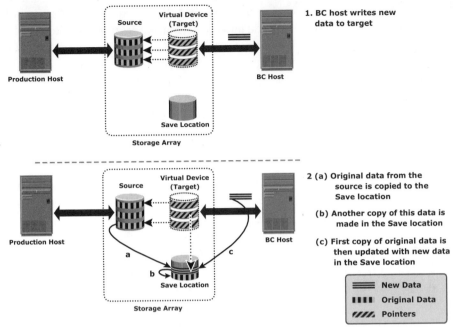

Figure 13-11: Pointer-based virtual replication – write to target

Data on the target is a combined view of unchanged data on the source and data on the save location. Unavailability of the source device invalidates the data on the target. As the target only contains pointers to data, the physical capacity required for the target is a fraction of the source device. The capacity required for the save location depends on the amount of expected data change.

13.5 Restore and Restart Considerations

Local replicas can be used to restore data to production devices. Alternatively, applications can be restarted using the consistent point-in-time copy of the data on the replicas.

A replica can be used to restore data to the production devices in the event of logical corruption of production devices — i.e., the devices are available but the data on them is invalid. Examples of logical corruption include accidental deletion of information (tables or entries in a database), incorrect data entry, and incorrect updating to existing information. Restore operations from a replica are incremental and provide a very small RTO. In some instances, applications can be resumed on the production devices prior to completion of the data copy. Prior to the restore operation, access to production and replica devices should be stopped.

Production devices may also become unavailable due to physical failures, such as production server or physical drive failure. In this case, applications can be restarted using data on the latest replica. If the production server fails, once the issue has been resolved, the latest information from the replica devices can be restored back to the production devices. If the production device(s) fail, applications can continue to run on replica devices. A new PIT copy of the replica devices can be created or the latest information from the replica devices can be restored to a new set of production devices. Prior to restarting applications using the replica devices, access to the replica devices should be stopped. As a protection against further failures, a "Gold Copy" (another copy of replica device) of the replica device should be created to preserve a copy of data in the event of failure or corruption of the replica devices.

Full-volume replicas (both full-volume mirrors and pointer-based in Full Copy mode) can be restored to the original source devices or to a new set of source devices. Restores to the original source devices can be incremental, but restores to a new set of devices are a full-volume copy operation.

In pointer-based virtual and pointer-based full-volume replication in CoFA mode, access to data on the replica is dependent on the health and accessibility of the original source volumes. If the original source volume is inaccessible for any reason, these replicas cannot be used for a restore or a restart.

Table 13-1 presents a comparative analysis of the various storage array–based replication technologies.

Table 13-1: Comparison of Local Replication Technologies

FACTOR	FULL-VOLUME MIRRORING	POINTER-BASED, FULL-VOLUME REPLICATION	POINTER-BASED VIRTUAL REPLICATION
Performance impact on source	No impact	CoFA mode - some impact Full copy - no impact	High impact
Size of target	At least the same as the source	At least the same as the source	Small fraction of the source
Accessibility of source for restoration	Not required	CoFA mode - required Full copy - not required	Required
Accessibility to target	Only after synchronization and detachment from the source	Immediately accessible	Immediately accessible

13.5.1 Tracking Changes to Source and Target

Updates occur on the source device after the creation of point-in-time local replicas. If the primary purpose of local replication is to have a viable point-in-time copy for data recovery or restore operations, then the target devices should not be modified. Changes can occur on the target device if it is used for non-BC operations. To enable incremental resynchronization or restore operations, changes to both the source and target devices after the point-in-time can be tracked. This is typically done using bitmaps, with one bit per block of data. The block sizes can range from 512 bytes to 64 KB or greater. For example, if the block size is 32 KB, then a 1 GB device would require 32,768 bits. The size of the bitmap would be 4 KB. If any or all of a 32 KB block is changed, the corresponding bit in the bitmap is flagged. If the block size is reduced for tracking purposes, then the bitmap size increases correspondingly.

The bits in the source and target bitmaps are all set to 0 (zero) when the replica is created. Any changes to the source or target are then flagged by setting the appropriate bits to 1 in the bitmap. When resynchronization or a restore is required, a *logical OR* operation between the source bitmap and the target bitmap is performed. The bitmap resulting from this operation (see Figure 13-12) references all blocks that have been modified in either the source or the target. This enables an optimized resynchronization or a restore operation, as it eliminates the need to copy all the blocks between the source and the target. The direction of data movement depends on whether a resynchronization or a restore operation is performed.

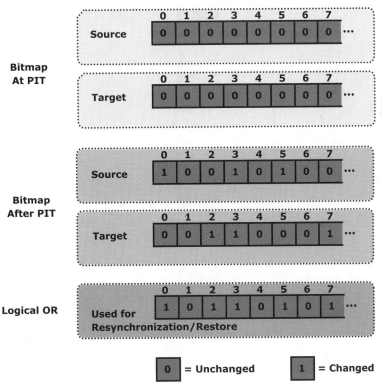

Figure 13-12: Tracking changes

If resynchronization is required, then changes to the target are overwritten with the corresponding blocks from the source. In this example, that would be blocks 3, 4, and 8 on the target (from the left).

If a restore is required, then changes to the source are overwritten with the corresponding blocks from the target. In this example, that would be blocks 1, 4, and 6 on the source. In either case, changes to both the source and the target cannot be simultaneously preserved.

13.6 Creating Multiple Replicas

Most storage array-based replication technologies enable source devices to maintain replication relationships with multiple targets. Changes made to the source and each of the targets can be tracked. This enables incremental resynchronization of the targets. Each PIT copy can be used for different BC activities and as a restore point.

Figure 13-13 shows an example in which a copy is created every six hours from the same source.

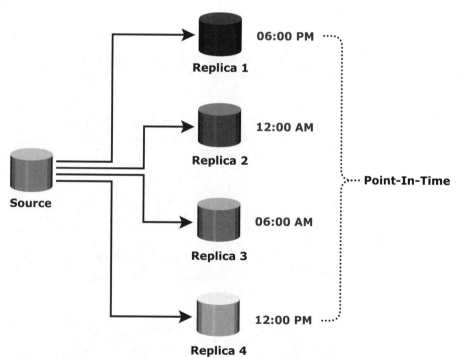

Figure 13-13: Multiple replicas created at different points in time

If the source is corrupted, the data can be restored from the latest PIT copy. The maximum RPO in the example shown in Figure 13-15 is six hours. More frequent replicas will reduce the RPO and the RTO.

Array local replication technologies also enable the creation of multiple *concurrent* PIT replicas. In this case, all replicas will contain identical data. One or more of the replicas can be set aside for restore or recovery operations. Decision support activities can be performed using the other replicas.

13.7 Management Interface

The replication management software residing on the storage array provides an interface for smooth and error-free replication. This management software interface provides options for synchronization, resynchronization, splitting, starting and stopping a replication session, and monitoring replication performance. In general, two types of interface are provided:

- **CLI:** An administrator can directly enter commands against a prompt in a CLI. A user can also perform some command operations based on assigned privileges. CLI scripts are developed to perform specific BC operations in a database or application environment.

- **GUI:** This type of interface includes the toolbar and menu bar options. A user can select an operation name and monitor performance in real time. Most of the tools have a browser-based GUI to transfer commands and are often integrated with other storage management suite products.

13.8 Concepts in Practice: EMC TimeFinder and EMC SnapView

EMC has several array-based specialized local replication softwares for different storage arrays. For Symmetrix array, the "EMC TimeFinder" family of products is used for full volume and pointer-based local replication. EMC SnapView and SnapSure are the solutions for CLARiiON and Celera storage arrays respectively.

TimeFinder family of product consists of two base solutions and four add-on solutions. The base solutions are TimeFinder/Clone and TimeFinder/Snap. The add-on solutions are TimeFinder/Mirror, TimeFinder/Consistency Groups,

TimeFinder/Exchange Integration Module, and TimeFinder/SQL Integration Module. Visit `http://education.EMC.com/ismbook` for the latest information.

TimeFinder is available for both open systems and mainframe. The base solutions support the different storage array–based local replication technologies discussed in this chapter. The add-on solutions are customizations of the replicas for specific application or database environments.

13.8.1 TimeFinder/Clone

TimeFinder/Clone is a point-in-time image of the full source volume in open systems that can be used for backups, decision support, data warehouse refreshes, or any other process that requires parallel access to production information. TimeFinder/Clone also includes a Mainframe SNAP facility that enables the creation of full-volume copies or dataset-level copies.

Clones can be protected using any type of supported protection scheme. Clones are available immediately for read and write access. TimeFinder/Clone also includes a "no copy" option, which enables performing a copy process only when the actual data is requested. As with all TimeFinder family of products, TimeFinder/Clone also supports the TimeFinder/Consistency Groups option to ensure data consistency between volumes and even across Symmetrix systems. TimeFinder/Clone is an ideal solution when high performance, RAID 5 protection, and highly functional point-in-time copies are required.

Clone Operation

A full-volume copy can be created by copying all data from the source as a background operation. When the copy is activated, data begins copying in the background. Track-by-track copying makes the target a clone of the source volume. While background copying, the state of the device pair is "CopyInProgress." When the operation completes, the state becomes "Copied." The copy session must be activated before the target host can access the data from the target volume. The Pre-Copy function starts copying tracks in the background, before the copy session is activated.

13.8.2 TimeFinder/Mirror

TimeFinder/Mirror performs local replication using full-volume mirroring. TimeFinder/Mirror uses special Symmetrix logical devices called *Business Continuance Volumes (BCVs)* for local replication. BCVs are dedicated devices for local replication and can be attached dynamically and nondisruptively with a *standard device*. All BCVs and their corresponding standard devices are of the same size and format.

TimeFinder/Mirror Operations

TimeFinder/Mirror performs four basic BCV operations — *Establish*, *Split*, *Restore*, and *Reestablish* — to preserve the mirror relationship between a standard device and a BCV:

- **Establishment of BCV pairs:** The TimeFinder establish operation is the first step in creating a TimeFinder/Mirror replica. The purpose of the establish operation is to synchronize the contents from the standard device to the BCV (see Figure 13-14[a]). The first time a BCV is established with a standard device, a full synchronization has to be performed. Any future resynchronization can be incremental in nature. The establish operation is a nondisruptive operation to the standard device. I/O to standard devices can proceed during an establish. However, all I/Os to the BCV device must be stopped before the establish operation is performed.

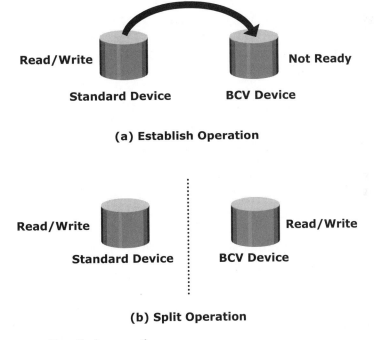

Read/Write   **Not Ready**

Standard Device   BCV Device

(a) Establish Operation

Read/Write   **Read/Write**

Standard Device   BCV Device

(b) Split Operation

Figure 13-14: TimeFinder operation

- **Split of BCV pairs:** The replica is associated with the time when the split operation is executed. The split operation detaches the BCV from the standard device and makes the BCV device available for host access through its own device address (see Figure 13-14[b]). After the split operation, changes made to the standard or BCV devices are tracked by the

Symmetrix Enginuity Operating Environment. EMC TimeFinder/Mirror ensures consistency of data on the BCV devices via the *consistent split* option, described next.

▪ **Consistent split of BCV pairs:** The TimeFinder/Mirror consistent split option ensures that the data on the BCV is consistent with the data on the standard device. Consistent split holds I/O across a group of devices using a single consistent split command; thus all the BCVs in the group are consistent PIT copies. It can be used to create a consistent PIT copy of an entire system, a database, or any associated set of volumes.

For ensuring consistency I/O can be held with either the EMC PowerPath multipathing software at the host level or with the Symmetrix Enginuity Consistency Assist at the array level. With a PowerPath-based consistent split executed by the host performing the I/O operation, I/O is held at the host before the split.

An Enginuity Consistency Assist (ECA) based consistent split can be executed by the host doing the I/O or by a control host in an environment containing distributed and/or related databases. I/O is held at the Symmetrix until the split operation is completed; therefore, ECA can be used to perform consistent splits on BCV pairs across multiple, heterogeneous hosts.

▪ **Restoration of BCV pairs:** The BCV can be used to restore data to standard devices. Restore is a recovery operation, so all I/O activity to the standard device needs to be stopped, and the device must be taken offline, just before this operation. The restore sets the BCV to a "Not Ready" state. Therefore, all I/O activity to the BCVs must be stopped before issuing the restore command. Operations on standard devices can resume as soon as the restore operation is initiated, even while synchronization of the standards from the BCV is still in progress. The query command is used to obtain the current status of standard or BCV volume pairs. This operation also provides options for full or incremental restores.

Note the important difference between TimeFinder/Clone and TimeFinder/Mirror: With the former, the target is immediately available after the copy session is activated, whereas in the latter, it is only available after splitting from the source.

13.8.3 EMC SnapView

SnapView is an EMC CLARiiON array-based local replication software that creates point-in-time views or point-in-time copies of logical volumes using SnapView snapshots and clones, respectively. Snapshots are pointer-based snaps that require only a fraction of the source disk space. Clones are full-volume copies that require disk space equal to the source.

SnapView Snapshot

A SnapView snapshot is not a full copy of the production volume; it is a logical view of the original production volume based on the time the snapshot was created. Snapshots are created in seconds, and can be retired when no longer needed. Up to eight read/write snapshots per source LUN can be created to suit the needs of multiple business processes. A snapshot "roll back" feature provides instant restore to the source volume. The key terminologies of SnapView snapshot are as follows:

- **SnapView session:** The SnapView snapshot mechanism is activated when a session is started, and deactivated when a session is stopped. A snapshot appears "offline" until there is an active session. It is an exact copy of the source LUN when a session starts. Multiple snapshots can be included in a session. The source LUN can be involved in up to eight SnapView sessions at any time.

- **Reserved LUN pool:** This is a private area, also called a save area, used to contain Copy on First Write (CoFW) data. The "Reserved" part of the name refers to the fact that the LUNs are reserved and therefore cannot be assigned to a host.

To keep the number of pointers and the pointer map at a reasonable size, SnapView divides the source LUN into data chunks of 64 KB. Any changes to data inside a chunk cause that chunk to be written to the Reserved LUN pool, if it is being modified for the first time. The total number of reserved LUNs is limited and model dependent. To create snapshots on the source LUN, SnapView sessions need to be started on these LUNs and the Reserved LUN pool should be assigned to the source LUN. Once a session starts, the SnapView mechanism tracks changes to the source LUN.

13.8.4 EMC SnapSure

EMC SnapSure is an EMC Celerra Network Server software feature that enables the creation and management of checkpoints, which are point-in-time, logical images of a production file system (PFS). SnapSure uses a "copy on first modify" principle. A PFS consists of blocks. When a block within the PFS is modified, a copy containing the block's original contents is saved to a separate volume called the SavVol. Subsequent changes made to the same block in the PFS are not copied into the SavVol. The original blocks from the PFS in the SavVol and the unchanged PFS blocks remaining in the PFS are read by SnapSure according to a bitmap and blockmap data-tracking structure. These blocks combine to provide a complete point-in-time image called a checkpoint. A checkpoint reflects the state of a PFS at the point of time it is created.

TimeFinder/FS

TimeFinder/FS is an implementation of EMC TimeFinder technology. It is specifically tailored for the Celerra Network Server attached to a Symmetrix storage array. TimeFinder/FS enables the creation of independently addressable, physical, point-in-time copies (snapshots) of a PFS and provides "mirroring" existing snapshot to resynchronize it (and maintain its synchronization) with the PFS, so that an exact mirror of the PFS is always available. The process of mirroring on an existing snapshot is less time consuming than creating a new snapshot. A snapshot in mirror mode can be "mirror off" and an updated snapshot is available immediately for mounting and exporting.

Summary

There are an immense number of uses for a local replica in both data center production and BC operations. This technology has become an integral part of day-to-day operations. Replication eliminates the backup window and provides a quick resource to ensure protection against data corruption during major updates to the source data.

This chapter took a detailed look at the local replication process and described the uses of a local replica. Local replication can be accomplished using various technologies, such as host-based local replication and storage array-based local replication. This chapter also described the restore operations for storage array-based local replication, as well as the creation and use of multiple replicas. The planning and design considerations for establishing viable local replication processes, and implementation examples, were also provided in this chapter.

Though duplication of data with a local replica ensures high availability, dispersal of the duplicates to different sites is a way to ensure continuous operation for data centers in the event of a disaster that could incapacitate the entire site. Establishing the replicas at the remote site with replication has now emerged as a mature technology. Remote replication is covered in detail in the next chapter.

EXERCISES

1. What is the importance of recoverability and consistency in local replication?

2. Describe the uses of a local replica in various business operations.

3. What are the considerations for performing backup from a local replica?

4. What is the difference between a restore operation and a resynchronization operation with local replicas? Explain with examples.

5. A 300 GB database needs two local replicas for reporting and backup. There are constraints in provisioning full capacity for the replicas. It has been determined that the database has been configured on 15 disks, and the daily rate of change in the database is approximately 25 percent. You need to configure two pointer-based replicas for the database. Describe how much capacity you would allocate for these replicas and how many save volumes you would configure.

6. For the same database described in Question 5, discuss the advantages of configuring full-volume mirroring if there are no constraints on capacity.

7. An administrator configures six pointer based virtual replica of a LUN and creates eight full volume replica of the same LUN. The administrator then creates four pointer based virtual replica for each full volume replica that was created. How many usable replicas are now available?

Chapter 14
Remote Replication

Remote replication is the process of creating replicas of information assets at remote sites (locations). Remote replicas help organizations mitigate the risks associated with regionally driven outages resulting from natural or human-made disasters. Similar to local replicas, they can also be used for other business operations.

The infrastructure on which information assets are stored at the primary site is called the *source*. The infrastructure on which the replica is stored at the remote site is referred to as the *target*. Hosts that access the source or target are referred to as *source hosts* or *target hosts*, respectively. This chapter discusses various remote replication technologies, along with the key steps to plan and design appropriate remote replication solutions. In addition, this chapter describes network requirements and management considerations in the remote replication process.

KEY CONCEPTS

Synchronous and Asynchronous Replication

LVM-Based Replication

Host-Based Log Shipping

Disk-Buffered Replication

Three-Site Replication

Data Consistency

14.1 Modes of Remote Replication

The two basic modes of remote replication are synchronous and asynchronous. In *synchronous remote replication*, writes must be committed to the source and the target, prior to acknowledging "write complete" to the host (see Figure 14-1). Additional writes on the source cannot occur until each preceding write has been completed and acknowledged. This ensures that data is identical on the source and the replica at all times. Further writes are transmitted to the remote site exactly in the order in which they are received at the source. Hence, write ordering is maintained. In the event of a failure of the source site, synchronous remote replication provides zero or near-zero RPO, as well as the lowest RTO.

However, application response time is increased with any synchronous remote replication. The degree of the impact on the response time depends on the distance between sites, available bandwidth, and the network connectivity infrastructure. The distances over which synchronous replication can be deployed depend on the application's ability to tolerate extension in response time. Typically, it is deployed for distances less than 200 KM (125 miles) between the two sites.

In *asynchronous remote replication*, a write is committed to the source and immediately acknowledged to the host. Data is buffered at the source and transmitted to the remote site later (see Figure 14-2). This eliminates the impact to the application's response time. Data at the remote site will be behind the source by at least the size of the buffer. Hence, asynchronous remote replication provides a finite (nonzero) RPO disaster recovery solution. RPO depends on the size of the buffer, available network bandwidth, and the write workload to the source. There is no impact on application response time, as the writes are acknowledged immediately to the source host. This enables deployment of asynchronous replication over extended distances. Asynchronous remote replication can be deployed over distances ranging from several hundred to several thousand kilometers between two sites.

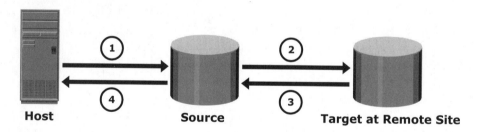

Host **Source** **Target at Remote Site**

(1) Host writes data to source

(2) Data from source is replicated to target at remote site

(3) Target acknowledges back to source

(4) Source acknowledges write complete to host

Figure 14-1: Synchronous replication

14.2 Remote Replication Technologies

Remote replication of data can be handled by the hosts or by the storage arrays. Other options include specialized appliances to replicate data over the LAN or the SAN, as well as replication between storage arrays over the SAN.

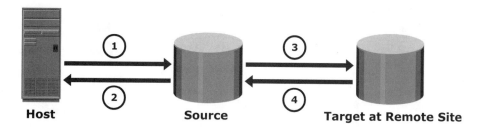

Host   **Source**   **Target at Remote Site**

① Host writes data to source

② Write is immediately acknowledged to host

③ Data is transmitted to the target at remote site later

④ Target acknowledges back to source

Figure 14-2: Asynchronous replication

14.2.1. Host-Based Remote Replication

Host-based remote replication uses one or more components of the host to perform and manage the replication operation. There are two basic approaches to host-based remote replication: *LVM-based replication* and *database replication via log shipping*.

LVM-Based Remote Replication

LVM-based replication is performed and managed at the volume group level. Writes to the source volumes are transmitted to the remote host by the LVM. The LVM on the remote host receives the writes and commits them to the remote volume group.

Prior to the start of replication, identical volume groups, logical volumes, and file systems are created at the source and target sites. Initial synchronization of data between the source and the replica can be performed in a number of ways. One method is to backup the source data to tape and restore the data to the remote replica. Alternatively, it can be performed by replicating over the

IP network. Until completion of initial synchronization, production work on the source volumes is typically halted. After initial synchronization, production work can be started on the source volumes and replication of data can be performed over an existing standard IP network (see Figure 14-3).

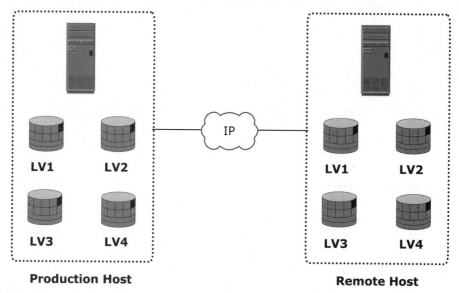

Figure 14-3: LVM-based remote replication

LVM-based remote replication supports both synchronous and asynchronous modes of data transfer. In asynchronous mode, writes are queued in a log file at the source and sent to the remote host in the order in which they were received. The size of the log file determines the RPO at the remote site. In the event of a network failure, writes continue to accumulate in the log file. If the log file fills up before the failure is resolved, then a full resynchronization is required upon network availability. In the event of a failure at the source site, applications can be restarted on the remote host, using the data on the remote replicas.

LVM-based remote replication eliminates the need for a dedicated SAN infrastructure. LVM-based remote replication is independent of the storage arrays and types of disks at the source and remote sites. Most operating systems are shipped with LVMs, so additional licenses and specialized hardware are not typically required.

The replication process adds overhead on the host CPUs. CPU resources on the source host are shared between replication tasks and applications, which may cause performance degradation of the application.

As the remote host is also involved in the replication process, it has to be continuously up and available. LVM-based remote replication does not scale well, particularly in the case of applications using *federated databases*.

Host-Based Log Shipping

Database replication via log shipping is a host-based replication technology supported by most databases. Transactions to the source database are captured in logs, which are periodically transmitted by the source host to the remote host (see Figure 14-4). The remote host receives the logs and applies them to the remote database.

Prior to starting production work and replication of log files, all relevant components of the source database are replicated to the remote site. This is done while the source database is shut down.

After this step, production work is started on the source database. The remote database is started in a standby mode. Typically, in standby mode, the database is not available for transactions. Some implementations allow reads and writes from the standby database.

All DBMSs switch log files at preconfigured time intervals, or when a log file is full. The current log file is closed at the time of log switching and a new log file is opened. When a log switch occurs, the closed log is transmitted by the source host to the remote host. The remote host receives the log and updates the standby database.

This process ensures that the standby database is consistent up to the last committed log. RPO at the remote site is finite and depends on the size of the log and the frequency of log switching. Available network bandwidth, latency, and rate of updates to the source database, as well as the frequency of log switching, should be considered when determining the optimal size of the log file.

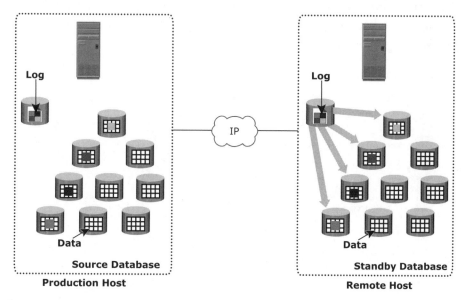

Figure 14-4: Host-based log shipping

Because the source host does not transmit every update and buffer them, this alleviates the burden on the source host CPU. Similar to LVM-based remote replication, the existing standard IP network can be used for replicating log files. Host-based log shipping does not scale well, particularly in the case of applications using federated databases.

14.2.2 Storage Array-Based Remote Replication

In *storage array-based remote replication*, the array operating environment and resources perform and manage data replication. This relieves the burden on the host CPUs, which can be better utilized for running an application. A source and its replica device reside on different storage arrays. In other implementations, the storage controller is used for both the host and replication workload. Data can be transmitted from the source storage array to the target storage array over a shared or a dedicated network.

Replication between arrays may be performed in synchronous, asynchronous, or disk-buffered modes. Three-site remote replication can be implemented using a combination of synchronous mode and asynchronous mode, as well as a combination of synchronous mode and disk-buffered mode.

Synchronous Replication Mode

In array based synchronous remote replication, writes must be committed to the source and the target prior to acknowledging "write complete" to the host. Additional writes on that source cannot occur until each preceding write has been completed and acknowledged. The array-based synchronous replication process is shown in Figure 14-5.

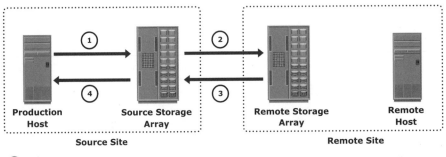

Figure 14-5: Array-based synchronous remote replication

In the case of synchronous replication, to optimize the replication process and to minimize the impact on application response time, the write is placed on cache of the two arrays. The intelligent storage arrays can de-stage these writes to the appropriate disks later.

If the network links fail, replication is suspended; however, production work can continue uninterrupted on the source storage array. The array operating environment can keep track of the writes that are not transmitted to the remote storage array. When the network links are restored, the accumulated data can be transmitted to the remote storage array. During the time of network link outage, if there is a failure at the source site, some data will be lost and the RPO at the target will not be zero.

For synchronous remote replication, network bandwidth equal to or greater than the maximum *write workload* between the two sites should be provided at all times. Figure 14-6 illustrates the write workload (expressed in MB/s) over time. The "Max" line indicated in Figure 14-6 represents the required bandwidth that must be provisioned for synchronous replication. Bandwidths lower than the maximum write workload results in an unacceptable increase in application response time.

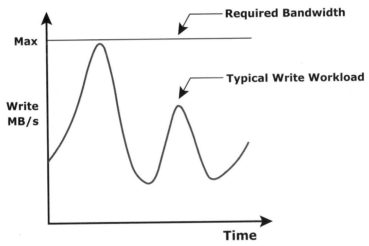

Figure 14-6: Network bandwidth requirement for synchronous replication

Asynchronous Replication Mode

In array-based *asynchronous remote replication mode*, shown in Figure 14-7, a write is committed to the source and immediately acknowledged to the host. Data is buffered at the source and transmitted to the remote site later. The source and the target devices do not contain identical data at all times. The data on the target device is behind that of the source, so the RPO in this case is not zero.

Similar to synchronous replication, asynchronous replication writes are placed in cache on the two arrays and are later de-staged to the appropriate disks.

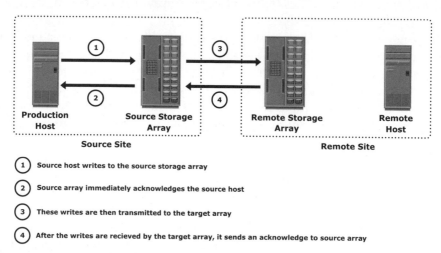

① Source host writes to the source storage array

② Source array immediately acknowledges the source host

③ These writes are then transmitted to the target array

④ After the writes are recieved by the target array, it sends an acknowledge to source array

Figure 14-7: Array-based asynchronous remote replication

Some implementations of asynchronous remote replication maintain write ordering. A time stamp and sequence number are attached to each write when it is received by the source. Writes are then transmitted to the remote array, where they are committed to the remote replica in the exact order in which they were buffered at the source. This implicitly guarantees consistency of data on the remote replicas. Other implementations ensure consistency by leveraging the dependent write principle inherent to most DBMSs. The writes are buffered for a predefined period of time. At the end of this duration, the buffer is closed, and a new buffer is opened for subsequent writes. All writes in the closed buffer are transmitted together and committed to the remote replica.

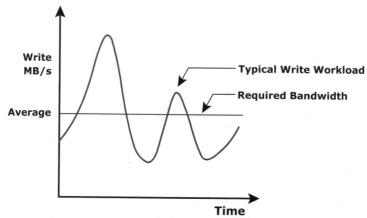

Figure 14-8: Network bandwidth requirement for asynchronous replication

Asynchronous remote replication provides network bandwidth cost savings, as only bandwidth equal to or greater than the average write workload is needed, as represented by the "Average" line in Figure 14-8. During times when the write workload exceeds the average bandwidth, sufficient buffer space has to be configured on the source storage array to hold these writes.

Disk-Buffered Replication Mode

Disk-buffered replication is a combination of local and remote replication technologies. A consistent PIT local replica of the source device is first created. This is then replicated to a remote replica on the target array.

The sequence of operations in a disk-buffered remote replication is shown in Figure 14-9. At the beginning of the cycle, the network links between the two arrays are suspended and there is no transmission of data. While production application is running on the source device, a consistent PIT local replica of the source device is created. The network links are enabled, and data on the local replica in the source array is transmitted to its remote replica in the target array. After synchronization of this pair, the network link is suspended and the next local replica of the source is created. Optionally, a local PIT replica of the remote device on the target array can be created. The frequency of this cycle of operations depends on available link bandwidth and the data change rate on the source device.

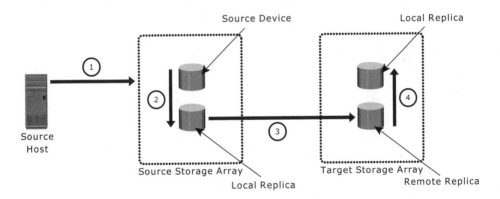

(1) Source host writes data to source device

(2) A consistent PIT local replica of the source device is created

(3) Data from local replica in the source array is transmitted to its remote replica in the target array

(4) A local PIT replica of the remote device on the target array is created

Figure 14-9: Disk-buffered remote replication

Array-based replication technologies can track changes made to the source and target devices. Hence, all resynchronization operations can be done incrementally.

For example, a local replica of the source device is created at 10:00 AM and this data is transmitted to the remote replica, which takes one hour to complete. Changes made to the source device after 10:00 AM are tracked. Another replica of the source device is created at 11:00 AM by applying track changes between the source and local replica (10:00 AM copy). During the next cycle of transmission (11:00 AM data), the source data has moved to 12:00 PM The local replica in the remote array has the 10:00 AM data until the 11:00 AM data is successfully transmitted to the remote replica. If there is a failure at the source site prior to the completion of transmission, then the worst-case RPO at the remote site would be two hours (as the remote site has 10:00 AM data).

Three-Site Replication

In synchronous and asynchronous replication, under normal conditions the workload is running at the source site. Operations at the source site will not be disrupted by any failure to the target site or to the network used for replication. The replication process resumes as soon as the link or target site issues are resolved. The source site continues to operate without any remote protection. If failure occurs at the source site during this time, RPO will be extended.

In synchronous replication, source and target sites are usually within 200 KM (125 miles) of each other. Hence, in the event of a regional disaster, both the source and the target sites could become unavailable. This will lead to extended RPO and RTO because the last known good copy of data would have to come from another source, such as offsite tape library.

A regional disaster will not affect the target site in asynchronous replication, as the sites are typically several hundred or several thousand kilometers apart. If the source site fails, production can be shifted to the target site, but there will be no remote protection until the failure is resolved.

Three-site replication is used to mitigate the risks identified in two-site replication. In a three-site replication, data from the source site is replicated to two remote data centers. Replication can be synchronous to one of the two data centers, providing a zero-RPO solution. It can be asynchronous or disk buffered to the other remote data center, providing a finite RPO. Three-site remote replication can be implemented as a cascade/multi-hop or a triangle/multi-target solution.

Three-Site Replication—Cascade/Multi-hop

In the *cascade/multi-hop* form of replication, data flows from the source to the intermediate storage array, known as a *bunker*, in the first hop and then from a bunker to a storage array at a remote site in the second hop. Replication between the source and the bunker occurs synchronously, but replication between the bunker and the remote site can be achieved in two ways: disk-buffered mode or asynchronous mode.

Synchronous + Asynchronous

This method employs a combination of synchronous and asynchronous remote replication technologies. Synchronous replication occurs between the source and the bunker. Asynchronous replication occurs between the bunker and the remote site. The remote replica in the bunker acts as the source for the asynchronous replication to create a remote replica at the remote site. Figure 14-10(a) illustrates the synchronous + asynchronous method.

RPO at the remote site is usually on the order of minutes in this implementation. In this method, a minimum of three storage devices are required (including the source) to replicate one storage device. The devices containing a synchronous remote replica at the bunker and the asynchronous replica at the remote are the other two devices.

If there is a disaster at the source, operations are failed over to the bunker site with zero or near-zero data loss. But unlike the synchronous two-site situation, there is still remote protection at the third site. The RPO between the bunker and third site could be on the order of minutes.

If there is a disaster at the bunker site or if there is a network link failure between the source and bunker sites, the source site will continue to operate as normal but without any remote replication. This situation is very similar to two-site replication when a failure/disaster occurs at the target site. The updates to the remote site cannot occur due to the failure in the bunker site. Hence, the data at the remote site keeps falling behind, but the advantage here is that if the source fails during this time, operations can be resumed at the remote site. RPO at the remote site depends on the time difference between the bunker site failure and source site failure.

A *regional disaster* in three-site cascade/multihop replication is very similar to a source site failure in two-site asynchronous replication. Operations will failover to the remote site with an RPO on the order of minutes. There is no remote protection until the regional disaster is resolved. Local replication technologies could be used at the remote site during this time.

If a disaster occurs at the remote site, or if the network links between the bunker and the remote site fail, the source site continues to work as normal with disaster recovery protection provided at the bunker site.

Synchronous + Disk Buffered

This method employs a combination of local and remote replication technologies. Synchronous replication occurs between the source and the bunker: A consistent PIT local replica is created at the bunker. Data is transmitted from the local replica at the bunker to the remote replica at the remote site. Optionally, a local replica can be created at the remote site after data is received from the bunker. Figure 14-10(b) illustrates the synchronous + disk buffered method.

In this method, a minimum of four storage devices are required (including the source) to replicate one storage device. The other three devices are the synchronous remote replica at the bunker, a consistent PIT local replica at the bunker, and the replica at the remote site. RPO at the remote site is usually in the order of hours in this implementation. For example, if a local replica is created at 10:00 AM at the bunker and it takes an hour to transmit this data to the remote site, changes made to the remote replica at the bunker since 10:00 AM are tracked. Hence only one hour's worth of data has to be resynchronized between the bunker and the remote site during the next cycle. RPO in this case will also be two hours, similar to disk-buffered replication.

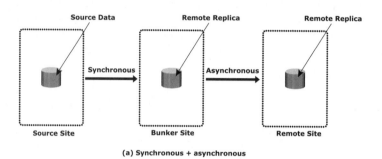

(a) Synchronous + asynchronous

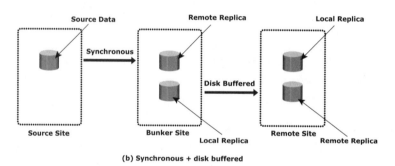

(b) Synchronous + disk buffered

Figure 14-10: Three-site replication

The process of creating the consistent PIT copy at the bunker and incrementally updating the remote replica and the local replica at the remote site occurs continuously in a cycle. This process can be automated and controlled from the source.

Three-Site Replication—Triangle/Multi-target

In the *three-site triangle/multi-target replication,* data at the source storage array is concurrently replicated to two different arrays. The source-to-bunker site (target 1) replication is synchronous, with a near-zero RPO. The source-to-remote site (target 2) replication is asynchronous, with an RPO of minutes. The distance between the source and the remote site could be thousands of miles. This configuration does not depend on the bunker site for updating data on the remote site, because data is asynchronously copied to the remote site directly from the source.

The key benefit of three-site triangle/multi-target replication is the ability to failover to either of the two remote sites in the case of source site failure, with disaster recovery (asynchronous) protection between them. Resynchronization between the two surviving target sites is incremental. Disaster recovery protection is always available in the event of any one site failure.

During normal operations all three sites are available and the workload is at the source site. At any given instant, the data at the bunker and the source is identical. The data at the remote site is behind the data at the source and the bunker. The replication network links between the bunker and remote sites will be in place but not in use. Thus, during normal operations there is no data movement between the bunker and remote arrays. The difference in the data between the bunker and remote sites is tracked, so that in the event of a source site disaster, operations can be resumed at the bunker or the remote sites with incremental resynchronization between the sites.

14.2.3 SAN-Based Remote Replication

SAN-based remote replication enables the replication of data between heterogeneous storage arrays. Data is moved from one array to the other over the SAN/WAN. This technology is application and server operating system independent, because the replication operations are performed by one of the storage arrays (the control array). There is no impact on production servers (because replication is done by the array) or the LAN (because data is moved over the SAN).

SAN-based remote replication is a point-in-time replication technology. Uses of SAN-based remote replication include data mobility, remote vaulting, and data migration. Data mobility enables incrementally copying multiple volumes over extended distances, as well as implementing a tiered storage strategy. Data vaulting is the practice of storing a set of point-in-time copies on heterogeneous remote arrays to guard against a failure of the source site. Data migration refers to moving data to new storage arrays and consolidating data from multiple heterogeneous storage arrays onto a single storage array.

The array performing the replication operations is called the *control array*. Data can be moved to/from devices in the control array to/from a remote array. The devices in the control array that are part of the replication session are called *control devices*. For every control device there is a counterpart, a *remote device*, on the *remote* array.

The terms "control" or "remote" do not indicate the direction of data flow, they only indicate the array that is performing the replication operation. Data movement could be from the control array to the remote array or vice versa. The direction of data movement is determined by the replication operation.

The front-end ports of the control array must be zoned to the front-end ports of the remote array. LUN masking should be performed on the remote array to allow access to the remote devices to the front-end port of the control array. In effect, the front-end ports of the control array act as an HBA, initiating data transfer to/from the remote array.

SAN-based replication uses two types of operations: *push* and *pull*. These terms are defined from the perspective of the control array. In the *push* operation, data is transmitted from the control storage array to the remote storage array. The control device, therefore, acts like the source, while the remote device is the target. The data that needs to be replicated would be on devices in the control array.

In the *pull* operation, data is transmitted from the remote storage array to the control storage array. The remote device is the source and the control device is the target. The data that needs to be replicated would be on devices in the remote array.

When a push or pull operation is initiated, the control array creates a protection bitmap to track the replication process. Each bit in the protection bitmap represents a data chunk on the control device. Chunk size may vary with technology implementations. When the replication operation is initiated, all the bits are set to one, indicating that all the contents of the source device need to be copied to the target device. As the replication process copies data, the bits are changed to zero, indicating that a particular chunk has been copied. At the end of the replication process, all the bits become zero.

During the push and pull operations, host access to the remote device is not allowed because the control storage array has no control over the remote storage array and cannot track any change on the remote device. Data integrity cannot be guaranteed if changes are made to the remote device during the push and pull operations. Therefore, for all SAN-based remote replications, the remote devices should not be in use during the replication process in order to ensure data integrity and consistency.

The push/pull operations can be either *hot* or *cold*. These terms apply to the control devices only. In a cold operation, the control device is inaccessible to the host during replication. Cold operations guarantee data consistency because both the control and the remote devices are offline to every host operation. In a hot operation, the control device is online for host operations. With hot operations, changes can be made to the control device during push/pull because the control array can keep track of all changes, and thus ensures data integrity.

When the hot push operation is initiated, applications can be up and running on the control devices. I/O to the control devices is held while the protection bitmap is created. This ensures a consistent PIT image of the data. The protection bitmap is referred prior to any write to the control devices. If the bit is zero, the write is allowed. If the bit is one, the replication process holds the write, copies the required chunk to the remote device, and then allows the write to complete.

In the hot pull operation, the hosts can access control devices after starting the pull operation. The protection bitmap is referenced for every read or write operation. If the bit is zero, a read or write occurs. If the bit is one, the read or write is held, and the replication process copies the required chunk from the remote device. When the chunk is copied, the read or write is completed. The control devices can be used after the pull operation is initiated and as soon as the protection bitmap is created.

In SAN-based replication, the control array can keep track of changes made to the control devices after the replication session is activated. This is allowed in the incremental push operation only. A second bitmap, called a *resynchronization bitmap,* is created. All the bits in the resynchronization bitmap are set to zero when a push is initiated, as shown in Figure 14-11 (a). As changes are made to the control device, the bits are flipped from zero to one, indicating that changes have occurred, as shown in Figure 14-11 (b). When resynchronization is required, the push is reinitiated and the resynchronization bitmap becomes the new protection bitmap, as shown in Figure 14-11 (c), and only the modified chunks are transmitted to the remote devices. If changes are made to the remote device, the SAN-based replication operation is unaware of these changes, therefore, data integrity cannot be ensured if an incremental push is performed.

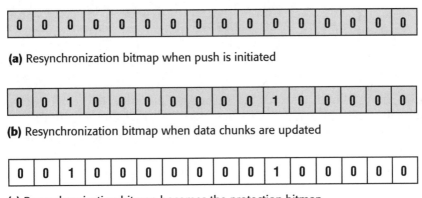

(a) Resynchronization bitmap when push is initiated

(b) Resynchronization bitmap when data chunks are updated

(c) Resynchronization bitmap becomes the protection bitmap

Figure 14-11: Bitmap status in SAN-based replication

14.3 Network Infrastructure

For remote replication over extended distances, optical network technologies such as dense wavelength division multiplexing (DWDM), coarse wavelength division multiplexing (CWDM), and synchronous optical network (SONET) are deployed.

14.3.1 DWDM

DWDM is an optical technology by which data from different channels are carried at different wavelengths over a fiber-optic link. It is a fiber-optic transmission technique that uses light waves to transmit data parallel by bit or serial by character. It integrates multiple light waves with different wavelengths in a group and directs them through a single optical fiber.

The multiplexing of data from several channels into a multicolored light stream transmitted on a single optical fiber has opened up the conventional optical fiber bandwidth by breaking it into many channels, each at a different optical wavelength. Each wavelength can carry a signal at a bit rate less than the upper limit defined by the electronics; typically up to several gigabits per second. Using DWDM, different data formats at different data rates can be transmitted together. Specifically, IP ESCON, FC, SONET and ATM data can all travel at the same time within the optical fiber (see Figure 14-12).

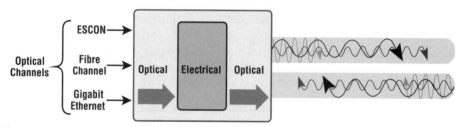

Figure 14-12: Dense wavelength division multiplexing (DWDM)

CWDM, like DWDM, uses multiplexing and demultiplexing on different channels by assigning varied wavelengths to each channel. Compared to DWDM, CWDM is used to consolidate environments containing a low number of channels at a reduced cost.

14.3.2 SONET

SONET (synchronous optical network) is a network technology that involves transferring a large payload through an optical fiber over long distances. SONET multiplexes data streams of different speeds into a frame and sends them across the network. The European variation of SONET is called synchronous digital hierarchy (SDH). Figure 14-13 shows the multiplexing of data streams of different speeds in SONET and SDH technologies.

SONET/SDH uses generic framing procedure (GFP) and supports the transport of both packet-oriented (Ethernet, IP) and character-oriented (FC) data.

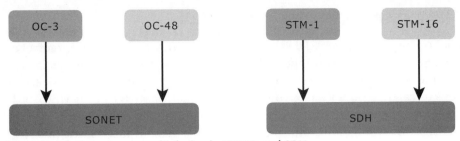

Figure 14-13: Data stream multiplexing in SONET and SDH

SONET transfers data at a very high speed (for example, OC-768 provides line rate up to 40 Gbps). The basic SONET/SDH signal operates at 51.84 Mbps and is designated synchronous transport signal level one (STS-1). The STS-1 frame is the basic unit of transmission in SONET/SDH. Multiple STS-1 circuits can be aggregated to form higher-speed links. STS-3 (155.52 Mb/s) is equivalent to SONET level OC-3 and SDH level STM-1.

14.4 Concepts in Practice: EMC SRDF, EMC SAN Copy, and EMC MirrorView

This section discusses three EMC products that use remote replication technology. EMC Symmetrix Remote Data Facility (SRDF) and EMC MirrorView are storage array–based remote application softwares supported by EMC Symmetrix and CLARiiON respectively. EMC SAN Copy is SAN-based remote replication software deployed in an EMC CLARiiON storage array. For the latest information, visit http://education.EMC.com/ismbook.

14.4.1 SRDF Family

SRDF offers a family of technology solutions to implement storage array-based remote replication technologies. The three Symmetrix solutions are:

- **SRDF/Synchronous (SRDF/S):** A remote replication solution that creates a synchronous replica at one or more Symmetrix targets

- **SRDF/Asynchronous (SRDF/A):** A remote replication solution that enables the source to asynchronously replicate data, incorporating delta set technology and dependent write consistency. A delta set enables write ordering by employing a buffering mechanism.

- **SRDF/Automated Replication (SRDF/AR):** A remote replication solution that uses both SRDF and TimeFinder/Mirror to implement disk-buffered replication technology

14.4.2 Disaster Recovery with SRDF

The source arrays have SRDF R1 devices (source devices), and the target arrays have SRDF R2 devices (replica devices). Data written to R1 devices is replicated to R2 devices, either synchronously or asynchronously. SRDF R1 and R2 devices can have any local RAID protection, such as RAID 1 or RAID 5. SRDF R2 devices are in a read-only (R/O) state when remote replication is in effect. Hence, under normal operating conditions, changes cannot be made directly to the R2 devices. The R2 devices can only receive data from their corresponding R1 devices on the source storage array.

SRDF uses dedicated adapters (controllers) to send data from the source to the target storage array. The supported adapters for remote replication are ESCON, FC, and GigE.

Shifting production work from the source site to the target site is done by the SRDF *failover* operation, whereas shifting the production work from the target site back to the source site is done by the SRDF *failback* operation:

- **Failover:** The failover operation is initiated if the SRDF R1 devices are unavailable and if BC operations need to restart on the R2 devices. The failover operation can also be performed for testing the disaster-recovery processes and for any maintenance tasks at the source site. Figure 14-14 shows the I/O status before and after failover. Before failover, the source allows the R/W operation, whereas a host accesses the target only in the R/O state. The failover process enables a host to perform R/W operations with the targets.

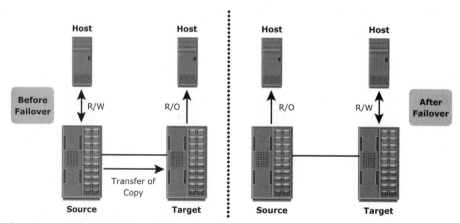

Figure 14-14: EMC SRDF - before and after failover

- **Failback:** The failback operation allows normal business operations to resume at the source site on the R1 device. When failback is invoked, the target becomes R/O, the source becomes R/W, and any changes that were made at the target while in the failover state are incrementally propagated back to the source, as illustrated in Figure 14-15.

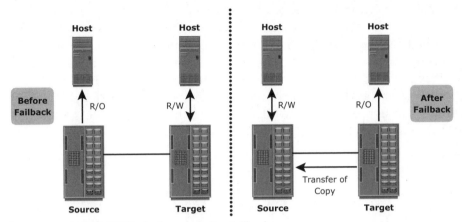

Figure 14-15: EMC SRDF - before and after failback

14.4.3 SRDF Operations for Concurrent Access

SRDF provides split operations to enable concurrent access to both source and target devices. The establish and restore operations are used to return the source-target pairs to the normal SRDF state.

In *split* operation, when R2 is split from R1, BC operations can be performed on R2. The split operation enables concurrent access to both the source and the target devices. In this operation, target devices are made R/W, and the SRDF replication between the source and the target is suspended, as shown in Figure 14-16. For the duration of the split, there is no remote data protection.

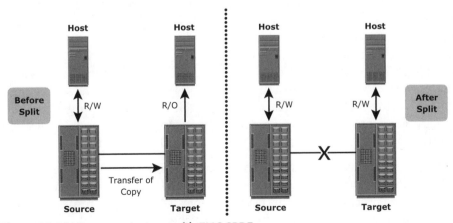

Figure 14-16: Concurrent access with EMC SRDF

During concurrent operations while in a SRDF split state, changes could occur on both the source and the target devices. Normal SRDF replication can be resumed by performing an *establish* or a *restore* operation. With either establish or restore, the status of the target device becomes R/O (see Figure 14-17).

The establish operation is used when changes to the target device should be discarded, while preserving changes that were made to the source device. The restore operation is used when changes to the source device should be discarded, while preserving changes that were made to the target device. Prior to a restore operation, all access to the source and target devices must be stopped. The target device switches to R/O status, while the data on the source device is overwritten with the data from the target device.

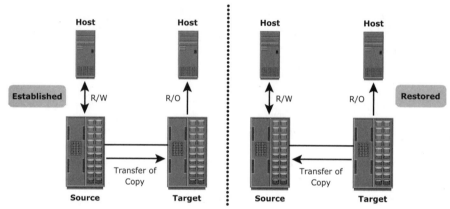

Figure 14-17: Restarting SRDF replication after concurrent access

14.4.4 EMC SAN Copy

SAN Copy is CLARiiON software that performs SAN-based remote replication between CLARiiON and Symmetrix or other vendor storage arrays. It enables simultaneous creation of one or more copies of source devices to target devices through a SAN. Source and target devices could either be on a single array or on multiple arrays. SAN Copy software on the CLARiiON (designated as the control storage array) controls the entire replication process. The source ports utilized during SAN Copy data transfer must be zoned to the target port, and LUN masking must be implemented on the target to perform remote replication. Additional features offered by SAN Copy include the following:

- **Automatic check pointing in the event of a link failure:** Checkpoints are written on the disk drive of the source CLARiiON at the administrator-defined time intervals. This feature enables SAN Copy to resume an interrupted replication session from the last checkpoint.

- **Transfer rate throttle:** The SAN Copy transfer rate can be controlled by throttling network bandwidth. The throttle value ranges from 1 (low) to 10 (high). The transfer rates of each concurrent replication session are adjusted to different throttle values depending on bandwidth requirements.

- **Incremental SAN Copy:** The target logical device is synchronized with the source logical device after an initial full copy replication session is over. After a full copy, SAN Copy establishes an incremental session to transfer only updated data to the target, which lowers the network bandwidth requirement. Changes at the source are tracked by a protection bitmap. The source device is R/O during a full-copy replication session, whereas the incremental session allows R/W at the source.

14.4.5 EMC MirrorView

EMC MirrorView is a CLARiiON-based software that enables storage array–based remote replication over FC SAN, IP extended SAN, and TCP/IP networks. MirrorView family consists of MirrorView/Synchronous (MirrorView/S), and MirrorView/Asynchronous (MirrorView/A). MirrowView software must be installed at both source and target CLARiiON in order to perform remote replication. Any CLARiiON running MirrorView can simultaneously house primary (source) LUNs for some applications and secondary (target) LUNs for others. MirrorView supports both synchronous and asynchronous replication of data on the same CLARiiON. It also supports consistency groups for maintaining data consistency across write-order dependent LUNs.

MirrorView Operations

Initial Synchronization is a replication process that is used for new mirrors (target) to create an initial copy of the primary/primary image (LUN on source CLARiiON containing production data). During the initial synchronization process, the primary images remain online whereas the secondary/secondary image (LUN that contains a mirror of the primary image) is inaccessible. Until the initial synchronization process is complete, secondary images are in the *synchronizing* state. If the synchronization were interrupted, the secondary image would be in the *out-of-sync* state indicating the secondary data is not in a consistent state. When synchronization completes, the mirror data state will be *in-sync*.

A *fracture* operation stops MirrorView replication. An administrator can initiate fracture to suspend the replication. MirrorView software can automatically fracture when it senses a connectivity failure between the primary and secondary LUNs. Replication can resume when the user executes the *synchronize* command.

In the event of a link failure, MirrorView recovery policy provides two options. An *auto-recovery* option starts synchronization as soon as the secondary image is reachable, or a *manual recovery,* where MirrorView waits for a synchronization request from the user.

MirrorView/S invokes a *fracture log* when the secondary image is fractured. The fracture log is a bitmap held in the memory of the storage processor that owns the primary LUN. When the secondary is reachable, using the fracture log, the primary and secondary LUNs can be synchronized by transmitting only the updated information to the secondary. MirrorView/S also uses a *write intent log*, but unlike the fracture log, which is enabled when the mirror is fractured, the write intent log is always active. The write intent log is stored persistently on the disk in the source CLARiiON. Before the primary and secondary LUNs are updated, an entry takes place at the write intent log to indicate locations at the primary LUNs where data changes will occur. In the event of a storage processor failure, the write intent log will be used to determine which locations must be synchronized from the primary LUNs to the secondary LUNs.

MirrorView/A does not use fracture and write intent logs, but it tracks locations (using SnapView technology) at the primary LUNs where updates occur. MirrorView/A utilizes the delta set mechanism to periodically transfer data to the secondary LUNs. MirrorView uses two bitmaps on the primary LUNs. For each update, one bitmap (the *tracking map*) tracks changes between updates, and the other bitmap (the *transfer map*) tracks the progress of the update when transferring to the secondary. The tracking and transfer maps are persistently stored at the reserved LUN pool before mirror operations are initiated.

A secondary image is *promoted* to the role of primary, when it is necessary to run production applications at the disaster recovery site. This may be in response to an actual disaster at the source site, part of a migration strategy, or simply for testing purposes.

Summary

This chapter detailed remote replication. As a primary utility, remote replication provides disaster recovery and disaster restart solutions. It enables business operations to be rapidly restarted at a remote site following an outage, with acceptable data loss.

Remote replication enables BC operations from a target site. The replica of source data at the target can be used for backup and testing. This replica can also be used for data repurposing, such as report generation, data warehousing, and decision support. The segregation of business operations between the source and target protects the source from becoming a performance bottleneck, ensuring improved production performance at the source.

Remote replication may also be used for data center migrations, providing the least disturbance to production operations because the applications accessing the source data are not affected.

This chapter also described different types of remote replication solutions. The distance between the primary site and the remote site is a prime consideration when deciding which remote replication technology solution to deploy. Asynchronous replication may adequately meet the RPO and RTO needs, while permitting greater distances between the sites.

Storage management solutions provide the capability to not only automate business continuity solutions, but also enable centralized management of the overall storage infrastructure. Organizations must ensure security of the information assets. The next chapter details storage security and management.

EXERCISES

1. An organization is planning a data center migration. They can only afford a maximum of two hours downtime to complete the migration. Explain how remote replication technology can be used to meet the downtime requirements. Why will the other methods not meet this requirement?

2. Explain the RPO that can be achieved with synchronous, asynchronous, and disk-buffered remote replication.

3. Discuss the effects of a bunker failure in a three-site replication for the following implementation:

   ▪ Multihop—synchronous + disk buffered

   ▪ Multihop—synchronous + asynchronous

   ▪ Multi-target

4. Discuss the effects of a source failure in a three-site replication for the following implementation, and the available recovery options:

   ▪ Multihop—synchronous + disk buffered

   ▪ Multihop—synchronous + asynchronous

   ▪ Multi-target

5. A host generates 8,000 I/Os at peak utilization with an average I/O size of 32 KB. The response time is currently measured at an average of 12 ms during peak utilizations. When synchronous replication is implemented with a Fibre Channel link to a remote site, what is the response time experienced by the host if the network latency is 6 ms per I/O?

6. Research the remote replication options in a NAS environment. Which type of replication is best suited in integrated and gateway NAS solutions?

Storage Security and Management

In This Section

Chapter 15
Securing the Storage Infrastructure

The Internet is a globally available medium for connecting personal computers, servers, networks, and storage, making it increasingly vulnerable to attacks. Valuable information, including intellectual property, personal identities, and financial transactions, is routinely processed and stored in storage arrays, which are accessed through the network. As a result, storage is now more exposed to various security threats that can potentially damage business-critical data and disrupt critical services. Securing storage networks has become an integral component of the storage management process. It is an intensive and necessary task, essential to managing and protecting vital information.

KEY CONCEPTS

Storage Security Framework

The Risk Triad

Denial of Service

Security Domain

Infrastructure Right Management

Access Control

This chapter describes a framework for storage security that is designed to mitigate security threats that may arise and to combat malicious attacks on the storage infrastructure. In addition, this chapter describes basic storage security implementations, such as the security architecture and protection mechanisms in SAN, NAS, and IP-SAN.

15.1 Storage Security Framework

The basic security framework is built around the four primary services of security: accountability, confidentiality, integrity, and availability. This framework incorporates all security measures required to mitigate threats to these four primary security attributes:

- **Accountability service:** Refers to accounting for all the events and operations that takes place in data center infrastructure. The accountability service maintains a log of events that can be audited or traced later for the purpose of security.

- **Confidentiality service:** Provides the required secrecy of information and ensures that only authorized users have access to data. This service authenticates users who need to access information and typically covers both data in transit (data transmitted over cables), or data at rest (data on a backup media or in the archives).

  Data in transit and at rest can be encrypted to maintain its confidentiality. In addition to restricting unauthorized users from accessing information, confidentiality services also implement traffic flow protection measures as part of the security protocol. These protection measures generally include hiding source and destination addresses, frequency of data being sent, and amount of data sent.

- **Integrity service:** Ensures that the information is unaltered. The objective of the service is to detect and protect against unauthorized alteration or deletion of information. Similar to confidentiality services, integrity services work in collaboration with accountability services to identify and authenticate the users. Integrity services stipulate measures for both in-transit data and at-rest data.

- **Availability service:** This ensures that authorized users have reliable and timely access to data. These services enable users to access the required computer systems, data, and applications residing on these systems. Availability services are also implemented on communication systems used to transmit information among computers that may reside at different locations. This ensures availability of information if a failure in one particular location occurs. These services must be implemented for both electronic data and physical data.

15.2 Risk Triad

Risk triad defines the risk in terms of threats, assets, and vulnerabilities. Risk arises when a threat agent (an attacker) seeks to access assets by exploiting an existing vulnerability.

To manage risks, organizations primarily focus on vulnerabilities because they cannot eliminate threat agents that may appear in various forms and sources to its assets. Organizations can install countermeasures to reduce the impact of an attack by a threat agent, thereby reducing vulnerability.

Risk assessment is the first step in determining the extent of potential threats and risks in an IT infrastructure. The process assesses risk and helps to identify appropriate controls to mitigate or eliminate risks. To determine the probability of an adverse event occurring, threats to an IT system must be analyzed in conjunction with the potential vulnerabilities and the existing security controls.

The severity of an adverse event is estimated by the impact that it may have on critical business activities. Based on this analysis, a relative value of criticality and sensitivity can be assigned to IT assets and resources. For example, a particular IT system component may be assigned a high-criticality value if an attack on this particular component can cause a complete termination of mission-critical services.

The following sections examine the three key elements of the risk triad. Assets, threats, and vulnerability are considered from the perspective of risk identification and control analysis.

15.2.1 Assets

Information is one of the most important *assets* for any organization. Other assets include hardware, software, and the network infrastructure required to access this information. To protect these assets, organizations must develop a set of parameters to ensure the availability of the resources to authorized users and trusted networks. These parameters apply to storage resources, the network infrastructure, and organizational policies.

Several factors need to be considered when planning for asset security. Security methods have two objectives. First objective is to ensure that the network is easily accessible to authorized users. It should also be reliable and stable under disparate environmental conditions and volumes of usage. Second objective is to make it very difficult for potential attackers to access and compromise the system. These methods should provide adequate protection against unauthorized access to resources, viruses, worms, Trojans and other malicious software programs. Security measures should also encrypt critical data and disable unused services to minimize the number of potential security gaps. The security method must ensure that updates to the operating system and other software are installed regularly. At the same time, it must provide adequate redundancy in the form of replication and mirroring of the production data to prevent catastrophic data loss if there is an unexpected malfunction. In order for the security system to function smoothly, it is important to ensure that all users are informed of the policies governing use of the network.

The effectiveness of a storage security methodology can be measured by two criteria. One, the cost of implementing the system should only be a small fraction of the value of the protected data. Two, it should cost a potential attacker more, in terms of money and time, to compromise the system than the protected data is worth.

TYPES OF PASSIVE ATTACKS

- **Eavesdropping:** When someone overhears a conversation, the unauthorized access is called eavesdropping.

- **Snooping:** This refers to accessing another user's data in an unauthorized way. In general, snooping and eavesdropping are synonymous.

Malicious hackers frequently use snooping techniques and equipment, such as key loggers, to monitor keystrokes, to capture passwords and login information, or to intercept e-mail and other private communication and data transmission. Organizations sometimes perform legitimate snooping on employees to monitor their use of business computers and to track Internet usage.

15.2.2 Threats

Threats are the potential attacks that can be carried out on an IT infrastructure. These attacks can be classified as active or passive. *Passive* attacks are attempts to gain unauthorized access into the system. They pose threats to confidentiality of information. *Active* attacks include data modification, Denial of Service (DoS), and repudiation attacks. They pose threats to data integrity and availability.

In a *modification* attack, the unauthorized user attempts to modify information for malicious purposes. A modification attack can target data at rest or data in transit. These attacks pose a threat to data integrity.

Denial of Service (DoS) attacks denies the use of resources to legitimate users. These attacks generally do not involve access to or modification of information on the computer system. Instead, they pose a threat to data availability. The intentional flooding of a network or website to prevent legitimate access to authorized users is one example of a DoS attack.

Repudiation is an attack against the accountability of the information. It attempts to provide false information by either impersonating someone or denying that an event or a transaction has taken place.

Table 15-1 describes different forms of attacks and the security services used to manage them.

Table 15-1: Security Services for Various Types of Attacks

ATTACK	CONFIDENTIALITY	INTEGRITY	AVAILABILITY	ACCOUNTABILITY
Access	X			X
Modification	X	X		X
Denial of Service			X	
Repudiation		X		X

15.2.3 Vulnerability

The paths that provide access to information are the most vulnerable to potential attacks. Each of these paths may contain various access points, each of which provides different levels of access to the storage resources. It is very important to implement adequate security controls at *all* the access points on an access path. Implementing security controls at each access point of every access path is termed as *defense in depth*.

Defense in depth recommends protecting all access points within an environment. This reduces vulnerability to an attacker who can gain access to storage resources by bypassing inadequate security controls implemented at the vulnerable single point of access. Such an attack can jeopardize the security of information assets. For example, a failure to properly authenticate a user may put the confidentiality of information at risk. Similarly, a DoS attack against a storage device can jeopardize information availability.

Attack surface, *attack vector*, and *work factor* are the three factors to consider when assessing the extent to which an environment is vulnerable to security threats. *Attack surface* refers to the various entry points that an attacker can use to launch an attack. Each component of a storage network is a source of potential vulnerability. All of the external interfaces supported by that component, such as the hardware interfaces, the supported protocols, and the management and administrative interfaces, can be used by an attacker to execute various attacks. These interfaces form the attack surface for the attacker. Even unused network services, if enabled, can become a part of the attack surface.

An *attack vector* is a step or a series of steps necessary to complete an attack. For example, an attacker might exploit a bug in the management interface to execute a snoop attack whereby the attacker can modify the configuration of the storage device to allow the traffic to be accessed from one more host. This redirected traffic can be used to snoop the data in transit.

Work factor refers to the amount of time and effort required to exploit an attack vector. For example, if attackers attempt to retrieve sensitive information, they consider the time and effort that would be required for executing an attack on a database. This may include determining privileged accounts, determining the database schema, and writing SQL queries. Instead, based on the work factor, they consider a less effort-intensive way to exploit the storage array by attaching to it directly and reading from the raw disk blocks.

Having assessed the vulnerability of the network environment to security threats, organizations can plan and deploy specific control measures directed at reducing vulnerability by minimizing attack surfaces and maximizing the work factor. These controls can be technical or nontechnical. Technical controls are usually implemented through computer systems, whereas nontechnical controls are implemented through administrative and physical controls. Administrative controls include security and personnel policies or standard procedures to direct the safe execution of various operations. Physical controls include setting up physical barriers, such as security guards, fences, or locks.

Based on the roles they play, controls can be categorized as preventive, detective, corrective, recovering, or compensating. The discussion here focuses on preventive, corrective, and detective controls only. The preventive control attempts to prevent an attack; the detective control detects whether an attack is in progress; and after an attack is discovered, the corrective controls are implemented. *Preventive* controls avert the vulnerabilities from being exploited and prevent an attack or reduce its impact. *Corrective* controls reduce the effect of an attack, while *detective* controls discover attacks and trigger preventive or corrective controls. For example, an Intrusion Detection/Intrusion Prevention System (IDS/IPS) is a detective control that determines whether an attack is underway and then attempts to stop it by terminating a network connection or invoking a firewall rule to block traffic.

15.3 Storage Security Domains

Storage devices that are not connected to a storage network are less vulnerable because they are not exposed to security threats via networks. However, with increasing use of networking in storage environments, storage devices are becoming highly exposed to security threats from a variety of sources. Specific controls must be implemented to secure a storage networking environment. This requires a closer look at storage networking security and a clear understanding of the access paths leading to storage resources. If a particular path is unauthorized and needs to be prohibited by technical controls, one must ensure that these controls are not compromised. If each component within the storage network is considered a potential access point, one must analyze the attack surface that each of these access points provides and identify the associated vulnerability.

In order to identify the threats that apply to a storage network, access paths to data storage can be categorized into three security domains: *application access*, *management access*, and *BURA (backup, recovery, and archive)*. Figure 15-1 depicts the three security domains of a storage system environment.

The first security domain involves application access to the stored data through the storage network. The second security domain includes management access to storage and interconnect devices and to the data residing on those devices. This domain is primarily accessed by storage administrators who configure and manage the environment. The third domain consists of BURA access. Along with the access points in the other two domains, backup media also needs to be secured.

To secure the storage networking environment, identify the existing threats within each of the security domains and classify the threats based on the type of security services—availability, confidentiality, integrity, and accountability. The next step is to select and implement various controls as countermeasures to the threats.

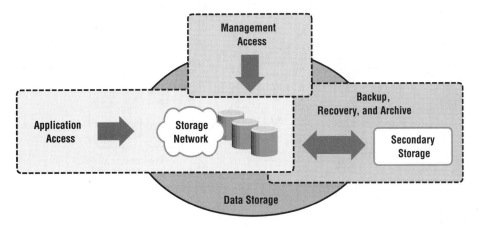

Figure 15-1: Three security domains of data storage

15.3.1 Securing the Application Access Domain

The application access domain may include only those applications that access the data through the file system or a database interface.

Figure 15-2 shows application access in a storage networking environment. Host A can access all V1 volumes; host B can access all V2 volumes. These volumes are classified according to access level, such as confidential, restricted, and public. Some of the possible threat in this scenario could be host A spoofing the identity or elevating the privileges of host B to gain access to host B's resources. Another threat could be an unauthorized host gain access to the network; the attacker on this host may try to spoof the identity of another host and tamper with data, snoop the network, or execute a DoS attack. Also any form of media theft could also compromise security. These threats can pose several serious challenges to the network security, hence they need to be addressed.

An important step for securing the application access domain is to identify the core functions that can prevent these threats from being exploited and to identify the appropriate controls that should be applied. Implementing physical security is also an important consideration to prevent media theft.

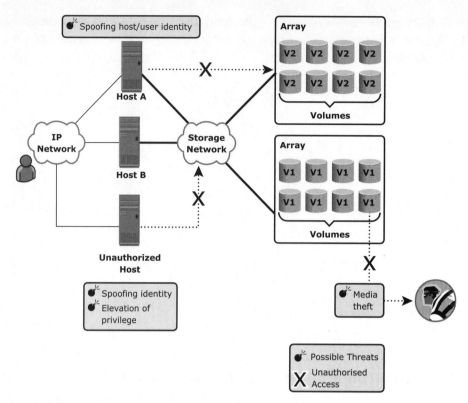

Figure 15-2: Security threats in application access domain

Controlling User Access to Data

Access control services regulate user access to data. These services mitigate the threats of spoofing host identity and elevating host privileges. Both of these threats affect data integrity and confidentiality.

Technical control in the form of user authentication and administrative control in the form of user authorization are the two access control mechanisms used in application access control. These mechanisms may lie outside the boundaries of the storage network and require various systems to interconnect with other enterprise identity management and authentication systems—for example, systems that provide strong authentication and authorization to secure user identities against spoofing. NAS devices support the creation of *access control lists* that are used to regulate user access to specific files. The Enterprise Content Management application enforces access to data by using Information Rights Management (IRM) that specify which users have what rights to a document. Restricting access at the host level starts with authenticating a node when it tries to connect to a network. Different storage networking technologies, such as iSCSI, FC, and IP-based storage, use various authentication mechanisms, such as Challenge-Handshake Authentication Protocol (CHAP), Fibre Channel Security Protocol (FC-SP), and IPSec, respectively, to authenticate host access.

After a host has been authenticated, the next step is to specify security controls for the storage resources, such as ports, volumes, or storage pools, that the host is authorized to access. *Zoning* is a control mechanism on the switches that segments the network into specific paths to be used for data traffic; *LUN masking* determines which hosts can access which storage devices. Some devices support mapping of a host's WWN to a particular FC port, and from there to a particular LUN. This binding of the WWN to a physical port is the most secure.

Finally, it is very important to ensure that administrative controls, such as defined policies and standards, are implemented. Regular auditing is required to ensure proper functioning of administrative controls. This is enabled by logging significant events on all participating devices. Event logging must be protected from unauthorized access because it may fail to achieve its goals if the logged content is exposed to unwanted modifications by an attacker.

Protecting the Storage Infrastructure

Securing the storage infrastructure from unauthorized access involves protecting all the elements of the infrastructure. Security controls for protecting the storage infrastructure address the threats of unauthorized tampering of data in transit that leads to a loss of data integrity, denial of service that compromises availability, and network snooping that may result in a loss of confidentiality.

The security controls for protecting the network fall into two general categories: *connectivity infrastructure integrity* and *storage network encryption*. Controls for ensuring the infrastructure integrity include a fabric switch function to ensure fabric integrity. This is achieved by preventing a host from being added to the SAN fabric without proper authorization. Storage network encryption methods include the use of IPSec, for protecting IP-based storage networks, and FC-SP, for protecting FC networks.

In secure storage environments, root or administrator privileges for a specific device are not granted to any individual. Instead, *role-based access control (RBAC)* is deployed to assign necessary privileges to users, enabling them to perform their roles. It is also advisable to consider administrative controls, such as "separation of duties," when defining data center procedures. Clear separation of duties ensures that no single individual is able to both specify an action and carry it out. For example, the person who authorizes the creation of administrative accounts should not be the person who uses those accounts. Securing management access is covered in detail in the next section.

Management networks for storage systems should be logically separate from other enterprise networks. This segmentation is critical to facilitate ease of management and increase security by allowing access only to the components existing within the same segment. For example, IP network segmentation is enforced with the deployment of filters at layer 3 by using routers and firewalls, as well as at layer 2 by using VLANs and port-level security on Ethernet switches.

Finally, physical access to the device console and the cabling of FC switches must be controlled to ensure protection of the storage infrastructure. All other established security measures fail if a device is physically accessed by an unauthorized user; the mere fact of this access may render the device unreliable.

Data Encryption

The most important aspect of securing data is protecting data held inside the storage arrays. Threats at this level include tampering with data, which violates data integrity, and media theft, which compromises data availability and confidentiality. To protect against these threats, encrypt the data held on the storage media or encrypt the data prior to being transferred to the disk. It is also critical to decide upon a method for ensuring that data deleted at the end of its lifecycle has been completely erased from the disks and cannot be reconstructed for malicious purposes.

Data should be encrypted as close to its origin as possible. If it is not possible to perform encryption on the host device, an encryption appliance can be used for encrypting data at the point of entry into the storage network. Encryption devices can be implemented on the fabric that encrypts data between the host and the storage media. These mechanisms can protect both the data at rest on the destination device and data in transit.

On NAS devices, adding antivirus checks and file extension controls can further enhance data integrity. In the case of CAS, use of MD5 or SHA-256 cryptographic algorithms guarantee data integrity by detecting any change in content bit patterns. In addition, the CAS data erasure service ensures that the data has been completely scrubbed from the disk before the disk is discarded. An organization's data classification policy determines whether the disk should actually be scrubbed prior to discarding it as well as the level of erasure needed based on regulatory requirements.

15.3.2 Securing the Management Access Domain

Management access, whether monitoring, provisioning, or managing storage resources, is associated with every device within the storage network. Most management software supports some form of CLI, system management console, or a web-based interface. It is very important to implement appropriate controls for securing storage management applications because the damage that can be caused to the storage system by using these applications can be far more extensive than that caused by vulnerability in a server.

Figure 15-3 depicts a storage networking environment in which production hosts are connected to a SAN fabric and are accessing storage Array A, which is connected to storage Array B for replication purposes. Further, this configuration has a storage management platform on Host B and a monitoring console on Host A. All these hosts are interconnected through an IP network. Some of the possible threats in this system are, unauthorized host may spoof the user or host identity to manage the storage arrays or network. For example, Host A may gain management access to array B. Remote console support for the management software also increases the attack surface. Using remote console support, several other systems in the network may also be used to execute an attack.

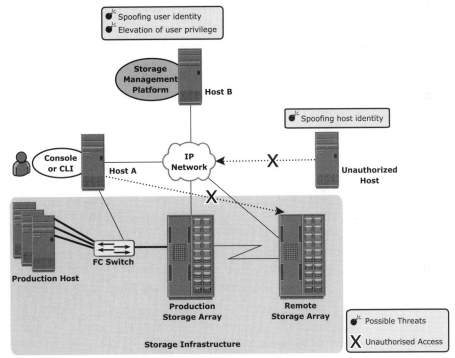

Figure 15-3: Security threats in management access domain

Providing management access through an external network increases the potential for an unauthorized host or switch to connect to that network. In such circumstances, implementing appropriate security measures prevents certain types of remote communication from occurring. Using secure communication channels, such as Secure Shell (SSH) or Secure Sockets Layer (SSL)/ Transport Layer Security (TLS), provides effective protection against these threats. Event log monitoring helps to identify unauthorized access and unauthorized changes to the infrastructure.

The storage management platform must be validated for available security controls and ensures that these controls are adequate to secure the overall storage environment. The administrator's identity and role should be secured against any spoofing attempts so an attacker cannot manipulate the entire storage array and cause intolerable data loss by reformatting storage media or making data resources unavailable.

Controlling Administrative Access

Controlling administrative access to storage aims to safeguard against the threats of an attacker spoofing an administrator's identity or elevating another user's identity and privileges to gain administrative access. Both of these threats affect the integrity of data and devices. To protect against these threats, administrative access regulation and various auditing techniques are used to enforce accountability. Every storage component should provide access control. In some storage environments, it may be necessary to integrate storage devices with third-party authentication directories, such as *Lightweight Directory Access Protocol (LDAP)* or Active Directory.

Security best practices stipulate that no single user should have ultimate control over all aspects of the system. If an administrative user is a necessity, the number of activities requiring administrative privileges should be minimized. Instead, it is better to assign various administrative functions by using RBAC. Auditing logged events is a critical control measure to track the activities of an administrator. However, access to administrative log files as well as their content must be protected. Deploying a reliable *Network Time Protocol* on each system that can be synchronized to a common time is another important requirement to ensure that activities across systems can be consistently tracked. In addition, having a Security Information Management (SIM) solution supports effective analysis of the event log files.

Protecting the Management Infrastructure

Protecting the management network infrastructure is also necessary. Controls to protect the management network infrastructure include encrypting management traffic, enforcing management access controls, and applying IP network security best practices. These best practices include the use of IP routers and Ethernet switches to restrict traffic to certain devices and management protocols. At the IP network layer, restricting network activity and access to a limited set of hosts minimizes the threat of an unauthorized device attaching to the network and gaining access to the management interfaces of all devices within the storage network. Access controls need to be enforced at the storage-array level to specify which host has management access to which array. Some storage devices and switches can restrict management access to particular hosts and limit commands that can be issued from each host.

A separate private management network must be created for management traffic. If possible, management traffic should not be mixed with either production data traffic or other LAN traffic used in the enterprise. Restricting traffic makes it easy for IDS to determine whether there is unauthorized traffic on the network segment. Unused network services must be disabled on every device within the storage network. This decreases the attack surface for that device by minimizing the number of interfaces through which the device can be accessed.

To summarize, security enforcement must focus on the management communications between devices, confidentiality and integrity of management data, and availability of management networks and devices.

15.3.3 Securing Backup, Recovery, and Archive (BURA)

BURA is the third domain that needs to be secured against attack. As explained in Chapter 12, a backup involves copying the data from a storage array to backup media, such as tapes or disks. Securing BURA is complex and is based on the BURA software accessing the storage arrays. It also depends on the configuration of the storage environments at the primary and secondary sites, especially with remote backup solutions performed directly on a remote tape device or using array-based remote replication.

Organizations must ensure that the DR site maintains the same level of security for the backed up data. Protecting the BURA infrastructure requires addressing several threats, including spoofing the legitimate identity of a DR site, tampering with data, network snooping, DoS attacks, and media theft. Such threats represent potential violations of integrity, confidentiality, and availability. Figure 15-4 illustrates a generic remote backup design whereby data on a storage array is replicated over a disaster recovery (DR) network to a secondary storage at the DR site. In a remote backup solution where the storage components are separated by a network, the threats at the transmission layer need to be countered. Otherwise, an attacker can spoof the identity of the backup server and request the host to send its data. The unauthorized host claims to be the backup server at the DR site, which may lead to a remote backup being performed to an unauthorized and unknown site. In addition, attackers can use the connection to the DR network to tamper with data, snoop the network for authentication data, and create a DoS attack against the storage devices.

The physical threat of a backup tape being lost, stolen, or misplaced, especially if the tapes contain highly confidential information, is another type of threat. Backup-to-tape applications are vulnerable to severe security implications if they do not encrypt data while backing it up.

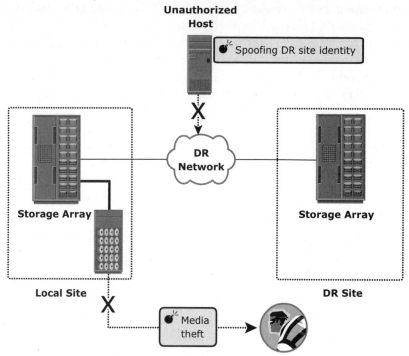

Figure 15-4: Security threats in a BURA environment

15.4 Security Implementations in Storage Networking

The following discussion details some of the basic security implementations in SAN, NAS, and IP-SAN environments.

15.4.1 SAN

Traditional FC SANs enjoy a natural security advantage over IP-based networks. An FC SAN is configured as an isolated private environment with fewer nodes than an IP network. Consequently, FC SANs impose fewer security threats. However, this scenario has changed with storage consolidation, driving rapid growth and necessitating designs for large, complex SANs that span multiple sites across the enterprise. Today, no single comprehensive security solution is available for SANs. Many SAN security mechanisms have evolved from their counterpart in IP networking, thereby bringing in mature security solutions.

FC-SP (Fibre Channel Security Protocol) standards (T11 standards), published in 2006, align security mechanisms and algorithms between IP and FC interconnects. These standards describe protocols used to implement security measures in an FC fabric, among fabric elements and N_Ports within the fabric. They also include guidelines for authenticating FC entities, setting up session keys, negotiating the parameters required to ensure frame-by-frame integrity and confidentiality, and establishing and distributing policies across an FC fabric. The current version of the FC-SP standard is referred to as FC-SP-1.

SAN Security Architecture

Storage networking environments are a potential target for unauthorized access, theft, and misuse because of the vastness and complexity of these environments. Therefore, security strategies are based on the *defense in depth* concept, which recommends multiple integrated layers of security. This ensures that the failure of one security control will not compromise the assets under protection. Figure 15-5 illustrates various levels (zones) of a storage networking environment that must be secured and the security measures that can be deployed.

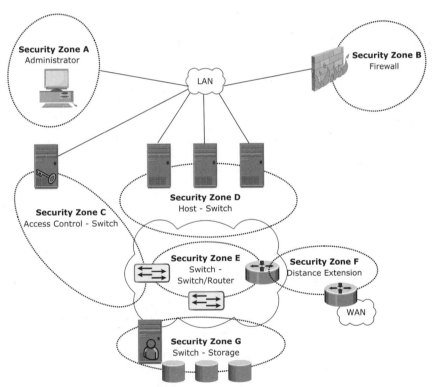

Figure 15-5: SAN security architecture

SANs not only suffer from certain risks and vulnerabilities that are unique, but also share common security problems associated with physical security and remote administrative access. In addition to implementing SAN-specific security measures, organizations must simultaneously leverage other security implementations in the enterprise. Table 15-2 provides a comprehensive list of protection strategies that must be implemented in various security zones. Note that some of the security mechanisms listed in Table 15-2 are not specific to SAN, but are commonly used data center techniques. For example, two-factor authentication is implemented widely; in a simple implementation it requires the use of a user name/password and an additional security component such as a smart card for authentication.

Table 15-2: Security Zones and Protection Strategies

SECURITY ZONES	PROTECTION STRATEGIES
Zone A (Authentication at the Management Console)	(a) Restrict management LAN access to authorized users (lock down MAC addresses) (b) Implement VPN tunneling for secure remote access to the management LAN (c) Use two-factor authentication for network access
Zone B (Firewall)	Block inappropriate or dangerous traffic by: (a) Filtering out addresses that should not be allowed on your LAN (b) Screening for allowable protocols—block well-known ports that are not in use
Zone C (Access Control Switch)	Authenticate users/administrators of FC switches using RADIUS (Remote Authentication Dial In User Service), DH-CHAP (Diffie-Hellman Challenge Handshake Authentication Protocol), etc.
Zone D (ACL and Zoning)	Restrict FC access to legitimate hosts by: (a) Implementing ACLs: Known HBAs can connect on specific switch ports only (b) Implementing a secure zoning method such as port zoning (also known as hard zoning)
Zone E (Switch to Switch/ Switch to Router)	Protect traffic on your fabric by: (a) Using E_Port authentication (b) Encrypting the traffic in transit (c) Implementing FC switch controls and port controls
Zone F (Distance Extension)	Implement encryption for in-flight data: (a) FCsec for long-distance FC extension (b) IPSec for SAN extension via FCIP
Zone G (Switch-Storage)	Protect the storage arrays on your SAN via: (a) WWPN-based LUN masking (b) S_ID locking: Masking based on source FCID (Fibre Channel ID/Address)

Basic SAN Security Mechanisms

LUN masking and zoning, switch-wide and fabric-wide access control, RBAC, and logical partitioning of a fabric (Virtual SAN) are the most commonly used SAN security methods.

LUN Masking and Zoning

LUN masking and zoning are the basic SAN security mechanisms used to protect against unauthorized access to storage. LUN masking and zoning were detailed earlier in Chapter 4 and Chapter 6. Standard implementations of storage arrays mask the LUNs that are presented to a front-end storage port, based on the WWPNs of the source HBAs. A stronger variant of LUN masking may sometimes be offered whereby masking can be done on the basis of source FCIDs. Note that the FCID typically changes if the HBA is relocated across ports in the fabric. To avoid this problem, major switch vendors offer a mechanism to lock down the FCID of a given node port regardless of its location.

Hard zoning or *port zoning* is the mechanism of choice in security-conscious environments. Unlike soft zoning or WWPN zoning, it actually filters frames to ensure that only authorized zone members can communicate. However, it lacks one significant advantage of WWPN zoning: The zoning configuration must change if the source or the target is relocated across ports in the fabric. There is a trade-off between ease of management and the security provided by WWPN zoning and port zoning.

Apart from zoning and LUN masking, additional security mechanisms such as port binding, port lockdown, port lockout, and persistent port disable can be implemented on switch ports. *Port binding* limits the number of devices that can attach to a particular switch port and allows only the corresponding switch port to connect to a node for fabric access. Port binding mitigates but does not eliminate WWPN spoofing. *Port lockdown* and *port lockout* restrict a switch port's type of initialization. Typical variants of port lockout ensure that the switch port cannot function as an E_Port and cannot be used to create an ISL, such as a rogue switch. Some variants ensure that the port role is restricted to only FL_Port, F_Port, E_Port, or a combination of these. *Persistent port disable* prevents a switch port from being enabled even after a switch reboot.

Switch-wide and Fabric-wide Access Control

As organizations grow their SANs locally or over longer distances there is a greater need to effectively manage SAN security. Network security can be configured on the FC switch by using *access control lists (ACLs)* and on the fabric by using fabric binding.

ACLs incorporate the device connection control and switch connection control policies. The device connection control policy specifies which HBAs and storage ports can be a part of the fabric, preventing unauthorized devices (identified by WWPNs) from accessing it. Similarly, the switch connection control policy specifies which switches are allowed to be part of the fabric, preventing unauthorized switches (identified by WWNs) from joining it.

Fabric binding prevents an unauthorized switch from joining any existing switch in the fabric. It ensures that authorized membership data exists on every switch and that any attempt to connect two switches by using an ISL causes the fabric to segment.

Role-based access control provides additional security to a SAN by preventing unauthorized management activity on the fabric for management operations. It enables the security administrator to assign roles to users that explicitly specify privileges or access rights after logging into the fabric. For example, the *zoneadmin* role is able to modify the zones on the fabric, whereas a basic user may only be able to view fabric-related information, such as port types and logged-in nodes.

Logical Partitioning of a Fabric: Virtual SAN

VSANs enable the creation of multiple logical SANs over a common physical SAN. They provide the capability to build larger consolidated fabrics and still maintain the required security and isolation between them. Figure 15-6 depicts logical partitioning in a VSAN.

Zoning should be done for each VSAN to secure the entire physical SAN. Each managed VSAN can have only one active zone set at a time. As depicted in the figure, VSAN 1 is the active zone set. The SAN administrator can create distinct VSANs other than VSAN 1 and populate each of them with switch ports. In the example, the switch ports are distributed over three VSANs: 1, 2, and 3—for the IT, Engineering, and HR divisions, respectively. A zone set is defined for each VSAN, providing connectivity for HBAs and storage ports logged into the VSAN. Therefore, each of the three divisions—Engineering, IT, and HR—has its own logical fabric. Although they share physical switching gear with other divisions, they can be managed individually as stand-alone fabrics.

VSANs minimize the impact of fabricwide disruptive events because management and control traffic on the SAN—which may include RSCNs, zone set activation events, and more—does not traverse VSAN boundaries. Therefore, VSANs are a cost-effective alternative for building isolated physical fabrics. They contribute to information availability and security by isolating fabric events and providing a finer degree of authorization control within a single fabric.

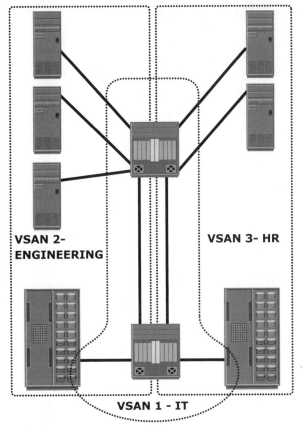

VSAN 2-
ENGINEERING

VSAN 3- HR

VSAN 1 - IT

Figure 15-6: Securing SAN with VSAN

15.4.2 NAS

NAS is open to multiple exploits, including viruses, worms, unauthorized access, snooping, and data tampering. Various security mechanisms are implemented in NAS to secure data and the storage networking infrastructure.

Permissions and ACLs form the first level of protection to NAS resources by restricting accessibility and sharing. These permissions are deployed over and above the default behaviors and attributes associated with files and folders. In addition, various other authentication and authorization mechanisms, such as Kerberos and directory services, are implemented to verify the identity of network users and define their privileges. Similarly, firewalls are used to protect the storage infrastructure from unauthorized access and malicious attacks.

NAS File Sharing: Windows ACLs

Windows supports two types of ACLs: *discretionary access control lists (DACLs)* and *system access control lists (SACLs)*. The DACL, commonly referred to as the ACL, is used to determine access control. The SACL determines what accesses need to be audited if auditing is enabled.

In addition to these ACLs, Windows also supports the concept of object ownership. The owner of an object has hard-coded rights to that object, and these rights do not have to be explicitly granted in the SACL. The owner, SACL, and DACL are all statically held as an attribute of each object. Windows also offers the functionality to inherit permissions, which allows the child objects existing within a parent object to automatically inherit the ACLs of the parent object.

ACLs are also applied to directory objects known as SIDs. These are automatically generated by a Windows server or domain when a user or group is created, and they are abstracted from the user. In this way, though a user may identify his or her login ID as "User1," it is simply a textual representation of the true SID, which is used by the underlying operating system. ACLs are set by using the standard Windows Explorer GUI, but can also be configured with CLI commands or other third-party tools.

NAS File Sharing: UNIX Permissions

For the UNIX operating system, a *user* is an abstraction that denotes a logical entity for assignment of ownership and operation privileges for the system. A user can be either a person or a system operation. A UNIX system is only aware of the privileges of the user to perform specific operations on the system, and identifies each user by a user ID (UID) and a user name, regardless of whether it is a person, a system operation, or a device.

In UNIX, a user can be organized into one or more groups. The concept of groups serves the purpose of assigning sets of privileges for a given resource and sharing them among many users that need them. For example, a group of people working on one project may need the same permissions for a set of files.

UNIX permissions specify the operations that can be performed by any ownership relation with respect to a file. In simpler terms, these permissions specify what the owner can do, what the owner group can do, and what everyone else can do with the file. For any given ownership relation, three bits are used to specify access permissions. The first bit denotes read (r) access, the second bit denotes write (w) access, and the third bit denotes execute (x) access. As UNIX defines three ownership relations, (Owner, Group, and All) a triplet (defining the access permission) is required for each ownership relationship, resulting in nine bits. Each bit can be either set or clear. When displayed, a set bit is marked by its corresponding operation letter (r, w, or x), a clear bit is denoted by a dash (-), and all are put in a row, such as rwxr-xr-x. In this example, the owner can do anything with the file, but group owners and the rest of the world can only read or execute.

When displayed, a character denoting the mode of the file may precede this nine-bit pattern. For example, if the file is a directory, it is denoted as "d"; and if it is a link, it is denoted as "l."

Authentication and Authorization

In a file-sharing environment, NAS devices use standard file-sharing protocols, NFS and CIFS. Therefore, authentication and authorization are implemented and supported on NAS devices in the same way as in a UNIX or Windows file-sharing environment.

Authentication requires verifying the identity of a network user and therefore involves a login credential lookup on a Network Information System (NIS) server in a UNIX environment. Similarly, a Windows client is authenticated by a Windows domain controller that houses the Active Directory. The Active Directory uses LDAP to access information about network objects in the directory, and Kerberos for network security. NAS devices use the same authentication techniques to validate network user credentials. Active Directory, LDAP, and Kerberos are discussed later in this chapter. Figure 15-7 depicts the authentication process in a NAS environment.

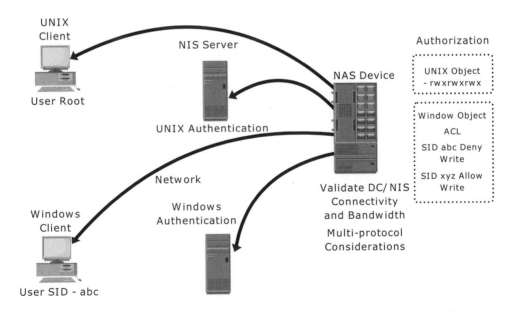

Figure 15-7: Securing user access in a NAS environment

Authorization defines user privileges in a network. The authorization techniques for UNIX users and Windows users are quite different. UNIX files use mode bits to define access rights granted to owners, groups, and other users, whereas Windows uses an ACL to allow or deny specific rights to a particular user for a particular file.

Although NAS devices support both of these methodologies for UNIX and Windows users, complexities arise when UNIX and Windows users access and share the same data. If the NAS device supports multiple protocols, the integrity of both permission methodologies must be maintained. NAS device vendors provide a method of mapping UNIX permissions to Windows and vice versa, so a multiprotocol environment can be supported. However, it is important to examine these complexities of multiprotocol support when designing a NAS solution. At the same time, it is important to validate the domain controller and/ or NIS server connectivity and bandwidth. If multiprotocol access is required, specific vendor access policy implementations need to be considered. Additional care should be taken to understand the resulting access rights for data being accessed by NFS and CIFS because the access techniques for Windows and UNIX are quite different.

Kerberos

Kerberos is a network authentication protocol. It is designed to provide strong authentication for client/server applications by using secret-key cryptography. It uses cryptography so that a client and server can prove their identity to each other across an insecure network connection. After the client and server have proven their identity, they can choose to encrypt all of their communications to ensure privacy and data integrity.

In Kerberos, all authentications occur between clients and servers. The client gets a ticket for a service, and the server decrypts this ticket by using its secret key. Any entity, user, or host that gets a service ticket for a Kerberos service is called a *Kerberos client*. The term *Kerberos server* generally refers to the Key Distribution Center (KDC). The KDC implements the Authentication Service (AS) and the Ticket Granting Service (TGS). The KDC has a copy of every password associated with every principal, so it is absolutely vital that the KDC remain secure.

In a NAS environment, Kerberos is primarily used when authenticating against a Microsoft Active Directory domain although it can be used to execute security functions in UNIX environments. The Kerberos authorization process shown in Figure 15-8 includes the following steps:

1. The user logs on to the workstation in the Active Directory domain (or forest) using an ID and a password. The client computer sends a request to the AS running on the KDC for a Kerberos ticket. The KDC verifies the user's login information from Active Directory. (Note that this step is not explicitly shown in Figure 15-8.)

2. The KDC responds with a TGT (TKT is a key used for identification and has limited validity period). It contains two parts, one decryptable by the client and the other by the KDC.

3. When the client requests a service from a server, it sends a request, consist of the previously generated TGT and the resource information, to the KDC.

4. The KDC checks the permissions in Active Directory and ensures that the user is authorized to use that service.

5. The KDC returns a service ticket to the client. This service ticket contains fields addressed to the client and to the server that is hosting the service.

6. The client then sends the service ticket to the server that houses the desired resources.

7. The server, in this case the NAS device, decrypts the server portion of the ticket and stores the information in a keytab file. As long as the client's Kerberos ticket is valid, this authorization process does not need to be repeated. The server automatically allows the client to access the appropriate resources.

8. A client/server session is now established. The server returns a session ID to the client, which is used to track client activity, such as file locking, as long as the session is active.

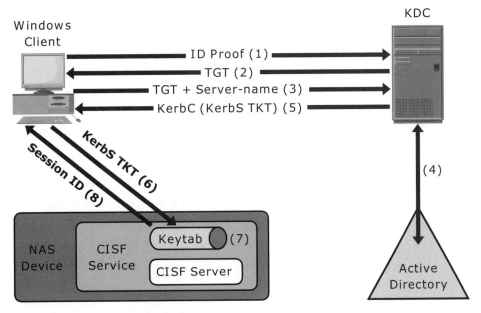

Figure 15-8: Kerberos authorization

Network-Layer Firewalls

Because NAS devices utilize the IP protocol stack, they are vulnerable to various attacks initiated through the public IP network. Network layer firewalls are implemented in NAS environments to protect the NAS devices from these security threats. These network-layer firewalls are capable of examining network packets and comparing them to a set of configured security rules. Packets that are not authorized by a security rule are dropped and not allowed to continue to the requested destination. Rules can be established based on a source address (network or host), a destination address (network or host), a port, or a combination of those factors (source IP, destination IP, and port number). The effectiveness of a firewall depends on how robust and extensive the security rules are. A loosely defined rule set can increase the probability of a security breach.

Figure 15-9 depicts a typical firewall implementation. Demilitarized zone (DMZ) is commonly used in networking environments. A DMZ provides a means of securing internal assets while allowing Internet-based access to various resources. In a DMZ environment, servers that need to be accessed through the Internet are placed between two sets of firewalls. Application-specific ports, such as HTTP or FTP, are allowed through the firewall to the DMZ servers. However, no Internet-based traffic is allowed to penetrate the second set of firewalls and gain access to the internal network.

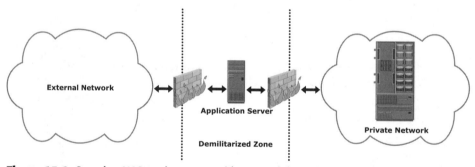

Figure 15-9: Securing NAS environment with network-layer firewall

The servers in the DMZ may or may not be allowed to communicate with internal resources. In such a setup, the server in the DMZ is an Internet-facing Web application that is accessing data stored on a NAS device, which may be located on the internal private network. A secure design would only serve data to internal and external applications through the DMZ.

15.4.3 IP SAN

This section describes some of the basic security mechanisms of IP SAN environments. The *Challenge-Handshake Authentication Protocol (CHAP)* is a basic authentication mechanism that has been widely adopted by network devices and hosts. CHAP provides a method for initiators and targets to authenticate each other by utilizing a secret code or password. CHAP secrets are usually random secrets of 12 to 128 characters. The secret is never exchanged directly over the wire; rather, a one-way hash function converts it into a hash value, which is then exchanged. A hash function, using the MD5 algorithm, transforms data in such a way that the result is unique and cannot be changed back to its original form. Figure 15-10 depicts the CHAP authentication process.

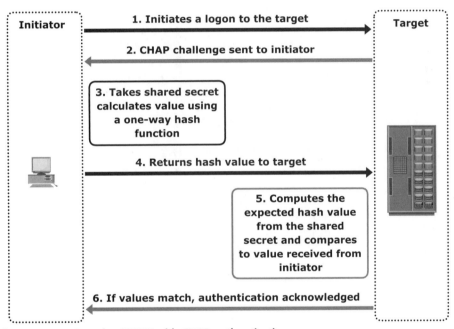

Figure 15-10: Securing IPSAN with CHAP authentication

If the initiator requires reverse CHAP authentication, the initiator authenticates the target by using the same procedure. The CHAP secret must be configured on the initiator and the target. A CHAP entry, comprising the name of a node and the secret associated with the node, is maintained by the target and the initiator.

The same steps are executed in a two-way CHAP authentication scenario. After these steps are completed, the initiator authenticates the target. If both authentication steps succeed, then data access is allowed. CHAP is often used because it is a fairly simple protocol to implement and can be implemented across a number of disparate systems.

iSNS discovery domains function in the same way as FC zones. Discovery domains provide functional groupings of devices in an IP-SAN. In order for devices to communicate with one another, they must be configured in the same discovery domain. State change notifications (SCNs) tell the iSNS server when devices are added or removed from a discovery domain. Figure 15-11 depicts the discovery domains in iSNS.

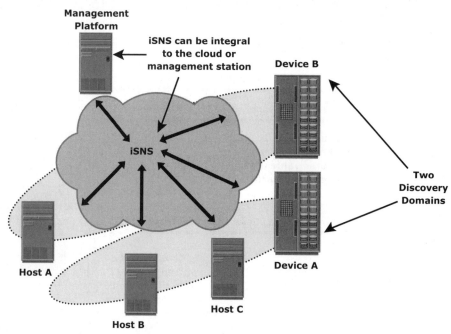

Figure 15-11: Securing IPSAN with iSNS discovery domains

Summary

The continuing expansion of the storage network has exposed data center resources and storage infrastructures to new vulnerabilities. The delineation between a back-end data center and a front-end network perimeter has become less clear. IP-based storage networking has exposed storage resources to traditional network vulnerabilities. Data aggregation has also increased the potential impact of a security breach. In addition to these security challenges, compliance regulations continue to expand and have become more complex. Data center managers are faced with addressing the threat of security breaches from both within and outside the organization.

This chapter detailed a framework for storage security and provided mitigation methods that can be deployed against identified threats in a storage networking environment. It also detailed the security architecture and protection mechanisms in SAN, NAS, and IP-SAN environments. Security has become an integral component of storage management, and it is the key parameter monitored for all data center components. The following chapter focuses on management of a storage infrastructure.

EXERCISES

1. Research the following security protocols and explain how they are used:
   ■ MD-5 algorithm
   ■ SHA-256 algorithm
   ■ RADIUS
   ■ DH-CHAP

2. A storage array dials a support center automatically whenever an error is detected. The vendor's representative at the support center can log on to the service processor of the storage array through the Internet to perform diagnostics and repair. Discuss the impact of this feature in a secure storage environment and provide security methods that can be implemented to mitigate any malicious attacks through this gateway.

3. Develop a checklist for auditing the security of a storage environment with SAN, NAS, and iSCSI implementations. Explain how you will perform the audit. Assume that you discover at least five security loopholes during the audit process. List them and provide control mechanisms that should be implemented to eliminate them.

Chapter 16
Managing the
Storage Infrastructure

Proliferation of applications, complexity of business processes, and requirements of 24×7 availability of information have put increasingly higher demands on IT infrastructure. Managing storage infrastructure is a key that enables organizations to address these challenges and ensures continuity of business.

KEY CONCEPTS
Alerts
Management Platform Standards
Internal Chargeback

Comprehensive storage infrastructure management requires the implementation of intelligent processes and tools. This ensures availability and performance of all storage infrastructure elements, greater data protection and security, centralized auditing, and meeting compliance requirements. It also ensures the consolidation and better utilization of resources, limiting the need for excessive investment in technology, and helps to efficiently leverage existing resources.

Managing the storage infrastructure comprises various activities including availability, capacity, performance, and security management. Each of these aspects are interrelated and must work together to maximize the return on investment. Virtualization technologies have dramatically changed the storage management scenario and have simplified the storage infrastructure management.

Monitoring is one of the most important aspects that forms the basis for managing a storage infrastructure. Monitoring provides status of various storage components and information to perform essential management activities.

The management of the storage infrastructure components begins with defining products and services followed by defining service levels for these products and services. The service level defines the scope of the service, the associated security definitions, level of criticality to the business, and severity or priority levels. It also defines the response time associated with each level, hours of normal operation, promises of quality, and speed of service. These service levels are defined with metrics that can be monitored and measured.

Establishing management processes and implementing appropriate tools is the key to meeting service levels proactively. The management process establishes procedures for efficient handling of incidents, problems, and change requests to the storage infrastructure environment. The tools help in monitoring and executing management activities on the infrastructure. It is imperative to manage not just the individual components, but the storage infrastructure end-to-end due to the components' interdependency.

This chapter details the monitoring and other management activities of the storage infrastructure; it also describes emerging standards in storage resource management tools.

16.1 Monitoring the Storage Infrastructure

Monitoring helps to analyze the status and utilization of various storage infrastructure components. This analysis facilitates optimal use of resources and proactive management. Monitoring supports capacity planning, trend analysis, and root cause/impact analysis. As the business grows, monitoring helps to optimize the storage infrastructure resources. The monitoring process also includes the storage infrastructure's environmental controls and the operating environments for key components such as storage arrays and servers.

16.1.1 Parameters Monitored

Storage infrastructure components should be monitored for accessibility, capacity, performance, and security.

Accessibility refers to the availability of a component to perform a desired operation. A component is said to be accessible when it is functioning without any fault at any given point in time. Monitoring hardware components (e.g., a SAN interconnect device, a port, an HBA, or a disk drive) or software components (e.g., a database instance) for accessibility involves checking their availability status by listening to pre-determined alerts from devices. For example, a port may go down resulting in a chain of availability alerts. A storage infrastructure uses redundant components to avoid a single point of failure. Failure of a component may cause an outage that affects application availability, or it may cause serious performance degradation even though accessibility is not compromised.

For example, an HBA failure can restrict the server to a few paths for access to data devices in a multipath environment, potentially resulting in degraded performance. In a single-path environment, an HBA failure results in complete accessibility loss between the server and the storage. Continuously monitoring for expected accessibility of each component and reporting any deviations helps the administrator to identify failing components and plan corrective action to maintain SLA requirements.

Capacity refers to the amount of storage infrastructure resources available. Examples of capacity monitoring include examining the free space available on a file system or a RAID group, the mailbox quota allocated to users, or the numbers of ports available on a switch. Inadequate capacity may lead to degraded performance or affect accessibility or even application/service availability. Capacity monitoring ensures uninterrupted data availability and scalability by averting outages before they occur. For example, if a report indicates that 90 percent of the ports are utilized in a particular SAN fabric, a new switch should be added if more arrays and servers need to be installed on the same fabric. Capacity monitoring is preventive and predictive, usually leveraged with advanced analytical tools for trend analysis. These trends help to understand emerging challenges, and can provide an estimation of time needed to meet them.

Performance monitoring evaluates how efficiently different storage infrastructure components are performing and helps to identify bottlenecks. Performance monitoring usually measures and analyzes behavior in terms of response time or the ability to perform at a certain predefined level. It also deals with utilization of resources, which affects the way resources behave and respond. Performance measurement is a complex task that involves assessing various components on several interrelated parameters. The number of I/Os to disks, application response time, network utilization, and server CPU utilization are examples of performance monitoring.

Monitoring a storage infrastructure for *security* helps to track and prevent unauthorized access and login failures, whether accidental or malicious. Security monitoring also helps to tracks unauthorized configuration changes of storage infrastructure elements. For example, security monitoring tracks and reports the initial zoning configuration performed and all subsequent changes. Physical security of a storage infrastructure is also continuously monitored using badge readers, biometric scans, or video cameras.

16.1.2 Components Monitored

Hosts, networks, and storage are components within the storage environment that should be monitored for accessibility, capacity, performance, and security.

Hosts

Mission-critical application hosts should be monitored continuously. The accessibility of a host depends on the status of the hardware components and software processes running on it. For example, an application crash due to host hardware failure can cause instant unavailability of the data to the user.

Servers are used in a cluster to ensure high availability. In a server virtualization environment, multiple virtual machines share a pool of resources. These resources are dynamically reallocated, which ensures application accessibility and ease of management.

File system utilization of hosts also needs to be monitored. Monitoring helps in estimating the file system's growth rate and helps in predicting when it will reach 100 percent. Accordingly, the administrator can extend (manually or automatically) the file system's space proactively to prevent a failure resulting from a file system being full. New provisioning technologies even enable the allocation of storage on demand as the need arises. Alternatively, system administrators can enforce a quota for users, provisioning a fixed amount of space for their files. For example, a quota could be specified at a user level, restricting the maximum space to 10 GB per user, or at a file level that restricts a file to a maximum of 100 MB.

Server performance mainly depends on I/O profile, utilization of CPU and memory. For example, if a server running an application is experiencing 80 percent of CPU utilization continuously, this suggests that the server may be running out of processing power, which can lead to degraded performance and slower response time. Administrators can take several actions to correct the problem, such as upgrading or adding more processors, shifting the workload to different servers, and restricting the number of simultaneous client access. In a virtualized environment, CPU and memory may be allocated dynamically from another physical server or from the same server.

Memory utilization is measured by the amount of free memory available. Databases, applications, and file systems utilize the server's physical memory (RAM) for data manipulation. Insufficient memory leads to excessive swapping and paging on the disk, which in turn affects response time to the applications.

Security monitoring on servers involves tracking of login failures and execution of unauthorized applications or software processes. Proactive measures against unauthorized access to the servers are based on the threat identified. For example, an administrator can block access to an unauthorized user if multiple login failures are logged.

Storage Network

The storage network needs to be monitored to ensure proper communication between the server and the storage array. Uninterrupted access to data over the storage network depends on the accessibility of the physical and logical components in the storage network. The physical components of a storage network include elements such as switches, ports, cables, GBICs, and power supplies. The logical components include constructs, such as zones and fabrics. Any failure in the physical or logical components may cause data unavailability. For example, errors in zoning such as specifying the wrong WWN of a port results in failure to access that port, which potentially prevents access from a host to its storage.

Capacity monitoring in a storage network involves monitoring the availability of ports on a switch, the number of available ports in the entire fabric, the utilization of the inter-switch links, individual ports, and each interconnect device in the fabric. Capacity monitoring provides all required inputs for future planning and optimization of the fabric with additional interconnect devices.

Monitoring the performance of a storage network is useful in assessing individual component performance and helps to identify network bottlenecks. For example, monitoring port performance is done by measuring receive or transmit link utilization metrics, which indicate how busy the switch port is, based on expected maximum throughput. Heavily used ports can cause queuing delays on the server.

For IP networks, monitoring performance includes monitoring network latency, packet loss, bandwidth utilization for I/O, network errors, and collisions.

Storage network security monitoring provides information for any unauthorized change to the configuration of the fabric—for example, changes to the zone policies that can affect data security. Login failures and unauthorized access to switches for performing administrative changes should be logged and monitored continuously.

Storage

The accessibility of the storage array should be monitored for its hardware components and various processes. Storage arrays configured with redundant components do not affect accessibility in the event of an individual component failure, but failure of any process can disrupt or compromise business continuity operations. For example, the failure of a replication task affects disaster recovery capabilities. Some storage arrays also provide the capability to send a message to the vendor's support center in the event of hardware or process failures, referred to as a *call home*.

Capacity monitoring of a storage array enables the administrator to respond to storage needs as they occur. Information about fan-in or fan-out ratios and the availability of front-end ports is useful when a new server is given access to the storage array.

A storage array can be monitored by a number of performance metrics, such as utilization rates of the various storage array components, I/O response time, and cache utilization. A high utilization rate of storage array components may lead to performance degradation.

A storage array is usually a shared resource, which may be exposed to security breaches. Monitoring security helps to track unauthorized configuration of the storage array or corruption of data and ensures that only authorized users are allowed to access it.

16.1.3 Monitoring Examples

A storage infrastructure requires implementation of an end-to-end solution to actively monitor all the parameters of its critical components. Early detection and instant alerts ensure the protection of critical assets. In addition, the monitoring tool should be able to analyze the impact of a failure and deduce the root cause of symptoms.

Accessibility Monitoring

Failure of any component may affect the accessibility of one or more components due to their interconnections and dependencies, or it may lead to overall performance degradation. Consider an implementation in a storage infrastructure with three servers: H1, H2, and H3. All the servers are configured with two HBAs, each connected to the storage array through two switches, SW1 and SW2, as shown in Figure 16-1. The three servers share two storage ports on the storage array. Path failover software has been installed on all three servers.

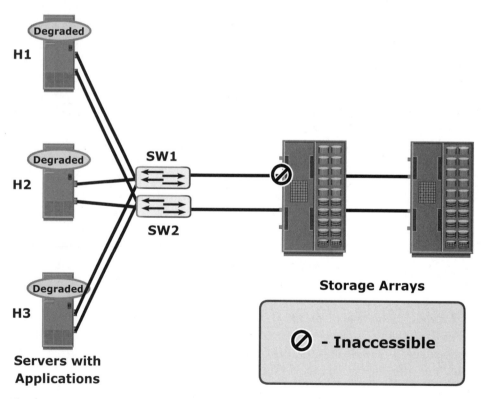

Figure 16-1: Storage array port failure in a storage infrastructure

If one of the *storage array ports* fails, all the storage volumes that were accessed through the switch connected to that port may become unavailable, depending on the type of storage array. If the storage volume becomes unavailable, path failover software initiates a path failover. However, due to redundant ports, the servers continue to access data through another switch, SW2. The servers H1, H2, and H3 may experience degraded performance due to an increased load on the path through SW2.

In the same example, if a single HBA fails on server H1, the server experiences path failure as shown in Figure 16-2. However, due to redundant HBAs, H1 can still access the storage device but it may experience degraded application response time (depends on I/O load).

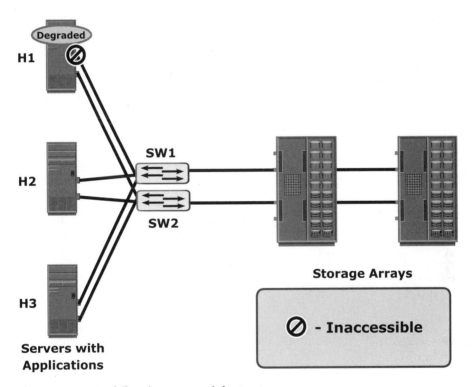

Figure 16-2: HBA failure in a storage infrastructure

Consider a scenario in which a number of servers with two HBAs each are connected to the storage array through two switches, SW1 and SW2, as shown in Figure 16-3. If SW1 fails, all the servers that were accessing the storage array through SW1 experience a path failure and data is redirected to SW2. The applications on all of the servers may experience degradation in response time depending on I/O workload. In this case, the failure of a single component has affected multiple storage infrastructure components.

Capacity Monitoring

In the scenario shown in Figure 16-4, each of the servers is allocated storage on the storage array. When a new server is deployed in this configuration, the applications on the new servers have to be given access to the storage devices from the array through switches SW1 and SW2. Monitoring the available capacity on the array helps to proactively decide whether the array can provide the required storage to the new server. Other considerations include the availability of ports on SW1 and SW2 to connect to the new server as well as the availability of storage ports to connect to the switches. Proactive monitoring also helps to identify the availability of an alternate fabric or an array to connect to the server.

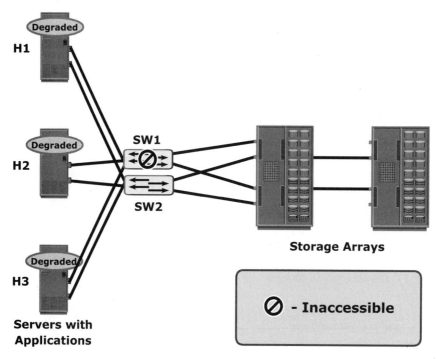

Figure 16-3: Switch failure in a storage infrastructure

The following example illustrates the importance of monitoring file system capacity on file servers. If file system capacity monitoring is not implemented, as shown in Figure 16-5 (a), and the file system is full, the application most likely will not function properly. Monitoring can be configured to issue a message when thresholds are reached on file system capacity. For example, when the file system reaches 66 percent of its capacity a warning message is issued, and a critical message when the file system reaches 80 percent of its capacity (see Figure 16-5 [b]). This enables the administrator to take action manually or automatically to extend the file system before the full condition is reached. Proactively monitoring the file system can prevent application outages caused by a lack of file system space. Applying trend analysis provides even more proactive help in dealing with such a scenario.

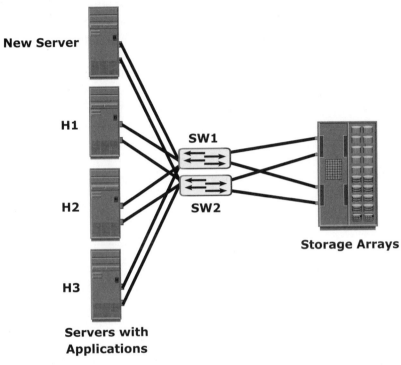

Figure 16-4: Monitoring storage array capacity

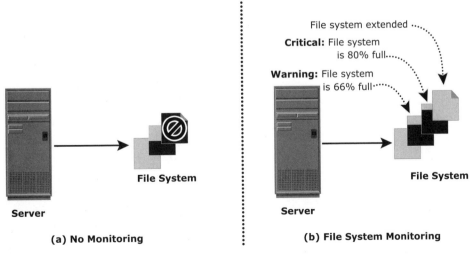

Figure 16-5: Monitoring server file-system space

Performance Monitoring

The example shown in Figure 16-6 illustrates the importance of monitoring performance on storage arrays. In this example, servers H1, H2, and H3 (with two HBAs each) are connected to the storage array through switches SW1 and SW2. The three servers share the same storage ports on the storage array. A new server, H4 running an application with high work load, has to be deployed to share the same storage ports as H1, H2, and H3.

Monitoring array port utilization ensures that the new server does not adversely affect the performance of the other servers. In this example, utilization for the shared ports is shown by the solid and dotted lines in the line graph for the storage ports. Notice that the port represented by a solid line is close to 100 percent utilization. If the actual utilization of both ports prior to deploying the new server is closer to the dotted line, there is room to add the new server. Otherwise, deploying the new server will affect the performance of all servers.

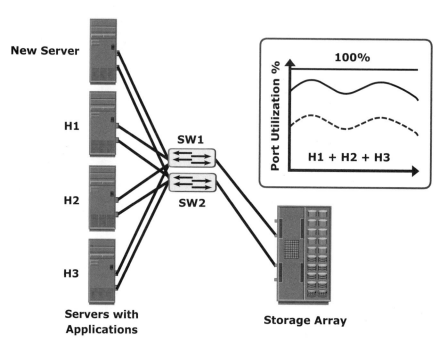

Figure 16-6: Monitoring array port utilization

Most servers offer tools that enable interactive monitoring of server CPU usage. For example, Windows Task Manager displays CPU and memory usage, as shown in Figure 16-7. These interactive tools are useful only when a few servers need to be managed. A storage infrastructure requires performance monitoring tools that are capable of monitoring many servers simultaneously. Although it is inefficient to monitor hundreds of servers continuously in real-time, this monitoring often uses polling servers at regular intervals. These monitoring tools must have the capability to send alerts whenever the CPU utilization exceeds a specified threshold.

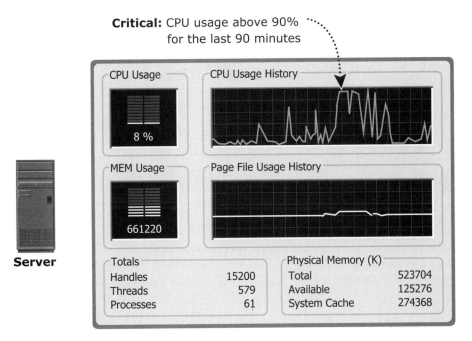

Figure 16-7: Monitoring the performance of servers

Security Monitoring

The example shown in Figure 16-8 illustrates the importance of monitoring security breaches in a storage array.

In this example, the storage array is shared between two workgroups, WG1 and WG2. The data of WG1 should not be accessible by WG2. Likewise, WG2 should not be accessible by WG1. A user from WG1 may try to make a local replica of the data that belongs to WG2. Usually, available mechanisms prevent such an action. However, if this action is not monitored or recorded, it is difficult to track such a violation of security protocols. Conversely, if this action is monitored, a warning message can be sent to prompt a corrective action or at least enable discovery as part of regular auditing operations.

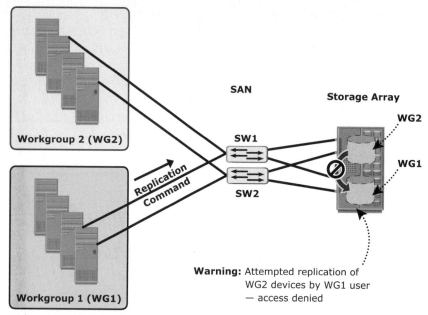

Figure 16-8: Monitoring security in a storage array

Example of host security monitoring involves login failures at the host. These login failures may be accidental (mistyping) or a deliberate attempt to access a server. Many servers usually allow two successive login failures, prohibiting additional attempts after three consecutive login failures. In most environments, login information is recorded in a system log file. In a monitored environment, three successive login failures usually triggers a message, warning of a possible security threat.

16.1.4 Alerts

Alerting of events is an integral part of monitoring. There are conditions observed by monitoring, such as failure of power, disks, memory, or switches, which may impact the availability of services that requires immediate administrative attention. Other conditions, such as a file system reaching a capacity threshold or a soft media error, are considered warning signs, and may also require administrative attention.

Monitoring tools enables administrators to assign different severity levels for different conditions in the storage infrastructure. Whenever a condition with a particular severity level occurs, an alert is sent to the administrator or triggers a script, or opens an incident ticket to initiate a corrective action. Alert classifications can range from information alerts to fatal alerts. *Information alerts* provide useful information that does not require any intervention by the administrator.

Creation of zone or LUN is an example of an information alert. *Warning alerts* require administrative attention so that the alerted condition is contained and does not affect accessibility. For example, when an alert indicates a soft media error on a disk that is approaching a predefined threshold value, the administrator can decide whether the disk needs to be replaced. *Fatal alerts* require immediate attention because the condition may affect overall performance or availability. For example, if a disk fails, the administrator must ensure that it is replaced quickly. Alerts can be assigned a severity level based on the impact of the alerted condition.

Continuous monitoring, in conjunction with automated alerting, enables administrators to respond to failures quickly and proactively. Alerting provides information to prioritize administrator's response to events.

16.2 Storage Management Activities

All the management tasks in a storage infrastructure can be broadly categorized into availability management, capacity management, performance management, security management, and reporting.

16.2.1 Availability management

The critical task in availability management is establishing a proper guideline for all configurations to ensure availability based on service levels. For example, when a server is deployed to support a critical business function, the highest availability standard is usually required. This is generally accomplished by deploying two or more HBAs, multipathing software with path failover capability, and server clustering. The server must be connected to the storage array using at least two independent fabrics and switches that have built-in redundancy. Storage devices with RAID protection are made available to the server using at least two front-end ports. In addition, these storage arrays should have built-in redundancy for various components, support backup, and local and remote replication. Virtualization technologies have significantly improved the availability management task. With virtualization in place resources can be dynamically added or removed to maintain the availability.

16.2.2 Capacity management

The goal of *capacity management* is to ensure adequate availability of resources for all services based on their service level requirements. Capacity management provides capacity analysis, comparing allocated storage to forecasted storage on a regular basis. It also provides trend analysis of actual utilization of allocated storage and rate of consumption, which must be rationalized against storage acquisition and deployment timetables.

Storage provisioning is an example of capacity management. It involves activities such as device configuration and LUN masking on the storage array and zoning configuration on the SAN and HBA components. Capacity management also takes into account the future needs of resources, and setting up monitors and analytics to gather such information.

16.2.3 Performance management

Performance management ensures the optimal operational efficiency of all components. Performance analysis is an important activity that helps to identify the performance of storage infrastructure components. This analysis provides the information — whether a component is meeting expected performance levels.

Several performance management activities are initiated for the deployment of an application or server in the existing storage infrastructure. Every component must be validated for adequate performance capabilities as defined by the service levels. For example, to optimize expected performance levels, activities on the server such as the volume configuration, designing the database, application layout configuration of multiple HBAs, and intelligent multipathing software must be fine-tuned. The performance management tasks on a SAN include designing sufficient ISLs in a multi-switch fabric with adequate bandwidth to support the required performance levels. The storage array configuration tasks include selecting the appropriate RAID type and LUN layout, front-end and back-end ports, and LUN accessibility (LUN masking) while considering the end-to-end performance.

16.2.4 Security Management

Security management prevents unauthorized access and configuration of storage infrastructure components. For example, while deploying an application or a server, the security management tasks include managing user accounts and access policies, that authorizes users to perform role-based activities. The security management tasks in the SAN environment include configuration of zoning to restrict an HBA's unauthorized access to the specific storage array ports. LUN masking prevents data corruption on the storage array by restricting host access to a defined set of logical devices.

16.2.5 Reporting

It is difficult for businesses to keep track of the resources they have in their data centers, for example, the number of storage arrays, the array vendors, how the storage arrays are being used, and by which applications. Reporting on a storage infrastructure involves keeping track and gathering information from various components/processes. This information is compiled to generate reports for trend analysis, capacity planning, chargeback, performance, and to illustrate the basic configuration of storage infrastructure components. Capacity planning reports also contain current and historic information about utilization of storage, file system, database tablespace, and ports. Configuration or asset management reports include details about device allocation, local or remote replicas, and fabric configuration; and list all equipment, with details such as their value, purchase date, lease status, and maintenance records. Chargeback reports contain information about the allocation or utilization of storage infrastructure components by various departments or user groups. Performance reports provide details about the performance of various storage infrastructure components.

16.2.6 Storage Management Examples

The discussion that follows details various storage management activities with examples.

Example 1: Storage Allocation to a New Server/Host

Consider a deployment of the new RDBMS server to the existing non-virtualized SAN environment. As a part of storage array management activities, the administrator needs to configure new volumes on the array and assign those volumes to the array front-end ports. In addition, a LUN masking configuration is performed on the storage array by assigning new servers and volumes to the storage group.

The installation and configuration of the HBA hardware (at least two to ensure redundancy) and driver has to be performed on the server before it can be physically connected to the SAN. Server reconfiguration may be required, depending on the operating system installed on the server, so it can recognize the new devices either with a *bus rescan* process or sometimes through a server reboot. Optional multipathing software can be installed on the server, which might require additional configuration.

The administrator configures the fabric's zoning policies for the new server's HBA, allowing the host to access the storage array port via the specific HBA port. This operation should probably be done at two or more fabrics to ensure redundant paths between the hosts and the storage array. The switches should have free ports available for the new server, and the array port utilization is validated against the required I/O performance of the server if the port is shared between many servers.

The volume management tasks involve the creation of volume groups, logical volumes, and file systems. The number of logical volumes or file systems to create depends on how the database or the application is expected to use the storage.

On the application side, whether it is a database or any other type of application, administrator tasks include installation of the database or the application on the logical volumes or file systems that were created. Other required activities to perform include the implementation of procedures to start the database or application. Figure 16-9 illustrates the individual tasks on the server, the SAN, and the storage arrays for this new allocation. It is a new trend in virtualization, where the application is already installed and sometimes already configured.

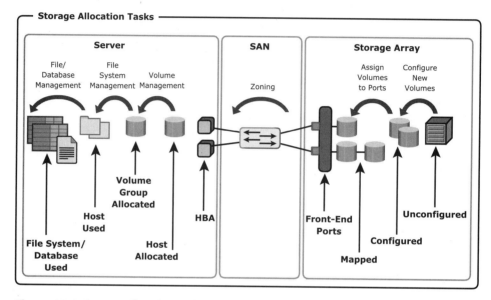

Figure 16-9: Storage allocation tasks

Example 2: File System Space Management

To prevent a file system from running out of space, administrators need to perform tasks to offload data from the existing file system. This includes deleting unwanted files and offloading files to backup media that have not been accessed for a long time.

Alternatively, an administrator can extend the file system to increase its size and avoid an application outage. The dynamic extension of file systems or a logical volume is dependent on the specific operating system or a logical volume manager (LVM) in use, and the volume management tasks detailed in the previous example may need to be commenced.

The steps and considerations for the extension of file systems are illustrated in the flow chart shown in Figure 16-10.

While extending the file system also consider whether the volume is replicated or not. If the application uses remote or local replication for business continuity operations and a new device is added to the volume group, it must be ensured that the new device is replicated as well.

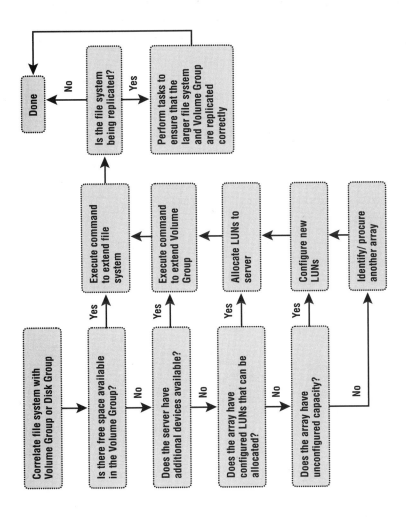

Figure 16-10: Extending a file system

Example 3: Chargeback Report

This example explores the storage infrastructure management tasks necessary to create a specific report.

Figure 16-11 shows a configuration deployed in a storage infrastructure. Three servers with two HBA each are connected to a storage array via two switches, SW1 and SW2. Individual departmental applications are running on each of the servers, and array replication technology is used to create local and remote replicas. The production volume is represented as A, local replica volume as B and the remote replica volume as C.

A report documenting the exact amount of storage resources used by each application is created using a chargeback analysis for each department. If the unit for billing is based on the amount of raw storage (usable capacity plus protection provided) configured for an application used by a department, the exact amount of raw space configured must be reported for each application. A sample report is shown at the bottom of Figure 16-11. The report shows the information for two applications, Payroll_1 and Engineering_1.

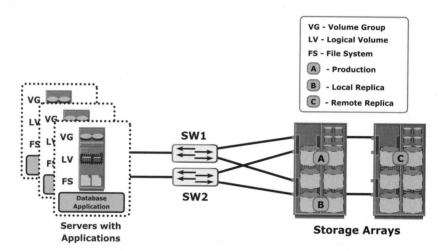

Application	Storage (GB)	Production Storage Raw (GB)	Local Replica Storage Raw (GB)	Remote Replica Storage Raw (GB)	Total Storage Raw (GB)	Chargeback Cost $ 0.25/Raw (GB)
Payroll_1	100	200	100	125	425	$ 106.25
Engineering_1	200	250	200	250	700	$ 175.00

Figure 16-11: Chargeback report

The first step to determine chargeback costs associated with an application is to correlate the application with the exact amount of raw storage configured for that application.

As indicated in Figure 16-12, the Payroll_1 application storage space is traced from file systems to logical volumes to volume groups to the LUNs on the array. When the applications are being replicated, the storage space used for local replication and remote replication is also identified. In the example shown, the application is using "Source Vol 1 and Vol 2" (in Array 1). The replication volumes are "Local Replica Vol 1 and Vol 2" (in Array 1) and "Remote Replica Vol 1 and Vol 2" (in the Remote Array). As the application grows, more file systems and storage space may be used; therefore, configuration changes are inevitable. Before a new report is generated, a correlation of the application to the array LUNs should be done to ensure that the most current information is used.

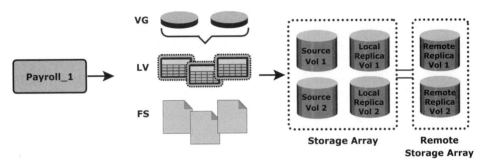

Figure 16-12: Correlation of capacity configured for an application

The amount of storage allocated to the application can be easily computed after the array devices are identified. In this example, if we assume that Source Vol 1 and Vol 2 are each 50 GB in size, the storage allocated to the application is 100 GB (50 + 50). The allocated storage for replication is 100 GB for local replication and 100 GB for remote replication. From the allocated storage, the raw storage configured for the application is determined based on the RAID protection that is used for various array devices. If the Payroll_1 application production volumes are RAID 1 protected, the raw space used by the production volumes is 200 GB. If we assume that the local replicas are on unprotected volumes and the remote replicas are protected with a RAID 5 configuration, the raw space used by local replicas is 100 GB, and 125 GB by the remote replicas. Therefore, the total raw capacity used by the Payroll_1 application is 425 GB. If provisioned capacity is equal to the consumed capacity, the total cost of storage will be $106.25 (assume cost per GB of storage is $0.25). This exercise must be repeated for each application in the enterprise to generate the required report.

Chargeback reports can be extended to include a preestablished cost for other resources, such as the number of switch ports, HBAs, and array ports in the configuration. Chargeback reports are used by data center administrators to ensure that storage consumers are well aware of the costs of the service levels they have requested.

16.3 Storage Infrastructure Management Challenges

Monitoring and managing today's complex storage infrastructure environment has become very challenging due to the number and variety of storage arrays, networks, servers, databases, and applications. There is a variety of storage devices varying in capacity, performance, and protection methodologies. Storage infrastructures deploy both SAN and IP networks and servers with different operating systems such as UNIX, LINUX, Windows, or mainframe. These products and services from multiple vendors may have interoperability issues which add complexity in managing storage infrastructure.

All of these components are provided with vendor-specific tools to manage and monitor them. However, in an environment where multiple tools are in use, it is difficult to understand the overall status of all the components and to be able to provide cross-component failure, impact, and behavior analysis. Ideally, monitoring tools should be able to correlate information from all components in one place. That way, analysis and actions are taken based on a holistic, end-to-end view of the environment and corrective measures can be taken proactively.

16.4 Developing an Ideal Solution

An ideal solution offers meaningful insight into the accessibility and status of the overall infrastructure and provides remedial solutions to each failure based on interdependencies and priorities, as discussed in the preceding section. There is value in building a central monitoring and management system that can work in a multi-vendor storage environment and is able to create an end-to-end view that includes various technology stacks and different deployment configurations. The other benefit of end-to-end monitoring is the ability to correlate one component's behavior to others. This will be helpful to debug or analyze a problem, where looking into each component individually might not be enough. The infrastructure management system should be able to gather information from all of the components and manage them through a single-user interface. It should also be able to perform root cause analysis and indicate the impact of individual component failure on various business applications/processes. In addition, it must provide a mechanism to notify administrators about various events using methods such as e-mail and SNMP traps, and generate monitoring reports or run automated scripts for task automation.

The ideal solution must be based on industry standards, leveraging common APIs, data model terminology, and taxonomy. This enables the implementation of policy-based management across heterogeneous classes of devices, services, applications, storage infrastructure, and deployed topologies.

The *SNMP* protocol was the standard used to manage multi-vendor SAN environments. However, SNMP was primarily a network management protocol and was inadequate for providing the detailed information and functionality required to manage the SAN environment. The unavailability of automatic discovery functions, weak modeling constructs, and lack of transactional support are some inadequacies of SNMP in a SAN environment. Even with these limitations, SNMP still holds a predominant role in SAN management, although newer open storage SAN management standards have emerged to monitor and manage these environments more effectively.

16.4.1 Storage Management Initiative

The Storage Networking Industry Association (SNIA) has been engaged in an initiative to develop a common, open storage, and SAN management interface. SMI-S is based on Web-Based Enterprise Management (WBEM) technology and the DMTF's Common Information Model (CIM). The initiative was formally created to enable broad interoperability among heterogeneous storage vendor systems and to enable better management solutions that span these environments. This initiative is known as the Storage Management Initiative (SMI). For more information, see www.snia.org.

The SMI Specification, known as SMI-S, offers substantial benefits to users and vendors. It forms a normalized, abstracted model to which a storage infrastructure's physical and logical components can be mapped, and which can be used by management applications such as storage resource management, device management, and data management for standardized, effective, end-to-end control of storage resources (see Figure 16-13).

Using SMI-S, the storage software developers have a single normalized and unified object model comprising the detailed document that contains information about managing the breadth of SAN components. Moreover, SMI-S eliminates the need for development of vendor-proprietary management interfaces, enabling vendors to focus on added value functions and offering solutions in a way that will support new devices as long as they adhere to the standard. Using SMI-S, device vendors can build new features and functions to manage storage subsystems and expose them via SMI-S. The SMI-S-compliant products lead to easier, faster deployment, and accelerated adoption of policy-based storage management frameworks.

The information required to perform management tasks is better organized or structured in a way that enables disparate groups of people to use it. This can be accomplished by developing a model or representation of the details required by users working within a particular domain. Such an approach is referred to as an *information model*. An information model requires a set of legal statements or syntax to capture the representation and expressions necessary to manage common aspects of that domain.

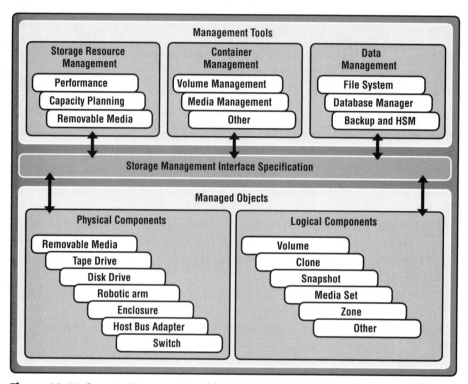

Figure 16-13: Storage Management Initiative Specification

The CIM is a language and methodology for describing management elements. A CIM schema includes models for systems, applications, networks, and devices. This schema also enables applications from different vendors working on different platforms to describe the management data in a standard format so that it can be shared among a variety of management applications.

WBEM is an initiative in the DMTF. It is a set of technologies that enables interoperable management of an enterprise. WBEM consists of CIM, an XML DTD defining the tags (XML encodings) to describe the CIM Schema and its data, and a set of HTTP operations for exchanging the XML-based information. The main objective of developing a WBEM is to unify the management of enterprise-computing environments that were traditionally administered through the management stacks, such as SNMP and Common Management Information Protocol (CMIP).

WBEM includes the CIM standard, the xmlCIM encoding specification, and a transport mechanism — CIM operation over HTTP.

The following features of SMI-S simplify SAN management:

- **Common data model:** SMI-S agents interact with an SMI-S-enabled device, such as a switch, a server, or a storage array, to extract relevant management data. They can also interact at the management layer to exchange information between one management application and another. They then provide this information to the requester in a consistent syntax and format.

- **Interconnect independence:** SMI-S eliminates the need to redesign the management transport and enables components to be managed by using out-of-band communications. In addition, SMI-S offers the advantages of specifying the CMI-XML over the HTTP protocol stack and utilizing the lower layers of the TCP/IP stack, both of which are ubiquitous in today's networking world.

- **Multilayer management:** SMI-S can be used in a multilayer and cross-domain environment—for example, server-based volume managers and network storage appliances. Many storage deployment environments currently employ this combination.

- **Legacy system accommodation:** SMI-S can be used to manage legacy systems by using a proxy agent or can be directly supported by the device itself. SMI-S can coexist with proprietary APIs and agents as well as providing integration framework for such mechanisms.

- **Policy-based management:** SMI-S includes object models applicable across all classes of devices, enabling a SAN administrator to implement policy-based management for entire storage networks.

A Common Information Model eases the huge tasks of interpreting relations and correlations of information across technology stacks and vendor devices. A CIM makes it easier for management applications as well as device/solution developers, as it creates normalized abstracted targets when both management and managed elements interact.

16.4.2 Enterprise Management Platforms

Enterprise management platforms (EMPs) are complex applications or suites of applications that provide an integrated solution for managing and monitoring an enterprise storage infrastructure. These applications proactively monitor many storage infrastructure components and are designed to alert users about any problems or the approach of a predefined threshold in monitored components.

These alerts are either shown on a console depicting the faulty component in a different color, or they can be configured to send the alert by e-mail or other means. In addition to monitoring functionality, the EMPs can provide the necessary management functionality, which can be natively implemented by code embedded into the EMP or may involve launching the proprietary management utility supplied by the target component manufacturer.

Other functionality enables easy scheduling of operations that must be performed regularly, such as the provisioning of resources, configuration management, and fault investigation. These platforms also provide extensive analytical, remedial, and reporting capabilities to ease storage infrastructure management. ControlCenter, described in this chapter, is an example of an EMP implementation.

16.5 Concepts in Practice: EMC ControlCenter

Businesses today are facing the challenge of managing storage resources. Management of storage environments has become complex due to the large number of physical and logical components from multiple vendors and complex technology stacks that involve physical, logical, structural, and virtualization concepts. Therefore organizations must need an integrated solution to effectively manage their storage resources from end to end.

EMC ControlCenter storage management suite provides an end-to-end integrated approach for dealing with multi-vendor storage reporting, monitoring, configuration, and control tasks. Using ControlCenter, administrators can see an end-to-end view of the storage infrastructure, understand how the infrastructure is performing, and do what is necessary to ensure that service levels are met. This results in better performance, improved productivity, and reduced costs.

EMC Navisphere Manager is a suite of management tools for managing EMC CLARiiON storage arrays (which is discussed briefly in Chapter 4). It enables access and management of all CLARiiON's advanced software functionality including Navisphere Quality of Service Manager, Navisphere Analyzer, SnapView, SAN Copy, and MirrorView. It can be launched from EMC Control Center. Visit http://education.EMC.com/ismbook for the latest information.

16.5.1 ControlCenter Features and Functionality

ControlCenter provides many features and functions to monitor and manage storage resources effectively. By supporting interoperability in a heterogeneous virtualized storage environment, it enables users to manage hardware, software and integrate resources, in multiple sites under a single management umbrella.

In addition, ControlCenter enables planning and provisioning of storage resources. It also provides customized monitoring and reporting using rule-based event alerting. Furthermore, ControlCenter provides enhanced security by enabling policy-based permission and authorization to grant controlled access to systems, operations, and information. In addition to helping to analyze and resolve existing failures, ControlCenter predicts failure scenarios and optimizes storage resource performance.

16.5.2 ControlCenter Architecture

ControlCenter is an n-tier, distributed application that consists of a user inter-face tier and a consolidation and analytics (infrastructure) tier as shown in Figure 16-14. The user interface tier is where user interactions are initiated and the results are reviewed for monitoring and managing the storage environment. The infrastructure tier is the data processing tier, consisting of the ControlCenter server, repository, store, and agents. Agents are software programs running on the host to collect and monitor host information and send it to the store in the infrastructure tier. In addition, the agent runs the user commands to configure and monitor activities of the storage environment components.

User Interface Tier

ControlCenter supports different types of interfaces to interact with users or administrators. A *console* is the primary interface to view, manage, configure, and handle reporting of various components (managed objects) and other required views. It is a Java-based application installed through a Web browser and launched from a desktop icon. For an object (storage infrastructure entity) to be displayed on the console, a ControlCenter agent must first discover it. Any command entered at the console is passed from the console to a ControlCenter server and then forwarded to the appropriate agent. The entities monitored and managed by various agents that appear on the console are organized into groups such as storage systems, hosts, and connectivity or may be manually managed in user-defined groups. Information about the objects is retrieved by a console from a repository or in real time directly from the agent.

The *Web console* is a web-based interface that provides support for remote or high latency local networks. It provides a portable solution because it does not require local installation.

The *StorageScope console* helps to view configuration, status, and usage informa-tion for individual objects, user-defined groups, or the entire enterprise storage environment. It is an interface to the StorageScope applications that monitor and report on all storage assets and their usage. StorageScope is bundled with ControlCenter as a Storage Resource Management (SRM) Tool. It enables users to collect high-level and detailed data about the storage components. It helps to view point-in-time snapshots of high-importance areas of your storage environment on StorageScope's customizable Dashboard page.

Infrastructure Tier

EMC ControlCenter's infrastructure tier has the following main components: ControlCenter server, Performance Manager server, Repository, Store, and StorageScope repository (refer to Figure 16-14). A *ControlCenter server* is the central component in the ControlCenter infrastructure and provides the primary interface for most components including the console. It retrieves data from the repository for the console to display and handles user-initiated requests for real-time data.

The *Repository* is a licensed, embedded Oracle 10g R2 database that holds current and historical information about both the storage environment and ControlCenter itself with the exception of performance data. This data includes configuration details, statistical data, alerts, and status information about any given device. It also contains general information about links, groups, metadata, alert definitions, components, and the data dictionary. The ControlCenter Store populates the repository with data sent by the agents. The ControlCenter Server processes transactions from the console for repository data, such as checking user group permissions. The repository has restricted access and can be updated only by the ControlCenter Server.

The *Store* is a process that populates the Repository with persistent data from the agents. It provides a store-and-retrieve interface between the agents and the Repository. ControlCenter can contain more than one store for load balancing and failover in large environments.

The *StorageScope Repository* is built on an Oracle 10g R2 and is populated with information that helps the business to make decisions about storage utilization and configuration. It provides managerial summaries and responses to online queries, and contains historical information that enables performance and utilization analysis over time. Moreover, it can be effectively used to reclaim storage resources by identifying unused or underutilized storage, as well as duplicate, rarely accessed, or nonbusiness files. It also facilitates chargeback and billing operations. StorageScope analytical modules determine future storage needs based on hierarchical usage and trends analysis.

The StorageScope Repository tables are populated through the extract, transform, and load (ETL) processes from the ControlCenter Repository.

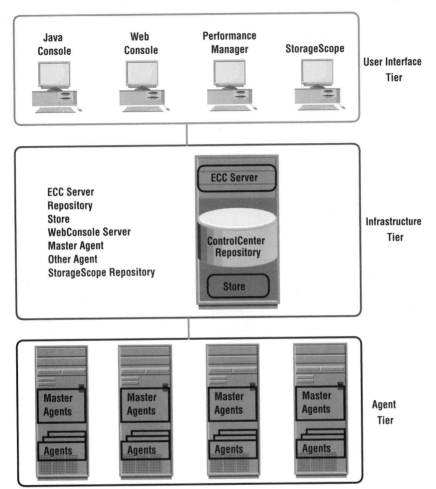

Figure 16-14: ControlCenter architecture

Agents

EMC ControlCenter uses agents installed on hosts to monitor and control the storage infrastructure components, or "managed objects" in ControlCenter. There are two type of agents; master agent and other agents. The master agent controls all other ControlCenter agents on a host by starting and stopping the agents and facilitates their remote installation and upgrade. In ControlCenter, only one master agent is required per host (object). The other agents run on the host to collect data and monitor the accessibility of storage infrastructure components. Multiple ControlCenter agents can exist on a host to monitor events and organize, analyze, and interpret collected information. In addition, the agents generate alerts when monitored events occur, passing information to the ControlCenter Store and the Server.

Different agent types manage different objects, such as storage agents for storage arrays, host agents for operating systems, and database agents for database applications. The agents collect data from the objects and analyze commands sent from the server. As defined by the agent policy, the store periodically polls every agent to retrieve updated information.

Each agent type has a predefined set of actions called a Data Collection Policy (DCP) specific to the type of objects it manages. New policies can be defined, or existing policies can be modified based on available templates. From these policies, an agent can collect five types of information about managed objects or components: discovery, configuration, status, performance, and system log data. The discovery data contains the discovered objects' names and types. Configuration data refers to an object's configuration, hierarchy, and subcomponents. The status data contains information about the state of objects and their components, with an additional explanation of their status. The status can be ok, offline, or error. Performance statistics indicate bandwidth, disk space, memory, and CPU performance.

The *Performance Manager* is packaged as part of the SRM monitoring and reporting offering. It is the ControlCenter performance analysis tool that provides the capability to quickly analyze and report on the performance and configuration data collected by the agents. Agents use data-collection policies to obtain historical, operational, or performance-related data. The Performance Manager function has an automated report generation and distribution feature supported by a job scheduler that can be displayed at the console. It is a Windows-based, post-processing tool that is invoked after data collection and processing is complete. Performance Manager helps to create data views of system performance and configuration. *Workload Analyzer Archiver,* a part of Performance Manager processes and stores the data collected by ControlCenter agents as performance archives, revolving collections, and analyst collections. The performance archives and collections are then available for viewing through Performance Manager Console and Performance Manager Automated reports. Figure 16-15 shows Window-based Performance Manager interface of ControlCenter.

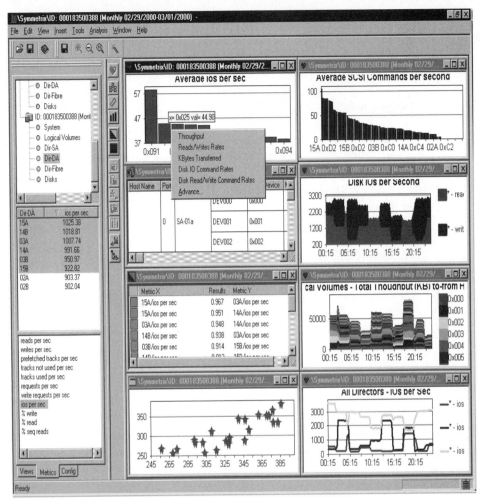

Figure 16-15: ControlCenter Performance Manager

ControlCenter Monitoring through Alerts

Each EMC ControlCenter agent can trigger predefined alerts based on monitoring various aspects of the distributed storage environment. These alerts enable the management of data availability and the proactive maintenance of various components. Alerts can be categorized as health, capacity, or performance alerts. Health alerts indicate the availability and status of ControlCenter components, capacity alerts specify the space availability of a volume or disk, and performance alerts indicate performance and usage of subsystems.

Agents trigger alerts based on a predefined alert matrix or conditions such as space availability or status of components. The alerts can be displayed on the console, or sent to the administrator or a user via e-mail, or directed to the management framework using the integration gateway or SNMP.

ControlCenter Add-on Products

ControlCenter can be effectively deployed to automatically build an accurate topology of different pieces of a multivendor SAN environment. Therefore, storage infrastructure administrators need to understand how these elements are interconnected and the nature of these interrelationships. They can monitor these elements and receive notifications when alert conditions are satisfied. ControlCenter helps to consistently manage multivendor SANs. Other products in the ControlCenter family, such as SAN Manager and SAN Advisor, provide additional functionality that facilitates administrators to enhance the overall monitoring and management processes. Some of this functionality includes LUN masking for EMC ControlCenter and other vendor storage and switch-zoning configuration setup capabilities for each major switch manufacturer. It also provides the capability to explore "what-if" scenarios, which administrators can use to quickly build an agile infrastructure that meets the needs of their business.

The provisioning of storage resources can be automated with the automated Resource Manager product. With many separate tasks being automated, the storage infrastructure can meet required service-level agreements while reducing management costs and the risk of error.

Summary

This chapter detailed the required proactive monitoring and management of storage infrastructure components that ensures established service levels are met for accessibility, capacity, performance, and security. The growing demand for storage coupled with heterogeneous operating environments has increased the complexity of monitoring and managing the storage environment. This chapter provided examples demonstrating the need for monitoring and management functionalities, and detailed industry standards, including SMI-S, that have emerged to minimize storage management interoperability concerns in the enterprise.

Visit `http://education.emc.com/ismbook` for additional reading materials.

EXERCISES

1. This chapter described how a storage array initiates a "call home," an automatic alert sent to the vendor's support team that enables the team to access the array to remotely fix an error. Discuss and detail the security implications of this procedure, and develop a procedure to mitigate any security threats that you may identify in providing access to remote support teams.

2. A performance problem has been reported on a database. Monitoring confirms that at 12:00 AM, a problem surfaced, and access to the database is severely affected until 3:00 PM every day. This time slot is critical for business operations and an investigation has been launched. A reporting process that starts at 12:00 PM contends for database resources and constrains the environment. What monitoring and management procedures, tools, and alerts would you establish to ensure accessibility, capacity, performance, and security in this environment?

3. Research SMI-S and write a technical paper on different vendor implementations of storage management solutions that comply with SMI-S.

Acronyms and Abbreviations

ACA	Auto Contingent Allegiance
ACL	Access Control List
AD	Active Directory
AES	Advanced Encryption Standard
AL-PA	Arbitrated Loop Physical Address
ALU	Arithmetic Logic Unit
ANSI	American National Standards Institute
API	Application Programming Interface
AR	Automated Replication
ARB	Arbitration Frame
AS	Authentication Service
ASCII	American Standard Code for Information Interchange
ASIC	Application-Specific Integrated Circuit
ATAPI	Advanced Technology Attachment Packet Interface
ATM	Asynchronous Transfer Mode
AUI	Application User Interface
AVM	Automatic Volume Management

BB_Credit	Buffer to Buffer Credit
BBU	Battery Backup Unit
BC	Business Continuity
BCP	Business Continuity Planning
BCV	Business Continuance Volume
BIA	Business Impact Analysis
BIOS	Basic Input/Output System
BLOB	Binary Large Object
BMR	Bare Metal Recovery
BURA	Backup, Recovery, and Archive
CA	Content Address
CAS	Content-Addressed Storage
CCS	Common Command Set
CD	Compact Disk
CDB	Command Descriptor Block
CDF	Content Descriptor File
CDP	Continuous Data Protection
CD-R	Compact Disk-Recordable
CD-ROM	Compact Disk Read-Only Memory
CD-RW	Compact Disc Rewritable
CE+	Compliance Edition Plus
CG	Consistency Group
CHAP	Challenge-Handshake Authentication Protocol
CHS	Cylinder, Head, and Sector
CIFS	Common Internet File System
CIM	Common Information Model
CKD	Count Key Data
CLI	Command-Line Interface
CmdSN	Command Sequence Number
CMI	CLARiiON Messaging Interface
CMIP	Common Management Information Protocol
CMIS	Common Management Information Service

COFA	Copy on First Access
COFW	Copy on First Write
CPC	Control Path Cluster
CPM	Content Protection Mirrored
CPP	Content Protection Parity
CPU	Central Processing Unit
CRC	Cyclic Redundancy Check
CS_CTL	Class-Specific Control
CSMA/CD	Carrier Sense Multiple Access/Collision Detection
CWDM	Coarse Wave Division Multiplexing
DAC	Discretionary Access Control
DACL	Discretionary Access Control List
DAE	Disk Array Enclosure
DART	Data Access in Real Time
DAS	Direct-Attached Storage
DBA	Database Administrator
DBMS	Database Management System
DCP	Data Collection Policy
DDR SDRAM	Double Data Rate Synchronous Dynamic Random Access Memory
DF-CTL	Data Field Control
DFS	Distributed File System
DHCP	Dynamic Host Configuration Protocol
D_ID	Destination ID
DMTF	Distributed Management Task Force
DMX	Direct Matrix
DMZ	Demilitarized Zone
DNS	Domain Name System
DoS	Denial of Service
DPC	Data Path Controller
DPE	Disk Processor Enclosure
DRM	Digital Rights Management
DSA	Directory System Agent

DVD	Digital Versatile Disk or Digital Video Disc
DVD-ROM	Digital Versatile Disk Read-Only Memory
DWDM	Dense Wave Division Multiplexing
ECA	Enginuity Consistency Assist
ECC	EMC Control Center
E_D_TOV	Error Detect Time Out Value
EE_Credit	End-to-End Credit
EIDE	Enhanced Integrated Drive Electronics
EMP	Enterprise Management Platform
EOF	End of Frame
E_Port	Expansion Port
ESCON	Enterprise Systems Connection
ETL	Extract, Transform, and Load
EUI	Extended Unique Identifier
EXT 2/3	Extended File System
FAT	File Allocation Table
FBA	Fixed-Block Architecture
FC	Fibre Channel
FC-AL	Fibre Channel Arbitrated Loop
F_CTL	Frame Control
FCIP	Fibre Channel over IP Protocol
FCP	Fibre Channel Protocol
FC-PH	Fibre Channel Physical and Signaling Interface
FC-PI	Fibre Channel Physical Interface
FC-SP	Fibre Channel Security Protocol
FC-SW	Fibre Channel Switched Fabric
FCWG	Fibre Channel Working Group
FDDI	Fibre Distributed Data Interface
FICON	Fibre Connectivity
FIFO	First In First Out
FLOGI	Fabric Login
FL_Port	Fabric Loop Port
F_Port	Fabric Port

FRU	Field Replaceable Unit
FSPF	Fabric Shortest Path First
FTP	File Transfer Protocol
GB	Gigabyte
GigE	Gigabit Ethernet
GBIC	Gigabit Interface Converter
GB/s	Gigabyte per Second
Gb/s	Gigabit per Second
GFP	Generic Framing Procedure
GFV	Global File Virtualization
GHz	Gigahertz
GMD	Global Memory Director
GUI	Graphical User Interface
HBA	Host Bus Adapter
HDA	Head Disk Assembly
HDD	Hard Disk Drive
HIPAA	Health Insurance Portability and Accountability Act
HIPPI	High Performance Parallel Interface
HSM	Hierarchical Storage Management
HTTP	Hypertext Transfer Protocol
HWM	High Watermark
IA	Information Availability
IDE/ATA	Integrated Device Electronics/Advanced Technology Attachment
IDS/IPS	Intrusion Detection/Intrusion Prevention System
IEEE	Institute of Electrical and Electronics Engineers
IETF	Internet Engineering Task Force
iFCP	Internet Fibre Channel Protocol
ILM	Information Lifecycle Management
I/O	Input/Output
IOPS	Input Output Per Second
IP	Internet Protocol
IP-SAN	Internet Protocol Storage Area Network

IPSec	Internet Protocol Security
iQN	iSCSI Qualified Name
IRM	Information Rights Management
iSCSI	Internet Small Computer Systems Interface Protocol
iSCSI PDU	ISCSI Protocol Data Unit
ISL	Inter-Switch Link
iSNS	Internet Storage Name Server
ISO	International Organization for Standardization
ITU	International Telecommunication Union
JBOD	Just a Bunch of Disks
KDC	Key Distribution Center
KVM	Keyboard, Video, and Mouse
LACP	Link Aggregation Control Protocol
LAN	Local Area Network
Lb	Least Blocks
LBA	Logical Block Addressing
LC	Lucent Connector
LCA	Link Capacity Adjustment
LCAS	Link Capacity Adjustment Scheme
LCC	Link Control Card
LDAP	Lightweight Directory Access Protocol
Lo	Least I/Os
LR	Link Reset
LRR	Link Reset Response
LRU	Least Recently Used
LUN	Logical Unit Number
LV	Logical Volume
LVDS	Low-Voltage Differential Signaling
LVM	Logical Volume Management
LWM	Low Watermark
MAC	Media Access Control
MAID	Massive Array of Idle Disks
MAN	Metropolitan Area Network

MD5	Message-Digest Algorithm
MIB	Management Information Base
MirrorView/A	MirrorView/Asynchronous
MirrorView/S	MirrorView/Synchronous
MLC	Multi-Level Cell
MMF	Multimode Fiber
MRU	Most Recently Used
MSS	Maximum Segment Size
MTBF	Mean Time Between Failure
MTTR	Mean Time to Repair
MTU	Maximum Transfer Unit
NACA	Normal Auto Contingent Allegiance
NAS	Network-Attached Storage
NDMP	Network Data Management Protocol
NFS	Network File System
NIC	Network Interface Card
NIS	Network Information Services
NMC	NetWorker Management Console
NL_Port	Node Loop Port
N_Port	Node Port
NTFS	New Technology File System
NTP	Network Time Protocol
OLTP	Online Transaction Processing
OS	Operating System
OSI	Open System Interconnection
OTF	Open Tape Format
OXID	Originator Exchange Identifier
PAgP	Port Aggregation Protocol
PCI	Peripheral Component Interconnect
PDU	Protocol Data Unit
PIT	Point in Time
PKI	Public Key Infrastructure
PRLI	Process Login

PV	Physical Volume
PVID	Physical Volume Identifier
QoS	Quality of Service
RADIUS	Remote Authentication Dial-In User Service
RAID	Redundant Array of Independent Disks
RAIN	Redundant Array of Inexpensive Nodes
RAM	Random Access Memory
R_A_TOV	Resource Allocation Time-Out Value
RBAC	Role-Based Access Control
R_CTL	Routing Control
RDBMS	Relational Database Management System
RFC	Requests for Comments
RLP	Reserved LUN Pool
ROI	Return on Investment/Information
ROM	Read-Only Memory
RPC	Remote Procedure Call
RPO	Recovery Point Objective
RR	Round-Robin
R_RDY	Receiver Ready
RSCN	Registered State Change Notification
RTD	Round-Trip Delay
RTO	Recovery Time Objective
R2T	Request to Transfer
R/W	Read/Write
RX	Receiver
SACK	Selective Acknowledge
SACL	System Access Control List
SAL	SCSI Application Layer
SAN	Storage Area Network
SAS	Serial Attached SCSI
SASI	Shugart Associate System Interface
SATA	Serial Advanced Technology Attachment
SC	Standard Connector

SCN	State Change Notification
SCSI	Small Computer System Interface
SDH	Synchronous Digital Hierarchy
SEC	Securities and Exchange Commission
SHA	Secure Hash Algorithm
SiS	Single-Instance Storage
SLA	Service Level Agreement
SLC	Single-Level Cell
SLED	Single Large Expensive Drive
SLP	Service Location Protocol
SLV	Symmetrix Logical Volume
SMB	Server Message Block
SMF	Single-Mode Fiber
SMI	Storage Management Initiative
SMTP	Simple Mail Transfer Protocol
SNIA	Storage Networking Industry Association
SNMP	Simple Network Management Protocol
SNS	Simple Name Server
SOF	Start of Frame
SONET	Synchronous Optical Networking
SP	Storage Processor
SPE	Storage Processor Enclosure
SPI	SCSI Parallel Interface
SPOF	Single Point of Failure
SPS	Standby Power Supply
SRDF	Symmetrix Remote Data Facility
SRDF/A	SRDF/Asynchronous
SRDF/AR	SRDF/Automated Replication
SRDF/CE	SRDF/Cluster Enabler
SRDF/CG	SRDF/Consistency Groups
SRDF/DM	SRDF/Data Mobility
SRDF/S	SRDF/Synchronous
SRM	Storage Resource Management

SSD	Solid-State Drive
SSH	Secure Shell
SSID	Service Set Identifier
SSL	Secure Sockets Layer
ST	Straight Tip
StatSN	Status Sequence Number
STPL	SCSI Transport Protocol Layer
STS	Synchronous Transport Signal
TB	Terabyte
TCO	Total Cost of Ownership
TCP	Transmission Control Protocol
TGS	Ticket Granting Service
TLU	Tape Library Unit
TOE	TCP/IP Offload Engine
TPI	Tracks per Inch
TX	Transmitter
UDP	User Datagram Protocol
UFS	UNIX File System
UID	User identifier
ULP	Upper-Layer Protocol
URL	Uniform Resource Locator
USB	Universal Serial Bus
VC	Virtual Circuit
VCAT	Virtual Concatenation
VG	Volume Group
VLAN	Virtual LAN
VPN	Virtual Private Network
VSAN	Virtual Storage Area Network
VTL	Virtual Tape Library
WAN	Wide Area Network
WBEM	Web-Based Enterprise Management
WDM	Wavelength-Division Multiplexing
WORM	Write Once, Read Many

WORO	Write Once, Read Occasionally
WWN	World Wide Name
WWNN	World Wide Node Name
WWPN	World Wide Port Name
XCM	Environmental Control Module
XML	Extensible Markup Language

8b/10b encoding An algorithm that converts 8-bit data into 10-bit transmission characters to avoid long sequences of zeros and ones.

Access control Services to regulate user access to resources.

Access Control List (ACL) A list of permissions that specifies who can access a resource and with what privileges.

Access node Provides connectivity to application servers through the network in CAS.

Accessibility Capability to access required information at the right place by the authorized user.

Accountability services A service that enables administrators to track activities performed on a system and link them back to individuals in such a way that there is little possibility for individuals to deny responsibility for their activities.

Active archive Category of data that is not likely to change or cannot be changed—often referred to as "fixed content" data.

Active attack Unauthorized alteration of information that may pose a threat to data integrity and availability.

Active changeable Category of data that is subject to change and can be changed is referred to as "changeable" data.

Active Directory (AD) Microsoft implementation used to provide central authentication and authorization services.

Actuator arm assembly An assembly to which all R/W heads are attached.

Adaptive copy mode A type of asynchronous replication that does not involve write ordering and data consistency while transferring the data.

Advanced Encryption Standard (AES) A block cipher (cryptographic algorithm) designated by the National Institute of Standards and Technology.

Agent A software program that manages specific objects (such as storage arrays, Fibre Channel switches, and hosts); monitors these objects for alert conditions; gathers information about object performance and configuration; and performs active commands.

Alert Notification of an event that may or may not need attention/action, depending on the type of alert.

Application Programming Interface (API) A set of function calls that enables communication between applications or between an application and an operating system.

Arbitrated Loop A shared Fibre Channel loop whereby each device contends with other devices to perform I/O operations; it is analogous to a token ring.

Arbitration A technique to determine which node gets control of the loop in FC-AL, when one or more nodes attempt to transmit data.

Archive A repository where fixed content is placed for long-term retention.

Array/disk array/storage array A group of hard disk drives that work together as a unit.

Asynchronous replication A write complete is acknowledged immediately to the source host. These writes are queued in the log, transmitted in the same order, and updated to the source. In SRDF it is termed *asynchronous mode*.

Asynchronous Transfer Mode (ATM) A switch-based connection-oriented technology that uses fixed-size cells (53 bytes, with a 48-byte payload and a 5-byte header) for data communication.

Attack surface Various ways in which an attacker can launch an attack.

Attack vector A series of steps necessary to complete an attack.

Authentication A process of verifying the digital identity of the sender in a communication.

Automatic path failover A seamless failover in the event of a path failure whereby I/O failover occurs on an available alternate path without disrupting application operations.

Autoprobe A PowerPath function that periodically tests inactive paths to identify failed paths before sending the I/O application.

Autorestore A PowerPath function that runs every five minutes and tests every failed or closed path to determine whether it has been repaired.

Availability An extent to which a component is available and will function according to business expectations during its specified time of operations.

Availability services Services that ensure reliable and timely access to data for authorized users.

Average queue size An average number of requests in a queue.

Average rotational latency One-half of the time taken for a full rotation of the disk drive platter.

Backup A copy of production data.

Backup catalog A database that holds information about backup processes and metadata.

Backup client A software that retrieves data from a production host and sends it to a storage node for backup.

Backup server A server that manages backup operation and maintains the backup catalog.

Backup to disk Use of disks to store backup data.

Backup window A period of time for which a source is available to perform a backup procedure.

Bandwidth (network) Maximum amount of data that can be transferred over a network in one second; expressed in Mbits/second (Mb/s).

Bare-metal recovery (BMR) A backup in which all metadata, system information, and application configuration is appropriately backed up for a full system recovery.

Battery Backup Unit (BBU) A battery-operated power supply used as an auxiliary source in the event of power failure.

BB_Credit Defines maximum number of frames that can be present over the link at any given point in time.

BC Planning (BCP) A disciplined approach enabling an organization's business functions to operate during and after a disruption.

Binary Large Object (BLOB) A bit sequence of user data representing the actual content of a file. It is independent of the name and physical location of the file.

Block A unit of contiguous fixed-size space on a disk drive.

Block-level access Basic mechanism for data access on the disk drive.

Block-level virtualization Provides an abstraction layer in the SAN between the hosts and the storage arrays.

Block size An application's basic unit of data storage and retrieval.

Bridged topology A topology that provides connectivity between an FC and IP network.

Buffer A temporary storage area, usually in RAM.

Bunker site An intermediate site between production and remote that is used in cascaded/multihop three-site replication to mitigate the risks associated with two-site replication.

Bus A collection of paths that facilitates data transmission from one part of the computer to another.

Business Continuance Volume (BCV) A copy of production volumes primarily used for recovery. It can also be used simultaneously for other business activities without affecting the production systems.

Business continuity (BC) Preparing for, responding to, and recovering from an outage that may adversely affect business operations.

Business Impact Analysis (BIA) A process of evaluating the effects of not performing a business function for a time period.

Cache A semiconductor memory where data is placed temporarily to reduce the time required to service I/O requests from the host.

Cache coherency Copies of the same data in two different cache addresses is maintained identical at all times.

Cache mirroring Each write to cache is held in two different memory addresses on two independent memory boards.

Cache vaulting The process of dumping the contents of cache into a dedicated set of physical disks during a power failure.

Call home Sends a message to the vendor's support center in the event of hardware or process failures.

Capacity management Ensures the adequate allocation of resources for all services based on their service level requirements.

Carrier Sense Multiple Access / Collision Detection (CSMA/CD) A set of rules specifying how network devices respond when two devices attempt to use a data channel simultaneously (called a *collision*).

Cascade/Multihop Replication whereby data flows from the source to the intermediate storage array, known as a *bunker*, in the first hop and then to a storage array at a remote site in the second hop.

C-CLIP A virtual container where CAS stores user data and its attributes as an object.

Challenge-Handshake Authentication Protocol (CHAP) Basic authentication used by initiator and target to authenticate each other via the exchange of a secret code or password.

Channel A high-bandwidth connection between a processor and other processors or devices.

Chargeback report A report that enables storage administrators to identify storage usage by an application/business unit in order to appropriately distribute storage costs across applications/business unit.

Checksum A redundancy check to verify data integrity by detecting errors in the data during transmission.

C-H-S addressing Use of physical addresses, consisting of the cylinder, head, and sector (CHS) number, for specific locations on the disk.

CLARiiON Messaging Interface (CMI) An interface used by the storage processors in a CLARiiON storage array to communicate with each other.

Class of Service (CoS) FC standards that differentiate between the quality of network services, treating each type as a class with its own level of service priority.

Client-initiated backup A manual/automatic backup process initiated by a client.

Client/server model A model in which a client requests and uses the services provided by a server that is capable of serving multiple clients at the same time.

Cluster (server) A collection of high-performance, interconnected computer servers working together as a single processing resource in an application environment in order to provide high availability.

Cold backup A backup that requires the application to be shut down.

Cold site A site where an enterprise's operations can be moved in the event of disaster—one with minimum IT infrastructure and environmental facilities in place, but not active.

Command Line Interface (CLI) An application user interface that accepts typed commands "one line" at a time in a command prompt window.

Command queuing An algorithm that optimizes the order in which received commands are executed.

Common Internet File System (CIFS) A Microsoft client/server application protocol that enables client programs to make requests for files and services on remote computers over TCP/IP.

Common Management Information Service (CMIS) A service that is used by network elements for network management.

Concatenation The process of logically joining address spaces of disks and presenting it as a single large address space.

Confidentiality Providing the required secrecy for information.

Consistency group A group of logical devices located on a single or multiple storage arrays and that need to be managed as a single entity.

Consistent split Multiple BCV mirrors are split simultaneously as one logical unit. This ensures data consistency across multiple volumes.

Console The primary interface to view, manage, configure, and handle reporting of various components (managed objects).

Content Address (CA) An identifier that uniquely addresses the content of a file and not its location.

Content Addressed Storage (CAS) An object-oriented system for storing fixed-content data. It provides a cost-effective networked storage solution.

Content authenticity Achieved at two levels: by generating a unique content address and by automating the process of continuously checking and recalculating the content address.

Content Descriptor File (CDF) An XML file that contains the content address and metadata of CAS objects.

Content handle A unique identifier of a CDF that contains the content address of the actual data in a CAS environment.

Content Protection Mirrored (CPM) The data object is mirrored for the total protection of data against failure.

Content Protection Parity (CPP) Data is transformed into segments, with an additional parity segment for the total protection of data against failure.

Continuous Data Protection (CDP) A technology whereby the recovery points or checkpoints are set with fine granularity so that data can be recovered without significant loss.

Control Path Cluster (CPC) A customized storage device with installed Invista software; it stores Invista configuration parameters.

Control station Provides dedicated processing capabilities to control, manage, and configure a NAS solution.

Copy on First Access (CoFA) A pointer-based full volume replication method that copies the data from source to target only when the write operation is issued on the source or a read/write operation is performed on the target for the first time. The replica is immediately available when the session starts.

Copy on First Write (CoFW) A pointer-based virtual replication method whereby data is copied to a predefined area in the array when a write occurs to the source or target for the first time.

Cryptography A technique for hiding information for the purpose of security.

Cumulative backup (differential backup) Copies the data that has changed since last full backup.

Cyclic redundancy check (CRC) A technique for detecting errors in digital data for verifying data integrity. In this method, a certain number of check bits, often called a checksum, are appended to the message being transmitted.

Cylinder A set of concentric, hollow, cylindrical slices through the platters in a HDD.

Data A piece of recorded information.

Data Access in Real Time (DART) Celerra's specialized operating system, which runs on the Data Mover.

Data center Provides centralized data processing capabilities to businesses. Its core elements are applications, databases, operating systems, networks, and storage.

Data Collection Policies (DCP) A predefined set of actions that an agent performs to gather information about objects.

Data compression The process of encoding information using fewer bits.

Data consistency The usability, validity, and integrity of related data components.

Data integrity The assurance that data is not modified unintentionally.

Data Mover An autonomous file server optimized for file serving used in EMC Celerra.

Data Path Controller (DPC) An intelligent SAN switch or director with Invista software installed. It receives I/O from the host and controls its attributes, such as target, LUN, and offset, within the logical unit.

Data security The means of ensuring both that data is safe from corruption and that its access is suitably controlled.

Data store The part of the cache that holds the data.

Data tampering Deliberate altering of data.

Data transfer rate The amount of data per second that a drive can deliver to the controller.

Defense in depth Implementing security controls at each access point of every access path.

Delta set Implementation of asynchronous replication uses large storage cache for temporarily buffering the outstanding writes assigned for the target. The buffered data represents the difference, or delta set, between the source and the target writes.

Denial-of-Service (DoS) attack An attack that denies the use of resources to legitimate users.

Dense Wave Division Multiplexing (DWDM) A technology that carries data from different sources together on an optical fiber, with each signal carried on its own separate wavelength.

Device driver Special software that permits the operating system and computer hardware device to interact with each other.

Differential split Synchronizes the primary mirror of a BCV device and its secondary mirror in a differential copy mode. This way, only tracks that changed on the standard device will propagate after the split to the other mirror of the BCV device.

Direct-attached backup A backup device attached directly to the backup client.

Direct-attached storage (DAS) Storage directly attached to a server or workstation.

Director Class of interconnection device that has large port count and redundant components for enterprise class connectivity requirements.

Directory A container in a file system that contains pointers to multiple files.

Directory service (DS) An application or a set of applications that stores and organizes information about a computer network's users and network resources. This enables network administrators to manage user access to the resources.

Directory System Agent (DSA) An LDAP directory that can be distributed among many LDAP servers. Each DSA has a replicated version of the full directory that is synchronized periodically.

Disaster recovery The process, policies, and procedures for restoring operations that are critical to the resumption of business, including regaining access to data.

Disaster recovery plan (DRP) A plan for coping with the unexpected or sudden loss of data access, with a focus on data protection. A part of business continuity planning.

Disaster restart The process of restarting business operations with consistent copies of data.

Discovery domain Provides a functional grouping of devices in an IP-SAN. In order for devices to communicate with one another, they must be configured in the same discovery domain.

Discretionary Access Control (DAC) An access policy determined by the owner of an object.

Disk-buffered replication A combination of local and remote replication technologies; it creates a local PIT replica first and then a remote replica of the local PIT replica.

Disk drive (HDD) A peripheral device used to store data persistently.

Disk partitioning The creation of logical divisions on a hard disk.

Distributed file system (DFS) A file system that is distributed across several computer nodes.

Domain Name System (DNS) Helps to translate human-readable host names into IP addresses.

Double buffering The buffering of data in two places. For example RDBMs use their own buffering along with file system buffering.

Downtime The amount of time during which a system is in an inaccessible state.

Dual-role node A node that provides both storage and access node capabilities.

Dynamic Host Configuration Protocol (DHCP) An approach to dynamically assigning an IP address to a host.

Encryption The process of transforming information using an algorithm (called a *cipher*) in order to make it unreadable to unauthorized users.

End-to-End Credit (EE-Credit) A mechanism that controls the data flow for class 1 and class 2 traffic using buffers.

Enterprise management platform (EMP) Integrated applications or suites of applications that manage and monitor the data center environment.

Enterprise Systems Connection (ESCON) An optical serial interface between IBM mainframe computers and peripheral devices.

Error-correction coding An encoding method that detects and corrects errors at the receiving end of data transmission.

Establish operation The process of attaching a BCV device to a standard device and synchronizing it with the standard device in TimeFinder/Mirror.

Expansion port (E_Port) A port used to connect two FC switches through an Inter-Switch Link (ISL).

Export Publishes the file system to UNIX clients that can mount or access the remote file system.

External transfer rate The rate at which data can be moved through the interface to the HBA.

Fabric A Fibre Channel topology with one or more switching devices.

Fabric Login (FLOGI) Login performed between an N_Port and an F_Port.

Fabric Loop port (FL_Port) A port on a switch that connects to a FC arbitrated loop.

Fabric port (F_Port) A port on the switch that connects an N_Port.

Fabric Shortest Path First (FSPF) Used in an FC network, a routing protocol that calculates the shortest path between nodes.

Failback This operation enables the resumption of normal business operations at the source site. Failback is invoked after a failover has been initiated.

Fan-in Qualified number of storage ports that can be accessed by a single initiator though a SAN.

Fan-out Qualified number of initiators that can access a single storage port though a SAN.

Fatal alert A warning about a condition requiring immediate attention because the condition may affect the overall performance or availability of the system.

Fault tolerance Describes a system or component designed in such a way that in the event of a failure, a backup component or procedure can immediately take its place with no loss of service.

Federated database A collection of databases that is treated as one entity and viewed through a single user interface.

Fibre Channel (FC) An interconnect that supports multiple protocols and topologies. Data is transferred serially on a variety of copper and optical links at a high speed.

Fibre Channel over IP protocol (FCIP) TCP/IP-based tunneling protocol for connecting Fibre Channel SANs over IP.

Field-Replaceable Unit (FRU) A component of a system that can be replaced only by a vendor engineer.

File-level access An abstraction of block-level access that hides the complexities of logical block addressing to the applications.

File-level virtualization Provides the independency between the data accessed at the file level and the location where the files are physically stored.

File Transfer Protocol (FTP) A network protocol that enables the transfer of files between computers over the Internet.

File server A server used to address file-sharing requirements.

File system A structured way of storing and organizing data in the form of files that represent a block of information.

Firewall A dedicated appliance, or software, that inspects network traffic passing through it and denies or permits passage based on a set of rules.

Firmware Software that is primed or embedded in a device.

Fixed-block architecture (FBA) A disk layout whereby each physical block on disk is the same size.

FLARE Special software designed for the operating environment of EMC CLARiiON.

Flushing The process of committing data from cache to disk.

Force flushing In case of a large I/O burst, this process forcibly flushes dirty pages onto the disk.

Frame A data stream that has been encoded by a data link layer for digital transmission over a node-to-node link.

Front-end controller Receives and processes I/O requests from the host and communicates with cache or the back end.

Front-end Port Provides the interface between the storage system and the host or interconnect devices (switch or director).

Full backup Copying of all data from source to backup device.

Full restore Entire data from the target is copied to the source. All data at the source is overwritten by the target data.

Full stroke The time taken by the read/write head to move across the entire width of the disk, from the innermost track to the outermost track.

Full-volume mirroring The target is attached to the source and established as the mirror of the source. This is accomplished by copying all the existing data and synchronously updating the target for each write on the source.

Gateway NAS A device consisting of an independent NAS head and one or more storage arrays.

Generic Framing Procedure (GFP) A multiplexing technique that enables the mapping of variable-length payloads into synchronous-payload envelopes.

Gigabit Interface Converter (GBIC) A transceiver that can convert electrical signals to optical signals and vice versa.

Global namespace Maps logical path names to physical locations.

Gold copy A copy of the replica device created prior to restarting applications using the replica device.

Graphical User Interface (GUI) An interface for issuing commands to a computer utilizing a pointing device, such as mouse, that manipulates and activates graphical images on a monitor.

Hard disk drive (HDD) A non-volatile storage device that stores digitally encoded data using rapidly rotating platters with magnetic surfaces.

Hard zoning/Port zoning Access to data is determined by the physical port to which a node is connected.

Heartbeat A messaging mechanism used by MirrorView software to determine whether a secondary device is available after it is determined unreachable.

Hierarchical Storage Management (HSM) Policy-based management that enables moving data from high-cost storage media to low-cost storage media.

High availability Ensures that no data is lost in the event of a disaster at the source.

High Performance Parallel Interface (HIPPI) A high-speed computer bus used to connect to a storage device.

High watermark The cache utilization level at which the storage system starts high-speed flushing of cache data.

Host A client or server computer that runs applications.

Host bus adapter (HBA) Hardware that connects a host computer to a storage area network or directly to a storage device.

Hot backup Backing up data when the application is up and running, with users accessing it.

Hot site A computer room with the required hardware, operating system, application, and network support to perform business operations in case of disaster or non-availability of an application.

Hot spare An idle disk drive that replaces a failed drive in any protected RAID group.

Hot swap The replacement of a hardware component with a similar one while the computer system using it remains in operation.

Hub An interconnectivity device that connects nodes in a logical loop whereby the nodes must share the bandwidth.

Hunt group Enables more than one port to respond to one alias address.

Idle flushing Continuous de-staging of data from cache to disk when the cache utilization level is between the high and low watermark.

In-band An implementation in which the virtualized environment configurations reside internal to the data path.

In-sync Implies that the primary logical device and secondary logical device contain identical data.

Incremental backup Copy of data that has changed since the last full or incremental backup, whichever has occurred more recently.

Information The knowledge derived from data.

Information Lifecycle Management (ILM) A proactive and dynamic strategy that helps businesses to manage the growth of information based on its business value.

Information Rights Management (IRM) A technology that protects sensitive information from unauthorized access; sometimes referred to as Enterprise Digital Rights Management.

Initiator A device that starts a data request.

Inode A data structure that contains information and is associated with every file and directory.

I/O burst A large number of writes that occur within a very short duration.

Input/Output channel (I/O channel) Provides the communication between the I/O bus and the CPU.

I/O controller Component that processes I/O requests one at a time.

Input Output per Second (IOPS) Number of reads and writes performed per second.

Integrated Device Electronics/Advanced Technology Attachment (IDE/ ATA) Standard interface for connecting storage devices inside personal computers.

Integrated NAS A self-contained NAS environment that bundles together all the components of NAS, such as the NAS head, storage, and management functions.

Integrity checking Ensures that the content of a file matches the digital signature (hashed output or CA).

Interface A communication boundary between two elements, such as software, hardware device, or a user.

Internal transfer rate The speed at which data moves from the disk surface to the read/write heads.

Internet Engineering Task Force (IETF) The body that defines standard Internet operating protocols such as TCP/IP.

Internet Fibre Channel Protocol (iFCP) A protocol that enables native Fibre Channel devices in remote locations to be connected via an IP network.

Internet Protocol (IP) A protocol used for communicating data across a packet-switched network.

Internet Protocol Security (IPSec) A suite of algorithms, protocols, and procedures used for securing IP communications by authenticating and/ or encrypting each packet in a data stream.

Internet Protocol Storage Area Network (IP SAN) Hybrid storage networking solutions that leverage IP networks.

Internet Small Computer System Interface protocol (iSCSI) An IP-based protocol built on SCSI. It carries block-level data over traditional IP networks.

Internet Storage Name Service (iSNS) A protocol that enables the automated discovery of storage devices on an IP network.

Inter-Switch Link (ISL) A link that connects two switches/fabrics through E_Ports.

Intrusion Detection/Intrusion Prevention System (IDS/IPS) A detection control that identifies intrusion in the IT systems and attempts to stop attacks by terminating a network connection or invoking a firewall rule to block traffic.

Jitter Unwanted variation in signal characteristics.

Journal file system A file system that uses a separate area called log or journal to track all the changes to a file system, enabling easy recovery in the event of a filesystem crash.

Jukebox Collections of optical disks in an "array" used to store and access fixed-content.

k28.5 A special 10-bit character used to indicate the beginning of a Fibre Channel command.

Kerberos A network authentication protocol that enables individuals communicating over a nonsecure network to prove their identity to one another in a secure manner.

Key Distribution Center (KDC) A Kerberos server that implements the authentication and ticket-granting services.

LAN-based backup Data to be backed up is transferred from the application server to the storage node over the LAN.

Landing zone The area of a hard disk where the R/W head rests on the platter near the spindle.

Latency Time delay between an I/O request and completion of that I/O.

Least Recently Used (LRU) A cache algorithm whereby addresses that have not been accessed for a long time are freed up or marked for reuse.

Level 1 (L1) cache An additional cache that is associated with the CPU. It holds data and program instructions that are likely to be needed by the CPU in the near future.

Lightweight Directory Access Protocol (LDAP) An application protocol for accessing an information directory over TCP/IP.

Link Aggregation Control Protocol (LACP) An IEEE standard for combining two or more physical data channels into one logical data channel for high availability.

Link Capacity Adjustment Scheme (LCAS) Specified in ITU-T G.7042, LCAS allows on-demand increases or decreases of the bandwidth of the virtual concatenated group.

Link Control Card (LCC) Provides connectivity among shelves of disks in a CLARiiON system. The LCC also monitors the field-replaceable units (FRUs) within the shelf and reports status information to the storage processor.

Load balancing A method of evenly distributing the workload across multiple computer systems, network links, CPUs, hard drives, or other resources in order to get optimal resource utilization.

Local Area Network (LAN) An IP based communication infrastructure that shares a common link to connect a large number of interconnecting nodes within a small geographic area (typically a building or campus).

Local bus or I/O bus A high-speed pathway that connects CPU and peripheral devices for data transfer.

Local replication The process of creating a copy of a production volume, within the same storage array (in the case of array-based local replication) or within the same data center (in the case of host-based local replication).

Log shipping A host based replication method whereby all activities at the source are captured into a "log" file and periodically shipped and applied to the remote site.

Logical arrays A subset of disks within an array that can be grouped to form logical associations—for example, a RAID set.

Logical Block Addressing (LBA) A method of addressing the location of a predefined storage space (block) using running numbers (ex: 1 to 65536) instead of cylinder-head-sector numbers.

Logical Unit Number (LUN) An identifier of a logical storage unit presented to a host for storing and accessing data on those units.

Logical volume Virtual disk partition created within a volume group.

Logical volume manager (LVM) Host-resident software that creates and controls host-level logical volumes.

Low watermark The point at which the storage system stops the forced flushing and returns to idle flush behavior.

LUN binding The process of creating LUNs within a RAID set.

LUN masking A process that provides data access control so that the host can see only the LUNs it is intended to access.

Magnetic tape A sequential storage medium used for data storage, backup, and archiving.

Mail or import/export slot A slot used to add or remove tapes from the tape-library without opening the access doors.

Management Information Base (MIB) A collection of objects in a (virtual) database used to manage entities (such as routers and switches) in a network.

Massive Array of Idle Disks (MAID) A system that uses a very large number of hard drives for near-line data storage. It is mostly used for write once, read occasionally applications.

Master agent Controls all agents on a host by starting and stopping the agents, and facilitates their remote installations and upgrades in an EMC ControlCenter environment.

Maximum Transmission Unit (MTU) A setting that determines the size of the largest packet that can be transmitted without data fragmentation.

Mean Time Between Failure (MTBF) A measure (in hours) of the average life expectancy of an individual component.

Mean Time To Repair (MTTR) The average time required to repair a faulty component.

Media Access Control (MAC) A mechanism to control physical media in a shared media network.

Memory virtualization A technique that gives an application program the impression that it has its own contiguous logical memory independent of available physical memory.

Metadata "Information about data" that describes the characteristics of data such as content, quality, and condition.

MetaLUN A logical unit that is expanded by aggregating multiple logical units.

Metropolitan Area Network (MAN) A large computer network usually spanning a city.

Mirroring A data redundancy technique whereby all the data is written to two disk drives simultaneously to provide protection against single-disk failure.

Mixed topology A backup topology that uses both LAN-based and SAN-based backup topologies.

Mixed zoning A combination of the WWN and port zoning technique.

Modification attack An unauthorized attempt to modify information for malicious purposes.

Monitoring The process of continuous collection of information and review of the entire storage infrastructure.

Most Recently Used (MRU) A cache algorithm whereby the addresses that have been accessed most recently are freed up or marked for reuse.

Mounting The process of making a file system usable by creating a mount point. The process of inserting a tape cartridge into a tape drive is also referred to as mounting.

Multicast Delivers frames to multiple destination ports at the same time.

Multimode Fiber (MMF) A fiber optic cable carrying multiple data streams in the form of light beams.

Multipathing Enables two or more data paths to be simultaneously used for read/write operations.

Multiplexing Transmitting multiple signals over a single communications line or channel.

Name server A host that implements a name service protocol.

Namespace An abstract container that provides context for the items it holds (e.g., names, technical terms, words).

Naviseccli A CLI-based (command-line interface) management tool to manage EMC CLARiiON.

Navisphere Analyzer A performance analysis tool for CLARiiON hardware components.

Navisphere Manager A GUI-based tool for centralized storage system management that is used to configure and manage CLARiiON.

Network A set of interconnected devices for resource sharing.

Network-attached storage (NAS) A dedicated file-serving device (with integrated or shared storage) attached to a local area network.

Network Data Management Protocol (NDMP) An open protocol used to control data backup and recovery communications between primary and secondary storage in a heterogeneous network environment.

Network File System (NFS) A common file-sharing method in UNIX environment.

Network Information System (NIS) Helps users identify and access a unique resource over the network.

Network Interface Card (NIC) Computer hardware designed for computers to communicate over an IP network.

Network latency Time taken for a packet to move from source to destination.

Network layer firewalls A firewall implemented at the network layer to examine network packets and compare them to a set of configured security rules.

Network portal A port to access any iSCSI node within a device.

Network Time Protocol (NTP) A protocol for synchronizing the clocks of computer systems over packet-switched, variable-latency data networks.

Network topology A schematic description of a network arrangement, including its nodes and connecting lines.

Network virtualization A technique for creating virtual networks, independent of the physical network.

Node A device or element connected in the network, such as a host or storage.

Node loop port (NL-Port) A node port that supports the arbitrated loop topology. This port is also known as the node loop port.

Node port (N-port) An end point in the fabric—typically a host port (HBA) or a storage array port that is connected to a switch in a switched fabric.

Non-protected restore A restore process in which the target remains attached to the source after the restore operation is complete and all the writes to the source are mirrored onto the target.

Non-repudiation Assurance that a subject cannot later deny having performed an action. Proof of delivery is provided in a communication for non-repudiation.

Normal Auto Contingent Allegiance (NACA) Controls the rules for handling an Auto Contingent Allegiance (ACA) condition caused by commands.

Offline mode (database replication) The database is not available for an I/O operation when replication takes place.

Online backup A form of backup in which the data being backed up may be accessed by applications.

Online Transaction Processing (OLTP) A system that processes transactions the instant the computer receives them and updates master files immediately.

Open file agents These agents interact directly with the operating system and enable the consistent backup of open files.

Operational backup Collection of data for the eventual purpose of restoring, at some point in the future, data that has become lost or corrupted.

Optical Disc Drive (ODD) A disk drive that uses laser light or electromagnetic waves near the light spectrum as part of the process of reading and writing data. It is a computer's peripheral device that stores data on optical discs.

Ordered set The low-level Fibre Channel (FC-1 layer) functions such as frame demarcation and signaling used for data transmission.

Out-of-band An implementation in which the virtualized environment configurations reside externally to the data path.

Out-of-sync Implies that the target data is not in a consistent state and requires full synchronization.

Packet loss When one or more packets of data traveling across a computer network fail to reach their destination.

Page A small unit of cache memory allocation.

Parity A mathematical construct that enables re-creation of the missing segment of data.

Parity bit An extra bit used in checking for errors in data bits during transmission. In modem communications, it is used to check the accuracy of each transmitted character.

Partition A logical division of the capacity of a physical or logical disk.

Passive attack An attempt to gain unauthorized access to information without altering it. Passive attacks may threaten the confidentiality of information.

Password A form of secret authentication data that is used to control access to a resource.

Payload Part of a data stream that represents user information and over-head, if any.

Performance Manager A performance analysis tool of EMC ControlCenter that provides the capability to quickly generate the performance and configuration reports.

Peripheral Component Interconnect (PCI) A standard bus for connecting I/O devices to a personal computer.

Platter One or more flat, circular disks found on a typical HDD. It is a rigid disk coated with magnetic material on both surfaces.

PLOGI (port login) Performed between one N_port (initiator) and another N_port (target storage port) to establish a session.

Point-in-time (PIT) copy A copy of data that contains a consistent image of the data as it appeared at a given point in time.

Port A physical connecting point to which a device is attached.

Portal group A group of network portals that can collectively support a multiple-connection session.

Pre-fetch (read ahead) In a sequential read request, a contiguous set of associated disk blocks that have not yet been requested by the host is read from the disk, and placed in cache in advance.

Primitive sequence An ordered set transmitted continually until a specified response is received, as defined in FC-1 layer.

Private loop An arbitrated loop without any switches.

Process login (PRLI) N_port to N_port login used to exchange service parameters. The PRLI verification process is dependent on the ULP.

Production data Data generated by an application hosted on a server.

Propagation Transmission (spreading) of signals through any medium from one place to other.

Propagation delay Amount of time taken by a packet to travel from its source to destination.

Protocol A set of rules or standards that enable systems or devices to communicate.

Protocol data unit (PDU) A message transmitted between two nodes on a network for communication.

Public Key Infrastructure (PKI) Software, hardware, people, and procedures that are used to facilitate the secure creation and management of digital certificates.

Public loop An arbitrated loop connected to a fabric through an FL_Port.

Quality of Service (QoS) A defined measure of performance in a data communication system.

Queue Location where an I/O request waits before it is processed by the I/O controller.

Quiescent state An application or device state in which the data is consistent. Processing is suspended, and tasks are either completed or not started.

Quota Restrictions specified at the user level about the maximum capacity allocated (e.g., the mailbox quota, the file system quota).

RAID controller Specialized hardware that performs all RAID calculations and presents disk volumes to host.

Random access memory (RAM) Volatile memory that allows direct access to any memory location.

Random I/O Consecutive I/O requests which do not access adjacent data locations in a storage system.

Raw partition A disk partition that is not managed by the volume manager.

Read-only memory (ROM) Non-volatile memory type in which data can be read but not written.

Read/write heads Components of the hard drive that read and write the data from or onto an HDD. Most drives have two read/write heads per platter, one for each surface of the platter.

Recoverability Ability of a replica to enable data restoration in order to resume business operations, with a predefined RPO and RTO, in the event of data loss or corruption.

Recovery Point Objective (RPO) Point in time at which systems and data must be recovered after an outage. It defines the amount of data loss that a business can endure.

Recovery Time Objective (RTO) Time within which systems, applications, or functions must be recovered after an outage. It defines the amount of downtime that a business can endure and survive.

Redundancy An inclusion of extra components (e.g., disk drive, HBA, link, or data) that enables continued operation if any of the working components fail.

Redundant Array of Independent Disks (RAID) Inclusion of a set of multiple independent disk drives in an array of disk drives, which yields performance exceeding that of a single large expensive drive.

Redundant Array of Inexpensive Nodes (RAIN) Data is replicated to multiple independent nodes to provide redundancy in CAS.

Registered State Change Notification (RSCN) Used to propagate information about changes in the state of one node to all other nodes in the fabric.

Reliability Assurance that a system will continue its normal business operations for a specific period under the given conditions.

Remote Authentication Dial-in User Service (RADIUS) An authentication, authorization, and accounting protocol for controlling access to network resources.

Remote backup A copy from the primary storage is performed directly to the backup media, which is located at another site.

Remote Procedure Call (RPC) A technology that enables a computer program to cause a subroutine or procedure to execute in another computer without the programmer explicitly coding the details for the remote interaction.

Remote replication Process of copying source data stored in a local storage array to an array located at a remote site.

Replica An image/copy of data usable by another application.

Repudiation attack An attack that denies or obfuscates the authorship of something.

Response time Amount of time a system or functional unit takes to react to a given input.

Restartability Determines the validity and usability of replicated data to restart business operations in the event of a disaster.

Restore To return data to its original or usable and functioning condition.

Resynchronization Process of restoring only the data blocks that are updated after the PIT is copied to the target.

Retention period Duration for which a business needs to retain the backup copies of data.

Reverse split Initiates a reverse data copy from the fixed BCV mirror to the primary mirror of a BCV upon the completion of a split operation. This PIT copy can then be used to recover the standard in the event of data loss or corruption.

Rewind time Time taken to rewind the tape to the starting position.

Risk analysis An analysis performed as part of the BC process that considers the component failure rate and average repair time, which are measured by MTTR and MTBF.

Robotic arms Component of a tape library, used for moving tapes from its slots to drive and back .

Role-based access control (RBAC) An approach to restricting system access to authorized users based on their respective roles.

Roll back Reverting a secondary replica to a previous point-in-time copy.

Rotation speed Speed at which a hard drive platter rotates.

Rotational latency Time taken by the platter to rotate and position the data location under the read/write head.

Round-robin I/O requests are assigned to each available path in rotation.

Round-trip delay (RTD) Delay between when data is sent and the acknowledgment is received from the remote site.

Router An inter-networking device that enables the routing of information between different networks.

SAN-based backup A method of backing up data over a SAN.

Save location A set of private LUNs that preserves PIT data just before it is updated at the source or the target by hosts.

SCSI Application Layer (SAL) An uppermost layer in the SCSI communication model, it contains both client and server applications that initiate and process SCSI I/O operations by using a SCSI application protocol.

SCSI Transport Protocol Layer (STPL) Contains the services and protocols that enable communication between an initiator and targets.

Sector Smallest individually addressable units of a disk drive on which data is physically stored.

Secure Shell (SSH) A network protocol that enables data to be exchanged over a secure channel between two computers.

Secure Sockets Layer (SSL) A cryptographic protocol that provides secure communications between a client and a server over the Internet, using public key cryptography.

Securities and Exchange Commission (SEC) A United States government agency that has the primary responsibility for enforcing the federal securities laws and regulating the securities industry/stock market.

Seek time The time required for the read/write heads in a disk drive to move between tracks of the disk.

Seek time optimization Commands are executed based on optimizing read/write head movements, which may result in improved response time.

Selective Acknowledge (SACK) With SACK, the data receiver can inform the sender about all segments that have arrived successfully, enabling the sender to retransmit only those segments that are actually lost.

SendTargetDiscovery A command issued by an initiator to begin the discovery process. The target responds with the names and addresses of the targets available to the host.

SEQ_ID An identifier of the frame as a component of a specific sequence and exchange as defined in FC-2 layer.

Sequence A contiguous set of frames that are sent from one port to another.

Serial Advanced Technology Attachment (SATA) A serial version of IDE/ATA, designed for serial transfer of data.

Server A computer system that provides services over the network to clients.

Server cluster Interconnected servers working together as a single processing resource in an application environment, for the purpose of high availability.

Server virtualization Enables multiple operating systems and applications to run simultaneously on different virtual machines created on a single or groups of physical servers.

Service-level agreement (SLA) An agreement between a provider and the consumer of a service.

Service Location Protocol (SLP or srvloc) A service discovery protocol that enables computers and other devices to find services in a local area network without prior configuration.

Service Set Identifier (SSID) A 32-character unique identifier attached to the header of packets sent over a WLAN that acts as a password when a mobile device tries to connect to the BSS.

Simple Mail Transfer Protocol (SMTP) The standard Internet e-mail protocol used for sending e-mail messages.

Simple Network Management Protocol (SNMP) A network management protocol used to monitor the health and performance of network-attached devices.

Single-instance Storage (SiS) Enables a system to avoid keeping multiple copies of user data by identifying each object using its unique object ID.

Single Large Expensive Drive (SLED) A single high-capacity, and generally more expensive, drive attached to a computer.

Single-Level Cell (SLC) A memory technology used in solid state drives that stores one bit on each memory cell, resulting in faster transfer speeds, lower power consumption, and higher cell endurance.

Single-mode fiber (SMF) A type of optical fiber that carries data in a form of a single ray of light projected at the center of the core.

Small Computer System Interface (SCSI) A popular storage interface used to connect a peripheral device to a computer and to transfer data between them.

Snapshot A point-in-time copy of data.

Snooping Unauthorized access to the data of another user or organization.

Soft zoning Use of WWNs to define zones. Also referred to as WWN zoning.

Solid-state drive (SSD) A data storage device that uses solid-state memory to store data persistently.

Source ID (S_ID) The standard FC address for the source port.

Spindle The part of the hard disk assembly that connects all platters and is connected to a motor.

Split operation Process of detaching a BCV from the standard device in TimeFinder/Mirror.

Spoofing A practice whereby one person or program successfully masquerades as another by falsifying data, thereby gaining an illegitimate advantage.

SRDF/Asynchronous (SRDF/A) A Symmetrix remote replication solution that enables the source to asynchronously replicate data, incorporating the delta set and dependent write consistency technology.

SRDF/Automated Replication (SRDF/AR) A Symmetrix remote replication solution that uses both SRDF and TimeFinder/Mirror to implement disk-buffered replication technology.

SRDF/Cluster Enabler (SRDF/CE) Enables server clustering whereby servers are distributed globally across multiple Symmetrix storage system environments, ensuring protection against site failure.

SRDF/Consistency Groups (SRDF/CG) A Symmetrix remote replication solution that ensures data consistency at the target in the event of a rolling disaster.

SRDF/Data Mobility (SRDF/DM) A Symmetrix remote replication solution that enables data center migration.

SRDF/Star A Symmetrix remote replication solution that implements three-site replication-triangle/multi-target technology.

SRDF/Synchronous (SRDF/S) A remote replication solution that creates a synchronous replica at one or more Symmetrix targets.

Standby Power Supply (SPS) A power supply that maintains power to cache for long enough to enable the content in cache to be copied to the vault.

State Change Notification (SCN) The notification sent to an iSNS server when devices are added or removed from a discovery domain.

Storage area network (SAN) A high-speed, dedicated network of shared storage devices and servers.

Storage array–based remote replication Replication that is initiated and terminated at the storage array.

Storage Management Initiative (SMI) A storage standard used to enable broad interoperability among heterogeneous storage vendor systems.

Storage Networking Industry Association (SNIA) A non-profit organization to lead the industry in developing and promoting standards, technologies, and educational services in order to empower organizations in the management of information.

Storage Node (Backup/Recovery) A part of the backup package that controls one or more backup devices (a tape drive, a tape library, or a backup to disk device) and receives backup data from backup clients.

Storage Node (CAS) Stores and protects data objects in a CAS system. Also referred to as back-end node.

Storage processor A component of CLARiiON array. Storage processors provide front-end and back-end connectivity and are configured in pairs for maximum availability.

StorageScope console A GUI-designed monitor that reports on all storage assets and their usage.

Store Receives data from agents, processes the data, and updates the repository.

Strip A group of contiguously addressed blocks within each disk of a RAID set.

Stripe A set of aligned strips that spans all the disks within a RAID set.

Stripe width Equal to the number of HDDs in the RAID array.

Striping The splitting and distribution of data across multiple HDDs.

Structured data Data that can be organized into rows and columns, and usually stored in a database or spreadsheet.

Stub file A small file, typically 8 KB, which contains metadata from the original file.

Superblock Contains important information about the file system, such as its type, creation and modification dates, size and layout of the file system, the count of available resources, and a flag indicating the mount status of the file system.

Swap file Also known as a page file or a swap space, this is a portion of the physical disk that is made to look like physical memory to the operating system.

Switched fabric A Fibre Channel topology whereby each device has a unique, dedicated I/O path to the device it is communicating with.

Switches More intelligent devices than hubs, switches directly route data from one physical port to another.

Switching A process of connecting network segments by using a hardware device called a *switch*.

Symmetrix Enginuity Symmetrix Enginuity is the operating environment for EMC Symmetrix.

Symmetrix Remote Data Facility (SRDF) Storage array–based remote replication software products supported by EMC Symmetrix.

Synchronous Digital Hierarchy (SDH) A standard developed by the International Telecommunication Union (ITU), documented in standard G.707 and its extension, G.708.

Synchronous Optical Networking (SONET) A standard for optical telecommunications transport whereby traffic from multiple subscribers is multiplexed together and sent out onto a ring as an optical signal.

System bus The bus that carries data between the processor and memory.

Tag RAM An integrated part of the cache that tracks the location of data in the data store; it is where the data is found in memory and where the data belongs on the disk.

Tape cartridges A device that contains magnetic tapes used for data storage.

Tape drive A data storage device that reads and writes data stored on a magnetic tape.

Target A SCSI device that executes a command to perform the task received from a SCSI initiator.

Target ID Uniquely identifies a target and is used as the address for exchanging commands and status information with initiators.

TCP/IP Offload Engine (TOE) card A TOE card offloads the TCP management functions from the host.

Threats Attacks that can be carried out on the IT infrastructure.

Throughput Measurement of the amount of data that can be successfully transferred within a set time period.

Tiered storage An environment that classifies storage into two or more tiers, based on differences in price, performance, capacity, and functionality.

Total Cost of Ownership (TCO) A financial estimate of direct and indirect costs for owning software or hardware.

Tracks The logical concentric rings on a disk drive platter.

Transfer rate throttle The SAN Copy transfer rate can be controlled by throttling network bandwidth. The throttle value ranges from 1 (low) to 10 (high).

Transmission code Used in FC primarily to improve the transmission characteristic of information across the fiber.

Transmission Control Protocol (TCP) A connection-based protocol that establishes a virtual session before information is sent from the source to the destination.

Transmission word A data transmission unit in FC-1 whereby each transmission word contains a string of four contiguous transmission characters or bytes.

Triangle/Multitarget A three-site remote replication process whereby data at the source site is replicated to an intermediate storage array (bunker) in the first hop and then to the remote storage array in the second hop.

Tunneling protocol A protocol that encapsulates the payload to a different delivery protocol in order to provide secure communication.

Universal Serial Bus (USB) A widely used serial bus interface to communicate with peripheral devices.

Unstructured data Data that has no inherent structure and is usually stored as different types of files.

Upper-layer protocol (ULP) Refers to a more abstract protocol when performing encapsulation.

User Datagram Protocol (UDP) A connectionless transport layer protocol used in IP.

User identifier (UID) Each user in a UNIX environment is identified using a unique UID.

Virtual Concatenation (VCAT) An inverse multiplexing technique to split the bandwidth equally into logical groups, which may be transported or routed independently.

Virtual LAN (VLAN) A switched network that is logically segmented by functions, project teams, or applications, regardless of the physical location of network users.

Virtual pools A logical group or cluster of resources.

Virtual private network (VPN) A secured dedicated communication network tunneled through another network.

Virtual storage area network (VSAN) A collection of ports from a set of connected Fibre Channel switches that form a virtual fabric.

Virtual tape library (VTL) Disk storage that is logically presented as tape libraries or tape drives to the application thorough emulation software.

Virtualization A technique of masking or abstracting physical resources by presenting a logical view of them.

Virus A malicious computer program that can infect a computer without permission or knowledge of the user.

Volume group (VG) A group of physical volumes (disk) from which a logical volume (essentially a partition) can be created.

Warning alert Conditions that require administrative attention in order to prevent the condition from becoming an event that affects accessibility.

Wavelength-Division Multiplexing (WDM) A technology that multiplexes multiple optical carrier signals on a single optical fiber by using different wavelengths of laser light to carry different signals.

Web-Based Enterprise Management (WBEM) A set of management and Internet standard architectures developed by the Distributed Management Task Force that leverages emerging web-based technologies.

Web console A web-based interface that enables remote as well as local network monitoring of the SAN.

Wide area network (WAN) Internetwork of computers that spans across geographical area (crossing metropolitan or even national boundaries); also used to interconnect multiple LANs.

World Wide Name (WWN) A vendor-supplied, 64-bit globally unique identifier number assigned to nodes and ports in a fabric.

World Wide Node Name (WWNN) A 64-bit node WWN used during fabric login.

World Wide Port Name (WWPN) A 64-bit port WWN used during fabric login.

Write aside size If an I/O request exceeds this predefined size, writes are directly sent to the disk, instead of written to cache. This reduces the impact of large writes consuming a large area of cache.

Write-back cache Data is placed in the cache and an acknowledgment is sent to the host immediately. Later, data from cache is committed (destaged) to the disk.

Write cache A portion of a cache set aside for temporarily storing data from a write operation before writing it to the disk for persistent storage.

Write Once Read Many (WORM) An ability of the storage device (such as optical disks) to write once and read many times.

Write penalty The I/O overhead in both mirrored and parity RAID configurations whereby every single write operation is manifested into additional write I/Os to the disks.

Write splitting A process of capturing writes and redirecting them—one to the source and one to the journal.

Write-through cache Data is placed in cache, written to the disk, and then acknowledged to the host.

ZIP A popular data compression and archival format.

Zone bit recording A method of recording data that takes advantage of the disk's geometry by storing more sectors per track on outer tracks than on inner tracks.

Zone set A group of zones that can be activated or deactivated as a single entity in a fabric. Zone sets are also referred to as *zone configurations*.

Zoning A fabric-level process that enables nodes within the fabric to be logically segmented into groups. Members of the zone can communicate only with each other.

Index

A

ACA (Auto Contingent Allegiance), 114, 425

access attacks, 338

access control, 340
  application, 341-344
  BURA, 347-348
  MAC, 135, 164, 186, 344, 423
  management, 344-347

access control lists (ACLs), 342, 351, 354

access nodes, 194

access time. *See* seek time

access time optimization, 74

accessibility. *See also* availability; high availability
  IA, 230
  monitoring, 364-365, 368-370

accountability service, 335-336. *See also* security

active attacks, 338

Active Directory, 161, 346, 355, 356, 407

active paths, 83

active-active arrays. *See* high-end intelligent storage systems

active-passive array configuration, 84. *See also* midrange intelligent storage systems

actuator arm assembly, 29

addressing. *See specific types of addressing*

advanced encryption standard (AES), 277, 408

alerts, 374-375, 391-392

ANSI (American National Standards Institution), 104, 105, 107, 118

API (application programming interface), 39

applications, 44-45
  as data center element, 4, 10, 11
  file serving, 9

application access domain, 341-344

application user interface (AUI), 11, 44, 395

application-specific integrated circuit (ASIC) , 23

Arbitrated Loop, FC. *See* FC-AL

Arbitrated Loop Physical Address (AL-PA), 126, 134

arbitration (ARB) frame, 126, 127

archives. *See also* CAS
  active, 407
  backups, 252-253
  compliance requirements, 192
  fixed content, 190, 407, 408

arithmetic logic unit (ALU), 22

arrival rate, 35

assets (risk triad), 336, 337

asynchronous remote replication, 310

ATM (Asynchronous Transfer Mode), 124, 133, 153, 324, 408

attack surface, 339